EMANCIPATION, THE UNION ARMY,
AND THE REELECTION OF ABRAHAM LINCOLN

CONFLICTING WORLDS:
NEW DIMENSIONS OF THE AMERICAN CIVIL WAR

T. Michael Parrish, Series Editor

EMANCIPATION
THE UNION ARMY
★★★★★★★★★★★ AND THE ★★★★★★★★★★★
REELECTION OF
ABRAHAM LINCOLN

JONATHAN W. WHITE

LOUISIANA STATE UNIVERSITY PRESS

BATON ROUGE

Published with the assistance of the V. Ray Cardozier Fund

Published by Louisiana State University Press
www.lsupress.org

Louisiana Paperback Edition, 2020

DESIGNER: Michelle A. Neustrom
TYPEFACE: Adobe Minion Pro

LIBRARY OF CONGRESS CATALOGING-IN-PUBLICATION DATA

White, Jonathan W., 1979–
    Emancipation, the Union army, and the reelection of Abraham Lincoln / Jona-
than W. White.
        pages cm. — (Conflicting worlds: new dimensions of the American Civil War)
    Includes bibliographical references and index.
    ISBN 978-0-8071-5457-1 (cloth : alk. paper) — ISBN 978-0-8071-5458-8 (pdf) —
ISBN 978-0-8071-5459-5 (epub) 1. Presidents—United States—Election—1864.
2. Soldiers—Suffrage—United States—History—19th century. 3. United States—
Politics and government—1861-1865. I. Title.
    E458.4.W554 2014
    973.7—dc23
                                                                    2013028459
ISBN 978-0-8071-7432-6 ; (paper ; alk. paper)

For Mark Neely,
who told me about the soldier vote when I was an undergraduate at Penn State,
and who taught me to challenge the reigning paradigms

The result of an election held in military camps, where the bayonets are all on one side of the question voted upon, can scarcely be considered as demonstrating popular sentiment.

—ABRAHAM LINCOLN, July 4, 1861

CONTENTS

EPILOGUE

ACKNOWLEDGMENTS

IN MANY WAYS, this book began as my first undergraduate research paper when I was a sophomore at Penn State. In 1998, I took a 300-level writing seminar entitled "Pennsylvania in the Civil War" with William Blair. In that class, I wrote about how Pennsylvania soldiers viewed the execution of deserters. I owe a great deal to Bill for teaching me how to conduct historical research, frame a research question, and convey my conclusions in written form.

This book was continued during my senior year at Penn State. On November 6 and 8, 2000, I drove from my dorm room in State College to Pittsburgh and Bethlehem to see two Bob Dylan concerts. The day in between the two shows was election day—the first presidential election in which I was old enough to vote. At the Pittsburgh show, on the eve of the election, I noticed a group around the arena carrying signs that read, "Honk if you love Al Gore" and "Gore-Lieberman." But they were all overshadowed by a heavyset man in a "Bob Dylan for President" T-shirt. For the third song of the evening, Bob played, "It's All Right Ma (I'm Only Bleeding)." When he got to the line: "But even the President of the United States sometimes must have to stand naked," the audience erupted in cheers.

Around 6:00 p.m. on the evening of November 7 (election day), a staunchly conservative friend of mine walked into my room to go to dinner. "If Bush wins Florida," he told me, "he'll win the whole thing." He had counted the electoral votes and predicted how each state would go (in those days I didn't pay much attention to national politics). To him, Florida was the only variable. We went to dinner and then came back to the room and settled in for a long night of watching the election returns come in on television. Exhausted, I went to bed sometime between 1:00 and 2:00 a.m.

The next morning I heard my roommates shuffling around, getting ready for class. I looked up from my bunk and said, "Who won?" "Bush," came the reply. "Gore conceded earlier this morning." I crashed my head down on my pillow and went back to sleep. A few hours later when I finally crawled out of bed, the political landscape had changed. Al Gore had taken back his concession and was contesting the election results in Florida. It would be several weeks of counts, recounts, and court decisions before George W. Bush was named the official winner. This, I thought, was un-American. I had never heard of a contested election before. Little did I know just how right my friend had been at dinner on election night.

During that same semester, I was auditing Mark Neely's course on the Civil War and Reconstruction. After many of the classes, Mark and I would go back to his office to chat (about the Civil War, Mark Twain, Bob Dylan, and any number of other things). I asked him if he would supervise an independent study for me in the spring and he agreed, but we had to find a viable topic. Mark suggested the soldier vote of 1864. The last—and only—book published on the subject had been privately printed in 1915. In light of the recent election fiasco in Florida, I thought an election-related topic sounded intriguing.

It turned out that the contested election in Florida was not the first in American history. Nor were Floridians the first to claim disfranchisement. I discovered dozens of contested elections around the country during the Civil War era, and I found that thousands of American voters faced disfranchisement when they donned the Union blue. Thus, the soldier vote was a very timely subject; the more I read about it, the more I became engrossed. I did not know at the time that Mark had been planning to have a chapter on the soldier vote in *The Union Divided* (2002); instead, he graciously gave the topic to me. During the spring semester of my senior year, I wrote a paper about the debate in Pennsylvania over permitting soldiers to vote.

As a master's student at the University of Maryland, I expanded on this research, writing seminar papers for David Grimsted, Leslie Rowland, and Alfred Moss. Herman Belz oversaw the completion of my master's thesis, and under his supervision I published articles on the soldier vote in *American Nineteenth Century History, Civil War History,* and *Pennsylvania Heritage.* Ira Berlin and Leslie Rowland also both generously served on my master's thesis committee.

My doctoral research took a step away from the issue of soldiers voting. I instead turned to the law of treason in the North during the Civil War. Studying the law of treason forced me to grapple with questions about the meaning of loyalty and disloyalty in the North during the Civil War. As I spent time reflecting on both treason and the soldier vote, I realized that these two topics were inextricably interconnected. At its root, the debate over permitting soldiers to vote was a debate about loyalty and citizenship. Soldiers, so Republicans argued, deserved to vote because they were making the greatest sacrifices on behalf of American democracy. Thus, while I have spent the past few years doing nothing but "think about treason," I am now back to the soldier vote, but I see a close connection between my work on treason and this book.

Several institutions provided funding for my research on this book. In 2001, the Department of History, the College of Liberal Arts, and the Richards Civil War Era Center at Penn State provided travel funds during the very early stages of this project. In 2005, I received a General and Mrs. Matthew B. Ridgway Research Grant at the U.S. Army Military History Institute, in Carlisle, Pennsylvania, as well as a Scholar-in-Residence grant at the Pennsylvania State Archives through the Pennsylvania Historical and Museum Commission. In 2006, I received four research travel grants: a C. Allan and Marjorie Braun Fellowship at The Huntington, in San Marino, California; a Gilder Lehrman Fellowship at the Gilder Lehrman Institute of American History in New York City; a research grant from the Friends of the Princeton University Library; and a Filson Fellowship from the Filson Historical Society, in Louisville, Kentucky. In 2007, I received a Littleton-Griswold Research Grant in Legal History from the American Historical Association, and an ABC-Clio Research Grant, which was administered by the Society for Military History. The Department of History at the University of Maryland and the Department of Leadership and American Studies at Christopher Newport University (CNU) both provided funding for travel and the purchase of research materials. The Office of the Provost at CNU awarded me a Faculty Development Grant in 2013 that was instrumental to the completion of this project. Finally, the University of Maryland, the Earhart Foundation, and the Lynde and Harry Bradley Foundation all provided funding for my graduate education, during which parts of this book were written.

Many archivists and librarians have assisted me in my research over the years. In particular, I thank Richard J. Sommers of the U.S. Army Military History Institute, Jill D'Andrea and Trevor Plante of the National Archives, Jonathan Stayer of the Pennsylvania State Archives, Diane Rofini of the Chester County Historical Society, and Olga Tsapina of the Huntington Library.

Several people generously opened up their homes to me during research trips. Steph Hahn allowed me to stay with her in Harrisburg for two weeks. I have fond memories of throwing a baseball in the backyard in the evenings. Ben Peets opened up his home to me for a month in Southern California and taught me how to surf, enjoy the nightlife, and navigate L.A. traffic. Jennie Reist gave me her spare bed for two weeks in New York City and showed me the highlights of the Big Apple. Linda and Dale Hyers welcomed a friend of their son's into their home during a week-long trip to Louisville. Mark Bieszka, Jeremy Rein, Anne Hall McKuhen, and Lee and Elizabeth Pitts all hosted me at their respective homes on numerous occasions during research trips to Washington, D.C. Finally, Dave and Irene Lepley welcomed a complete stranger into their home for three weeks in Carlisle. To Jake I am particularly grateful, since he gave up his own room during that time.

Several friends, colleagues, and students at CNU have been instrumental in the completion of this book. CNU students Maddie Popham, Kat Forbes, Ben Coffman, Erin Bello, Ashley Blatt, Oliver Thomas, and Meghan Butler conducted research for me. Jesse Spencer was able to track down many resources through Interlibrary Loan. Nathan and Elizabeth Busch have my enduring gratitude for founding CNU's Center for American Studies. The Center has been a wonderful place to exchange ideas with scholars and friends who are interested in America's history and form of government. My fellow Civil War scholars in the Department of Leadership and American Studies, Sean Scott and Sean Heuvel, are always eager to discuss our current research in the office, which I heartily enjoy. Dean Bob Colvin allowed me to teach courses on "Treason in America," "Civil Liberties in Wartime," and "The Experience of Civil War Soldiers," all of which helped me think about the content of this book. I also thank the Jack Miller Center and Provost Mark Padilla for funding my two-year postdoctoral fellowship at CNU, and Provost Padilla for creating a tenure-track line for me at such an excellent institution.

My parents, Bill and Eileen White, have always supported my dream to write history. My friend, Rich Ransom, has encouraged me almost daily over the past decade as I have pursued a career in academia. And my wife, Lauren, and our daughter, Charlotte, have graciously endured many long hours of research and writing.

I owe a great debt to the scholars and friends who have helped and encouraged me along the way. At Penn State, Bill Blair, John Frantz, and Wilson Moses each read and provided useful comments on early drafts of my work on Pennsylvania. Tim Orr of Old Dominion University answered numerous emails about enlistments and recruiting and read chapters 2 and 3. Aaron Sheehan-Dean, Stephen Berry and the participants at the 2012 Society for Military History conference offered helpful feedback on chapter 2. Steve Towne, associate university archivist at the Indiana University–Purdue University Indianapolis, kindly answered many questions about Indiana during the Civil War and generously shared some of his current research with me. The peer reviewer for LSU Press gave the manuscript a close reading and provided me with very useful suggestions for tightening my argument. At Christopher Newport University, Quentin Kidd lent his statistical expertise for the tables and appendix. William Thro, general counsel at the University of Kentucky, read chapter 5 and offered helpful ideas for revision. At the University of Maryland, Alfred Moss, Whit Ridgway, David Grimsted, Ira Berlin, James Henretta, Leslie Rowland, Mark Graber, and my fellow graduate students (now professors!) Chris Esh and Trisha Posey all read and offered valuable suggestions on portions of this project. Herman Belz cordially took me on as his student and worked with me through each chapter of my master's thesis and doctoral dissertation. Mike Parrish heard me speak on the soldier vote of 1864 at the first biennial meeting of the Society of Civil War Historians at the Union League of Philadelphia in 2008. He offered me a book contract for this project and has been a generous mentor throughout the process of writing and revising this book, just as he was with *Abraham Lincoln and Treason in the Civil War*. Finally, Mark Neely gave me this topic and, over the years, has invested an immense amount of time in me. I thank him for his friendship and scholarly example.

EMANCIPATION, THE UNION ARMY,
AND THE REELECTION OF ABRAHAM LINCOLN

INTRODUCTION

IN 1864, AS REPUBLICANS in northern states were passing legislation granting Union soldiers the right to vote, President Abraham Lincoln ordered his commanders in the field: "Tell the soldiers."[1] Lincoln, like most Republican politicians, wanted the soldiers to know that the Republicans were their true political allies at home. Regardless of their enfranchisement by Republicans, however, Democratic soldiers were critical of this brazen partisan jockeying. "Mr. Lincoln has telegraphed the news down himself! I suppose he thought to make himself popular by so doing, and perhaps he will," wrote one Democratic soldier, "but for myself I think it would be more becoming the dignity of the President to telegraph his thanks after a victory than such small news." Lincoln's actions, according to this soldier, "will open a door for political discussion and influence which may be very damaging to discipline." This soldier's ideas paralleled those of the Democratic opposition in many northern state legislatures, articulating a vision of limited government and the doctrine of separation of powers: "A soldier's business is to obey; he forms a part of the executive, not of the legislative force in the country."[2] Like many Democratic politicians across the North, this soldier believed that allowing soldiers to vote would undermine the safety of the country.[3]

Views like those of this soldier are rarely discussed in the historical literature. Most scholars who have looked at the soldiers' votes of 1864 have taken the outcome of the presidential election at face value, concluding that because soldiers voted so overwhelmingly Republican they had adopted Republican war policies as their own, regardless of antebellum political affiliations. Seventy-eight percent of the soldiers' votes cast in the field, after all, were for Lincoln and Johnson. Jean H. Baker referred to Democratic soldiers as "switchers" during the election of 1864, and Harold M. Hyman concluded that "Union soldiers decided that the War should continue on the basis of the Republican platform, including permanent abolition of slavery and rejection of any contrived 'armistice' with

1

the Confederacy that might allow rebel governments to outlast hostilities." Like Hyman, James M. McPherson has used the results of the soldier vote to suggest wide-scale acceptance of the Republican policy of emancipation: "When Lincoln ran for reelection on a platform pledging a constitutional amendment to abolish slavery, he received almost 80 percent of the soldier vote—a pretty fair indication of army sentiment on slavery by that time." Jennifer L. Weber, McPherson's student, claims to trace "the politicization of Union soldiers . . . into lifelong Republicans," although she offers no evidence from the postwar period to substantiate her position.[4]

The argument that soldiers became Republicans, or at least had adopted Republican war aims by 1864, has appeared in many histories of the war. In her recent *What This Cruel War Was Over*, Chandra Manning goes a step further, arguing that "a large and growing number of ordinary soldiers" came to support emancipation as early as 1861. "Throughout the rank and file, as enlisted soldiers decided that only elimination of the war's cause could end the rebellion and prevent its recurrence, they championed the destruction of slavery a full year ahead of the Emancipation Proclamation, well before most civilians, political leaders, or officers did." "By the end of the war," she concludes, "white northern opinions about racial equality and civil rights, intractable though they had seemed in 1861, were far more malleable and vulnerable to intense self-scrutiny among Union troops than anyone could have imagined when the war began." Manning, like McPherson, points out that when Union "soldiers voted in 1864, nearly 80 percent of them cast their ballots for Lincoln," thus demonstrating that they "believed that Lincoln shared their vision of the war's cause and purpose, even when nobody else at home seemed to understand."[5]

McPherson's *For Cause and Comrades* is the most important study to argue that Union soldiers had converted to Republicanism by 1864, but he has developed the thesis throughout his many works on the Civil War. In his 1982 *Ordeal by Fire*, McPherson writes: "Although McClellan's name still evoked enthusiasm among many officers and men in the Army of the Potomac, few soldiers wished to vote for a Democratic party that declared the war a failure. A Democratic victory, wrote one veteran officer, would mean 'inglorious peace and shame, the old truckling subserviency to Southern domination.' Another soldier, a lifelong Democrat, said that 'we all want peace, but none *any* but an honorable one. I had rather stay out here a lifetime (much as I dislike it) than consent to a division of our country.'"[6] The implication is obvious. The latter soldier—"a lifelong

Democrat"—voted for Lincoln because the president stood for reunion and an honorable peace, whereas the Democratic Party and its nominee, Gen. George B. McClellan, stood for disunion and slavery. Like many other voters in the army, McPherson implies, this Democratic soldier cast his ballot for Lincoln.

But such was not the case—at least not with this soldier. And McPherson's misuse of this quotation entirely distorts the soldier's true political position. Not only did this soldier vote for General McClellan, he did so enthusiastically. When news reached the army that McClellan had received the Democratic nomination, this soldier reported that there were nine cheers in the army for him, "and three for those who nominated him with the exception of the peace on any terms men. The nomination pleases me as much as anything could. . . . I feel confident the General will give us peace six months after taking the [presidential] chair." This soldier loathed the dishonorable Peace men of his party. Accordingly, he refused to vote the Democratic state ticket. And if the choice had been between a Copperhead presidential candidate and Lincoln, he would have grudgingly voted for the incumbent. But Little Mac, in his mind, was no traitor. "I shall do my best to make him President," he wrote. "I support the [Lincoln] administration in the field but oppose it at the ballot-box."[7]

This soldier's political views—fully articulated—are remarkably more complex than how McPherson presents them. The nuance in his position—and in that of many other Union soldiers—thus ought to force a rethinking of one of the reigning paradigms in Civil War historiography. For generations—really, since the Civil War itself—historians have assumed that the Union armies overwhelmingly supported Lincoln and his war policies. But while the soldier vote was cast overwhelmingly Republican in the presidential election of 1864, it may not be an altogether reliable index of the army's ideological motivation or political sentiment. Historians have failed to account for the myriad reasons that may have caused a soldier to vote for or against Abraham Lincoln. Historians have also neglected the nonpresidential elections of 1864, as well as voter turnout. Who did not vote may, in fact, be as important as who did.

This book seeks to tell a new story about the relationship between Union soldiers, emancipation, and the reelection of Abraham Lincoln. Chapter 1 sets up the story, describing the unity that existed among most northerners at the beginning of the war and the political divisions that emerged as Lincoln moved toward a more vigorous prosecution of the war. Issues like emancipation, restrictions on civil liberties, and centralization of the government divided northerners and exacerbated party tensions. By 1862, party lines were redrawn as though the unity that had existed in April 1861 had only been a mirage. As partisanship increased, the issue of soldier suffrage became increasingly important. With so many voters away from home for the first time in American history, politicians had to determine a way to extend the ballot to them. Republicans came to believe that the soldiers—more than any other citizens—deserved the right to vote. They also understood that soldiers' votes might become crucial to future Republican majorities.

Union soldiers were keenly aware that the Democratic Party had opposed extending the ballot to the battlefield. Democratic positions on other war-related issues also often appeared to be anti-soldier. As a consequence, when soldiers voted or voiced their opinions about elections during the war, they tended to vote overwhelmingly against the Democratic Party. This opposition to the Democrats did not necessarily signify a conversion of the soldiers to the Republican Party; rather, it conveyed the disgust that many Republican and Democratic soldiers felt for a party that routinely appeared unpatriotic and anti-soldier.

Chapters 2 and 3 examine the dynamics that emerged when divisive political issues intersected with army life. As the war moved from being a war for the Union to what Democrats feared was also becoming a war for slave emancipation, many northern soldiers felt betrayed. They claimed to have enlisted for one reason but that they were now being forced to fight for another. Many soldiers consequently resigned or deserted rather than fight in a war for slave liberation; others spoke out publicly against President Lincoln and his emancipation policy. As political opposition increased among the soldiery, federal officials searched for ways to inspire acquiescence—or coerce submission—to the North's changing war aims. Soldiers who resigned or deserted after Lincoln issued the Emancipation Proclamation, or who spoke out against Lincoln's decision, were court-martialed and publicly punished in order to dissuade other soldiers from acting alike.

Many scholars have emphasized the political conversion of Union soldiers to the Republican cause. In truth, the army may have seen more of a transformation in composition than a conversion in political sentiment. As Democrats deserted, resigned, or refused to reenlist, the nature and character of the army changed. Moreover, top-down political pressure caused many Democratic soldiers to fall into silence. Indeed, Democratic soldiers were often afraid to voice their opinions, sometimes even in private letters. In the face of Republican leadership—and a Republican-controlled U.S. Senate that might reject any promotion of an outspoken Democrat—Democrats in the army learned to keep their opinions to themselves rather than risk personal embarrassment or political injury.

The apex of this story is the presidential election of 1864. By the summer of 1864, as Union military fortunes were being dragged through the muddy trenches around Petersburg and Atlanta, the Democratic Party was hopelessly divided between its Peace and moderate wings.[8] The time should have been ripe for Democrats to regain power, but three years into the war, the party still could not settle on what position it should take in the crisis. Moderate Democrats supported a war for reunion, but they opposed Lincoln's policies of emancipation, conscription, and military arrests.[9] Members of the Peace wing of the party—often called "Copperheads"—by contrast, either called for an armistice or for Lincoln to let the South depart. Both factions battled for the soul and voice of the party. As the number of battlefield deaths increased in May, June, and July of 1864—with little progress to show for them—the Peace wing of the party became more vocal. Ultimately, this was bad news for the Democrats as a whole because no matter how terribly the war was going, most northerners were unwilling to vote for a party that seemed intent upon surrender.

Behind the leadership of Clement L. Vallandigham, the Democrats placed Gen. George B. McClellan, a moderate, pro-war, pro-slavery Democrat, on a Peace platform with a Peace Democratic running mate. Perhaps Democratic leaders believed that such triangulation was the best way to appeal to a wide array of war-weary voters. Perhaps they believed this was the best compromise they could reach. But when William Tecumseh Sherman's army finally took Atlanta on September 1, 1864, an exhausted North awoke from its demoralization and defeatism. Northern voters realized that victory, reunion, and the defeat of southern treason could soon be within their grasp. Most northern voters would not vote for a party and platform they believed to be treasonable (the Democratic platform labeled the war a "failure"). Now that victory and an honorable peace again seemed attainable, northern voters rejected the Democratic Party, lock, stock, and barrel.

Chapter 4 examines how Union soldiers responded to the political tempest that was brewing in the North in 1864. Soldiers from every northern state voted in the state, congressional, and presidential elections of 1864 (some in the field, some by mail, and some who were furloughed home to vote). Most scholars who have written about "the soldier vote" focus only on the presidential election, and they dwell on one simple but deceiving fact: that 78 percent of the soldiers' votes were cast for Lincoln.

The story is more complex than how it is typically told. To be sure, many soldiers were ardent and enthusiastic supporters of President Lincoln and emancipation, including some who had opposed Lincoln in 1860 and emancipation in 1863. Numerous Democrats in the Union army converted to the Republican Party during the war. But the number of these soldiers has been overemphasized in the scholarly literature. Historians who see a steadily building wave of support for emancipation that eventually turned the soldiers into "lifelong Republicans" oversimplify what happened. Soldier support for Lincoln and his policies rose and fell as the prospects for victory rose and fell. And even after the fall of Atlanta and Mobile Bay in September 1864, many still could not bring themselves to vote for him.

The more precise way to state the 78 percent statistic is to say that 78 percent *of the soldiers who voted* cast their ballots for Lincoln. At least 20 percent of the soldiers who were eligible to vote in the presidential election chose not to; even more abstained from voting in the state and congressional elections that year. Among these were Democrats who could not bring themselves to vote for a party that had called their efforts in the field a "failure." Other Democratic soldiers abstained from exercising the franchise out of fear. Voting in the nineteenth century was a public act. When a man went to vote in 1864, his comrades knew exactly how he voted. Each party printed its own ballots, and they usually bore distinctive colors and symbols. As a consequence, many Democratic soldiers silenced themselves rather than vote an unpopular, allegedly treasonous ticket.[10]

Chapters 2, 3, and 4 have an important subsidiary point to make regarding the civil liberties issue during the Civil War. Scholars who study Lincoln and civil liberties tend to focus only on Lincoln's treatment of civilians and irregular combatants. But to truly understand this issue, more attention needs to be given to the Lincoln administration's response to Democrats in the army as well. Lincoln and the Republicans' handling of anti-emancipation soldiers mirrored the treatment accorded to antiwar Democrats at home. Following the issuance of the Emancipation Proclamation, Lincoln and the War Department punished Democratic soldiers who spoke out against the president; during election season, soldiers who wanted to vote the Democratic ticket often faced strong pressure and intimidation.

To be sure, soldiers naturally possessed fewer rights than civilians at home—so it should not be surprising that some political speech would be silenced among the troops. But the Articles of War appeared to leave plenty of room for some political discussion around the campfire. The Fifth Article of War prohibited soldiers from using "contemptuous or disrespectful words" against the president, vice president, Congress, or governor and legislature of any state in which the troops were quartered. The Seventh and Eighth Articles of War prohibited soldiers from participating in "any mutiny or sedition." The Tenth Article of War required soldiers to swear to "observe and obey the orders of the President of the United States." And the Fifty-Seventh Article of War prohibited "holding correspondence with, or giving intelligence, to the enemy."[11] Beyond these limitations, soldiers believed that they possessed a broad latitude to discuss political matters as well as the war policies of the government.

Nevertheless, many Republicans supported restrictions upon the political speech of Democratic soldiers. As one Indiana officer put it, albeit rather hyperbolically, in February 1863: "Then let a vigorous, bloody, annihilating policy be inaugurated, both at home and in the army. Let every man, who dares to resist by word or deed suffer death instantly." Only through the enforcement of strict pro-Union policies did this soldier believe that the North would be unified enough to defeat the southern traitors.[12]

While this soldier's colorful language overstates the policies actually adopted by Lincoln, it demonstrates the drastic measures that some Republicans believed were necessary not simply to silence Democrats at home, but also to restrict the speech rights of Democrats in the field. As will be seen in chapters 2, 3, and 4, Democratic soldiers were frequently punished for articulating their party's political positions, while Republican soldiers could speak and publish their viewpoints with impunity. The limiting of Democratic soldiers' voting and speech rights is all the more ironic since Republicans championed the right of soldiers to vote based on the premise that soldiers deserved the full rights of citizenship.

Chapter 5 traces the legacies of the Civil War soldier vote, arguing that the North's wartime legislation had several profound effects on American history. In his masterful narrative of suffrage in America, Alexander Keyssar argued that the soldier vote was one of the "lesser effects" of the Civil War. This is a bit ironic since an image of Pennsylvania soldiers voting in October 1864 graces the front cover of Keyssar's book.[13] Nevertheless, Keyssar's view misses the extraordinary importance of the soldier vote during the Civil War. First, the rhetoric surrounding the soldier vote laid the groundwork for black suffrage in the early postwar period. Second, in the postwar years the Republican Party exploited the rationale for permitting soldiers to vote to disfranchise soldiers who had deserted from the Union armies. Congress and several northern states passed legislation depriving northern deserters of "the rights of citizenship"—most notably, the right to vote. These debates articulated new understandings of citizenship, suffrage, and the role of the federal government in electoral affairs. The postwar decitizenizing legislation also laid the groundwork for some of the most hotly contested debates in late-twentieth- and early-twenty-first-century American jurisprudence.

The Union soldier, above all others, could claim the mantle of "loyal citizen." After all, the volunteers were sacrificing their safety and their lives for the preservation of the nation. Yet the loyalty issue became complicated once Lincoln issued the Emancipation Proclamation on January 1, 1863. Now Republicans widely claimed that loyalty to the Union also entailed adherence to emancipation.[14] This seemingly clear line between loyalty and disloyalty became muddled, however, when it was applied to soldiers who opposed emancipation.

Large numbers of soldiers opposed Lincoln's war policies, especially emancipation. Did that mean that Democratic soldiers were traitors? If so, must they be punished or chastised for their political beliefs? An exchange between two officers in 1864 captured the contradiction that emerged when soldiers were willing to fight in a war that had goals they did not support. One Democratic colonel related an encounter he had with a like-minded general to illustrate the "contempt" that McClellan men in the army had for "the slang phrases of the day." Shortly before the presidential election of 1864, he wrote: "One of these Genls. whom I had not before met finding me a McClellan man said, 'Do you believe in prosecuting the War against the Rebellion to the last dollar and the last man?' 'I do!' 'Do you believe a nigger to be better than a white man?' 'I do not.' Extending his hand he exclaimed, 'I hail thee brother Copperhead!'"[15] Democratic soldiers like these frequently professed to be loyal Unionists, and they vehemently resented accusations of disloyalty. Nevertheless, many were punished for "disloyalty" for expressing their political opposition to Lincoln and emancipation.

Many Democratic soldiers wanted to restore rather than abandon the party of their youth. "I love the Democratic Party," wrote one Pennsylvania soldier, "but oh! God, when I see men who call themselves Democrats, who abuse and misuse the word democracy for a cloak to hide their damnable purpose, my heart burns within me with indignation. . . . I can be a Democrat and a Union man—but I hold that no man can be a true Democrat—a peace man and a rebel at the same time."[16] Soldiers like this *may* have voted against their party in certain wartime elections, but they did not necessarily become "lifelong Republicans."

This book is an attempt to understand the meaning of politics and elections during the Civil War, particularly as politics and elections related to Union soldiers. Many books have been written on these subjects, but most have come to remarkably similar conclusions—namely, that as the war progressed, Union soldiers came to support Lincoln, emancipation, and the contribution of African American troops. This study, by contrast, argues that Union soldiers' political decisions can be better explained by understanding what soldiers were *against* rather than what they were *for*. To give a concrete example that is explored in greater detail in the pages that follow, I argue that Union soldiers were more likely to vote for Republican candidates during the war because of their hatred for Copperheads than their support for Republican war policies.

Much of this book focuses on questions about how Union soldiers viewed slavery and emancipation during the Civil War. To be clear, the argument put forth in this book is *not* that slavery had little to do with the war. The war, in my view, came about because of the intractable issue of how to deal with slavery in the national territories.[17] Moreover, in the latter half of the war Lincoln used emancipation as a military measure to help win the war and restore the Union. Clearly, slavery is central to any right understanding of the war's causes and consequences. The central thesis of this book, however, is that the Union armies—while becoming de facto armies of liberation—did not necessarily have an ideological conversion to the Republican war measure of emancipation. For many northern soldiers, restoring the Union was the only true goal of the war from beginning to end.[18]

A NOTE ON METHODOLOGY

While working on my dissertation—which focused on the law of treason in the North during the Civil War—I became interested in civilians who were tried for treason in military courts. I contacted Tom Lowry and asked him to search for "treason" in his database of court-martial and military commission case files. The result yielded 107 cases. I expected all of these trials to involve civilian defendants, but upon reviewing the cases I found that nineteen were the cases of Union soldiers who were court-martialed for some treasonous offense, six of whom had exulted in the assassination of President Lincoln.

This discovery prompted me to search for more soldiers who were punished for crimes of disloyalty. Tom conducted a number of searches for me, including "disloyalty," "sedition," "nigger war," "abolition," "slave," "slavery," and "fifth article of war," which criminalized criticizing the president, Congress, or other government officials. As I went through the records, I began to uncover a pattern whereby the Union high command punished and sought to silence soldiers who vocally opposed Republican war policies, particularly emancipation.

Tom's database is indispensable to court-martial research—and more scholars ought to take advantage of it.[19] But the results of searches within the database cannot be taken as definitive, which I discovered in the course of going through the case files at the National Archives.

Court-martial records are organized in folders, with each case having an alpha-numeric case number. A box may contain anywhere from part of one large case file to more than twenty or thirty small cases. When a researcher requests a case file at the National Archives, the researcher will receive a box that may contain any number of other cases.

As time permitted, I often perused all of the case files in the boxes that were pulled for me, not only the cases I had requested. As is so often the case, serendipity played a significant role in my research. A number of the cases I discuss in chapters 2, 3, and 4 were cases that I found "by luck" while browsing through the records at the Archives. They did not come up in my searches in the Lowry database—although some of them presumably should have. As a result, it is impossible to quantify with precision the number of cases involving anti-emancipation soldiers. The evidence I give in this book amounts to the most thorough examination of these cases that is possible without replicating Tom and Beverly Lowry's ten-year project of reading every case file.

Other unique source materials in this book are voting statistics from the state and presidential elections of 1864. Using election returns in conjunction with regimental morning reports, I estimate the voter turnout in several of those elections (an explanation of the methodology can be found with table 1). These records reveal that more than 40 percent of the soldiers did not vote for Lincoln's reelection (either by voting for the Democratic nominee or by abstaining from voting); an even larger percentage did not vote for the Republican ticket in the state elections held in September, October, and November 1864. This analysis calls into question some of the reigning paradigms in Civil War historiography—most particularly, that the soldiers overwhelmingly supported Lincoln and that they had come to support the Republican Party and its policy of emancipation.

As supplemental materials, this book utilizes more than three hundred collections of soldiers' letters and diaries. Scholars have long recognized the pitfalls of using these sources to assess soldiers' motivation for enlisting and fighting during the Civil War. Joseph T. Glatthaar has recently summed up the problem of relying on these sorts of sources:

> I believe that to a great extent Civil War scholarship that focuses on soldiers is stuck. In the case of Civil War soldiers, we have gotten caught in a game of "he said, she said." We pluck something from a soldier's letter, diary, or memoir and make claims that this opinion represents most or even a substantial portion of those soldiers. If a scholar searches long enough, he or she will find evidence to justify virtually any contemporary attitude and buttress virtually any argument the scholar may pose, regardless of its representativeness. For that reason, valid statistics may break that scholarly logjam.[20]

Glatthaar is certainly correct. Any number of opinions will be found among the writings of Civil War soldiers, and it is important not to overgeneralize based on a few cherry-picked quotations. Nevertheless, these resources are essential for any study of Civil War soldiers. As Glatthaar wrote in an earlier study, "Civil War letters, diaries, and reminiscences are probably the single best source of mid-nineteenth-century attitudes."[21] Such materials thus make up an important portion of the evidence in this book.

As I began to notice patterns of intimidation of Democratic soldiers—both in the court-martial records and during the elections of 1864—I started seeking out letters and diaries by Democrats in the army. I make no claim that my sample of soldiers' personal writings is representative of the Union army as a whole. Unlike other scholars who lay out how many collections they read, the demographic portraits of their samples, and how representative they believe their samples to be, I had a different purpose in consulting "the soldier's pen." My goal was to add flesh and blood to the election returns, and to find first hand reactions to the intimidation that pervaded the army in the wake of the Emancipation Proclamation. If 22 percent of the soldiers voted against Lincoln, and another 20 percent or more chose not to vote at all, I wanted to find the voices of the more than 40 percent of the soldiers who exercised their franchise in these ways. Naturally, these accounts would more likely be found among the writings of Democratic soldiers.

1

"THAT THE PURITY AND SANCTITY
OF THE BALLOT BOX SHALL BE PRESERVED"

Civil War Politics and the Troops

MEMBERS OF BOTH POLITICAL PARTIES enthusiastically supported Lincoln's April 1861 call for volunteers. When Illinois senator Stephen A. Douglas visited his old rival at the White House, he told the president: "Our Union must be preserved. Partisan feeling must yield to patriotism. I am with you, Mr. President, and God bless you."[1] Such genuine bipartisanship was felt throughout the North in April 1861. "Great excitement exists in this community in regard to the war question," wrote one man in Pittsburgh to Pennsylvania's Republican governor, Andrew G. Curtin. "The feeling is Intense, and the most gratifying evidence of the loyalty of men of all parties is apparent on all sides." The writer proceeded to tell Curtin that even the Democratic newspaper in Pittsburgh published "a manly article on the subject fully up to the tune of the Republican journals. In this quarter the People are a unit." A day later, Pennsylvania Supreme Court justice John M. Read urged Governor Curtin to accept a volunteer regiment composed largely of Democrats: "A number of the officers and men of this Regiment are Democrats," Read stated, "but are all strong Union men and highly patriotic."[2]

To be sure, there were a few advocates for peace, but following the firing on Fort Sumter on April 12, 1861, cries for peace in the North were almost entirely silenced. Philadelphia diarist Sidney George Fisher naively believed that this unanimity in the North would endure. "The streets are all of a flutter with flags, streaming from windows, hotels, stores, &c.," he wrote. While there were a few "suspected" secessionists in the city, "Fortunately, the sentiments of the people are so generally loyal to the government that, tho we are to have the curse of civil war, we are not likely to suffer from the greater evil of partizan war among ourselves."[3] Orville Hickman Browning, soon to be Stephen Douglas's replacement in the Senate, likewise observed that the southern "traitors must be astounded at the unanimity of feeling in the North," while a Republican senator from Wisconsin noted that in his state all citizens spoke with "one voice." "Democrats stand shoulder to shoulder with Republicans now, ready to maintain the government at all hazards."[4] In the spring of 1861, mention of "traitors" universally referred to southern secessionists; by the following year, however, it would be employed to refer to northern Democrats, perhaps more frequently than it was used to denote southern rebels.

Most northerners were united in defense of the Union in 1861. In fact, during the autumn 1861 elections, Republicans and Democrats forewent antebellum party differences and joined hands to run on tickets called the "No-Party" ticket or the "Union" ticket. Devotion to the Union seemed to supersede earlier partisan squabbles.[5] To be sure, some northern Democrats and citizens from the Border States had opposed the war from the beginning, but it was not until the passage of the Confiscation Acts (August 1861 and July 1862), the announcement of an emancipation policy (September 1862 and January 1863), and the adoption of national conscription (March 1863) that the Democratic opposition to the Republican war effort really congealed. Once they decided to oppose the administration, however, Democrats then had to decide just what form that opposition would take.

Even after emancipation and conscription, many moderate Democrats still claimed to support the war, but only to oppose the way the administration was handling it. Others, forming the Peace wing of the party, insisted that it was impossible for war to restore the Union.[6] Democrats in the moderate wing of the party had to be careful with whom they associated in the Peace wing. National party chairman August Belmont warned Democratic financier Samuel L. M. Barlow in 1862 not to associate his name with certain Peace men because they "are disloyal & unreservedly express their sympathy with the Rebels.—I tell you this as a friend, because I know that you do not share their treasonable views."[7]

Being divided on the major questions of the war, Democrats were also divided among themselves as to the best ways to effect their policy positions. Some moderate Democrats hoped that they could "come up and possess the ear of the President," rather than leave Lincoln to the influence of Radical Republicans. If the Democratic Party would only act patriotically and openly support the Union war effort, they believed, Lincoln would turn his back on the Radicals of his own party and form a coalition with pro-war members of the opposition. But rather than take this approach, Democratic leadership generally "bull[ied] the Federal power," and their "opposition became tainted with rancor, partisanship, & some treason."[8] Consequently, Lincoln found that the opposition party could not be trusted, and Democrats may have lost a unique opportunity to exert their influence on presidential decision making.

ENACTING SOLDIER VOTING LEGISLATION

Permitting soldiers to vote during the Civil War was not an entirely novel idea, but the grand scale of the movement to permit soldiers to vote in the 1860s was unprecedented. During the American Revolution, New York's Committee of Safety permitted New York soldiers to vote in the gubernatorial election of 1777, but the state legislature never incorporated any provisions for soldier suffrage into the state's law books. As a consequence, this first experiment in absentee balloting in America was short-lived and has been largely forgotten. During the War of 1812, Pennsylvania and New Jersey both enfranchised their soldiers, but New Jersey repealed its law in 1820. At times in the antebellum period, such as during the Dorr War in Rhode Island in 1842, soldiers voted illegally in places in which they were stationed but were not qualified voters. But generally, soldiers were not permitted to vote in antebellum America. Thus, when the Civil War began, Pennsylvania was the only state with a law on the books permitting soldiers to vote.[9]

In October 1861, thousands of Pennsylvania soldiers voted at their camps in Pennsylvania and as far away as Virginia. Fraud permeated the elections. According to one report, one regiment cast a nine-hundred-vote majority for a Republican candidate from Philadelphia even though the regiment had only sixty or seventy men from the city.[10] "The frauds were very gross," noted Philadelphia diarist Sidney George Fisher, and "all parties were guilty."[11] Several contested elections came before the state legislature and judicial system. Reports of fraud were so widespread that Republican jurist John M. Read lamented that "great and grievous frauds upon the elective franchise have been perpetrated at the last general election, under the cover of alleged elections by the volunteers."[12]

Neither party took an official position on the issue; in some cases, Democrats challenged the soldier vote, while in others, the Republicans wanted the army vote thrown out. Moreover, many political observers believed that politics should be kept out of the camps. "Soldiers engaged in the service of the country, with an enemy almost within sight, should not be disturbed by electioneering politicians," opined the *Philadelphia Bulletin,* a Republican daily. "It is evident that they think so themselves, for in some regiments no polls were opened, and in those where they were opened, scarcely half the men voted. This proves that when men go to fight, they do not care to vote, and probably not one volunteer in twenty would consider himself injured by being deprived of the right of suffrage while in the army." The newspaper added, without any evidence: "The officers of the army, we know, from the Commander-in-Chief down, condemn the law, and it was contemplated, at one time, to forbid voting in the camps."[13]

Several court battles arose in Pennsylvania challenging the legitimacy of the soldier vote. Initially the state supreme court upheld the right of soldiers to vote, but in May 1862, in a case called *Chase v. Miller,* the court ruled that the law permitting soldiers to vote violated the text and spirit of the state constitution. Writing for the majority, Justice George W. Woodward, a Democrat, derided the soldier voting act as "careless legislation," "repugnant," "jargon," and "downright nonsense." According to Woodward, it was wholly inconsistent with the Pennsylvania constitution, which required voters to maintain "residence" within the state and to cast their ballots in election districts.[14] Specifically, the constitution stipulated that a voter must reside for ten days prior to an election "*in the election district where he offers to vote*" (emphasis added by Woodward). These districts must be bound by state lines, Woodward noted, and neither the legislature nor any military officer possessed the right to create an election district outside the borders of Pennsylvania. "The constitution meant, rather, that the voter, *in propria persona,* should offer his vote in an appropriate election district, in order that his neighbours might be at hand to establish his right to vote if it were challenged, or to challenge it if it were doubtful."[15]

Woodward also pointed out that the election law was internally inconsistent. Although one section of the act authorized soldiers to vote, a subsequent section prohibited all troops, "either armed or unarmed," from attending any polling place. Such contradictions demonstrated the negligence of the legislators who had framed the law. Finally, Woodward asserted that voting in the field "invites" and "opens a wide door for the most odious frauds"—a fear that Democrats would emphasize repeatedly for the duration of the war. The state supreme court's decision in *Chase v. Miller* arose out of a contested election for district attorney in Luzerne County. The court, in this case, vacated a Republican's victory, making Democrat Ezra B. Chase district attorney for the county.[16]

In another case a few months later, the Supreme Court of Pennsylvania upheld its earlier decision, this time ruling in favor of a Republican.[17]

Democrats immediately praised the court's ruling even while acknowledging that it meant Republicans would gain several offices across the state. The *Harrisburg Patriot and Union* proclaimed Woodward's opinion "so exhaustive and conclusive that it cannot fail to receive the concurrence of the public." Though the court "may have regretted the necessity of this decision, it obviously could not have determined otherwise consistently with its duty to expound, and not to make, the fundamental law."[18] Republican papers, on the other hand, paid little attention to the landmark decision.[19] Still not seeing any practical significance in the soldier vote, Republicans would not become fully aware of the repercussions of the ruling until after the setbacks of the October 1862 elections.

While the Supreme Court of Pennsylvania was busy disfranchising its state's volunteers, a few midwestern states extended the ballot to their soldiers in the summer and fall of 1862. The Illinois constitutional convention permitted Illinois soldiers to vote in the referendum on the proposed state constitution in June 1862. That same month, the provisional government in Missouri adopted an ordinance permitting its state's volunteers to vote in general elections "during the present war." In 1861, a bipartisan group of state legislators in Iowa rejected a proposal to enfranchise Hawkeyes in the army, but after the governor took a strong public stance in favor of such a measure in September 1862, the legislature adopted a soldier suffrage bill in a bipartisan manner.[20] Wisconsin and Minnesota also enacted soldier suffrage legislation in September 1862. Enfranchising Minnesota volunteers was initially proposed by a Democratic newspaper in St. Paul, but soon thereafter became a Republican effort. Although Democrats now claimed that enfranchising soldiers would be unconstitutional, a majority of Democrats in the legislature voted in favor of the bill in an attempt to avoid a political backlash. Likewise, the Wisconsin measure was generally supported by the Republicans and opposed by the Democrats. Both laws were passed just weeks prior to the 1862 elections.[21] In May 1862, Ohio Democrats sought to enfranchise soldiers from the Buckeye State, but Ohio Republicans blocked the measure.[22] Outside of Missouri and the Old Northwest, however, the states of the Union were not yet concerned about enfranchising their soldiers in the field.[23]

In the fall elections of 1862, Democrats made sweeping gains, picking up more than thirty seats in Congress, the governorships of New York and New

Jersey, and the legislatures in Pennsylvania, Illinois, and Indiana. These elections seemed to indicate a sea change in northern sentiment as each of these states had gone for Lincoln in 1860. Just before the autumn elections Lincoln had issued a preliminary Emancipation Proclamation, declaring that if the rebels did not lay down their arms by January 1, 1863, he would use his executive authority to abolish slavery in those portions of the southern states controlled by the Confederacy. Democrats thus interpreted their victories as the groaning of a northern public dissatisfied with the war and upset with Lincoln's changing war aims. They chastised the president for his infringements of civil liberties, for his apparent mangling of the Constitution, for his meddling into the "domestic institutions" of the southern states, and for his poor management of the war.[24]

Following the Democratic victories of 1862, Republicans almost unanimously decided that soldiers ought to have the right to vote.[25] "The National cause lost the advantage of the late State elections," wrote a Republican politician to Pennsylvania governor Andrew Curtin, "just because the men who fight, were not allowed to vote. The soldiers who cannot be defeated by armed traitors in the field, may be defeated by unarmed traitors, like the Woods, in the councils."[26] After Democrat Horatio Seymour was elected governor of New York in 1862, one soldier from the Empire State complained of "the *bad news, bad news,* that old Seymour is elected Governor of the state. Oh! that the warriors had been home I do not believe it would have been so."[27] A Republican state legislator from Ohio believed the Republicans lost because "Four fifths of the forces sent into the field are from the Union [Republican] ranks."[28] In the White House, President Lincoln lamented that the "democrats were left in a majority by our friends going to the war."[29] A Republican soldier echoed his commander in chief: "The cause of the elections going Democratic is the Republicans are away fighting the war and the Army did not vote this year."[30]

Many Democrats believed that the war-weary North would continue to elect Democrats to office; some Republicans also feared that result. "Change" became a powerful, if somewhat hollow mantra by the midpoint of the war. "We are impatient, dissatisfied, disgusted, disappointed," complained New York City diarist George Templeton Strong. "We are in a state of dyspepsia and general, indefinite malaise, suffering from the necessary evils of war and from irritation at our slow progress. We take advantage of the first opportunity of change, for its own sake, just as a feverish patient shifts his position in bed, though he knows he'll be none the easier for it. Neither the blind masses, the swinish multitude, that rule us under our accursed system of universal suffrage, nor the case of typhoid, can be expected to exercise self-control and remember that tossing and turning weakens and does harm."[31] Democratic politicians hoped to capitalize on this despair. "Discontent always seeks relief in *change*," wrote a former Democratic congressman to Charles J. Biddle of Philadelphia, and discontent must "work to our advantage."[32]

In their moment of triumph following the 1862 elections, Democratic leaders overreached. Believing that the northern populace was turning toward the Peace movement, they ran three archconservatives for the governorships of Connecticut, Ohio, and Pennsylvania in 1863. At least two of these candidates were men who had openly criticized the war, one had refused to vote to fund the war, and one had advocated "peaceable secession" before the war began. (The Pennsylvania and Ohio gubernatorial elections of 1863 are discussed later in this chapter.)

Republicans were horrified by the Democrats' choices. "I blush for my native state that such sentiments can be uttered here," wrote one Connecticut Republican when describing the "treasonable" Democratic nominating convention in his state. "At the same time I think it will be much more easy, politically, to defeat the 'anti-*war*' party than it would have been to defeat an 'anti-*administration*' party." In other words, despite Lincoln's lagging popularity when the war was going badly, this Republican believed that most voters still supported a war to preserve the Union. Consequently, Republicans felt confident that they could defeat antiwar candidates at the polls. "The democratic party consists of a few able, designing, ambitious leaders who drag after them an immense combination of ignorant, thoughtless & vicious voters, misled by popular watch-cries, & caring nothing for the foundations of the republic. There is a very small head to the party, and an immense tail"—the writer here alluding to Connecticut Democrats as disloyal Copperheads. "May Heaven defend us from their harm!"[33]

Democratic politicians increasingly discouraged their constituents from enlisting in the service. Ezra B. Chase, the Pennsylvania Democrat who had won his office when the state supreme court ruled Pennsylvania's soldier voting law unconstitutional, delivered a stump speech in which he urged his audience "not to go to the war but to stay home and to go to the polls" so that they could elect "men who would . . . bring the Southern Confederacy back into the Union without any fighting." Republicans, of course, thought this attitude was treasonable and had Chase arrested.[34] To counter these schemes by the political opposition, and to regain electoral majorities, Republican lawmakers in Pennsylvania as well as many states across the North began pushing for legislation that would extend the right of suffrage to the soldiers in the field.

In 1863 and 1864, Republicans nationwide championed the cause of gaining soldiers the right to vote. Ohio Republicans now took the lead, adopting a soldier suffrage law in April 1863. This law, in many ways, proved the most significant soldier voting statute of the war, for it allowed the boys in blue to vote against the North's most infamous and outspoken Copperhead. Clement L. Vallandigham, the notorious Ohio congressman, ran for governor of Ohio in October 1863 from exile in Canada after having been arrested for disloyalty by the military and convicted by a military commission. Throughout the war, Vallandigham had vocally criticized the Lincoln administration and the war effort; in Congress he had even refused to vote funding for the troops. The soldiers wreaked their vengeance on "Valliant Val," casting 94.8 percent of their votes against him, although fewer than 30 percent of Ohio soldiers actually voted in the election.[35]

The road to enfranchising soldiers took longer in other states. Some states simply passed legislation extending the ballot to the battlefield; other states, like Pennsylvania, had to amend their constitutions to permit their soldiers to vote. Throughout 1863 and 1864, debates over permitting soldiers to vote were ubiquitous in the North. Republicans claimed the mantle of the true friend of the soldier, while Democrats argued that they supported the rights of soldiers but that taking the ballot to the battlefield would be bad for American democracy. Fraud, corruption, misinformation, and intimidation were the political accusations and outrages of the day. "I am in favor of allowing the soldiers to vote," declared one Democratic politician. "I am aware that it is important that the soldier should vote; but . . . there is a still more important matter to the liberties of this country—that the purity and sanctity of the ballot box shall be preserved."[36] Indeed, some Democrats believed that the Republicans would control the army vote "to gain some great advantage to their party in the future."[37] Others claimed that it would be impossible (if not illegal) to regulate elections and prevent fraud outside of a state. "The most learned and able" legislator "cannot devise a code of law that will efficiently or even partially protect the purity of the ballot box, if it be carried to the army, outside of the Commonwealth," argued a state senator from Pennsylvania.[38]

Beyond the fear of fraud, Democrats argued that soldiers gave up both the rights and capacities of citizenship when they donned the Union blue. New York governor Horatio Seymour asserted that it "would be worse than a mockery to allow those secluded in camps or upon ships to vote, if they are not permitted to receive letters and papers from their friends, or if they have not the same freedom in reading public journals, accorded to their brethren at home."[39] Taking the argument a step further, Pennsylvania state senator William A. Wallace concluded that the soldier "disfranchises himself when he ceases to be a citizen, and takes upon himself the duties of a soldier" because "the acts of the soldier . . . are, from their nature, incompatible with the right of suffrage." Soldiers, Wallace argued, are taught to listen and obey; they consequently lose the ability to think and reason for themselves.[40] The *New York World* echoed Wallace's concern when it declared that "the first duty of a soldier, is absolute obedience to his superior officers," while a Maryland Democrat claimed that a man "lays aside his civil rights and is placed under martial law" when he enlists in the service.[41]

Democrats claimed that it made little sense to permit soldiers to vote if they were uninformed about the party platforms and candidates. If soldiers were not educated about the canvass, their votes might be easily controlled by their commanding officers, thus rendering them "worthless as soldiers and corrupt and depraved as citizens."[42] Permitting soldiers to vote could thus endanger the republic. Consequently, despite the risk of appearing unfriendly to the soldiers, Democrats held firm against legislation that would take the ballot to the field. The soldiers, Democrats argued, should only be allowed to vote at home, in their own election districts.[43]

Such arguments persuaded many Democratic voters—and nonvoters, for that matter. "I believe it would be better not to let the soldiers vote this fall," wrote Jennie Cleland, an Ohio woman, to her brother in the Union army, "because the soldiers most places only get to hear one side of the question (that is the Abolition side)." Echoing the assertions of hometown Democratic newspapers and politicians, Cleland complained that "Democratic papers are not allowed in the army very much" and that "if the soldiers do get to vote they will not . . . be allowed to vote their sentiments."[44]

The Republicans responded to the Democratic position with resoundingly patriotic appeals. They defended soldier suffrage on the grounds that soldiers, above all others, deserved the right to wield the ballot. Soldiers were "the flower of our population," one New York legislator announced in 1863. To deny them the ballot would be an unjust act of "high-handed tyranny."[45] A Republican newspaper in New Jersey argued that denying soldiers the vote would "degrade" them "to the level of the negro, so far as political rights are involved."[46] Such a degradation would be unacceptable in America. "I believe the American citizen, when he becomes a soldier, is . . . the American citizen more nobly developed," declared one Maryland Republican. "When he becomes a soldier he is only in a position to express differently his rights as an American citizen, and to defend them as a soldier." Another Maryland Republican chastised the Democrats for wanting to disfranchise those "who have gone to the front to defend your institutions" while placing "the destinies of your land into the hands of the traitors that remain behind." Striking at what he believed to be the heart of the issue, this Republican declared that the Democrats opposed permitting soldiers to vote "because he knows that every soldier . . . will vote for the prosecution of this war, for sustaining the government of this country, and for sustaining the principles of republican liberty of which the gentleman professes to be fond."[47] Democratic opposition to soldier voting, in other words, stemmed from the Democrats' own disloyal hearts.

Republicans hammered home their true affection for the soldier. The Pennsylvania House of Representatives adopted a resolution with language that unmistakably expressed the Republican Party line. "The gallant sons of Pennsylvania" had "voluntarily sacrificed the pleasures and endearments of home, endured the hardships and braved the diseases incident to camp life, [and] boldly faced death itself on the stormy battle-field, in defense of our imperiled Government." Their "unsurpassed valor" was an honor to the state, and had "wreathed Pennsylvania's brow with fadeless laurels, and added imperishable lustre to her former renown." Nevertheless, these brave soldiers were being "deprived of a citizen's highest privilege." To rob "the patriot soldier, who heroically risks life itself to perpetuate free Government" of "his right to have his voice heard" was grossly unjust.[48] Republicans refused to accept the Democratic premise that the soldiers would not be at perfect liberty to vote as they pleased. No red-blooded American soldier would ever permit his superior officers to interfere with his exercise of the franchise.

The Democrats' wartime definition of soldiers as mentally incompetent noncitizens and uninformed mercenaries was highly unpopular with northern voters. One central Pennsylvania farmer recorded in his diary that "treachery is at the root" of the Democratic position. "This amounts to such Democracy that whenever a citizen leaves his home in order to defend his privileges and his Country he is disenfranchised—loses his citizenship."[49] Similarly, a Philadelphia physician saw Democratic opposition to the soldier vote as "the shame of the great Democratic Party . . . Shame! Shame! on them."[50] The Republicans' popular justification for soldier voting made Democratic opposition seem dishonorable, disloyal, undemocratic, and dangerous to the existence of the nation.

The Republicans' expansive rhetoric of citizenship carried the day. By 1864, nineteen northern states had successfully enacted legislation permitting soldiers in the field to vote.[51] Specifically linking suffrage to the rights of citizenship, and citizenship to soldiers made it easy for northern Republicans to persuade the northern populace to support permitting soldiers to vote. Moreover (as is discussed in chapter 5), the linkage between soldiering, suffrage, and citizenship would have enduring consequences for the meaning of citizenship in the United States into the postwar period.

In addition to pressing the citizenship issue, the soldier vote enabled Republicans to place the franchise under broader federal control. Democrats noticed this trend and responded with derision. New York state legislator John Van Buren, for example, sarcastically recommended calling his state's law "An Act to Transfer the Elective Franchise from the Qualified Voters of This State to the Commander-in-chief of the Army and the Navy of the United States."[52] Indeed, some Republicans hoped that Congress could exercise some control over the state-level right of suffrage. Following the Democratic victories in the elections of 1862, congressman Thaddeus Stevens of Pennsylvania argued that "Congress can authorize" soldiers to vote in congressional elections, establish the residence of soldiers "wherever they are," and regulate "the mode" of elections. Even further, after Pennsylvania soldiers had not been allowed to vote in 1862, Stevens suggested that Congress "could pass an act allowing those who have not voted at this election to vote and be counted in the canvass." Federal tampering with an election even to this extraordinary extent, he supposed, "would be constitutional," though he doubted it would be "politic."[53] Another Republican congressman who lost his seat in 1862 wondered if Congress could pass a law fixing a day when soldiers from all states could vote.[54] This last proposition was almost as unprecedented as Stevens's postelection voting scheme. At the time of the Civil War, the states determined their own election calendars, with the exception of the presidential election. Such a congressional intrusion into the timing of elections most likely would have been perceived by many Americans as unwarranted.

A debate soon emerged among Republican members of Congress in January 1863 over the question of whether Congress should pass a law permitting all

Union soldiers to vote. Ohio congressman William Parker Cutler's description of a closed-door meeting is telling:

> A uniform election law for members of Congress—approved but voting of soldiers disapproved—on the ground of impracticability and that it would make the army dangerous in elections[.] It was asserted that the Army of the Potomac had been drilled into an anti-Republican engine & that not one in a thousand would vote for a Republican—[which I dont believe]—That large numbers of the Herald & World are circulated gratuitously among the soldiers while other papers are practically excluded.[55]

This Republican opposition to congressional legislation permitting the soldiers to vote reveals that some Republicans were unwilling to extend the ballot to Union soldiers because they believed that the soldiers would not vote Republican. In other words, Republican views toward soldier suffrage were sometimes rooted in pragmatism as much as they were in patriotism.

Ultimately most Republicans nationwide came to believe that the soldiers should have the right to vote *and* that the soldiers would vote overwhelmingly Republican. In one case, Congress did claim statutory control over permitting soldiers to vote. The act of Congress authorizing the territory of Nevada to write a state constitution declared that "citizens [who] are enlisted in the army of the United States, and are still within said territory, . . . shall be permitted to vote at their place of rendezvous; and [if] any are absent from said territory, by reason of their enlistment in the army of the United States, they shall be permitted to vote at their place of service."[56] Such a law was clearly constitutional, as Article IV of the U.S. Constitution permits Congress to pass legislation for the territories.[57]

The federal government exerted other forms of control over the soldier vote during the Civil War, particularly in the form of War Department orders furloughing soldiers home to vote at local, state, and federal elections. Typically only Republicans were selected to go home. One Connecticut Republican watched with horror as his regiment lost ten officers and ninety-four enlisted men who were ordered by the War Department to return to Connecticut to vote in that state's 1863 gubernatorial election. "Now Father is this *right*?" he wrote incredulously. This soldier expressed much admiration for the Republican incumbent, William A. Buckingham, but said, "I would almost rather see him defeated than to see him elected in a foul way," for the men selected for furlough were "with hardly an exception, . . . *Republicans* & men who will vote for Gov. B." Such a way of carrying elections—by having the War Department select only Republican soldiers to go home to vote—set "a very bad precedent" in the mind of this soldier, "for our party may not be *always* in power, and if the opposition *should* be successful we cannot consistently blame them for following our example." This soldier also warned his father that the troops were heading home "*fully armed and equipped.* I fear that our Nation is rapidly drifting toward a *military despotism.* The abuse of arbitrary power in a free land & people will work incalculable mischief. When I view the corruption and wickedness in the country I tremble for our future."[58]

Most politicians and soldiers were not as intellectually honest as this one. To many Republicans, the Civil War provided the federal government with an incredible and unprecedented tool for electioneering. The federal government could mobilize a powerful voting bloc in the army, and when necessary could use the army to help control opposition at the polls.

THE OHIO AND PENNSYLVANIA ELECTIONS OF 1863

The eyes of the North watched closely as voters in Pennsylvania and Ohio went to the polls on October 13, 1863, to select a governor in each state. The Democratic nominee in Ohio, former congressman Clement L. Vallandigham, was the most notorious Copperhead in the North. In Congress he had repeatedly denounced the war. In May 1863, he had been arrested by the military for disloyal speech. Following a conviction by a military commission, Lincoln banished Vallandigham to the Confederacy. But the wily agitator escaped to Canada and ran for governor of Ohio from exile.

Republicans in Ohio had to make a strategic decision in choosing their nominee to oppose Vallandigham. Ohio Republicans had grown dissatisfied with incumbent governor David Tod, an antebellum Democrat who had been elected on the Republican-Union ticket in 1861, because Tod opposed emancipation and appointed only Democrats to offices in the state. Rather than renominate Tod, Ohio Republicans chose War Democrat John Brough because of his support for emancipation. Still, the Republican platform that year was quite conservative—it was silent on the slavery issue—and the other leading candidates on the ticket were conservative Republicans rather than Radicals.[59]

Historians generally characterize the Ohio election as a significant blow to the Democratic Party. "Vallandigham was buried under a 100,000-vote majority in the 1863 Ohio gubernatorial election, in which 94 percent of the soldier vote went to his Republican opponent," writes James M. McPherson.[60] But such analysis misrepresents the true nature of the contest. The choice in Ohio was not between a Republican and a Democrat; it was actually between two Democrats. "We have a ticket for the lovers of the Union," wrote one antebellum Democrat to his abolitionist son in the army. "John Brough is an old Hickory Democrat but loves his country."[61] Within this context, the lopsided victory for Brough makes more sense. To Republicans and pro-war Democrats, the choice was between a loyal Democrat and a disloyal one. Thus, one Ohio soldier—who "never was, can or will be a supporter of 'honest old Abe'"—apparently stuffed ballot boxes for Brough at the October election, writing home that he added "twenty tickets in our regiment and three or four times that number in other regiments against the Val. ticket."[62] Democratic soldiers could therefore vote for Brough in good conscience because they were actually voting for a member of their own party.[63]

Most Union soldiers hated Vallandigham more than any other northern politician—perhaps even more than any rebel. One Ohio soldier told his parents that "if the arch traitor was turned loose in Ohio" the soldiers "would kill him boldly."[64] Indeed, the soldiers overwhelmingly supported Brough, giving him 41,467 votes to Vallandigham's 2,298. More than a decade later, James A. Garfield recalled voting against Vallandigham in October 1863: "While we were voting, the shells from the batteries of armed enemies of the United States were bursting over our heads, and some of our voters were killed while in the exercise of the right of suffrage as citizens of Ohio."[65] The act of voting against a northern traitor, for Garfield, was a heroic military sacrifice equal in importance to the fighting Union soldiers did against rebel forces in the field.

The election in Pennsylvania pit incumbent governor Andrew G. Curtin against George W. Woodward, the justice of the state supreme court who had struck down Pennsylvania's law enfranchising soldiers in 1862. Curtin was a conservative Republican who had been an antebellum Democrat and would return to the Democratic fold in the postwar period.[66] Though unquestionably supportive of the Lincoln administration's war against the rebellion, Curtin was a state-centered nationalist—so much so that historian William Blair has characterized Pennsylvania's role in federal military mobilization as that of "a problem child."[67] In the hope of forming a Union coalition that would unite all Pennsylvanians behind a strong pro-war candidate, Curtin publicly indicated that he would not seek reelection and recommended that Gen. William B. Franklin, a War Democrat, receive the nomination of both parties. The more radical Simon Cameron wing of the state party began working hard to place an abolitionist at the head of the Republican ticket, causing Curtin to rethink his decision not to run. At the Republican nominating convention, Curtin outmaneuvered Cameron's choice for governor and won the nomination on the first ballot. Cameron and his supporters were sorely disappointed by Curtin's renomination but they unified around him in order to ensure a Republican victory on election day.[68]

George W. Woodward, the Democratic nominee, was a conservative Jacksonian who had served on the state supreme court since 1852. State Democratic leaders chose him because they believed that he steadfastly adhered to Democratic policies and constitutional principles.[69] Because so many Democrats had been branded "Copperheads" for publicly speaking out against the Lincoln administration's handling of the war, Woodward's few public statements appeared to make him an ideal candidate. Democrats likely believed that there was little material for Republicans to use against his candidacy.

Clement L. Vallandigham cast a long shadow over the Pennsylvania gubernatorial contest of 1863. In the wake of his arrest, Democrats throughout the North cast their lot with Vallandigham, hosting indignation meetings, rallies, and parades to protest the Lincoln administration's handling of his case. Democrats in Pennsylvania even included a pro-Vallandigham plank in their state platform that year. In short, the moderate wing of the party unified around the Peace wing's leading spokesman. This political decision paid terrible dividends for the party. In a practical sense, all Democrats who decried Vallandigham's arrest opened themselves up to charges of disloyalty and Copperheadism. And since soldiers hated treason in both North and South, this unity among the Democrats cost the party significant support among the troops.

Republicans worked hard to paint Woodward as a disloyal sympathizer with southern treason. Central to their claim was that he was anti-soldier. At a Republican rally in Pittsburgh, one T. J. Bigham claimed that Woodward went to Gettysburg shortly after the battle to find his son, Maj. George A. Woodward, who had been wounded in the foot. According to Bigham, the judge believed his son "might be thankful he got off so well" because he "ought to have been wounded in the heart for fighting in such a cause."[70] Major Woodward refused to allow this libel to go unanswered. He immediately penned a letter to Bigham calling his statement "a wicked and deliberate falsehood." Major Woodward had, as a consequence of earlier battlefield wounds and confinement in Libby Prison, become "crippled for life." After being paroled, he returned to his parents' home, where he was cared for by his father, mother, and sisters. For four months he was confined to his bed, "suffering intensely," but "no father could be more kind, more solicitous for a son's welfare, than was mine."[71]

During that period of recuperation, the judge and his son had "almost daily conversations" related to the war, "and, although he freely criticised, and often condemned, the manner in which the war was managed by the Administration," according to the son, "never did he utter a sentiment in sympathy with the doctrine of secession, nor a syllable of approval of the course taken by the people of the South; and never did he say aught which was not calculated to encourage me in the performance of my duty as a soldier." Major Woodward concluded his letter by pointing out how disheartening it was for soldiers who were "toiling and fighting for their country" to know that "lying politicians at home are using them as instruments of their partisan malice."[72]

Bigham replied with an insulting public letter to Judge Woodward: "I have not the honor of [your son's] acquaintance, and unless he fights better than he writes, the active service has not lost much by his retirement." After repeating his accusations of disloyalty, Bigham suggested that Woodward's views on the war might even merit impeachment from the Supreme Court of Pennsylvania. All this did not stem from "personal unkindness toward you," Bigham assured the judge, but only "what I deem my duty to my country."[73]

Contrary to the false stories about his two sons in the army, Woodward took great pride in their service to the country. In fact, when the judge heard rumors that one of his sons had been promoted, Woodward wrote to the Curtin administration to ascertain whether the rumors were true. "I have understood that his superior officers give an excellent account of George," wrote Woodward with great satisfaction, "and I should feel highly gratified to know that he had been promoted."[74] When, during the gubernatorial campaign, Woodward sat on a train next to Republican politician and journalist Alexander K. McClure, the Republican asked the Democrat "whether he or I in the opposing positions with the soldiers was best supporting the cause of the soldiers in the field. He answered with visible pride that his sons were soldiers, and as soldiers they would do their duty."[75] McClure's recollection may be tainted—it was recorded more than forty years after the fact. But even so, the words he attributed to Woodward comport with Woodward's private correspondence during and after the war. Such were not the sentiments of a man who sought to aid the rebels, as the Republicans frequently charged.

Like T. J. Bigham, other Republican speakers, pamphleteers, and newspaper editors accused Woodward of being a traitor and "an open, avowed Secessionist" who would "repeal" the Union's victory at Gettysburg.[76] A vote for Woodward was a disloyal act. "Traitors . . . will support the Rebellion by voting for its friend, George W. Woodward," wrote the editors of the *Pittsburgh Daily Commercial.* "Vote by all means, for Curtin and the right, if you are a patriot, or for Woodward and treason if you are a traitor."[77] Most of the Republican attacks were based on a December 1860 speech Woodward had given at Independence Hall in which he advocated letting the South depart in peace. To be sure, Woodward was ardently pro-slavery, had studied and revered the doctrines of John C. Calhoun as a young man, and blamed abolitionist agitation for the coming of the war. But his advocacy of peaceable secession before the outbreak of hostilities was a viable (albeit improbable) constitutional position. It did not mean that he was "the candidate of Jeff. Davis" and was "counseling rebellion," as his Republican opponents frequently charged.[78]

In one instance, Republican creativity in the Curtin–Woodward contest had lasting consequences, influencing voters in the presidential election the following year. The *Pittsburgh Daily Commercial* declared that Gen. George B. McClellan "makes no secret of his earnest desire that Andrew G. Curtin should be [re]elected" and that he would campaign and vote for the governor.[79] John Forney's *Philadelphia Press* made similar specious claims. Pennsylvania Democrats were furious, and they convinced a reluctant McClellan to rebut the blatant falsehoods. McClellan penned a letter to Woodward's campaign manager, Charles Biddle, saying that while he had hoped to stay out of partisan politics, he could no longer remain silent in the face of such gross "misrepresentations." Contrary to the news reports, after having had a lengthy conversation with the judge, McClellan concluded that Woodward's election was in the best interest of the nation. "I understand Judge Woodward to be in favor of the prosecution of the war with all the means at the command of the loyal states, until the military power of the Rebellion is destroyed," wrote McClellan. Both Woodward and McClellan believed that while the war ought to be "waged with all possible decision and energy," the government ought not to assail citizens' "rights and property not demanded by military necessity and recognized by military law among civilized nations." Lastly, both Woodward and McClellan agreed that "the *sole* great objects of this war are the restoration of the unity of the nation, the preservation of the Constitution, and the supremacy of the laws of the country." Believing that he and the judge "entirely agree upon these points," wrote McClellan, "I would, were it in my power, give to Judge Woodward my voice and my vote."[80]

McClellan's letter was widely circulated on October 13, but, coming as it did, on election day, it had very little effect. Ironically, McClellan's letter proved detrimental to his presidential campaign the following year, as many northern observers believed it linked his opinions to those of an "avowed Secessionist." Indeed, Republicans saw McClellan's letter as evidence that he had "joined the Copperheads," endorsed "the Rebel calumny," and thrown his support behind northern treason.[81] A schoolteacher near Philadelphia noted that McClellan's letter revealed the general to be not only a "nincompoop," but "a little traitor, a little fool, and not much of anything."[82]

McClellan was not the only Union general falsely portrayed as supporting Governor Curtin. On August 28, 1863, Curtin made a sword presentation to Gen. George Gordon Meade. Prior to the ceremony, a Republican politician approached Meade and said, "If you can say anything in favor of Curtin, it will help us greatly." Meade replied that he did not know what was meant by "helping you" and that it was common knowledge that "I have nothing to do with politics." Of course, Meade continued, he did intend to "allude to Governor Curtin and his services in behalf of the volunteers of Pennsylvania." "Well, that is all we want," replied the Republican. Upon the stage, Meade delivered an address praising "the gallant officers and brave soldiers" of his corps, particularly those who had fallen in battle. Strangely enough, however, when Meade read the reports of his speech in the newspapers the following day, he found that they did not fully represent the opinions he had expressed: "The speech is accurately reported, with one exception, and that is where I am made to say, 'I hoped the people of Pennsylvania would re-elect Governor Curtin.' I said nothing of the kind, and made no allusions to elections." Meade went on to complain that some members of the press were editorializing in favor of Curtin, "quoting my speech in italics." Republican newspapers across the North picked up the misquoted speech, italicizing the section calling for Curtin's reelection, thus emphasizing the one passage that was not true.[83]

The issue of soldier suffrage became central to the gubernatorial campaign of 1863. The Republicans included a plank in their platform calling for an amendment to the state constitution to allow Pennsylvania soldiers to vote, and they pointed to Woodward's 1862 opinion in *Chase v. Miller* as key evidence of his animus toward the soldiery.[84] Congressman Thaddeus Stevens took to the stump to deride Woodward and his colleague, Chief Justice Walter H. Lowrie (who was up for reelection), for their decision. "As the surest way to aid their rebel friends, and punish those who oppose them," proclaimed Stevens at a Republican rally in Lancaster, "both Judge Woodward and judge Lawry, have denied the soldiers the right to vote."[85] Democrats in the army, like Fitz-John Porter, noted that the Republicans made use of Woodward's ruling in *Chase v. Miller* "to prejudice soldiers against him—and successfully," though Porter believed that Woodward's decision in that case had been the correct one.[86]

The soldier vote thus became a galvanizing issue for the Republican Party, and Republicans worked hard "to bring the influence of the disfranchised soldiers in the field into practical effect upon the fathers, brothers and immediate friends at home."[87] Indeed, soldiers' letters flooded post offices and Republican newspapers saying that Curtin's defeat at the polls would be worse than a Union defeat in the field.[88] Writing before the election, one soldier claimed, "It is as necessary to defeat Woodward as it is to defeat Lee."[89]

Although soldiers could not vote in the field, they were still allowed to vote *"within the limits of Pa."*[90] A massive drive thus ensued to get soldiers and government officials sent home to vote.[91] Governor Curtin wrote to Lincoln asking for extensions for "our friends from the Army" who were already on furlough in Pennsylvania prior to the election.[92] Meanwhile, Secretary of War Edwin M. Stanton ordered 1,500 convalescents from military hospitals back to Pennsylvania, noting that it "is my desire to do everything that can be properly done to carry the election in Pennsylvania." Stanton also directed military commanders "to grant furloughs and give transportation, home and back, to all electors who may be in your command, and may desire to exercise the elective franchise next Tuesday."[93]

Soldiers heard reports "that everything possible is being done" to get the troops home to vote. "The rumor now is that 500 leaves of absence are to be granted to the Division about the elections which is an absurdity."[94] One Republican physician near Philadelphia worried that the Union armies were "in great danger" with so "many thousands of soldiers having come away to be in the state elections in Ohio and Pa. Everything here yields now to the contest for Governor."[95] Some politicians sent letters to the Curtin administration with names of soldiers who ought to be furloughed to return home to vote for the governor's reelection, noting that the soldiers were "good talkers and will make good use of the time given them." One Pennsylvanian even reported that ten imprisoned deserters who were "Rank Democrats," members of the Knights of the Golden Circle, and "life long locofoco[s]," would vote for Curtin if they were discharged from prison.[96] Indeed, some soldiers' votes could be bought. Pvt. Henry G. Conser, an enlisted man who had received a medical discharge from the 148th Pennsylvania Infantry in March 1863, wrote to Governor Curtin a week before the election that he had not yet received all of the pay that was due him. "My intention was to vote the Union ticket this fall and to support it as much as my influence allows," he wrote the governor, "but I can not do so unless I receive full satisfaction about my money from some one." Conser was confident that Curtin "can get it if you try." And if the governor did so, "then I will vot[e] the ticket." "Shall I be cheated out of it and support the same party," he asked the governor rhetorically. "No sir!"[97]

Politicians understood the importance of appealing to voters' personal interests, including their base pecuniary motives. One Republican called on an official in the Curtin administration to use "all proper means to obtain a majority of votes for our Governor." All proper means, according to this correspondent, included making sure that draftees received the pay that was due them and having Curtin "connect his name as having moved in the matter, to obtain the pay."[98] Indeed, Republican politicians sought to make their candidate appear most friendly to the soldiers in the field. When soldiers were furloughed home, they were told that Curtin had secured the furloughs and travel expenses.[99] Republican leaders would leave no stone unturned in ensuring that Republican soldiers got home to vote. "Our business is to elect the ticket," wrote one Pennsylvania Republican. "It can and must be done regardless of work and expense." Victory could only be accomplished, according to this partisan, "by bringing every regiment into Penna for the *purpose of voting*," and the federal government must be brought to see the necessity of such an action.[100]

Some of the greatest electioneering took place in Centre County, where Republican politicians worked vigorously to bring loyal soldiers home to vote. "A vote here might do us more good tha[n] killing rebels on the battle field," wrote one Centre County Republican. "We have some hopes of beating the Rebs in Centre Co. but cannot do it without help."[101] In order to ensure that only Republican soldiers obtained furloughs to return home for the election, Centre County lawyer Hugh McAllister requested Col. James A. Beaver of the 148th Pennsylvania Volunteers to send him "a list of the men in your regiment.—voters in Centre county—who can render most aid at and before the Election. Place them in the order of their relative importance proposing *democrats* in case they can be relied upon." Such cooperation of the soldiers in the field, along with the effort being put forth by Republicans at home, gave McAllister "strong hopes of carrying our ticket in this county."[102]

Colonel Beaver regretted that military operations prevented his regiment from going home to vote, but the soldiers did their part by sending letters home in support of the Republicans, and many did receive furloughs.[103] Soldiers who received furloughs apparently gained other perks in addition to being able to exercise the full rights of citizenship. "I herd that some of the solders that went home to vote stood a good chance whith the girls," wrote one soldier in Colonel Beaver's command.[104] Following the election, Democratic newspapers from Centre County were outraged by the Republicans' duplicity. "They pretend that no pledge was exacted from any soldier, and that *Democratic* and Republican soldiers were sent home indiscriminately," the editor of the *Bellefonte Democratic Watchman* angrily exclaimed. "The radical journals have no readers so stupid as to believe that 'cock and bull story.'"[105]

In truth, the Democrats should not have expected to win much support from the soldiers. Many Pennsylvania soldiers had had a favorable predisposition toward Governor Curtin since the time of their enlistment. Curtin was well known among the troops as "The Soldier's Friend" for the attention he paid to their needs and the needs of their families.[106] More importantly, Pennsylvania soldiers came to believe that Curtin's reelection was essential for Union victory. The election of a Democrat would "prolong the war" by giving hope to the rebels that a disloyal party might gain control in the North and negotiate a disgraceful peace with the Confederacy.[107]

Equally important, many soldiers resented Woodward and the Democrats for depriving them of the franchise. One Democrat in the Eighty-Fourth Pennsylvania Volunteers who ardently supported George B. McClellan for president as early as 1863, wrote angrily that "Woodward and Lowrie made out that the soldiers had no right to vote for govner[.] if they aint got no right to vote they aint got no right to fight." This soldier wondered if Woodward might like to try joining the army: "let woodward come out and fight himself and see how he likes it[.] I will Bet he will Pull Back and say let them fight it out." This soldier could not support a Copperhead like Woodward in 1863, but he would write several newspaper articles in September 1864 supporting McClellan for president.[108] Another soldier, who may have been a Democrat, criticized Democratic leaders for showing sympathy toward the rebels but not Union soldiers. "They talk of giving the South her rights, just as if a traitor had any rights. They have two rights. A Constitutional right to be *hung* and a Divine right to be *Damned*. . . . Southern men are traitors out and out, but those contemptible leaders of a deluded set of men, Fernando Wood, Vallandigham, Woodward &c are a cross between Traitor and Dam Fools." Yet this soldier noted that Woodward was too smart to be considered a fool, "for he was sharp enough to deprive us of the right to vote against him."[109]

When word reached the army that Curtin had won, most soldiers exulted in the news.[110] The Republicans had successfully persuaded the troops that Democrats like Woodward were disloyal, which was easy to do when a candidate could be seen as hostile to the rights of the troops. Most soldiers came to believe what the Republican press had told them: that Woodward's election would "send a thrill of joy throughout the desolated land of traitors."[111] The Republican strategy to win the support of the troops by claiming the mantle of loyalty and charging the Democratic nominee with treason was crucial to Governor Curtin's victory in 1863.

In truth, Pennsylvania Democrats made themselves vulnerable to charges of treason by including a plank in their platform sympathizing with Vallandigham. Thoughtful Democrats recognized that the "Vallandigham resolution in the platform hurt us a little while it could do us no possible good."[112] After the election, another Democrat wrote to the editor of the *New York World* that their party had erred in linking Woodward to the Ohio Copperhead. While Vallandigham had been "greatly wronged," the party could not allow his "mischievous errors" to damage the cause of the whole Democratic Party. As this Democrat saw it, "the nomination of Val. has identified the whole Party with him throughout the Country & no doubt caused . . . disastrous results" throughout the North. If the Democratic Party hoped to regain electoral majorities, it could not follow Peace men like Vallandigham but rather "such calm & wise Counsellors" as Horatio Seymour of New York and George Woodward of Pennsylvania. "There is no mistake about one point," continued the writer, "the democratic party must plant itself immovably on the war footing—that is it must distinctly & inexorably take the ground of prosecuting the war until the rebellion is subdued—cost what it may of time, money or men. It must do this so plain that there can be no cavil about it & those who cannot unite with us in this must be cut loose & sent a drift."[113] In short, the Democrats had chosen the wrong standard-bearer since Vallandigham had ostentatiously chosen not to vote for supplies for the troops.

Ohio soldiers voted more than 17 to 1 in favor of John Brough over Vallandigham.[114] Had Pennsylvania soldiers been allowed to vote, they would likely have supported Curtin by similar margins. But such overwhelmingly lopsided statistics can be misleading. These election results do not reveal a conversion of the soldiers to Republicanism, but rather a rejection of Copperheadism. John Brough, after all, was a War Democrat. And Andrew Curtin was a conservative Republican who had supported a War Democrat for the Republican nomination before deciding to run for reelection; he only entered the race when it became apparent that an abolitionist would likely win the nomination if he retired. Curtin had been a Democrat before the war and he rejoined the party in the postwar period.

When the soldiers voted in 1863—or told their fathers, brothers, and uncles at home how to vote—they were in essence choosing between disloyal Peace Democrats and loyal pro-war Democrats. Their choice was to reject the Copperheads. One Pennsylvania soldier who had known the Woodward family personally concluded that the reelection of Curtin was "at once the most politic, and the most certain way to end the war speedily," though he felt "some regret that I can't sympathize with Judge Woodward's family, who always received me in the politest manner possible."[115] Another Pennsylvania soldier described his experience going home to vote: "I was home at the election to vote for the war but not for Curtin[.] I voted against the Copper Head Woodward."[116] This soldier's vote for Curtin was not a vote *for* the Republican Party but a vote *against* the Peace Democrats.[117]

When soldiers opposed the Democrats in 1863 and supported the Republican candidates, they did so because they believed it was in their interest to do so. Most soldiers believed that Democrats like Woodward and Vallandigham were anti-soldier and anti-Union, while Republicans, like Curtin, were "The Soldier's Friend." Many Democratic soldiers were pushed into the Union-Republican coalition by the Copperheads at home. Their votes were more against the Peace wing of the Democratic Party than anything else. A telling letter from a New York soldier, written in December 1863, is worth quoting at length:

You may enquire then why there were not more Democrats home [on furlough]. The reason is they are a very scarce article in the Army at present. The past six months have made a great change politically in the Army. Men who a year ago were bitterly against the Administration have failed to find even sympathy, much [less] encouragement in any other party. You may say they haven't received these from the Administration. I think they have. At least they haven't received open opposition from it, and they have from all other parties. The ground the Democratic party took in the Vallandigham affair disgusted every soldier. He was as much a traitor as Jeff Davis, and have your constitutional rights and liberties become so sacred that such a rebel cannot be arrested and taken out of town until some Justice of the Peace has decided whether he is loyal or not? Oh, fudge! Where is the loyalty and patriotism of the North? I don't believe there is any. Vallandigham ought to have been hung with a tarred rope, and there are others [in the] north nearly as bad.

The author of this letter, a Democrat, retained his party affiliation despite his reservations about the power of the Peace wing within his party. "Now perhaps you think I am an Administration man, but it is not so," he continued.

I know how things worked last winter at Washington, and I don't think they have changed much. But I do think the Democratic party has gone back on the soldiers. A year ago the soldiers thought the Democrats were their only friends, but the New York riot and the figuring of some men in evading the draft has changed the feeling greatly. And in regard to hiring Negro soldiers, I don't know a man so fond of soldiering that he is not willing to let the Negroes have the honors if they want them at $7 per month. And every one who has ever seen them acknowledges that they are the soldiers for this climate.

Democrats like this soldier felt betrayed by the Copperhead leaders of their own party. Men like Vallandigham, from their perspective, were just as culpable for their suffering in this bloody war as Jefferson Davis was. In some ways, antiwar Democrats were worse than the rebels since they lived in the Union but appeared to disregard the nation and the needs of its soldiers. "I tell you, we will soon end the fighting here and if the traitors north don't keep quiet we will fix them," concluded this soldier. "Well, I guess this is nonsense enough, but I tell you it [is] the feeling of the soldiers."[118]

The Democratic Party made fateful errors in Pennsylvania and Ohio when it picked nominees who could easily be painted as anti-soldier. Opposing the needs and rights of the soldiers would brand the most qualified candidate as disloyal. To the extent that Union soldiers "became" Republicans during the war, for many it was merely a temporary switch that enabled them to vote for a party that supported them in the field and upheld their rights as citizens.

CONCLUSION

The initial calls for unity in the North proved short-lived. As the war moved forward, Lincoln made many controversial decisions; he also found himself needing to do things that he had earlier pledged not to do. In 1861, he suspended the privilege of the writ of habeas corpus and used the military to detain northern civilians. Within a few months, he would be trying northern civilians before military commissions, a practice that continued well into Reconstruction. In 1862, he issued his preliminary Emancipation Proclamation, fundamentally altering the nature of the war. Now the war would no longer be about just Union, but freedom and the liberation of 4 million slaves as well. Emancipation became a means to the end of Union, and it was a means that Lincoln would hold to tenaciously for the remainder of his life. Other Republican war policies also engendered divisions within northern society—the passage of the Legal Tender Act, which created a system of paper money known as greenbacks; the National Bank Act, which centralized the banking system in America; and the conscription act, which many likened to slavery since it forced northern civilians into involuntary service in the Union armies. The war, which had been entered by the North with great fanfare and unity, had changed in ways that few had anticipated.

The divisiveness of wartime politics emerged not only in the legislative halls, but also in the field. Politicians and soldiers alike debated confiscation, emancipation, and conscription. And just as there was political intimidation at the polls during election season, it also existed within the ranks.

2

"YOU MUST HAVE LEARNED . . . OF MY
OFFICIAL DECAPITATION"

Emancipation and Intimidation in the Union Ranks

THE ARREST AND HUMILIATION of Brig. Gen. Charles P. Stone in the wake
of the Ball's Bluff debacle is well known among Civil War historians. Stone, a
pro-slavery Democrat, became the scapegoat for the Union defeat and the death
of Edward D. Baker, a Union general, U.S. senator, and personal friend of the
president. On the Senate floor, Charles Sumner chastised Stone for returning
two fugitive slaves to their master. Sumner referred to Stone's actions as "vile and
unconstitutional," an "outrage," an "indignity," an "abuse," and "an act unworthy
of our national flag." In response, Stone challenged Sumner to a duel, but such
a confrontation never occurred. Instead, Sumner and his Republican colleagues
used their powerful political influence to destroy Stone's personal reputation and
military career. Stone was brought before the congressional Joint Committee on
the Conduct of the War, but neither he nor his lawyer was allowed to see the
charges or testimony against him. On the committee's recommendation, Secretary of War Edwin M. Stanton arrested Stone and sent him to Forts Lafayette and
Hamilton in New York, where he remained imprisoned for six months. Republican newspapers howled with glee. "His punishment must be open and prompt,"
editorialized one Philadelphia paper, "whether that punishment is merely military disgrace *or the death that a traitor in arms* should have without delay" (emphasis added). Stone was later restored to active duty but was dismissed in 1864.
In a private letter, Sumner proudly informed Ralph Waldo Emerson that he was
responsible for Stone's dismissal.[1]

Charles Stone was one of several Union commanders to be disgraced before the meddling and highly partisan congressional committee. While the joint
congressional committee sought to root out disloyalty at the national level, Republican military officers did an equal share of the work at the company, regimental, brigade, division, corps, and army levels. Officers and enlisted men who

expressed disapproval of the president's war measures or who criticized the commander in chief (in violation of the Fifth Article of War) found themselves recipients of an order for summary dismissal, or, even worse, arrest and court-martial.[2] In fact, Congress, in July 1862, authorized President Lincoln "to dismiss and discharge from the military service . . . any officer, for any cause which, in his judgment, either renders such officer unsuitable for, or whose dismission would promote, the public service."[3] Opposition to emancipation soon became one such reason. The efforts of civilian and military leadership to suppress and punish anti-emancipation soldiers thus demonstrates the top-down nature by which soldiers were taught to fight in a war that required slave liberation to save the Union.

The self-emancipation thesis argues that emancipation was a bottom-up process—that the slaves taught the soldiers, who taught their officers, who taught their commanders, who taught Lincoln, that emancipation had to be adopted as a Union war measure. According to Ira Berlin, the slaves "taught common soldiers" that they needed to emancipate southern slaves. This "lesson" eventually worked its way up the chain of command so that many northerners, from army privates up to the commander in chief, "learned" that they needed to abolish slavery. "The burden of teaching that lesson fell upon the slaves," argues Barbara J. Fields. "Their stubborn actions in pursuit of their faith gradually turned faith into reality. It was they who taught the nation that it must place the abolition of slavery at the head of its agenda."[4]

The self-emancipation thesis is thus predicated on the assumption that the common soldiers learned directly from the slaves that the slaves needed to be freed. These soldiers then taught that lesson up the Union chain of command. Much evidence from the field, however, suggests that the Union high command had at least as much—if not more—influence on the common soldiers as the soldiers had on their leaders. Indeed, the Lincoln administration, the Republican majority in Congress, and the commanding officers in the field instilled in their soldiers—sometimes by force, sometimes by intimidation, sometimes by persuasion, and sometimes through the deprivation of opposing viewpoints— a belief that emancipation was a worthy war aim that needed to be pursued, that freeing the slaves would benefit the white soldiers who were fighting for the Union, and that African Americans should be permitted to join the Union army. In April and May 1863, for example, Adjutant General Lorenzo Thomas addressed white troops in the western theater regarding the government's new policy of enlisting black regiments. At Helena, Arkansas, he declared: "The policy of the Administration must be carried out, and no opposition on the part of officers and soldiers will be allowed. Even the stars [denoting a general's rank] will be no protection to the officer, who by act or word opposes the policy of the Government." Of course, not all soldiers responded positively to Thomas's message. The Ninetieth Illinois Volunteers, an Irish regiment, hissed after hearing Thomas announce the new policy, at which point the officers of the regiment were promptly arrested.[5]

In the months following Lincoln's issuance of the Emancipation Proclamation, Union military leaders repressed officers and ordinary soldiers within their jurisdictions who expressed dissatisfaction with Lincoln's emancipation policy, or with the president himself. To be sure, many of these soldiers voiced their disaffection in hyperbolic language that was sufficiently inflammatory—even to the extent of expressing ill will toward the president or wishing success to the rebel cause—to warrant punishment. Others complained that they would never have enlisted had they known that the war would become a conflict over slavery. Disgruntled officers tendered their resignations rather than fight in a war for emancipation. Enlisted men deserted. (Resignations and desertions are discussed in chapter 3.)

Union military leaders could not stand idly by while the army slowly disintegrated. Dissatisfaction among the troops could easily snowball—particularly in light of the recent disaster at Fredericksburg in December 1862 and Maj. Gen. Ambrose Burnside's subsequent "Mud March." Morale in the Union armies was reaching an all-time low during the winter of 1862–63, and Democratic propaganda against Lincoln and emancipation was falling on listening ears. As a consequence, the army—from the top down—moved to silence this opposition. Democratic newspapers were banned from Union camps, antiwar letters sent to soldiers were confiscated and their authors were arrested for disloyalty, and Democratic soldiers who voiced their displeasure with Lincoln were arrested, court-martialed, and punished. One judge advocate in the army argued that soldiers could not use the "right of free discussion" to criticize Lincoln, emancipation, or the war. "While a soldier still remains a freeman," claimed this officer, "neither civilian nor soldier has the right to use such language in the presence of the men of the Army, as will cause discontent, create distrust, encourage desertion, and dampen the ardor and enthusiasm of our soldiers."[6] An officer in the Fourteenth Rhode Island Heavy Artillery, a black regiment, similarly believed that "disloyal" speech should be silenced in wartime: "I don't object to free speech in a way, but it is a military necessity that speech of that kind shouldn't be quite so free at this time and so I say suspend it as you would the writ of habeas corpus, which copperheads make so much fuss about."[7] And soldiers who violated such principles must be punished. "All *ignorant, dissipated, disloyal, & cowardly* officers must be dismissed if we are to succeed," wrote one New York civilian to Maj. Gen. Joseph Hooker in February 1863.[8]

The punishments devised for anti-emancipation officers and enlisted men were designed to be spectacles that would dissuade other soldiers from acting alike. Some soldiers were publicly drummed out of camp, others were reprimanded while their comrades stood in formation listening, and still others were penalized through humiliating practices that would be witnessed day after day by their peers. The most final of all punishments, execution, was meted out on a few deserters who left their posts because of their opposition to emancipation. All of these punishments combined to teach the common soldier that he ought to reconsider any feelings he might have in opposition to emancipation—or to keep his personal views to himself.

These policies for dealing with dissent rested on the premise that good military order was necessary if the army was going to be successful in the field. In May 1863, Gen. Ambrose Burnside articulated these views when defending his arrest of former congressman Clement L. Vallandigham:

> If I were to indulge in wholesale criticisms of the policy of the Government, it would demoralize the army under my command, and every friend of his country would call me a traitor. If the officers or soldiers were to indulge in such criticisms, it would weaken the army to the extent of their influence; and if this criticism were universal in the army, it would cause it to be broken to pieces, the Government to be divided, our homes to be invaded, and anarchy to reign. My duty to my Government forbids me to indulge in such criticisms; officers and soldiers are not allowed so to indulge, and this course will be sustained by all honest men.[9]

In Burnside's view, criticism from within the ranks or officer corps could lead to the demoralization of the army and the final destruction of the Union. For Burnside, dissent had to be stifled at home just as it had to be silenced among the troops.

Republican members of Congress agreed with Burnside's assessment and sought to set a positive example for disaffected soldiers. The issue of soldiers exercising their free speech rights in opposition to Republican war measures arose on the floor of the House of Representatives in April 1864, when that body debated the expulsion of Democratic congressman Alexander Long of Ohio for saying that the South should be allowed to go in peace. The Republican majority believed that speech sometimes must be limited in wartime. Republican Robert C. Schenck of Ohio, a former Union general who had done much to silence pro-Confederate viewpoints in Maryland (and who had won Vallandigham's congressional seat in 1862), argued that soldiers would be shot for advocating the views that Long had articulated in Congress. If a soldier "should turn to one of his comrades about him, saying to one, 'We cannot beat the enemy;' to another, 'We had better lay down our arms;' to another, 'Our cause is wrong; we never can conquer;' and to another, 'Let us demand of our commanding officer to stop shedding blood, and have a truce between the two armies'—if a soldier at such a time should talk thus in the ranks, what would you do with him? You would shoot him!"[10] Having had the experience of discipline at the battlefield, Schenck argued for absolute loyalty on the home front as well as in the field. Setting such an example, Schenck maintained, would encourage the troops and demoralize the rebels.

Even Gen. George B. McClellan publicly declared that anti-emancipation speech could not be tolerated in the army. When word of Lincoln's edict reached McClellan in late September 1862, he fumed that it was "almost impossible for me to retain my commission & self respect at the same time" and that he could not bring himself "to fight for such an accursed doctrine as that of a servile insurrection," which he believed would be the result of emancipation. McClellan drafted a letter protesting Lincoln's actions; but upon calm reflection and the receipt of wise counsel, he burned it. Instead, on October 7, 1862, McClellan issued General Order No. 163, in which he reminded the officers and soldiers of the Army of the Potomac that the civil authorities in Washington possessed authority over the military and would determine national policy. He wrote: "Discussions by officers & soldiers concerning public measures determined upon and declared by the Government when carried at all beyond temperate and respectful expressions of opinion tend greatly to impair & destroy the discipline & efficiency of troops by substituting the spirit of political faction for that firm steady & earnest support of the Authority of the Government which is the highest duty

of the American soldier." The soldiers, in other words, were to silence their criticisms of the president and his policies. If they did not like emancipation, they
could vote the current administration and members of Congress out of office.[11]
McClellan silenced his own views out of deference to military order.

SUMMARY DISMISSALS FOR DISLOYALTY

Immediately following the issuance of the Emancipation Proclamation, the Lincoln administration began taking steps to weed anti-emancipation officers out
of the Union army. Some officers were summarily dismissed without the benefit
of a court-martial for language they had been overheard saying against the proclamation. The most well known of these was Maj. John J. Key of Gen. Henry W.
Halleck's staff, who was reported to have said that the object of the war was not
to gain "any decisive advantage" but for both sides to be "tired out" so that "a
compromise may be made by which we can save slavery." Upon hearing of Key's
remarks, Lincoln wanted "the matter examined" to determine whether Key's
"head should go off." When called before the president, Key did not deny having
said such things, so Lincoln immediately dismissed him from the service. "You
may think about that as you please," Lincoln told the soldier, "but no man shall
bear a commission of mine, who is not in favor of gaining victories over the
rebels, at any and all times."[12]

In an anonymously published newspaper editorial, Lincoln's private secretary, John Hay, defended Key's dismissal: "It is to be hoped that the example
of the luckless Major, who was only more indiscreet than others, will result in
good to those ardent young persons who garrison Willard's, and evade the liquor
ordinance in quiet places of the Capital. *Striking him down may silence others
like him,* as a stone dropped into the noisiest frog pond will reduce to instant
reticence the whole batrachian orchestra" (emphasis added). When Key sent
Lincoln a "bundle of letters" protesting his dismissal and asking for reinstatement, Lincoln replied that he bore no ill will toward Key and he did not suspect
Key of disloyalty, but "an example" had to be made of officers who adhered to
Key's view of the war.[13]

Lincoln acted with prudence in dismissing Key and then having Hay dis-
seminate a news item publicizing and justifying the dismissal. The president
could have allowed the matter to drop quietly with little effect on the military

other than the loss of one staff officer. Hay's writing made the story national news and offered a warning to other like-minded officers to heed their words carefully even when speaking in private or out of anger. Secretary of the Treasury Salmon P. Chase used the Key case as an opportunity to shore up support for the president's new emancipation policy among the Union high command. "I hope you endorse heartily—not merely acquiesce in the Presidents proclamation," he wrote to Gen. William Starke Rosecrans in October 1862. "Let every body understand that Slavery is to end: and that the sooner masters pay wages & so secure willing service from free men the better for all concerned." Chase asked Rosecrans for his views on the subject and then added, "It was Buell's proslaveryism I verily believe that caused more than half his halting."[14]

Historians have mistakenly believed that Key's dismissal was anomalous. David Brion Davis and Steven Mintz, for example, write: "Key was the only officer to be dismissed from [the] service for uttering disloyal sentiments."[15] If such were the case, the Key affair would be an insignificant moment in which the Lincoln administration dismissed one otherwise unknown officer for opposition to the administration's new emancipation policy. But other dismissals soon followed. About a month after Key's dismissal, Lt. William S. Johnson of the Seventeenth Kentucky Volunteers was dismissed "for disloyalty and insubordination."[16] These two cases were only the beginning. In 1863 and 1864, the Lincoln administration and the Union high command punished many other officers in an attempt to enforce support for emancipation among the troops. In other words, Lincoln took many opportunities to teach the soldiers that they needed to support emancipation.

Following the issuance of the Emancipation Proclamation, the Union high command mounted a concerted effort to find and remove anti-emancipation officers from the army. In February 1863, Maj. Gen. Ulysses S. Grant established a board of examiners to remove disloyal officers from the Army of the Tennessee. The president of the board, Col. Thomas W. Bennett of the Sixty-Ninth Indiana Volunteers, colorfully described the work of the board in a letter to Indiana's adjutant general. "We are having a good time," he wrote. "We will give the army a good *purge* and a healthy *puke* of all 'Copperheads.' Resignations are 'played out' with such fellows, they are to be *kicked out*." Once he had accomplished the work of "*weeding* out the infernal scoundrels," Bennett predicted that "the army shall be purified."[17]

Work like that done by Bennett's board near Vicksburg was accomplished throughout the Union armies nationwide. In rare instances, it even occurred in Confederate prisoner of war camps. At least one Union officer believed he should prefer charges against any of his fellow prisoners who criticized Lincoln and his policies. "I occasionally hear an officer here denouncing the President of the U.S. and the Administration just as a *civilian* would have a right to do," wrote an Illinois officer at Libby Prison in August 1863. "Now they are especially prohibited from so doing by laws which they have positively sworn to obey, and I am determined hereafter to prefer charges against every man or officer in the service who I hear so denouncing the President."[18]

A number of officers were dismissed in 1863 and 1864 for criticizing President Lincoln, emancipation, or the enlistment of black soldiers. Maj. Charles J. Whiting of the Second U.S. Cavalry was dishonorably dismissed in November 1863 "for disloyalty and for using contemptuous and disrespectful words against the President of the United States." In public conversations, Whiting had been overheard saying that the Republican emancipation policy would divide the North and unite the South and that Lincoln had violated the Constitution by freeing the slaves and suspending the writ of habeas corpus. Maj. Granville O. Haller, a friend of Major Whiting's, was summarily dismissed in 1863 for allegedly toasting to separate northern and southern confederacies "while Lincoln is President" in December 1862.[19]

Some officers took the initiative to have "disloyal" subordinates removed from their regiments. On January 13, 1863, the colonel of the Sixty-Third Indiana Infantry held a "private interview" at Indianapolis with Gov. Oliver P. Morton, informing him that Capts. Horatio R. Claypool and William McFall of the Sixty-Third were disloyal. Based on this conversation with the colonel, Governor Morton wrote to Secretary of War Edwin M. Stanton seeking the captains' dismissal, adding that he believed each of them to be "a member of a secret and treasonable society organized in this State," although he admitted that this "fact cannot be proved." Based on this correspondence alone, Stanton dismissed both officers "for disloyalty" on March 7, 1863.[20]

Other officers similarly received the axe that spring and summer. Col. Joseph D. Hatfield of the Eighty-Ninth Ohio Volunteer Infantry, Col. John Vanvalkenburg of the Twentieth Indiana Volunteers, and Lt. D. R. Wilson of the Sixteenth U.S. Infantry were all dismissed during the spring of 1863 for speaking disloyally.[21]

Lincoln summarily dismissed Col. William W. Caldwell and Capt. Andrew J. Howard of the Eighty-First Indiana Volunteers on July 6, 1863, for "uttering disloyal sentiments."[22] Fifteen days later, Lt. Manuel B. DeSilva of the Sixteenth Ohio Infantry was dismissed from the service by order of the president for writing newspaper editorials critical of the Lincoln administration (more cases like this are discussed below).[23] An Illinois surgeon was arrested twice and then dismissed for disloyalty.[24] Lt. William G. McConnell of the Sixty-Second Illinois was summarily dismissed for criticizing the president in violation of the Fifth Article of War.[25] An Ohio officer was dismissed for saying he "did not recognize these nigger officers" at a social gathering on New Year's Day, 1864.[26] Alexander Montgomery, a quartermaster in Pittsburgh, was summarily dismissed from the army in July 1863 for allegedly saying that *President Lincoln ought to have his dam'd black heart cut out for issuing his proclamation of Emancipation,* but after several prominent Pennsylvanians—including Gen. George G. Meade, Simon Cameron, Sen. Edgar Cowan, and Gov. Andrew G. Curtin—and Postmaster General Montgomery Blair, wrote to Lincoln on behalf of Montgomery, he was reinstated.[27]

In some instances, Lincoln dismissed officers because of petitions he received from civilians on the home front. The Union League of York, Pennsylvania, sent a petition to Secretary of War Edwin M. Stanton in December 1863 claiming that Capt. Charles Garretson, a quartermaster in Washington, D.C., was disloyal. The petition was accompanied by a letter from Congressman Thaddeus Stevens that claimed that Garretson "has always been disloyal since this war began" and that his "removal . . . is demanded by healthy public opinion of Penn." Lincoln weighed the evidence and dishonorably dismissed Garretson from the service in March 1864.[28]

Stunned and bewildered, Garretson wrote to Lincoln claiming that the charge of disloyalty was "totally false and groundless." "I have always been a firm and faithful supporter of my Government, both by actions and words," Garretson continued, "and have done every thing in my power to aid the Administration and the Service in every measure presented, to crush this cursed rebellion." Following the war, his dishonorable dismissal was changed to an honorable discharge, and Garretson was reinstated in the army in 1866.[29]

Private civilians and enlisted men also petitioned members of the Union high command seeking the dismissal of disloyal officers. In December 1862, an enlisted man in the 108th Illinois Volunteers complained to Secretary of War Edwin M. Stanton that his regiment's colonel, John Warner, had been overestimating the number of recruits he had raised so that his regiment would appear to be filled. A few months later, on March 7, 1863, a private citizen in Peoria, Illinois, wrote to Gen. Ulysses S. Grant that Colonel Warner's wife "expresses disloyal sentiments and alleges that her husband entertains the same views with herself and will resign his position if negroes are enlisted in the service." Less than a week after this second letter, on March 13, Warner was summarily dismissed from the service.[30]

In one instance, a postal error led to the dismissal of an anti-emancipation officer. On February 27, 1863, Lt. John M. Garland of the Forty-Second New York Volunteers sent a private letter to an Anglican missionary friend in China. Garland put only thirty-six-cents' worth of postage on the letter, although it required ninety cents in stamps to reach Shanghai. As a consequence, the letter was opened at the post office "with a view to its restoration to the writer." Upon reviewing the letter, the postal employees discovered a slew of disloyal content, some merely anti-emancipation, some overtly pro-Confederate. In the letter, Garland blasted Lincoln's Emancipation Proclamation as "unconstitutional" and "unjust" and proclaimed that "the Administration have at last shown their hands, and that their principles and their hearts are blacker than the 'nigger' they are fighting for." He rejoiced that he had recently been transferred to the Ambulance Corps, which he claimed would prevent him "from coming into actual contact with the South" and would enable him during battle "to render the same assistance to the other side as well as his own." He recalled the "pleasure" of caring for "a large number of Confederates" at Antietam and how he "cried like a child" when he witnessed the shelling of Fredericksburg in December 1862.[31]

Recognizing the danger of expressing such sentiments publicly, Garland wrote, "Were it known that these were my sentiments, I would not only be summarily dismissed the service, but probably boarded, at the expense of Uncle Sam, in Fort Lafayette, or some other sea-side prison, for the benefit of my health, until the war is over." He was partly right, at least. Such disloyal sentiments could not be tolerated in the service. Lincoln dishonorably dismissed him, and the War Department declared in a general order that "no public interest can be safe in the hands of an officer so hostile to the Administration charged with the conduct of the war, and so profoundly sympathizing with the rebels." While Garland's sympathy for the South had so far "manifested itself only in weeping when one of the enemy's strongholds was bombarded, and in rejoicing when ministering to the wants of wounded rebels," the War Department feared that there was "no guaranty" that his "sympathy would not take a more active and manly, and, for the government, a far more fatal form of development."[32] Garland was then ordered by Quartermaster General Montgomery C. Meigs "out of the Department of Western Virginia under guard."[33]

At Hilton Head, South Carolina, Maj. Gen. David Hunter read of Garland's dismissal in the War Department's general order. Hunter wrote to Lincoln praising him for dismissing the disloyal officer as well as for the president's active support for raising black troops. "Believe me that I exaggerate nothing in saying that these indications of a thoroughly vigorous war policy, with all its necessary consequences, are more than sufficient to compensate for any temporary reverses sustained in the field or on the water," wrote Hunter to the president. Believing in the benefits of such policies, Hunter asked the president for the authority to raise black regiments and also "that I may have authority to deal promptly and finally with all officers who oppose a vigorous prosecution of the war or any of its necessary measures."[34]

In some cases, officers were dismissed without ever knowing the reason for their dismissal. One regular army officer, who almost certainly was a Democrat, complained of his "official decapitation" in a private letter in 1862: "I did not know that I was even *accused* of *anything*—the official 'orders' announcing my name as 'stricken from the Rolls of Army,' was the *first hint* of anything wrong." He wrote that "*I am not* & *never was* a disloyal man or officer" and insisted, "'The Constitution & the Laws' *never had* & *never will have* a firmer supporter & advocate than" himself.[35] In like manner, a surgeon with the Eighty-Second Illinois Infantry—who described himself as "a Douglas Democrat" in private correspondence—was summarily dismissed in July 1863 without knowing the charges against him.[36] Others claimed that the reasons given for their dismissals were mere pretexts. One soldier complained privately, "In December, 1863, I was dismissed [from] the army, owing to enemies I made for having and asserting my own opinions, though a charge of bribery was trumped up, and facts being maliciously perverted, I was summarily dismissed without trial or court-martial of any kind."[37]

COURTS-MARTIAL AND PUNISHMENT FOR DISLOYALTY

While many officers were summarily dismissed for their opposition to Lincoln and his emancipation policy, others were punished only after being tried and convicted by courts-martial.[38] An ordnance sergeant in the nation's capital was court-martialed and dishonorably dismissed for saying that he would no longer fight for "a Black Republican and nigger war" and that the Lincoln administration and "this rotten hole (meaning the city of Washington) ought to be blowed to hell."[39] In a similar vein, Lt. Effingham T. Hyatt of the Thirty-Fifth Missouri Infantry was dishonorably dismissed from the service for having said in January 1863 that General McClellan "ought to have march[ed] his Army into Washington and driven Old Abe and those damned Abolitionists out of Washington and taken the reins of Government in his own hands."[40]

Capt. Josiah McCaddon of the Thirty-Seventh Iowa Infantry was cashiered by a military court for uttering a string of disloyal language. He said that President Lincoln was indecisive; that Gens. Benjamin F. Butler and John A. Dix and Sen. Charles Sumner were "demagogues of the blackest water"; that secession was legal; that Congress was destroying the nation; that Lincoln's emancipation policy was "a very weak and foolish move"; and that all free blacks in the North "should be slaves," among other things. McCaddon's sentence declared that he was "utterly disabled from having or holding any office or employment in the service of the United States."[41] Lt. Aaron M. Wagner of the Fifth Indiana Cavalry was court-martialed, cashiered, and declared "utterly disqualified from having or holding any office or employment of profit or trust under the Government of the United States" in February 1863 for saying that "This is nothing but an Abolition war—we are fighting to free the Negroes" and "if I could get a better position on the other side (rebel side) damned if I wouldn't take it," among other things.[42]

Military authorities had little patience for officers who criticized the president or his war measures in front of their men. Capt. John Gibson of the 114th Illinois said that he would rather "sink to Hell" than fight to free "the God damned negroes," that "Old Abe Lincoln is a God damned Old Shit," and that he did not know whether he would rather vote for Lincoln or Jefferson Davis. Gibson was charged with "Using mutinous and seditious language in the presence of the Officers and men of Co. 'I' 114th Regt. Ills. Vols." and using disrespectful language toward the president.[43]

A court-martial found Gibson guilty of all of the charges and specifications preferred against him and sentenced him to be dismissed from the service and to forfeit all pay due him. On May 1, 1863, shortly after his conviction, Gibson wrote a letter claiming that personal illness and difficulties at home caused him to say indiscreet things, but that "I am as good a Union man as any man . . . and

I think I would go as far and do as much as any other man to save this Union." Nevertheless, Gens. William T. Sherman and Ulysses S. Grant approved the findings and sentence of the court.

Other Union officers and enlisted men were punished for articulating antiemancipation sentiments in private conversations. Charles Steck, a Pennsylvania artilleryman, was court-martialed and dismissed for saying that the president was wrong to pursue emancipation, that the press in Russia was more free than it was in the United States, that the southern states were only fighting to protect their property, and that he might fight for the southern army if they paid him on time. Steck was found guilty of violating the Fifth Article of War for his antiemancipation speech and was sentenced to be dismissed from the service.[44]

Steck wrote to President Lincoln complaining about illegalities in the proceedings against him. In a letter to Secretary of War Edwin M. Stanton, Judge Advocate General Joseph Holt called Steck's language "no more than an earnest and somewhat rude enunciation by the accused of his convictions upon political subjects. . . . But it is quite evident that an officer holding and declaring these sentiments and convictions is an unfit person to be allowed to remain in the service of the Government. Language more treasonable, or radically disloyal, could hardly be uttered than was much of that which is testified as having been repeatedly used by the accused." Holt recommended summary dismissal, and Stanton approved the recommendation on June 8, 1864.[45]

Carrying out punishments in camp could have a salutary effect on the troops. Indeed, soldiers who opposed Lincoln's emancipation policy could find themselves brought before courts-martial and made the objects of punishments that subjected them to public censure and possible ridicule. New York artillerist August Fickel was convicted of violating the Fifth Article of War for saying in the presence of a number of officers and men on March 13, 1863, that he would hang President Lincoln "and his whole crowd." Fickel claimed that these words had been said in jest in response to another soldier who called him a "Black Republican" for doing "nigger-work" on a fortification. Fickel pleaded guilty and was sentenced to be "severely reprimanded in General Orders"—orders, which, of course, would be publicly read to his fellow soldiers.[46]

Assistant surgeon Charles Woodward of the Twenty-Sixth Illinois Infantry was court-martialed in March 1863 for violating the Fifth Article of War for saying that Lincoln "was attempting to raise a degraded race on an equality with a superior race," among other things. Witnesses testified to various statements he had made between October 1862 and February 1863. Woodward was convicted and sentenced to be "severely reprimanded" in general orders that would "be read on dress parade to every regiment and detachment throughout the division," as well as to forfeit sixty dollars of his monthly pay. Upon reviewing the case, Brig. Gen. William S. Smith expressed surprise and dismay "at the leniency of the sentence" since Woodward had uttered sentiments "unworthy of an officer in the service of our Government." According to Smith, an officer's duty was to obey orders, "not . . . to dictate to the chief executive his policy."[47] Nevertheless, Smith approved the sentence and ordered that it be carried out. Even if Woodward did not receive the harsh punishment that Smith believed he deserved, at least a strong message would reach thousands of troops that opposition to Lincoln's policies would not be tolerated.

Sgt. Hower Fitzsimmons of the Third Missouri Cavalry was court-martialed for encouraging desertion and uttering disloyal sentiments for saying on March 12, 1863, "That the Army of the United States was engaged only to free negroes, and that rather than do that, for his part the Union might go to Hell," and "that he considered that he was violating his oath by continuing in the army in its present state, more than by deserting." During the trial, one witness claimed that Fitzsimmons called Copperheads "pretty good men." He was found guilty of all of the charges and specifications and was sentenced "to be reduced to the ranks, to have his stripes taken off at a Regimental dress parade, and that the sentence of the court be read to the whole Regiment in line."[48]

Pvt. Philip Kirland of the Eleventh Iowa Volunteers was court-martialed in February 1863 for violation of the Fifth Article of War for saying in front of his company "that the President of the United States was a d—d abolition son of a B—h and that he would like to shoot him." Kirland pleaded not guilty and said that if he had said such things he had no recollection. The court found Kirland guilty and sentenced him to "walk the beat with the Sentinel at the Regimental Guard House every alternate two Hours, from reveille to Retreat, for thirty days, with twenty five pounds in weight strapped on his back, and a placard on his breast with the words in letters three inches long 'Violation of the 5th Article of War' printed on it, and forfeit all pay and allowances in the next six months."[49]

Fickel, Woodward, Fitzsimmons, and Kirland surely deserved to be punished for their foolish words, but these punishments were less about the penalty inflicted than they were about the message that was sent to their comrades in arms—that dissent would not be tolerated and that the soldiery should be dissuaded from speaking in a similar manner. The public nature of these punishments had its desired effect. A soldier in another Iowa regiment took note of Kirland's punishment in his diary: "One man in the 11th Iowa [was court-martialed] for *cussing* the name of the President of the United States and calling him a G—d [d—d] s—n of a B—h and a black abolitionist and said [if] he had the power he would *shoot* him—has now to carry a 20 lb ball 2 hours per day."[50] Everyone in the brigade knew what Kirland had said and comprehended the severity of his punishment.

Other soldiers received less conspicuous punishments, although word of their sentences must have been widely discussed among their comrades. Pvt. David Bailey of the Second Virginia (Union) Cavalry was sentenced to forfeit all of the pay due him and to perform hard labor with a ball and chain attached to his leg for the rest of his enlistment for calling the conflict "a damned Abolition war and if I was to see Jeff Davis and Abe Lincoln together I would rather shoot Lincoln than Jeff Davis."[51] Pvt. Matthias Kenyon of the Fifty-Fifth Pennsylvania made similar comments and was also sentenced to hard labor with a ball and chain for one year and to lose his pay for that period.[52] Daniel Rutherford of the Tenth Indiana Cavalry was court-martialed and sentenced to hard labor for uttering treasonable sentiments—"that he never intended to fire a ball out of his gun for the purpose for which he enlisted"—while brandishing his loaded gun.[53] In a few rare instances, military courts convicted enlisted men of uttering disloyal language but then recommended that their sentences be vacated. One Wisconsin soldier was sentenced to hard labor and loss of pay for uttering disloyal sentiments, but the officers serving on the court-martial wrote to the commanding general asking for remission of the penalty on account of his prior good service. The commanding general remitted the punishment.[54] Such instances were the exception, however.

The military punished vocal dissenters in the army to prevent seditious sentiments from spreading among the soldiery. Pvt. Charles Weickert of the Sixty-Eighth New York was court-martialed for "causing sedition" in his camp and for making noise while saying "I shit on the colonel and the General & also on the President of the United States." Weickert was found innocent of causing sedition but guilty of disobeying orders. He was sentenced to hard labor for six months (ten days out of each month he had to wear a ball and chain), and loss of pay during that time.[55] Other soldiers were court-martialed and punished for cursing or otherwise disrespecting the American flag, an action that had obvious political import.[56]

A court-martial convicted Lt. Hugh H. McClune of the 135th Pennsylvania of disloyally criticizing the government for "waging an abolition war against the South." McClune had said these things while stationed on Capitol Hill in early October 1862, just two weeks after Lincoln issued the preliminary Emancipation Proclamation. Hoping to make an example of McClune, the court sentenced him to be "cashiered and be deprived from ever holding any office or post of honor or trust under the United States, and that he be confined by imprisonment in the Old Capitol Prison, or such other place as the commanding General may direct, during the present rebellion, *and that this sentence be published throughout the United States.*"[57] Such a punishment would send a message to soldiers and civilians who might be considering making a public statement against Lincoln and Republican war aims. It became important to military leaders that punishments for such political insubordination be not only punitive but also preventive.

Even at the highest levels of the military hierarchy Union generals were punished, denied promotion, or dismissed from the service for opposing emancipation. Brig. Gen. James G. Spears of Tennessee was court-martialed twice for opposing emancipation. In October 1862, he requested a fellow officer to write a newspaper editorial in opposition to the Emancipation Proclamation, declaring, "if this is to be the policy of the Government, I'll be God-damned if I do not lead my brigade out of the service." Spears was found not guilty of the charges against him. But soon thereafter he was tried again, this time for "using disloyal language" in opposition to emancipation. The military court found Spears guilty and ordered him dismissed from the service. The case came before President Lincoln for review. On August 17, 1864, Lincoln closed Spears's case file and military career with the words, "Summary dismissal."[58]

Some dismissals may have accidentally targeted loyal Republicans. Gen. Joseph Hooker ordered the dismissal of Lt. William Berdine of the Thirty-Eighth New Jersey Volunteers for disloyalty. According to testimony at his court-martial, Berdine had said that he was going to resign, go home, run for mayor of his town, and hire a local newspaper "to have this damned Negro war pasted up as it ought to be." Frantic and beside himself, Berdine wrote to Lincoln decrying the public disgrace he would face when he returned home "to my family with the odor of the foulest crime known to a soldier, resting upon me." Berdine assured the president that he had not only "ever been a firm & faithful upholder of the great principles of our Government, its Constitutions & its laws," but also that he had "ever been a Republican in principal as well as in politics and since the first organization of the party have used every effort to promote its aims and purposes & to secure the success of those ends. . . . Hence I have ever been a firm and faithful supporter of your administration & of its avowed policy."[59] The president thought it "a curious case" and was "incline[d] to think there is some mistake in this case," but did not restore Berdine's commission.[60]

Courts-martial cases that ended in acquittal could still be used to teach enlisted men that anti-emancipation speech was unacceptable in the army. During the presidential election campaign of 1864, Capt. Edward G. Mathey of the Eighty-First Indiana Volunteers said that he would rather resign than "fight to free the negro" and that "the Emancipation Proclamation was in direct violation of the Constitution." Although Mathey made these statements during the Atlanta campaign in the summer of 1864, he was not court-martialed until February 1865, after the presidential election. Now that the heat of the campaign was over and Lincoln was reelected, the court decided not to attach any criminality to his statements. Mathey walked away a free man. Nevertheless, Gen. Nathan Kimball, an antebellum Whig and Republican, took the opportunity to teach his soldiers the importance of not speaking against Lincoln or his war policies. On April 7, 1865, after approving of Mathey's acquittal, Kimball wrote: "but the General Commanding takes this opportunity of reminding all Officers in his command, that, neither jest or political excitement, is an excuse for disregarding his duties as an Officer." As "a Citizen," a soldier "is at liberty to think and vote as he pleases, yet as an Officer in the Armies of the United States, he is bound by the articles of war to which he has subscribed."[61] Soldiers, in short, must not criticize the president or his war measures. Still, the timing of Mathey's acquittal—after the presidential election was won and Union victory seemed imminent—was telling. It showed that the military leadership's concern was more about preserving support for Lincoln and his war measures than with actually punishing a disloyal officer.

Not all soldiers court-martialed for criticizing emancipation were found guilty,[62] but most were, and the prospect of being punished for voicing one's political views was certain to have a chilling effect on political discussion among the troops. One Massachusetts Democrat worried that if he voiced his political opinions he would be called "a Copperhead and perhaps a *poor cuss* like me might get shot."[63] Mum was the word for many Democratic soldiers who feared punishment for being part of the political opposition.[64]

PUBLIC OPINION AND THE POLITICS OF PROMOTION

Throughout the war, politicians on the home front looked to the army for soldiers who could help publicize and legitimize their political positions. Soldiers home on furlough were often invited to address political gatherings or write letters in favor of a given candidate. Many soldiers also worked as embedded reporters for their hometown newspapers. Because most newspapers at the time were unabashedly partisan, Republican soldiers tended to correspond with Republican newspapers, while Democrats wrote home to their party press. At times, editors themselves enlisted in the Union armies, in which case they guaranteed for themselves a voice among the people at home. A double standard arose, however, in how Republican and Democratic soldiers were treated for expressing their views. Republican soldiers could correspond with politicians and editors at home with impunity. Democratic soldiers who sought to influence voters at home—either in print or through public speaking—were frequently punished for the public expression of their views.

Republican authorities in Washington and Union officers in the field mounted a concerted effort to keep Democratic papers from reaching the troops.[65] "They send nothing but abolition documents here," complained Pvt. John Riggs of the Seventh Connecticut to his father in January 1863, "and I should like to see some old Democratic papers and some speaches."[66] The suppression of opposition newspapers frightened and angered northern Democrats. "A party that can silence opposition and muzzle the press is the worst kind of tyrant," wrote Col. Charles J. Biddle shortly after his resignation from the Forty-Second Pennsylvania Infantry.[67] In addition to prohibiting anti-emancipation materials among the troops, Republican officers arrested and punished Democratic soldiers who corresponded with their hometown newspapers.

While Republican soldiers had no difficulty writing to their hometown papers, Democratic soldiers often found themselves in hot water. In August 1864, Pvt. Newton B. Spencer of the 179th New York Infantry wrote a letter to his local newspaper, of which he had previously been editor, the *Penn Yan Democrat*, claiming that the "Abolition mania for employing 'nigger' soldiers has culminated in the worst disaster of the whole campaign and discouraged and nearly demoralized the whole army." Spencer believed that it "was to glorify the sooty abolition idol, that upon a Division of raw and worthless black poltroons, was devolved the most important part of the whole conflict—in the hope evidently that they would crown our temporary success, with decisive victory, and bear off the hard won laurels, of the white fighting men." Spencer was charged with conduct prejudicial to good order and military discipline, contempt and disrespect for his commanding officer, violation of the Fifty-Seventh Article of War (giving intelligence to the enemy), and "giving aid and comfort to the enemy," which was essentially a charge of treason. Spencer admitted writing the letter but pleaded not guilty to each of the charges.

In his defense, Spencer argued that the Articles of War had never been publicly read in his company and that he was ignorant of their requirements. The court-martial found him guilty of the first two charges, but not guilty of aiding the enemy or violating the Articles of War. He was sentenced to be returned to his regiment and "to be publicly reprimanded by his Regimental Commander, in the presence of his Company and Regiment." He also lost more than half of his monthly pay for the next six months. The commanding general believed that Spencer ought to have been convicted of the third and fourth charges and to have received a harsher sentence, but on reconsidering the case, the military court declined to change any of its findings.[68]

Pvt. Charles L. Paul of the Twelfth U.S. Infantry was charged with insubordination, disobedience of orders, and "using disrespectful words against the President of the United States" for an article he sent to a newspaper in Saratoga Springs, New York, in early 1863 in which he said that the army was demoralized by its loss at Fredericksburg and by the issuance of the Emancipation Proclamation. According to Paul, the war would last longer if the North was fighting "to *free these cursed niggers*." Paul was found guilty of writing the letter but was acquitted of the charges.[69] B. L. Hovey, a surgeon with the 136th New York Infantry, was court-martialed for writing a letter to the *Dansville Advertiser* in February 1863 in which he said that the soldiers had enlisted "to sustain the Constitution," not to abolish slavery. He was found guilty and sentenced to be reprimanded in general orders that would be read publicly "in the presence of the officers of the Brigade."[70] In like manner, Sgt. William B. Gillespie of the Twenty-Eighth New York Infantry was convicted by court-martial for publishing a newspaper article in January 1863 in which he said that the Emancipation Proclamation "will be the cause of a large number of our best officers resigning, and of a large number of desertions," to which he added that the freed people should all be "shipped to Washington that their Massa Linkum and Cabinet might give them a hearty welcome and cordial embrace." Gillespie was sentenced to be reduced to the ranks and then drummed out of the service, although Maj. Gen. Joseph Hooker mitigated the latter part of the sentence on account of Gillespie's good service during the first two years of the war.[71]

Some officers were summarily dismissed from the service or even threatened with arrest for writing newspaper editorials critical of the Lincoln administration. In September 1861, the State Department ordered the arrest of Col. Isaac J. Wistar of the Seventy-First California (Pennsylvania) Regiment. Wistar had written a public protest of Gen. John C. Fremont's emancipation edict in Missouri. "While we cheerfully admit the universal right to freedom of thought and expression," wrote Wistar on behalf of his regiment, "yet we protest that *we* are not Abolitionists, and will not be used as tools for the propagation of that wicked and pernicious doctrine." It was only by the efforts of Wistar's commanding officer, Sen. Edward D. Baker, that he was spared imprisonment at Fort Lafayette in New York harbor.[72] In January 1863, Wistar's promotion to brigadier general faced stiff opposition in Congress, according to one congressman, "on the ground of sentiments expressed by you, in disapproval of the Proclamation."[73] Wistar recalled thirty years later in his autobiography how his political opponents "confined their charges and imputations to the troublesome theme of my 'loyalty,' it being an axiom with the plundering scoundrels of that day that any coolness or deficiency in partisan Republican profession in itself constituted the most formidable kind of 'disloyalty.'"[74]

Most Democrats rejected emancipation as a war policy. Yet those who said so publicly—especially if they did so as newspaper correspondents—found themselves in a predicament. Capt. Thomas Barrett of the Ninetieth Illinois Volunteers was summarily and dishonorably dismissed for publishing a letter in the *Chicago Times* on May 25, 1863, critical of Lincoln's policy of enlisting black soldiers. The *Boston Pilot* remarked that Barrett was the "victim" of an "official injustice" by a "demagogue in epaulettes," referring to Adjutant General Lorenzo Thomas, the person who ordered his dismissal.[75]

One soldier who was convicted by court-martial for writing a letter to his hometown Democratic newspaper claimed that soldiers possessed the same right to criticize a president's policies as any other citizen. "The policy of an American administration has always been subject to the criticism of the people," he wrote. "My remarks applied to Legislative policy, and not to acts of Military Commanders." This soldier pointed out that he was "a sincere lover of the Union and that, although always a Democrat," he had left his "comfortable home and a remunerative practice" to support the nation in its time of need. Moreover, he surmised that his articles to a small-town newspaper far away from the battle-field could have "but a limited influence over the soldier."[76] In other words, he claimed not to have committed any actual crime against the military, and that he possessed the full rights of a citizen to criticize the government. This soldier was mistaken. Union soldiers did not possess the full rights of citizenship—at least as they pertained to free speech, free press, and the issue of emancipation.

Even if they were not punished by the military, Democratic soldiers might be shunned by their neighbors at home for sending editorials to local newspapers. One New York soldier was astonished at the reaction his letters to a Democratic daily received at home:

> Capt. Reynolds told me that my letters to the *Union* were considered "*treason-able*," by "my friends!" Think of that, your brother George in the army, and has been for sixteen months or more, fighting for his country, an obedient soldier and officer in every respect, . . . ready now as ever to fight the battles of his country, and if need be, give his life for that country. Guilty of *Treason!* Whew, what an unenviable reputation I must be obtaining in Rochester. Per-haps, a committee will be sent to have me arrested and put into some bastile for the utterance of sedition and treasonable sentiments, because for[th]with I have very mildly taken exceptions to the emancipation proclamation.

This soldier concluded this February 1863 letter by noting how "abolitionized" people were "disposed to call every one traitorous and disloyal because his ideas about slavery don't happen to chime with their exalted but fallacious notions on the subject." More than a year later—after Lincoln's reelection in November 1864—this soldier decided to resign his commission in the army: "About January [1865], if I am spared till then, look out for a Copperhead and a Traitor in the family, who has repeatedly been called such, by patriotic Republican officers in the field. It is surely dangerous, and 'prejudicial to good military discipline,' to have such a person of treasonable sentiments as I am in the army and confront the enemy." He was tired of the war and believed that abolitionism had changed the nature of the conflict to something for which he was no longer willing to fight. "Do you know of any good, loyal, and devoted Republican in Rochester who will come and fill my place for three years or during the war?" he asked. "I don't want a substitute. I want a *bona fide,* out and out Republican, who abominates a Copperhead, and is down on the Chicago Platform and George H. Pendleton, who is a true exponent of Mr. Lincoln and his policy."[77]

Even soldiers who were not newspaper correspondents might still get punished for their connections to Democratic organs. During Ohio's gubernatorial election of 1863, Capt. Benjamin F. Sells of the 122nd Ohio Volunteers criticized the Emancipation Proclamation and the arrest of Clement Vallandigham. Sells was arrested for circulating Democratic election pamphlets and copies of the stridently conservative *Columbus Crisis* among the troops. In February 1864, Sells was court-martialed on charges of "using contemptuous and disrespectful language against the President of the United States" and conduct prejudicial to good order and military discipline. Found not guilty of the first charge but guilty of the second, he was sentenced to dismissal from the military service.[78]

Like Colonel Wistar, other Democratic officers faced difficulty attaining promotions they believed they had earned. Letters flooded the desks of northern governors and congressmen warning that officers seeking promotion had familial ties to the South, had voted the wrong way in previous elections, held pro-slavery views, or were even members of the Knights of the Golden Circle.[79] Democratic soldiers who hoped for promotion learned that they had to keep their political opinions out of the public eye. One Massachusetts officer critical of the Lincoln administration asked his mother to "keep shady about this letter, or it might cost me [my] commission, as I suppose the despotism at Washington will be making as many victims as after the last wholesale butchery of this poor army."[80]

Col. W. W. H. Davis, a Democratic newspaper editor and the commander of the 104th Pennsylvania, knew that his opposition to Lincoln and emancipation kept him from being promoted, but he stayed in the service for the sake of "my poor afflicted country." In a private letter, he wrote:

> I have no love for the [Lincoln] administration, and am *very* unsound on their goose. [Editor of the *Philadelphia Press* John] Forney is my political enemy, and does not consider me a loyal man because I will not swallow the darkie raw. I must have him partly cooked, at least, and well seasoned. I well know that I am *not* to be promoted, because I dont vote right, when I vote at all. . . . I have done the duty of a Brigadier for 18 months on the pay of a Colonel.

Despite this injustice and his misgivings about the president, Colonel Davis believed that Jefferson Davis was "*infinitely* worse" than Lincoln, "for he is a traitor to his country by heading an armed rebellion against the government. Every claim of interest and duty protests against a peace that leaves us a divided country."[81] Democrats, like Davis, who were willing to put winning the war above their personal interests, suffered what they believed were partisan disadvantages for the good of the cause.

Democratic officers were often frustrated by their inability to gain promotions from Republican politicians. One Pennsylvania officer noted in September 1863 that he "cannot give up my political opinions to gain a position to which I am entitled in the regular order of military promotion." A year later, as the presidential election was approaching, he told his brother, "I have had intimations from several sources that if I were to change my political views and make a few stump speeches on the other side it would be greatly to my advantage." But he would not sacrifice his political principles. "I shall not avail myself of these offers or any of them. I have done so many things wrong in my life that I cannot afford to carry with me the consciousness of having been actually sold."[82]

Col. Francis T. Sherman of the Eighty-Eighth Illinois Infantry, a War Democrat whose father was the Peace Democrat mayor of Chicago, believed that he was denied promotion to brigadier general because of his family's political affiliations. In his letters home, Colonel Sherman claimed not to have become an abolitionist, but over time he did come to believe that the war could not end until "the fire brand of slavery is utterly quenched." Like many moderate Democrats, Sherman castigated "the extremists in both parties," but he became increasingly critical of the Peace faction of his own party and expressed particular delight when that "miserable traitor" Clement Vallandigham lost the Ohio gubernatorial election in 1863.[83]

Despite this change of heart on the slavery issue, Sherman continually reassured his father, "I am as good a Democrat as ever," and he remained in the Democratic fold for the rest of his life. Sherman's rejoicing at the defeat of Copperhead candidates like Ohio's Vallandigham and Pennsylvania's Woodward was not a rejection of the Democratic Party but an expression of hope for his party's restoration and renewal to its true positions, principles, and former greatness. "'Hurrah' say I for the patriots who at the pass have come forth nobly in defense and put down the subtletrys of treason under the guise of Democracy," he told his father. "Our party is redeemed from disgrace, and will be once more looked upon as the true *War* party which cannot be led astray by any logic or sophistry by such men as Val and Merrick and others of his ilk."[84]

Still, it was Sherman's party affiliation that thwarted his "quest for a star." He lamented to his family: "If the policy is kept up by the administration of promoting only those who are out-and-out Republicans and ignoring those who are Democrats and making politics the test of merit the country will lose the services of hundreds of able and patriotic Democrats who hold commissions. If this rebellion is to be crushed there must be no political preferences, and men fighting to preserve this government from the hands of traitors must be recognized for their merits and nothing else."[85] It was only in the postwar period that Sherman received the promotion he had so desperately sought during the war.

Not all Democratic officers were as patient as Cols. Davis and Sherman. Col. Isham N. Haynie of the Forty-Eighth Illinois had been an antebellum Democrat in the Illinois state legislature and a presidential elector for Stephen A. Douglas in 1860. In November 1862, Haynie was appointed a brigadier general, but the Senate refused to confirm his nomination. "For now Seventeen months I have been devoting my time, energies and whatever of ability I possess to aiding an administration I did not help to Elect in its efforts to subdue the rebellion," he wrote to Sen. Lyman Trumbull of Illinois. "I have never allowed the inquiry as to who was President, or what political party was dominant to direct me from the true issue made by the treasonable Efforts of the states in rebellion." But after the Republican majority in the Senate snubbed him, Haynie resigned his commission on March 6, 1863.[86] In like manner, Col. William Batchelder Greene of the First Massachusetts Heavy Artillery resigned his commission in October 1862, claiming to be "the victim of an unmerited, unmerciful, and unrelenting persecution on the part of the influential members of the Republican Party in Massachusetts and on the part of political influences which prevail in Washington."[87]

Democratic officers often claimed that promotions and dismissals were based on partisan politics and the Lincoln administration's desire to win elections rather than on the actual merit or malfeasance of the officer. Historian Michael F. Holt points out that Lincoln appointed prominent Democrats to high military command but that he only "retained them . . . as long as they might lure Democratic votes to the Union parties in the northern states." Following the October and November 1862 elections, Lincoln dismissed Democratic generals such as Don Carlos Buell.[88] One New York soldier noted despondently after McClellan's November 1862 removal from command: "Probably all Democratic generals will be removed now."[89] Indeed, two of McClellan's staff officers were arrested shortly after McClellan's dismissal, with one observer noting, "Charges as usual unknown to outsiders."[90] Historian T. Harry Williams described the situation following Lincoln's adoption of an emancipation policy: "Secretary of War Stanton, an ardent radical, started a campaign in 1863, aided by the Committee [on the Conduct of the War], to remove Democratic officers, particularly those who had voiced opposition to the emancipation proclamation."[91] Dismissals continued throughout 1863 and 1864, with a rash of dismissals taking place around the time of the presidential election of 1864 (see chapter 4).

Partisanship may have led to some dismissals in cases in which actual disloyalty or anti-emancipation sentiment could not be proved. Lt. Mordecai P. Bean of the 111th Ohio was court-martialed in the spring of 1863 for having debated the affirmative side of a resolution that claimed that "the Southern States had just cause to secede from the union." Bean was also charged with drunkenness, playing cards with the enlisted men in his company, and other ungentlemanly conduct. He was acquitted of disloyalty because some witnesses testified that Bean's company had a "debating society" in which questions were raised and both sides were argued, but he was convicted of the other charges against him. He was sentenced to be cashiered.[92]

Even though he was acquitted of the political charges against him, Bean's status as a Democrat likely contributed to his dismissal. Bean returned home to Fremont, Ohio, where he edited a Democratic newspaper and ran for county office. A Republican editor in nearby Sandusky wrote to Judge Advocate General Joseph Holt asking him for a transcript of the testimony from Bean's trial. The editor informed Holt that Bean was now "publishing a 'copperhead' paper, and is also a candidate for Co. Clerk on the copperhead, Vallandigham ticket." By publishing the testimony against Bean, "I think . . . this traitor (he is nothing less— call him a sympathizer with traitors) may be defeated."[93]

While partisanship and politics certainly influenced some, if not many of the courts-martial cases and dismissals, there can be little doubt that many of those punished had earned their stripes. Lt. Edward H. Underhill, a New York artilleryman, was court-martialed and docked six months' pay for criticizing the "damned Lincoln nigger government."[94] Capt. Charles Arthur of the Fifth New York Cavalry was court-martialed and dismissed for calling Lincoln "a loafer and a traitor."[95] Soldiers who returned fugitive slaves to their masters were especially liable to punishment, including dismissal for officers.[96] Returning slaves to their masters after the issuance of the Emancipation Proclamation went beyond anti-administration speech; it constituted flagrant disobedience of both military and civilian policy.[97] When the Ninth New Jersey Volunteers, angered by the issuance of the Emancipation Proclamation, burned a slave shantytown in North Carolina in February 1863, Gen. David Hunter cut their rations and drilled them continuously for a month.[98] Once emancipation had become the official Union military policy, it could not be undermined by the troops; violation of the policy needed to be punished.

Arrests, courts-martial, dishonorable dismissals, and other forms of corporal punishment were effective ways of teaching the soldiers the importance of supporting emancipation and respecting the use of black troops. When an Irish soldier stationed at Folly Island, South Carolina, called a black infantryman a "nigger" in March 1864, he was arrested and sent to the provost guard "accompanied by at least two files of good brave colored soldiers." A black soldier in the Fifty-Fifth Massachusetts remarked on the good that such an arrest and humiliating punishment could have on other white soldiers who might be prone to think or act alike: "A few cases like this will teach these fellows to attend to their own business and let other folks alone."[99]

LINCOLN TEACHES A SOLDIER

Officers who, on political grounds, spoke out against the enlistment of African American troops also faced punishment for their words against the Union policy. Col. Frank Wolford of the First Kentucky Cavalry was dishonorably dismissed from the service in March 1864 for publicly opposing the enlistment of black soldiers. He was arrested later that year and sent to Washington to meet with President Lincoln, who he believed showed nothing but partisan malice in the handling of the matter. Wolford, like many Democrats who felt deceived by the changing nature of the war, believed himself fully loyal to the Union cause. Republicans, by contrast, saw him as nothing but a traitor.

In 1861, Kentucky adopted a policy of armed neutrality in the sectional conflict because many of the state's leaders believed disunion and civil war would have calamitous social and economic effects on the state.[100] Many northerners saw Kentucky's position as traitorous. President Lincoln for example, argued that neutrality was "treason in effect" because it "recognizes no fidelity to the Constitution, [and] no obligation to maintain the Union."[101] One Kentuckian who had concurred with Lincoln was Frank Wolford, who quickly raised a cavalry regiment at his own expense and mustered it into the Union army. Wolford, a lawyer and Mexican War veteran, served honorably for two years, was wounded in battle six times, and played a part in the capture of Confederate cavalry raider John Hunt Morgan.[102]

On March 10, 1864, a group of Kentucky Unionists chose to honor Colonel Wolford with a beautiful presentation sword. In his acceptance speech, Wolford castigated the Lincoln administration and its policies of emancipation and the arming of black soldiers. Wolford also lampooned the Confederates for their treason, but Unionists worried that his speech was "producing a good deal of division in the ranks of the Union party." Some correspondents frantically warned Lincoln that Wolford would lead his troops against the Union army.[103]

Kentucky Unionists were bewildered by Wolford's address. "Was this the good Union man, and gallant soldier, whose services to the country they wished to acknowledge in public by a present?" wrote a Kentucky woman in her diary. "Was this the man to whom they would be proud to bestow a sword? Why had they not known this before? Why had they been deceived into giving to a traitor the sword intended for a gallant patriot whom Ky wished to honor? Why had they been put to blush before all the world, and what possessed him that he dared to talk of treason, before Union men? Had he been bought over by the rebels; or had he caught the negrophobia and knew not what he did?"[104]

Military leaders began to worry that "mischief will result" from these "seditious speeches."[105] A few days after the sword presentation ceremony Wolford was arrested and sent to Knoxville, Tennessee, to be tried by a military court, but the army decided not to bring his case to trial and chose rather to dishonorably dismiss him. General Grant reinstated Wolford to his command, but the Kentucky colonel continued to vocally protest Lincoln's handling of the war. On June 27, 1864, after several months of delivering anti-Lincoln and anti-emancipation stump speeches, Wolford was again arrested by the military and sent to Washington, D.C., to be tried by a military court.[106] About this same time, on July 5, 1864, Lincoln suspended the writ of habeas corpus in Kentucky. The text of Lincoln's suspension order clearly showed that Wolford and others like him were on the president's mind. Lincoln noted that the rebels were having success in the Bluegrass State, in part, because of the "aid and comfort furnished by disaffected and disloyal citizens of the United States residing therein."[107]

On July 7, Wolford and Lincoln signed a parole giving Wolford the liberty to travel to Louisville, Kentucky, to await his military trial "and that in the mean time I will abstain from public speaking, and every thing intended or calculated to produce public excitement." Ten days later Lincoln offered to discharge Wolford from military custody and the terms of his earlier parole if the soldier would pledge "that I will neither do or say anything which will directly or indirectly tend to hinder, delay, or embarrass the employment and use of colored persons, as soldiers, seamen, or otherwise, in the suppression of the rebellion, so long as the U.S. government chooses to so employ and use them." Lincoln enclosed with the new parole a printed copy of his April 1864 letter to Albert Hodges in which he had defended the constitutionality of military emancipation.[108] Lincoln attempted to take on the role of teacher to one of his wayward pupils in the field.

Upon receipt of Lincoln's message, Wolford's temper exploded. He penned a sixteen-page diatribe (plus an enclosure) to Lincoln explaining why he could never assent to such an offer. "I cannot bargain for my liberty, and the exercise of my rights as a freeman, on any such terms," he told the president. "I have committed no crime," nor broken any law of Congress, the state of Kentucky, or the U.S. military. He claimed to be fully loyal to the Union cause and wholeheartedly against the rebellion, but he could not assent to the administration's policy of enlisting black troops. In language that must have been jarring to the kindhearted president, Wolford wrote:

> You, Mr President, if you will excuse the bluntness of a soldier, by an exercise of arbitrary power have caused me to be arrested and held in confinement contrary to law, not for the good of our common country—but to increase the chances of your reelection to the presidencey [*sic*]—and otherwise to serve the purposes of the political party whose candidate you are, and, now, you ask me to stultify myself by signing a pledge where by I shall virtually admit, your right to arrest me—and virtually support you in deterring other men from criticising the policy of your Administration. No Sir! much as I love liberty, I will fester in a prison, or die on a gibbet, before I will agree to any terms that do not abandon all charges against me, and fully acknowledge my innocense.
> . . . [I]mpartial history, in attesting the goodness and severity of god, will write you down [as] the greatest tryrant [*sic*] that ever lived.

Wolford offered a point-by-point refutation of Lincoln's "Hodges Letter," again stated his support of the enlistment of white soldiers but his opposition to the enlistment of black ones, and claimed that the constitutional freedoms enumerated in the First Amendment extended to every citizen the right to "the unrestricted discussion of the merits and demerits of every candidate for office, yourself among the rest,—to the criticism of your whole course [of] conduct and policy, the policy of enlisting slaves not excepted. You must undergo the same tests that are applied to other candidates," he lectured the president. "If not, our system of free government is a mockery."[109]

Wolford's case never went to trial; instead, he again took to the stump, castigating the Lincoln administration at every turn and urging his fellow Kentuckians to vote for George B. McClellan, the Democratic nominee for president. As a further affront to Lincoln, Kentucky Democrats selected Wolford to serve as a member of the Electoral College in the upcoming election.

After Lincoln's great national triumph in November 1864 (although he lost the state of Kentucky), Colonel Wolford and Kentucky's lieutenant governor, Richard T. Jacob (another former Union soldier), were arrested and imprisoned for disloyalty. In accordance with an order of Gen. Stephen Burbridge, Lieutenant Governor Jacob was sent to the South and informed that he would be executed if he returned to Kentucky during the war. Jacob protested to Lincoln that he was "forced by necessity into the Confederate lines, to accept the hospitality and protection of a people that I had fought against."[110] Unconditional Unionists in Kentucky believed that if Lincoln would support these arrests, they would do "incalculable good" by causing the "leading conspirators of the state" to "succumb; [and] the State will have quiet."[111]

In truth, the arrests of Wolford and Jacob were propagated on testimony of dubious reliability. A deposition taken by order of General Burbridge reveals the use of leading questions that were necessary to secure adequate evidence to warrant arrest.

> QUESTION. Did or did you not hear Wolford denounce the President of the United States? If so, state the terms he used in denouncing him.
> ANSWER. He did denounce the President severely, but I do not remember the terms used.
> QUESTION. Do you not remember that he applied the terms "fool," "tyrant," "usurper," &c., to him?

ANSWER. I think that he did, to the best of my knowledge. . . .

QUESTION. Did he refer to the enlistment of negroes at Lebanon? If so, did he not denounce the action of the provost marshal on enlisting negroes as "contrary to law and order, and disgraceful"?

ANSWER. I do not remember that he denounced the provost marshal at Lebanon, but he denounced the enlistment of negroes as "contrary to law, against order, and disgraceful." . . .

QUESTION. Do you remember what he (Wolford) said directly before he threatened the arrest?

ANSWER. I do not.

QUESTION. Did he not call [the] attention of the people to the fact that a poll had been opened in Lebanon for the enlistment of slaves; that it was contrary to law, disgraceful, and against order; and did he not call attention to the provost marshal to this fact?

ANSWER. I think he did.

The interview continued for some time but stopped abruptly after the questioner asked the witness whether Wolford had denounced the rebellion. "He did," replied the witness, "in severe terms." With that the interview was brought to a close, for the testimony only probed Wolford's loyalty to "the Constitution as it is and the Union as it was," meaning a restored Union with slavery still intact.[112]

Back in Washington, Sen. Lazarus W. Powell of Kentucky introduced a resolution in the Senate calling on the president to state the reasons for the arrests and detentions of Wolford and Jacob. The resolution initially met with opposition from radical senator Henry Wilson of Massachusetts but passed the following day. Lincoln complied with the request for information on February 1, 1865, about a month later. With such national attention brought to these cases, and with, in Lincoln's words, "the *passion-exciting* subject of the election . . . past," Lincoln permitted Jacob and Wolford to return home.[113]

Col. Frank Wolford was emblematic of many of the Union soldiers who had left the Union army by the time of the election of 1864. He supported suppression of the rebellion, but only through the use of white soldiers and without the military measure of emancipation. Wolford, like many of his former comrades, never came to realize the truth that Lincoln knew so well: that emancipation was a double-edged sword that both helped the Union and hurt the Confederacy.[114] In this case, Lincoln's "Hodges Letter" fell on deaf ears.

In 1863, Lincoln had sent a public letter to his old friend James C. Conkling to be read at a mass Union meeting in his home state of Illinois. Knowing that many in the audience might be conservative Unionists who opposed a war for black liberation, Lincoln implored them to understand the necessity of emancipation as a military aim. To those who still denied this necessity, he wrote: "You say you will not fight to free negroes. Some of them seem willing to fight for you; but, no matter. Fight you, then, exclusively to save the Union. I issued the proclamation on purpose to aid you in saving the Union. Whenever you shall have conquered all resistance to the Union, if I shall urge you to continue fighting, it will be an apt time, then, for you to declare you will not fight to free negroes." He reminded them that any help the former slaves ceased to be to the rebels would be help to the white Union soldiers, and therefore "just so much less for white soldiers to do, in saving the Union. Does it appear otherwise to you? But negroes, like other people, act upon motives. Why should they do any thing for us, if we will do nothing for them? If they stake their lives for us, they must be prompted by the strongest motive—even the promise of freedom. And the promise being made, must be kept."[115]

Lincoln knew—and he assured his audience—that "there will be some black men who can remember that, with silent tongue, and clenched teeth, and steady eye, and well-poised bayonet, they have helped mankind on to this great consummation; while, I fear, there will be some white ones, unable to forget that, with malignant heart, and deceitful speech, they strove to hinder it." Men like Colonel Wolford may have believed that they were helping the Union cause by discouraging black enlistments, but Lincoln knew otherwise. He tried to teach them. Many learned; others did not.[116]

3

"I AM AFRAID I AM SOMETHING OF A 'COPPERHEAD'"

Resignations and Desertions in the Union Army Following Emancipation

IN LATE FEBRUARY 1863, Maj. Henry F. Kalfus of the Fifteenth Kentucky Volunteer Infantry submitted his resignation because, as he saw it, the war was being fought "for the elevation of the negro race, or rather for the *degradation of the white man* . . . and for the subversion of the rights and institutions of the states." Rather than accept his resignation, Gen. William Starke Rosecrans ordered Kalfus to be arrested and dishonorably dismissed "for using treasonable language in tendering his resignation." Col. John Beatty—a Republican who had supported John C. Fremont for president in 1856, had been a presidential elector for Lincoln in 1860, and would serve two terms as a Republican in Congress after the war—gladly carried out the arrest and punishment, seeking both to humiliate the offender and to warn other soldiers against articulating similar ideas. After being paraded through camp, Kalfus had his shoulder straps cut, his dishonorable discharge publicly read, and then was escorted from camp by soldiers with their muskets bayoneted. A veteran of the Forty-Second Indiana Volunteer Infantry recalled years later: "This circumstance put a stop to all criticisms by subordinate officers of the line of the Forty-second respecting the federal government, or the conduct of the war. It had a wonderful and excellent effect throughout the whole army also."[1]

Democrats believed that Lincoln's emancipation policy was an illegal measure that expanded executive power beyond what the Constitution allowed. Moreover, as a military measure, the Emancipation Proclamation essentially forced Union soldiers to fight for "Negro freedom"—an idea that they found unpalatable. Some Union officers were so distraught by the changing war policies that they resigned their commissions shortly after Lincoln issued the Emancipation Proclamation. Enlisted men deserted. "Abe Lincoln has broken his oath," declared an Illinois sergeant on March 4, 1863, the second anniversary of Lincoln's inauguration, "and I have a right to break mine." Union authorities, both in Washington and in the field, could not tolerate such a disregard of duty (this Illinois sergeant was sentenced to six months hard labor, to be reduced to the ranks, and then to be dishonorably discharged).[2] Nor could federal authorities allow regimental commanders to set this sort of example for the troops they commanded. Consequently, many of the officers who resigned to protest the Union's new emancipation policy were arrested, court-martialed, and punished.[3]

RESIGNATIONS AND EMANCIPATION

In February 1863, Lt. James McDaniel of the Thirty-First Missouri Volunteers attempted to resign his commission because he opposed fighting in a war for abolition. When his letter of resignation reached Maj. Gen. William T. Sherman, the general wrote a brief dissertation on the dangers that such outspoken officers like McDaniel posed to the service. "The whole theory of Army Discipline would be destroyed if subordinate officers 'sworn to obey the orders of the President of the U.S. & officers appointed over him' be permitted to reflect on the policy of the General Government," wrote Sherman. He conceded that McDaniel "should be permitted to explain the terms" of his resignation, but that if he truly held the views he expressed and was "found engaged in spreading them among his associates, he merits condign punishment." Sherman stated that McDaniel's request to resign met "with my entire disapproval," and he called on Gen. Ulysses S. Grant to adopt "some rule . . . in such cases." He concluded, "He merits severe punishment & I refer this paper that such punishment may be ordered as will be exemplary."[4]

Sherman clearly understood the damage this officer could cause and that only by making an example of McDaniel could the danger to the service be stemmed. The punishment must be not only "condign" and "severe" but "exemplary." It must serve a larger purpose—not simply to punish one disloyal soldier but to dissuade others from acting alike. General Grant agreed with Sherman and recommended dishonorable dismissal. Secretary of War Edwin M. Stanton concurred and dismissed McDaniel for disloyalty on March 25.[5] The point in all this was clear. After January 1, 1863, the Republican standard for loyalty included support of emancipation; dissent from that standard could earn an officer dishonorable dismissal from the service.

While Kalfus and McDaniel were summarily dismissed, other officers were arrested and court-martialed for resigning in protest to emancipation. Lt. George D. Wiseburn of the 133rd New York Infantry resigned his commission at Baton Rouge, Louisiana, on February 4, 1863, telling his superior officer: "When I entered the Volunteer Army of the United States it was for the sole purpose of maintaining the Government and upholding the supremacy of the Law against Rebellion since then the Executive has seen proper to make it the Emancipation of the Negro Slaves which I do not concur in." Wiseburn was further incensed by Lincoln's decision to allow African American men to enlist in the army, "thus making the Negro my equal." The colonel commanding the brigade disapproved of Wiseburn's request and recommended that all other officers who tendered their resignation "on similar grounds, be detailed for special duty, during their unexpired term of service, on Ship Island." Brig. Gen. Cuvier Grover disapproved of this recommendation because such a punishment would not draw enough attention to the offender.[6]

Wiseburn's letter was forwarded to Maj. Gen. Nathaniel P. Banks, who immediately ordered that Wiseburn be court-martialed. He was charged with using contemptuous and disrespectful language against the president and his superior officers as well as conduct prejudicial to good order and military discipline. Wiseburn admitted to writing the letter but pleaded not guilty to the charges. The court found Wiseburn guilty of all charges and specifications and sentenced him "to receive a public reprimand to be published before the Army of the Gulf" and to be sent to Ship Island, Mississippi, to finish out his duty there. General Banks recommended dismissal by the president, and Lincoln concurred.[7]

Near Winchester, Virginia, Lt. Frank B. Smith, a Pennsylvania cavalryman, was charged with disloyalty and three charges of disrespect and insolence toward his commanding officer, for wanting to resign in the wake of the Emancipation Proclamation. He was found not guilty of disloyalty but guilty of some of the other charges and was sentenced to be dismissed. Brig. Gen. Benjamin F. Kelley disapproved of the court's finding and sentence: "I am of the opinion that the evidence adduced would have warranted the court in finding the accused guilty as charged [with disloyalty] and that the sentence awarded is totally inadequate to the offence of which he was found guilty." But since it was "impracticable to reconvene the Court," General Kelley sent the record of the proceedings forward to President Lincoln "with the recommendation that Lieut. Smith be dismissed from the service of the United States." Judge Advocate General Joseph Holt concurred and recommended dishonorable dismissal. Lincoln agreed and dismissed Lieutenant Smith from the service in April 1864.[8]

In western Tennessee, Lt. Charles W. Mann of the Sixty-First Illinois was dishonorably dismissed for attempting to resign after the Emancipation Proclamation was issued. In his letter of resignation, Mann wrote: "I hereby respectfully tender to you the immediate and unconditional resignation of my commission . . . on account of being dissatisfied with the service and the conduct of the present Administration—and the Emancipation Proclamation of President A. Lincoln—of Jany. 1st 1863." For this letter, Mann was charged with "Tendering his resignation in disloyal language and writing and expressing disloyal sentiments," "Inciting discontent and disloyalty in his Regiment," and violating the Fifth Article of War. The record seems to indicate that there was no trial; the letter was submitted as evidence and the court-martial found him guilty, sentencing him to be dishonorably dismissed and to lose all pay. Gen. Ulysses S. Grant approved the finding and sentence.[9]

Back east, near Falmouth, Virginia, Lt. Joseph Nichols of the Nineteenth Maine Infantry wrote a letter of resignation to the lieutenant colonel of his regiment on January 12, 1863, claiming that if he had known that emancipation would become a war aim, he never would have entered the service. The Emancipation Proclamation, in his view, was inexpedient and unconstitutional. "I cannot as a volunteer Officer, conscientiously and zealously serve under it," he concluded.[10]

Nichols was arrested and brought before a court-martial, where he was arraigned on two charges:

CHARGE 1ST. Conduct prejudicial to good order and military discipline.

SPECIFICATION. In this that the said Joseph Nichols . . . did tender his resignation while near the enemy under an allegation or pretext of the inexpediency and unconstitutionality of a Proclamation of the President of the United States: thereby affording an example deeply injurious to the service and meddling with the war policy of the Government with which he has nothing to do.

CHARGE 2ND. Disloyalty to the Government

SPECIFICATION. In this: that he . . . entertains ideas in opposition to the Government, expressing his belief of the inexpediency and unconstitutionality of one of its leading measures and stating further that he cannot serve conscientiously and zealously under it, the said measure being expressly intended to weaken the enemies of the United States.

All this at Camp near Falmouth on or about the 12th of January 1863.

These charges and specifications, which were based on Maj. Gen. Oliver Otis Howard's assessment of the case, went beyond simply stating Nichols's alleged crimes; they made substantive claims about the duties of a soldier. Soldiers, in Howard's view, were not to render opinions against federal policies because such "meddling" was "injurious to" the federal war effort and thus worked to aid the enemy.[11]

In his defense, Nichols claimed to possess "the same right to entertain his own opinions as to the expediency or constitutionality of any measure of the government as other citizens in civil life." Political "expression," he argued, "is not disloyalty, for the civil [law] which defines disloyalty permits such expressions. Whatever is disloyalty here [in the army] is disloyalty everywhere." Nichols maintained that if he could be punished for what he said in camp, then every political opponent of Lincoln's who held "the same opinion or belief, is guilty of the same crime and liable to [be] arraigned and convicted before a civil court on the same charge as that one which the accused is arraigned before this Court." Moreover, Nichols claimed, "it is not within the province of military law to define the crime of disloyalty."[12]

Nichols's arguments did not persuade the judges. The court-martial found him guilty of the first charge (except for the words "and meddling with the war policy of the Government with which he has nothing to do") and of the specification of the second charge (except the words "the said measure being expressly intended to weaken the enemies of the United States"), although he was acquitted of disloyalty. He was sentenced to be dismissed from the service but to receive his pay and allowances.[13]

Major General Howard was livid when he read the proceedings of the court. Howard saw "no propriety in excepting the words 'the said measure being expressly intended to weaken the enemies of the United States,' since this clause is merely descriptive & explanatory of what precedes." But to avoid injury to the service by prolonging the case, he approved the proceedings on January 20, 1863, and forwarded them to Maj. Gen. Darius Couch.[14]

Major General Couch disapproved of the sentence of the court, and his superior, Maj. Gen. Edwin V. Sumner, agreed. Nichols's punishment, in their view, was not strong enough. "I earnestly recommend that this officer be dishonorably dismissed [from] the service with the loss of all pay and allowance," wrote Sumner on the case file, before forwarding it on to Washington. In the nation's capital, Judge Advocate General Holt summarized the facts of the case on January 31 and sent the file to Secretary of War Edwin M. Stanton. Stanton, in turn, dishonorably discharged Nichols on February 2, 1863.[15]

Nichols's dismissal had a profound effect on his men. Writing in the early twentieth century, a corporal who had served under Nichols recalled: "He was a pleasant and lovable man and the officers and a great many of the men were very fond of him. He left the Regiment regretted by all who knew him." Still, the dismissal accomplished what Nichols's superiors hoped. Soldiers throughout the army learned that anti-emancipation speech would not be tolerated in the field. An officer in the Fourteenth Indiana Volunteers observed, "They handle all such chaps without gloves in the army."[16]

At least one officer escaped punishment when resigning in protest of Lincoln's emancipation policy. Lt. Col. Robert A. Constable of the Seventy-Fifth Ohio Infantry submitted his resignation to Maj. Gen. Franz Sigel on January 9, 1863. In his letter, Constable claimed to be motivated by patriotism—that he "cherish[ed] none but devoted feelings of attachment to the Constitution and the Union, and have no desire but that the one may be sustained and the other restored." But he now believed that he could no longer remain in the army in good conscience. "I can not conscientiously endorse and carry out the Emancipation Proclamation of our Commander-in-Chief—the President of the United States," he wrote to Sigel. On January 10, Brig. Gen. Julius Stahel disapproved of Constable's "reprehensible" request. Two days later, Sigel forwarded Constable's letter to the War Department with the recommendation that he be dismissed from the service. For some unknown reason, however, the War Department accepted Constable's resignation. An enlisted man in the Seventy-Fifth caustically noted the difference between officers and enlisted men who opposed emancipation. Constable, he wrote, "did not come out to fight for the Damned niggers, so he got a free pass to Ohio."[17]

Some officers resigned in order to escape looming punishment for anti-emancipation speech. Capt. Martin Van Buren Bennett of the Fortieth Iowa, an outspoken critic of the Lincoln administration, resigned his commission before he could be punished and dishonorably discharged from the military.[18] In like manner, Col. John Beardsley of the Ninth New York Cavalry resigned in March

1863 to avoid several pending charges, including "uttering disloyal sentiments and language tending to demoralize his command."[19] Others simply resigned without giving an explanation but became vocal spokesmen for the Democratic Party when they got home. Col. John C. Groom of the One Hundredth Ohio Infantry, for example, resigned his commission in May 1863 and went home to campaign for Vallandigham.[20] Many soldiers must have known officers like these. Indeed, a group of Union soldiers stationed in Illinois encountered a former officer of theirs in October 1864—"a renegade soldier," one called him, "who says he left the Army because he couldnt fight for the Niggar."[21]

Still other officers resigned quietly, only expressing their disdain for emancipation in private correspondence. "*I* for one (and I think it is so with a large portion of the Army) am disgusted with this war & its management. And shall be very glad when my time is out, they will not get me into it again," wrote one angry officer from New York in January 1863. He continued:

> I did not come out to fight for the nigger or abolition of slavery. Much less to make the nigger *better* than white men, as they are every day becoming in the estimation and treatment of the powers at Washington. I would sooner see every nigger now free, *in* slavery, than see slavery abolished. And yet the *latter* seems to be the sole object of the Govt.—I believe that 9/10th of the Army would today if they could lay down their Arms & go home, and positively refuse to have anything more to do with this war, on the principles on which it is now being carried on. . . . Our Officers & Soldiers have no heart for carrying on a war on the principles those men & their followers advocate. It is not what they joined the service for, and they will not fight for them.[22]

While this soldier certainly overestimated the amount of disaffection among the troops as a whole, he lived up to his own pledge and resigned his commission shortly thereafter. Privately he called the war "a bad cause—Although I suppose it would not do to say so, openly." When his abolitionist uncle later asked him to raise another regiment for the Union, he replied, "I shall do nothing of the kind, as I do not wish to go with the Army again, unless compelled to do so."[23]

Other soldiers expressed similar sentiments in their private correspondence. Connecticut artillerist Stephen Whitney, a lieutenant in the Fourth U.S. Artillery, wrote in January 1863, "I am utterly and entirely disgusted with the way things are going and came so near resigning that there was no fun in it last week and now I cant say that I am any more contented." He noted that many officers had been disheartened since the dismissal of Fitz-John Porter. Lincoln's Emancipation Proclamation only further disillusioned him. "Now what let me ask is a man to gain by serving such an administration? The nigger is not exactly what I entered the service for." Whitney soon would decide that he had had enough of army life; he resigned his commission later that year.[24]

Such sentiments compelled other officers to resign as well, although they may not have said so publicly at the time. Three officers from the Ninetieth Illinois Volunteers resigned in January 1863 in protest of the Emancipation Proclamation.[25] Col. Owen Jones of the First Pennsylvania Cavalry, an antebellum Democrat who had served in Congress in the 1850s, resigned his commission in January 1863. While the published records do not state the reason for his resignation, historians of his regiment note that he "resigned in order to defend his reputation at home and because the emancipation proclamation had moved the war beyond his aim, as a loyal Democrat, of preserving the Union as it was."[26] In like manner, postwar writings reveal that Col. John C. Cochran "and other officers" of the Fourteenth Kentucky Infantry resigned in January 1863 "because of the president's emancipation proclamation," although Cochran's letter of resignation made no mention of political matters.[27]

Lincoln's final Emancipation Proclamation caused a stark transformation in some Union officers. On December 17, 1862, Lt. Richard M. Goldwaite of the Ninety-Ninth New York Infantry told his wife that he could not leave the army, for "as long as my country is in danger and calls on me to do my duty, I must submit to these deprivations and fight for the right" so that "our country [may] once more be placed in union and peace. Until this is done, I cannot be satisfied to come home." But things changed on January 1, 1863. "I have made up my mind to leave the Army in the Spring, if I can get out of it," he told his wife on January 24—a month after he had pledged to fight until the war was won. "I shall try hard to get out. . . . I am sick and tired of this Nigger War. A soldier has nothing to encourage him to fight for a lot of Nigger lovers at home." As was common with letters of this sort, Goldwaite added a postscript asking his wife not to show it to anyone and to "burn all of these kind of letters." Within two weeks, Goldwaite submitted his resignation; he returned home to his family later that spring.[28]

Goldwaite was eventually joined by a number of enlisted men from his regiment. During the summer of 1864, 178 other men in the Ninety-Ninth New York Volunteer Infantry opted to muster out rather than reenlist, leaving just enough men for four companies, which was then reduced to three in September 1864.[29] This is not to suggest that these 178 men were all Democrats who opposed Lincoln's war policies, but certainly some were.

THE EFFECTS OF EMANCIPATION ON DESERTION
AND REENLISTMENTS

Unlike officers who could submit a letter of resignation, a healthy enlisted man's only real options for leaving the service early were faking illness, self-mutilation, or desertion. Several Delaware soldiers contacted one of their U.S. senators in January 1863 "to see if I could aid them in getting discharged. They claim to be on the ground of health, but I found they were opposed to the abolition policy[,] sick of the war, & said they had been deceived in their enlistment."[30] Similarly, Capt. David Acheson of the 140th Pennsylvania Volunteer Infantry wrote home that two men in his company were "making themselves sick purposely by eating fried crackers, fat meat, &c, to a sufficient amount to make the strongest man sick. They are both working for discharge."[31] Cases like these were common. Many others simply deserted.

Recent scholarship has tended to underestimate the significant impact of emancipation upon desertion in the Union armies. Chandra Manning, for example, argues that soldiers' reactions to the Emancipation Proclamation "were not nearly as negative or simplistic as has long been supposed" (it will be recalled that Manning argues that many Union soldiers came to support emancipation as early as 1861). Moreover, she claims that emancipation had little impact on the military's low morale in the winter of 1862–63. "Timing does not support a link between emancipation and demoralization," she writes. "If soldiers' low spirits resulted from the preliminary or final Emancipation Proclamation, then morale should have dropped at the same time throughout the entire Union Army, right after one or the other of the proclamations." Instead, she maintains that the Army of the Potomac faced its lowest morale in November and December 1862, while the western armies were not demoralized until February 1863. "Demoralization, in short, struck eastern and western armies at different times in response to local circumstances, not as the result of emancipation, which troops everywhere had known was coming since September." Taking her argument one step further, she concludes that "when the preliminary and final proclamations came, many soldiers regarded them less as unwelcome surprises than as evidence that a tardy federal government was finally catching up to what soldiers had known for more than a year."[32]

Manning's account glosses over the significant opposition to emancipation that existed in the Union armies in the winter of 1862–63, as well as the ways that Union leaders coerced adherence to the cause of emancipation. As is evident in chapter 2, Union military authorities publicly punished officers and enlisted men for speaking out against emancipation, most of which took place after January 1, 1863. Moreover, the officers who resigned out of opposition to emancipation did so after the final Emancipation Proclamation was issued—not after Lincoln issued his preliminary edict in September 1862. In other words, although they knew that it was coming, they still viewed emancipation as an unwelcome surprise. And when it came, they were no longer willing to fight under Lincoln's command. Finally, just like their officers, many common soldiers deserted rather than fight in a war for abolition.

President Lincoln intuitively understood the connection between desertion and the proslavery, antiwar wing of the Democratic Party. In his famous exchange with Erastus Corning in June 1863, Lincoln claimed that Clement Vallandigham had been arrested for inhibiting Union enlistments and for encouraging desertion. "Mr. Vallandigham avows his hostility to the war on the part of the Union; and his arrest was made because he was laboring, with some effect, to prevent the raising of troops, to encourage desertions from the army, and to leave the rebellion without an adequate military force to suppress it."[33] In response to Lincoln's letter, a group of Ohio Democrats accused Lincoln—not Vallandigham—of encouraging desertion through his emancipation policy: "If it were proper to do so in this paper, [we] might suggest that the measures of the Administration and its changes of policy in the prosecution of the war have been the fruitful sources of discouraging enlistments and inducing desertions," they boldly told the president.[34]

The Democrats' claim that emancipation caused desertions only half-explained the situation. Yes, many soldiers deserted following Lincoln's issuance of the Emancipation Proclamation on January 1, 1863. But, as Lincoln argued, soldiers continued to desert when Democratic politicians spoke out against emancipation, conscription, or his other war policies, as Clement Vallandigham had done. Thus, Lincoln did not need to prove that Vallandigham had specifically encouraged soldiers to desert. Vallandigham had never overtly done such a thing. But in criticizing Lincoln's policies, Vallandigham implicitly encouraged soldiers to give up the fight. He thus opened himself up to punishment. "He was warring upon the military," argued Lincoln, "and this gave the military constitutional jurisdiction to lay hands on him."[35] While this may have been a weak constitutional argument, Lincoln's overall point was clear: Copperhead speech was tantamount to discouraging enlistments and encouraging desertion and therefore needed to be silenced.

Some officers in the Union army recognized the ill effects that Copperheads could have on war-weary soldiers. Col. Thomas W. Bennett of the Sixty-Ninth Indiana Volunteers complained that desertions from his regiment were resulting from the letters his men received from home—letters that criticized the government and that included such statements as "it's an abolition war" and "Lincoln is played out."[36] To counter the effects of such letters from home, military authorities arrested some civilians who sought to demoralize the troops. Buckeye Democrat John O'Connell, for example, was sentenced to death by a military tribunal for sending a "Copperhead" letter to a soldier in the Seventy-Fourth Ohio. Other civilians were arrested and tried in civil courts.[37] Army leaders believed that the influence of Copperhead family members and politicians had to be kept to a minimum if the army was to remain an effective fighting force. The army therefore court-martialed several soldiers who had been induced by Copperheads to desert, hoping to prevent them from further spreading their Democratic views.[38] In calling for the execution of one deserter, Col. Milton S. Robinson of the Seventy-Fifth Indiana Volunteers declared: "It is known that disloyal men of the loyal states are exerting such powerful influences to bring about desertions, and disaffection in the Army."[39]

Military authorities used the punishment of deserters to reinforce the idea that soldiers ought to disregard the disloyal speech of Democratic politicians. Pvt. Barnabas Carter of the Ninety-First Ohio Volunteers deserted on January 15, 1863, because of the influence of his "pretended friends . . . as they are inclined to be disloyal." He was apprehended, court-martialed, and sentenced to hard labor. Although Carter died before his sentence could be carried out, the brigadier general commanding would not lose this opportunity to remind the troops that they ought not to heed the calls to desert from the traitors in the rear. "The proceedings & findings must be read to the troops," the general added to the case file.[40]

Pvt. William Delaney of the Twenty-Seventh Ohio Infantry deserted about January 19, 1863, shortly after the Emancipation Proclamation was issued. He remained absent until February 1864, when he was arrested in Illinois and brought back to his regiment. Delaney was arraigned before a court-martial and charged with desertion and "working, or acting very zealously with a political party popularly known as the Copperhead party." Delaney was found guilty of desertion but not of being a Copperhead. Nevertheless, the timing of his desertion and the accusation of Copperheadism suggest that Delaney was one of the many soldiers who left the army in early 1863 because they refused to fight for emancipation. He was sentenced to hard labor for two years and to forfeit all pay that was or would come due him.[41]

Soldiers could not help but notice the large numbers of men fleeing the ranks in early 1863. "There is much dissatisfaction existing in the army on account of the President's proclamation. Desertions are numerous and frequent," wrote one New Jersey soldier. "As the slaves become free only as our army advances, then who can deny we are fighting for the confounded nigger? . . . The proclamation has done more to demoralize the army of the North than any good, practically or morally, that can possibly result from it. The nine months men are looking anxiously to the time when they can return home. I'm one of them."[42] Indeed, one nine-month cavalryman from New York wrote in late 1863: "I have only nine months to serve and Uncle Sam may get all the nigger soldiers he can raise and scrape." Another New Yorker echoed his comrade's sentiments: "The soldiers are down on the President's Proclamation, and our reg. is getting thinned out pretty fast by deserters. . . . The soldiers swear they will never fight by the side of the damned Niggers."[43]

Conservatives in the ranks felt deceived by the changing nature of the war and believed that desertion was a justifiable response. One Michigan artillerist told his parents in November 1862: "I hope to Run away for all wee fiting for is to free the god dam Negros and that dont suit this Child by god . . . I would Rather bea dishonerabel discharged than to stay in a disgrasful army." He went absent without leave in June 1863.[44] Pvt. Carter M. Fentriss of the Sixty-Fifth Indiana felt alike. He deserted on March 10, 1863, because, he said, he "did not enlist in the war to free the negroes." Fentriss was captured four days later, convicted by a court-martial, and sentenced to hard labor for the remainder of his enlistment, with a ball and chain for a year of that time, and to be branded with the letter "D."[45] In January 1863, George Sinclair of the Eighty-Ninth Illinois said that the Emancipation Proclamation "only exasperates the rebs to fight the harder making an enemy for the Union where it had a friend before. . . . I will come home and let some abolitionist take my place, *in the good work.*" He wanted to find out whether he was fighting "for the *nigger* or the *Union* and Constitution *as it was*. If the nigger is the object and Abe Lincoln's Proclamation [is] still to be the main feature and guide for the prosecution of this unholy war against our own countrymen, then I am out of it forever and shall act conscientiously in leaving the army." Sinclair, feeling "swindled" and "deceived" by the changing nature of the war, believed "the nigger loving" people of the North should join the army "to fight their abolition battles." Sinclair received a discharge after suffering a battle wound in June 1863.[46]

One Vermont soldier noted in January 1863 that "Old Abe['s] stock is clear down" and that the soldiers "unanimously want to go home and let the Southern Confederacy, Negroes, our own administration, and all go to the devil together."[47] Several regiments faced near-mutinous responses to the Emancipation Proclamation. A Wisconsin soldier observed that many border state soldiers "are deserting & going home every day they say they didn't come down here to free the niggers." He also noted that the 128th Illinois Volunteers "has entirely broken up & gone home."[48] According to one historian, "the regiment virtually disintegrated. At one time it was reported that only 35 men reported for morning muster."[49] Another Illinois regiment, the 109th Infantry, was disbanded for disloyalty in April 1863. Over the previous few months, 348 men had deserted from the 109th, and one contemporary observer claimed that "the regiment was composed almost exclusively of members of the knights of the Golden Circle."[50] Company H of the 107th New York faced a similar problem. One soldier in that regiment noted in mid-January 1863: "There was four men belonging to our company Deserted last night. This makes 12 in all that had Deserted our company. We have Twenty-Six in Hospitals. This leaves our Co. with but 49 Enlisted men now. When we left Elmira we had 98 Enlisted men and three commissioned officers. Now we have but one Commissioned officer and 49 Enlisted men—quite a difference."[51] The Fifty-First New York encountered the same problem. Wrote one soldier on January 17:

> The troops are loud in their denunciations against the President & the Abolition Cabinet generally & I have a faint idea that there will soon be a general uprising in the North to put an end to this war & decapitate some of the leading men in the Cabinet. Soldiers are constantly deserting & say that they will not fight to put niggers on a par with white men—that they had been duped

& that they only enlisted for the preservation of the Union & nothing else. Our Regt alone has lost 27 men by desertion since the last fight.[52]

In like manner, an Illinoisan observed in January 1863: "Desertions are not infrequent here. About 20 left the Kansas 1st & about as many more the 95th [Illinois] & some from nearly all of the Reg*ts* that left Memphis to come on this expedition I guess."[53]

Company I of the Thirty-Fourth Ohio Volunteer Infantry saw a similar spike in desertions in early 1863. On February 2, 1863, nine noncommissioned officers and enlisted men in the Thirty-Fourth deserted. They were captured, court-martialed, found guilty, and sentenced to be executed. Two officers also faced charges. Capt. James Anderson of Company I was court-martialed for uttering disloyal language, encouraging desertion, and assisting soldiers in deserting, and Lt. I. C. Fair of the First Ohio Independent Battery was charged with using "disloyal language" for saying: "This is a negro war. If I had known, I would never have joined. The Emancipation Proclamation is unconstitutional." One witness accused Anderson of publicly espousing the formation of a Northwest Confederacy that would join with the South to form a new slave nation. The witness also accused Anderson of giving copies of the *Cincinnati Enquirer,* a Copperhead newspaper, to his soldiers "stating that it contained Vallandigham's late speech in Congress—That it contained the sentiments of a loyal and patriotic man: for them to read it and ponder it well, and so be governed—that it was a severe blow upon the present corrupt and traitorous administration." In addition, the witness accused Anderson of giving a citizen's pass to a private so that he could desert. Like the enlisted men in his command, Anderson was found guilty, but he and Lieutenant Fair were only sentenced to dismissal from the service.[54]

In his defense, Anderson argued that he had not violated any military law or article of war. "It is quite evident that no article of war defines any punishment for such an offence," he argued, "therefore it can be no crime, nor can it be said that disloyal language is Treason." Anderson pointed out that the U.S. Constitution requires that treason "must consist of 'overt acts,' not words or language." He therefore claimed that he could not be convicted of a crime simply for uttering "words" of which his superiors disapproved. "A Court Martial cannot entertain such a charge as uttering disloyal language, much less inflict a punishment not clearly defined by law." Moreover, Anderson argued that citizens did not forfeit their right to free speech when they joined the military.[55]

Anderson's argument did not persuade the court, but because of a technicality, Maj. Gen. Robert C. Schenck, the commanding general, disapproved and annulled the findings and sentences of the court-martial, restoring the men to their duties. According to Schenck, the colonel who had called the court had not been authorized to do so and that while the "gravity of the charges and the force of the testimony would justify" the calling of a new court-martial, Schenck hoped that the experience and threat of execution would cause the men to reflect on their experience and act with more wisdom in the future. Indeed, Schenck hoped for a salutary effect "as well in regard to others as the parties themselves."[56] Thus, in this case military authorities did not believe it was necessary to inflict a punishment in order to send a message to the troops about desertion.

Other officers also facilitated desertions from their commands. Capt. John Brown of the Twenty-Eighth Illinois Volunteers was court-martialed for disloyalty and for aiding soldiers in his company to desert in January and February 1863. While he was acquitted of aiding desertion, he was found guilty of saying "that he could not blame any of the men for deserting, and that he would not report any soldier for deserting" and of lying about the whereabouts of deserters from his company. Brown was immediately cashiered from the army.[57]

These regiments and companies were not the norm, but they reveal that political dissatisfaction with Lincoln's war policies had a significant impact on many Union soldiers' decisions to desert. One Pennsylvania officer informed his father in February 1863 that the army had many "Grunters" who caused trouble for the troops.

Every regiment has some of them, but New York ones the most. These men are always shirking duty. They are never at their posts in the hour of danger. When the army goes into battle they stay back, and if their side is defeated, they are the first to cry out against their leader. I saw hundreds of them loitering and camping in the woods during the last move. These men take every opportunity to run down the administration and complain of the hardships which they have to endure. The N.Y. troops are especially noted for bragging and grumbling. Take a man that has never known what we are fighting about, place him where he can hear N.Y. troops talk, and he'll come to the conclusion that New York is doing all the fighting, and that there are more hardships than ever were in war before. We've been thrown in connection with these New Yorkers very often on Picket and the only talk is "Damn the nigger war"; "Abe ought to be hung"; "Wish the war was over."[58]

Some groups of soldiers articulated these views en masse. Several Iowa regiments, for example, adopted resolutions condemning the Emancipation Proclamation.[59]

Actions like these had to be stopped before they had a negative effect on the troops. A captain in the Fifth Indiana Cavalry arrested six noncommissioned officers on January 2, 1863, for circulating "a Mutinous Petition."[60] And when six men fled from the Sixty-Ninth Indiana in February 1863—"and others were contemplating it"—the regiment's colonel delivered a speech to his men in which he said that if he heard any more complaints against the government's policies or talk of desertion, "I should begin to shave heads and drum out." He reported proudly to his state's adjutant general, "Since then not a word has been uttered out of the way."[61]

Unlike other types of deserters (such as those who deserted to care for loved ones or to tend to the harvest), men who deserted because of their views of emancipation likely had no intention of returning to the service. Pvt. Dala Kritzer deserted from the Seventieth Indiana and was recaptured several times in 1863. On one such occasion, February 3, he got drunk and handed his musket to his captain, saying, "I want you to take it, I aint agoing to fight any more for this damned abolition war. . . . I am going home." True to his word, that night he deserted and went home. A few months later, Kritzer was arrested, returned to his regiment, court-martialed, and sentenced to execution by firing squad. Fortunately for him, however, Gen. William Starke Rosecrans recommended commuting the sentence to loss of all pay and confinement at hard labor for the remainder of his enlistment.[62]

Some officers even deserted rather than resign. Lt. George D. Farrar of the Ninety-Fourth Ohio deserted in November 1862. He returned to his regiment and persistently voiced his opposition to this "damned Abolition War," even going so far as to wear "a 'Butternut' emblem, denoting opposition to the government." Farrar was dishonorably dismissed, forfeited all pay that was or would come due him, and spent six months in a military prison.[63]

Many soldiers who deserted because of emancipation were shrewd enough not to say so publicly. Indeed, deserters' Democratic views can sometimes only be deduced from their private correspondence. Sharpshooter William B. Greene loathed the idea of "freeing the niggers" and tried every trick he could to get out of the service. He deserted for a short period in October 1862 and upon returning lied about his mother being sick to avoid punishment. He deserted again sometime between November 1862 and March 1863 and went to Wisconsin, where he assumed an alias. After he was arrested in October 1863 and returned to his regiment, he continued to seek new ways to leave the service. And when his brother considered enlisting, the sharpshooter told him, "Just as sure as you enlist and come out here I'll shoot you, for by G—d, if after I have told you all about it, you want a canteen, you had ought to be shot."[64]

When given the chance, some Union soldiers fled into rebel lines hoping to find sanctuary. Upon reaching the Confederate army, a lieutenant from the 110th Ohio Infantry told the rebels that there was "much dissatisfaction among the troops on account of the emancipation proclamation" and that "many would follow his example if insured kind treatment by our Government." Upon hearing of this story, Confederate general Robert E. Lee gladly hoped to encourage further Union desertion by authorizing his subordinates "to offer kind treatment to all who come into your lines."[65] Although he grossly overestimated the number who would desert to the enemy, this Ohio lieutenant's views correctly gauged the mass discontent that plagued many northern camps. On January 4, 1863, one Illinois soldier noted despondently that "patriotism . . . is about played out among the soldiers generally."[66]

A small but notable minority of soldiers—many of whom came from border slave states like Kentucky—were so incensed by the Emancipation Proclamation and Lincoln's other war policies that they left their posts and joined the rebel forces. A few also became spies for the Confederacy. When captured by their former comrades, these men usually faced the gallows, a firing squad, or hard labor with a ball and chain.[67] Some were also punished for threatening such action. Sgt. Peter Haring of the Third Potomac Home Brigade was convicted by court-martial for saying on January 15, 1863, that he would rather fight in the rebel army and that he "would never raise his rifle again in favor of a nigger."[68] The threat of Union soldiers deserting to the enemy could not go without punishment. The Union army simply could not tolerate such acts of treason.

Trials for desertion spiked between January and March 1863.[69] Indeed, the period from October 1862 to February 1863 saw the highest number of desertions during the war.[70] On February 17, 1863, General Rosecrans lamented, "The effect of the state of party agitation at the North is to encourage desertion." To counteract this evil in the army, Rosecrans recommended "promptly executing sentence[s] of death for desertion" and detailing officers and men to arrest and return deserters to their regiments. The problem in the Army of the Cumberland in February 1863 was grave indeed. "There are 40,000 absentees from this army to-day," Rosecrans informed Gen. Henry Wager Halleck.[71]

The massive desertion problem placed President Lincoln in a difficult position. On the one hand, he had an army to mobilize and he had to ensure good order, discipline, and minimal absenteeism. On the other hand, Lincoln is widely known for his kindness and compassion toward common soldiers. He pardoned many deserters who had been sentenced to be shot. In fact, the record reveals that Lincoln was almost always prone toward mercy. In the first two years of the war, Lincoln in some way lessened the punishment of 77 percent of the deserters whose court-martial case files he reviewed; from 1863 to 1865, he lightened the sentences of 95 percent.[72] When Gen. Benjamin F. Butler pressed Lincoln in early 1863 to execute every soldier who deserted, the president responded: "How can I have a butcher's day every Friday in the Army of the Potomac?" "Better have that," replied Butler, "than have the Army of the Potomac so depleted by desertion that good men will be butchered on the other days than Friday."[73] But enough blood was being spilled on a daily basis. Lincoln's tendency was to not pardon soldiers who committed heinous crimes, particularly those that violated women and children.[74]

Lincoln often waited until the last minute to issue a reprieve. Pvt. Henry Andrus of the 124th Ohio Infantry deserted on January 1, 1863—the day that the proclamation was issued. He turned up back in Ohio a few days later publicly saying that Lincoln was "a d—d curse, a d—d abolitionist, and a d—d scoundrel"; that the Lincoln administration was "more corrupt and contemptible than that of Jeff Davis"; that "I wish I had Lincoln's d—d old head"; and that "I hope the slaves will murder many Union men as Lincoln is encouraging them to murder." Andrus was found guilty and sentenced to be shot on January 8, 1864. Maj. Gen. Ambrose Burnside approved the sentence, as did Judge Advocate General Joseph Holt, who believed Andrus's "words & conduct were those of a man wholly disloyal." But on January 7, 1864, Lincoln commuted the death sentence to imprisonment at hard labor for the duration of the war. The soldier's life was spared, but in the postwar period his comrades were less forgiving. The regimental history for the 124th Ohio, published several decades after the war, wiped Andrus's memory from the record.[75]

On occasion, Lincoln approved the death sentences of soldiers who deserted because of the changing nature of the war. Pvt. Thomas Clifton, a twenty-five-year-old native of Maine who joined the Second California Cavalry in San Francisco in 1861, deserted on October 23, 1862. He was captured and tried before a court-martial, where he testified: "I took an oath that as soon as the war was for the abolition of slavery, I would take no further part. At the first opportunity, I took my chance to remain neutral." Clifton was found guilty and sentenced to be shot. Lincoln approved the sentence in July 1863.[76]

Thomas Clifton was a simple-minded soldier boy Lincoln was willing to shoot. Indeed, executing some opponents of emancipation could have very positive consequences. "There has been a good deal of deserting since the Proclamation, but I guess it will stop now," wrote one soldier in the Twenty-Fifth Illinois. "I understand that the law is to be executed to the limit on deserters, & that means death—for my part I would rather as soon die any other way as to be set up against a stump & shot at."[77] Honorable soldiers would rather die facing the enemy than sitting on a coffin before a firing squad. An Ohio soldier told his wife in late January 1863: "If a man Deserts and is caught he is punished even unto death for it. Rather would I have my Dear little children Dear as they are to me say that Pa was killed in War rather than have it thrown up to them that yo[u]r father was a *Deserter* and had to wear the chain and ball for thre[e] years as many are paying for the same crime here."[78]

Witnessing an execution was a solemn experience that placed an indelible mark on the memory of a soldier. Many Union soldiers recorded vivid accounts of executions in their letters, diaries, and memoirs. They never forgot the scene. Maj. Gen. George G. Meade remarked to his wife: "I trust the example made of five deserters, who were shot on Saturday, will check the evil of desertion. This execution was witnessed by a very large number of soldiers, and I am told the only remark made was, 'Why did they not begin this practice long ago?' Not a murmur against the justice or the propriety of the act was heard. Indeed, the men are the most anxious to see this great evil cured, as they know their own security will be advanced thereby."[79] Indeed, when one Democrat deserted from the Fifteenth Pennsylvania Cavalry in the spring of 1863, an unsympathetic comrade wrote: "Henry [is] a copperhead. . . . I hope he will be caught as a deserter and treated as such. It would be good for him."[80]

Soldiers intent on deserting had to be very careful that their intentions were not discovered. Military authorities had no qualms with punishing a soldier for disloyalty or conduct prejudicial to good order and military discipline if they found out about a soldier's plans. One officer in the Sixty-First Illinois was reduced to the ranks, confined at hard labor for the rest of his enlistment, lost all pay, and was dishonorably discharged at the end of his term of service. His crime was having written a personal, anti-emancipation letter in January 1863 that found its way into the hands of Union authorities. "I am well satisfied that it is a fight for the freedom of the Negro," he told his correspondent. "With or without a resignation I am determined to leave the army, unless there is a change of way of prosecuting this war, though I would much rather leave in honor. If old Illinois secedes from the New England States, I am with her. These sentiments are from my heart, *though I can't express myself here.*"[81] Despite the fact that these sentiments were contained only in a private letter, this soldier's punishment was swift, severe and public.

Several soldiers were punished for openly praising the rebels after they had deserted their posts. Wesley Hampton, a wagoner in the 117th Illinois, deserted in late 1862 and went to hear a Confederate speaker whom he thought was "one of the smartest men he had ever heard speak and that a great deal of his speech he could endorse that it was the true Doctrine." He was dishonorably dismissed for saying so.[82] Pvt. Washington Venom deserted from an Ohio hospital in October 1862. He was arrested at Wheeling, [West] Virginia, in February 1863 for "shouting for 'Jeff Davis, and the Southern Confederacy.'" The military court sentenced him to be shot, but Gen. Benjamin F. Kelley suspended his execution because of Lincoln's March 1863 proclamation that granted amnesty to deserters who returned to their regiments. Kelley also took into account the fact that Venom was drunk when he huzzahed his treason.[83] Others were similarly punished for speaking foolishness. George W. Schultz, a saddler in the Eighteenth Pennsylvania Cavalry, was dishonorably discharged and imprisoned at Fort Delaware at hard labor for the remainder of his term of enlistment for saying that he would like to desert to England and that if the rebels "were to surround him 'he would not fire a shot.'"[84]

A personal connection to Lincoln helped one common soldier avoid the firing squad after he was caught deserting and uttering disloyal language. Pvt. Adam K. Daines of the Sixty-Third Indiana deserted from his regiment in September 1862; he was discovered almost a year later—in August 1863—at a saloon in Indianapolis drunkenly shouting that he was a "Vallandigham and a Jeff. Davis man." Daines was court-martialed and sentenced to be executed on October 1. Fortunately for him, an officer in his regiment had known Lincoln back in Illinois in the 1850s. The officer wrote to Lincoln, enclosing a petition signed by a number of Indiana soldiers which claimed that Daines was "ignorant and illiterate" and had fallen under the influence of disloyal men. Upon receiving the petition, Lincoln commuted the sentence to imprisonment at the Dry Tortugas.[85]

Of course, not all soldiers who threatened desertion followed through with their plans.[86] In 1861, Theodore Parks of the 147th Pennsylvania hoped that members of both political parties would work together to restore the Union. An antebellum Democrat, Parks believed it was time to "let party lines and platforms become extinct" so that the North could unify for victory. In January 1863, Parks noted how the Emancipation Proclamation "dampens the ardor of the army somewhat. Much as I detest desertion, when ever they organise Negro Regiments, and expect me to fight by the side of an African, I will either desert or shoot niggers instead of rebels. Those who volunteered for 'glory' will then have it heaped-up." Despite his threats, Parks opted not to desert—it is also unlikely that he shot at black Union soldiers. But Lincoln's shift in war policy reignited his partisanship for the Democratic Party. In September 1864, Parks noted that if McClellan "had the moral courage to denounce the Peace faction that took so conspicuous a part in the Chicago convention, nothing under heaven would prevent his election."[87]

Other soldiers felt like Parks. In November 1862, Sergeant Onley Andrus of the Ninety-Fifth Illinois hoped that the rebels would sue for peace before the Emancipation Proclamation went into effect "to keep the Niggers where they belong . . . in Slavery." His views did not appear to change much with the war. On March 4, 1864, he told his wife that he wished this "was the last day" of his enlistment. He then added sarcastically: "I think I see myself reenlisting to help to make the Nigger my superior. . . . I expect to stay my time out and not one minute longer."[88]

Sgt. Symmes H. Stillwell, a New Jersey Republican in Lincoln's army, was a violent racist, a harsh critic of the abolitionists, and a virulent opponent of emancipation. In March 1863, Stillwell called "the arming of negroes a confession of weakness, a folly, an insult to the brave Soldier, and a crime against humanity and civilization" and he hoped that "the President will have to recall his proclamation." By November 1863, Stillwell had decided that he would not reenlist once his time in the service was up. In September 1864, he still believed that the "proclamation should never have been issued," although he acknowledged that revoking it now would be a sign of "weakness." When the chance came to reenlist in October 1864, Stillwell remained true to his earlier pledge and mustered out of the army. He refused to fight any longer in a war for emancipation.[89]

Stillwell was not alone among his comrades. Indeed, less than 15 percent of the Union army reenlisted between November 1, 1863, and November 1, 1864. Of an estimated 922,155 soldiers who were eligible to reenlist during this time period, only 136,507 chose to do so. More than 85 percent (785,648) opted not to reenlist.[90] Such a vast number of soldiers leaving the Union army marked a major shift in the composition of the troops. Certainly a fair number of these men, like Stillwell, chose not to keep fighting because they disapproved of the direction that Lincoln was taking the war. Pvt. Jacob Young of the Thirty-First New Jersey Volunteers mustered into the Union army on September 17, 1862, five days before Lincoln issued his preliminary Emancipation Proclamation. This new policy turned Private Young against the president and the war effort. "When I was at home I was a Lincoln man," he told his father on January 4, 1863, "but I am set against him now for yesterday and day before yesterday there was a lot of niggers came through our camp and they said they was a-going to Washington. I thought they was a-going to take New Year's dinner with old Abe." Private Young mustered out with his regiment in June 1863 after only nine months' service.[91]

Some soldiers wondered whether wanting to quit the army would mark them as disloyal. Upon telling a superior officer that he would not reenlist, one New York cavalryman remarked, "I am afraid I am something of a 'Copperhead' for I don't think as much of the administration as—well as I do of Gens Peck & Parmer & thats the worst I *can* say aint it?" This soldier hoped for a Democratic victory in 1864, but like many other Democratic soldiers, he hated the Peace men of his party. Of Clement Vallandigham and the Wood brothers of New York, he wrote: "I dont believe in them at all."[92]

ARMY RESOLUTIONS

By January and February 1863, politicians at home and Republican officers in the field were beginning to recognize the harm that Democratic influences were having on the troops. Behind closed doors, Republicans in Congress discussed ways to keep Democratic papers from reaching the hands of soldiers and to furnish the troops with Republican messages.[93] One Union paymaster distributed "Uncle Abe's Photographs" to members of the Sixth Kentucky Infantry in March 1863 while he was doling out four months' pay. A soldier in the regiment figured this was "probably to keep our memories sharpened in regard to that great and good man."[94] Some generals took the proactive step of banning Democratic newspapers from their commands. In February 1863, one brigadier general banned the sale or circulation of the *Chicago Times* in his military district. Such a "dose of medicine," remarked Capt. Charles W. Wills of the 103rd Illinois, "will do an immensity of good to the army, and if the President will only suppress the paper and several others of the same stripe, and hang about 200 prominent copperhead scoundrels in the North, we may then hope that the army will once more be something like its former self."[95]

Captain Wills recognized that officers like himself had to devote "a great deal more of my time than I wish to, in talking patriotism at the boys and doing good, round, solid cursing at the home cowardly vipers, who are disgracing the genus, man, by their conduct." With "proper action of the officers for a few days," he believed, the "whole regiment . . . will denounce copperheadism" and it would "be the officers['] fault if we don't. If we were only officered properly throughout there would never have been a word of dissatisfaction in the regiment." Moreover, Wills "advised my men to whip any enlisted man they hear talking copperheadism, if they are able, and at all hazards to try it," and if he heard any officers talking disloyally "that I think I can't whale, I'm going to prefer charges against him." Only by proactively instilling patriotism in his men did Wills believe he could conquer the evils of desertion and disaffection in early 1863.[96]

In order to shore up support for the president and his emancipation policy, to discourage desertions, and to express their disgust with the antiwar Democrats back home, many Union officers led their regiments in public declarations of support for the president and emancipation. One Illinois soldier recalled that in the spring of 1863, "there had been great dissatisfaction, and desertions were quite frequent" to the point that if soldiers were allowed to continue this "agitation and these expressions of discontent" desertions might reach a dangerous level. "To meet this growing discontent," he recalled, "a meeting of the Field, Staff and Line Officers of the Brigade was held . . . [and] a committee was appointed to draft resolutions expressive of the sentiments of those present."[97] Some regiments even threatened to march back home to punish disloyal politicians. These army resolutions have traditionally been interpreted as frightening demonstrations of the army's resolve to promote loyalty at home.[98] But they were more than that. Indeed, army resolutions were also intended to apply political pressure on soldiers who were not in line with the Lincoln administration's changing policies for the war.

Between January and April 1863, as the contending armies rested between military campaigns, a number of Union regiments adopted resolutions condemning the actions of Copperheads on the home front, threatening "to return and crush out Treason" in the North. According to historian Mark E. Neely Jr., most Democratic newspapers offered no answer to these resolutions. The *York (Pa.) Gazette* printed several "critical letters purportedly from Pennsylvania soldiers," although it did not identify their names or regiments. According to Neely, "One of the letters maintained that officers threatened anyone who opposed the resolutions with being put in the front rank in the next battle. Another said that officers called only for ayes but not for nays, and still another maintained that no one voiced opposition in his unit because of fear of arrest for mutiny."[99]

As far-fetched as these complaints may seem, court-martial records and private correspondence from a variety of regiments and states substantiate these claims of intimidation. "Political Resolutions were gotten up for the express purpose, as one of the committee said, to make us show our hands, and those who did not endorse them, *'they would make the service too hot to hold them,'*" wrote one Ohio soldier in a private letter. This soldier refused to vote for his regiment's resolutions and was subsequently "arrested for disloyalty" and sentenced to dismissal.[100] Soldiers like this one, who simply refused to support their regiment's resolutions, might face punishment or public humiliation for their actions. Indeed, at least one Indiana regiment published the name of an officer who refused to sign its resolutions.[101]

Officers and enlisted men could face serious consequences for opposing regimental resolutions. One Illinois sergeant opposed the resolutions introduced in his regiment, calling them an "Abolition trick." In stating his opposition to the resolutions, the sergeant proclaimed "the President has broken his oath, and I have a right to break mine." He was court-martialed and convicted of violating the Fifth and Seventh Articles of War (criticizing the president and inciting mutiny). He was sentenced to be reduced to the ranks, confined to hard labor for six months, and then dishonorably discharged.[102]

In March 1863, the 176th Pennsylvania Militia adopted a series of resolutions in support of the Emancipation Proclamation, but one officer, David Schaad, refused to sign them. On March 27, 1863, four of his fellow officers protested to Maj. Gen. David Hunter that Schaad "is a very disloyal officer, and a traitor to his country—deeply opposed to every act of the Administration having for its object the prosecution of the war; and we beg that he may be relieved of his command, without pay, &c." Three days later, Hunter issued an order dismissing Schaad from the service, pending the president's approval.[103]

Lincoln doubted the propriety of Hunter's order. After all, Schaad had devoted considerable energy to raising troops for the Union war effort earlier in the war. "All this should not retain him in the service," Lincoln conceded, "if, since then, he has given himself in any way, to the injury of the service." But Lincoln insisted on knowing what Schaad had done or said that was illegal. "If, as is claimed for him, he is guilty of nothing, but the withho[l]ding his vote or sanction, from a certain resolution or resolutions, I think his dismissal is wrong, even though I might think the resolution itself right, and very proper to be adopted by such as choose."[104]

Mortified by what was transpiring, Schaad requested a court of inquiry to clear his name. At the court, Schaad was accused of saying, "I will not fight alongside of a negro. I would not allow a negro to save my life in battle" and that he did not "know who to shoot, negro soldiers or the rebels." Schaad also allegedly suggested that if Lincoln had been shot before he was elected, then "we could all have remained at home." One witness stated that Schaad's loyalty was doubtful because of "his opposition to the acts of government to suppress the rebellion, and his refusal to endorse those resolutions." Indeed, the resolutions were central to the case against him. In his defense, Schaad argued that "I was put in arrest on a certain day that I refused to sign some long winded ill concerned, badly written resolutions gotten up by the Colonel of my Regiment. . . . Had I given my consent and approbation to the empty declamations of the Colonel, this Court would never have met."[105]

The officers on the court castigated Schaad for his disloyal language but decided not to punish him. The court declared that his speech "was grossly improper" for having been spoken "sometimes in the presence of enlisted members of his own Company." Moreover, what he had said "was mischievous and criminal, and in its tone, and tendency clearly disloyal." However, the court made "great allowance for Capt. Schaad's ignorance, and want of correct ideas of discipline, and military subordination." Thus, while the court considered him "open to the severest censure," it acquitted him of "intentions to encourage disloyalty, and still less to enact himself the part of a traitor to his government, and his country." Schaad returned to his unit and served out the rest of his term; he was mustered out with his company on August 18, 1863. Prior to this incident, Schaad had expressed a willingness to reenlist in the service; now he was unwilling.[106]

Evidence from the field suggests that support for these resolutions was not always as "unanimous" as Republican officers and newspapers claimed.[107] In some instances, Democratic soldiers adopted conservative counterresolutions in favor of things such as "a vigorous prosecution of the war for restoration of the Union and for no other purpose."[108] In other cases, soldiers were not given the opportunity to vote against the resolutions. This way regimental officers could report that support for the resolutions was without dissent even though the support was not unanimous. In at least one instance, an officer threatened to "shoot anyone who refused to sign" his resolutions.[109] Intimidation, in short, was a factor at many of the dress parades in which soldiers voted on these resolutions.

In March 1863, the colonel of the Fifteenth Iowa Volunteers called his regiment together and read them a series of pro-emancipation resolutions, calling for the soldiers to vote viva voce. According to one Republican soldier in the regiment: "About one half of the men voted *Yea* about one fourth *Nay* and the bal[ance] did not vote at all. When the *nays* had voted the Col asked them to step out to the *front* and 28 men did so. Many of the *nays* not knowing what was up did not come to the *front*." The colonel ordered the remainder of the men back to the tents. Some of them "groaned as they passed the brave 28."[110]

The twenty-eight men were marched to the adjutant's tent and were questioned by the colonel. "Some of the men said they were dissatisfied with one of the Resolutions which favored the 'Proclamation of Emancipation[.]' Some thought themselves better than a 'nigger.'" Eventually the colonel lost control of the meeting, which was finally settled down when another officer "raising his voice above the din proposed '*three* cheers for the Union.' . . . This ended the affair which otherwise might have ended in a most disagreeable manner."[111]

Some officers bypassed such dissension by not allowing Democratic soldiers to vote on the resolutions. At dress parade on the evening of March 2, 1863, the colonel of the Ninety-Sixth Illinois had pro-emancipation resolutions read to the troops and then called out: "As many of the soldiers of the Ninety-Sixth Illinois as indorse the resolutions just read, will manifest by saying 'aye.'" He then sent the men back to their tents and forwarded copies of the resolutions to the newspapers with a note that they had been adopted "without a dissenting voice." One man who witnessed the scene recalled, "The ayes were numerous and enthusiastic, but, strange to say, not universal." And while it was "literally true" that they had been adopted without dissent, "the Colonel afterward declared that he dared not put the negative for fear the nays would be so numerous as not to look well for a Regiment from the State which was President Lincoln's home."[112]

These soldiers' resolutions served several important functions in the winter and spring of 1863. First, they warned disloyal politicians at home to remain loyal to the Union. Second, they became campaign tools for the Republican Party in the spring of 1863. Many newspapers published them, and the Indiana state government collected the memorials and resolutions of twenty-three Indiana regiments into a ninety-page pamphlet (most likely at the behest of Republican governor Oliver P. Morton). Third, and most importantly, the process of adopting these resolutions was an important tool for ensuring the loyalty of Union soldiers to the Republican war aim of reunion and war measures of conscription and emancipation.

When viewed as a whole, the regimental resolutions exhibit an unmistakable resemblance to one another—so much so that historian Mary R. Dearing suggests that they may have been ordered from the top down. "Republicans insisted that these expressions were spontaneous," she writes, "but the striking similarity of their phraseology suggests that this was not the case."[113] Indiana Democrats believed that the resolutions sent to their state legislature had been solicited by embattled governor Oliver P. Morton.[114] Evidence from the archives supports this contention. In mid-January 1863, one of Governor Morton's friends "advised . . . the governor to procure" expressions of support from the army. A few days later, Morton's military secretary, W. H. H. Terrell, wrote to Col. John T. Wilder of the Seventeenth Indiana Volunteers complaining that Democrats in the state were doing all they could "to vilify, abuse, embarrass & annoy" Governor Morton "in every possible way and shape." From the correspondence, Wilder appears to have already intimated a plan to rally support among the troops for the governor. Terrell therefore asked him to have the soldiers "raise their voices in his [Morton's] favor in such an hour as this." Such an action, he wrote, would be "peculiarly appropriate" and the governor would "never forget this mark of approbation." Soon thereafter, resolutions from Indiana soldiers began to circulate among the troops. By February 3, Governor Morton "had procured the memorials & protests of over 50 Regiments of our Indiana Soldiers." He also received word that other military units "would likewise express similar opinion."[115]

Indiana officers also "boasted" of the effects their resolutions had on enlisted men. Historian Thomas E. Rodgers describes the process among the Ninety-

Seventh Indiana Volunteers in which "fervently Republican soldiers did not fail to try to convert others to the views they held so strongly." They circulated pro-Union materials while "muzzling . . . Democratic views." The Republicans in the regiment thus persuaded Democrats and other discontented soldiers "to reverse their opinion and support the proclamation. Soon the men of the 97th were giving unanimous approval to resolutions in favor of Lincoln's policy, resolutions that were sent off to Hoosier Republican newspapers for publication."[116]

Sometimes the persuasion in a regiment could include threats of punishment. A soldier in the Twenty-Seventh Indiana Volunteers informed his father that there were anti-emancipation officers in his regiment who had been stirring up dissension among the troops. The colonel of the regiment "has had to Call Some of them to account & gave them to understand their fate if they persisted Which has had the effect to rather Smother things a little in our midst."[117] These resolutions, in short, were part of a mechanism for raising morale, discouraging desertion, and attempting to transform the ideological beliefs of the soldiery.

CONCLUSION

"I never in my life felt more certain that I was doing right than I do in signing this paper," Lincoln said as he prepared to sign the Emancipation Proclamation. "If my name ever goes into history it will be for this act, and my whole soul is in it."[118] Indeed, on January 1, 1863, Lincoln transformed the nature of the war and changed the direction of the country for all future time.[119] Yet many men in the army were unprepared for this change, and many others at home sought to discourage soldiers from fighting for emancipation. Rumblings in the army portended disaster should Union leaders not find a way to win support among the troops for Lincoln's new policy.

Union military officials could not allow the army to disintegrate in the winter and spring of 1863. Morale was already low in the Eastern Theater in the wake of Fredericksburg and the Mud March. When army officers began to resign their commissions in January and February 1863 because of their opposition to Lincoln's proclamation, the Union high command decided to make examples of them so that other officers would not follow suit.

Union leaders also sought to diminish the influence of Democratic politicians on the troops.[120] During the cold, hard months of winter in 1862 and 1863, common soldiers were susceptible to negative influences from antiwar politicians and family members. Many soldiers deserted because they believed that the Emancipation Proclamation was unconstitutional and had changed the nature of the war. Some did so by their own volition; others followed the voices of Copperhead politicians and newspaper editors. Just as military leaders punished officers who resigned out of opposition to emancipation, they also disciplined ordinary soldiers who expressed their dissatisfaction with the president's policy, or who deserted because they were not willing to fight for black freedom. The public nature of these punishments was intended to stifle dissent among the troops and stop the proverbial bleeding.

Within this context, dozens of Union regiments adopted anti-Copperhead resolutions in March 1863, just before the spring and summer season of fighting commenced. These resolutions sought to counteract the influence of antiwar politicians and to persuade Union soldiers to support emancipation. Equally important, they also helped solidify the growing hatred that soldiers felt toward Copperheads. As was seen in chapter 1 and will be seen in chapter 4, Democratic soldiers were willing to turn against their own party when they believed their party was acting disloyally.

4

"FOR MY PART I DONT CARE WHO IS ELECTED PRESIDENT"

The Union Army and the Elections of 1864

AS THE PRESIDENTIAL ELECTION of 1864 was rapidly approaching, the eyes of all northern politicians turned toward the armies of the Union. Over the previous few years, nineteen northern states had passed legislation permitting volunteers from their states to vote in the field, and many politicians believed that the soldiers' votes would determine whether or not Abraham Lincoln would be reelected. Never before had absentee voting existed on such a grand scale in the United States. Consequently, the votes of the soldiers became central to winning the election. "Everything depends on Pa. and upon the army vote of that State," wrote a prominent New York banker to the Democratic candidate for president, George B. McClellan.[1]

THE PARTIES AND THE NOMINEES

Within Republican ranks, radicals and abolitionists had been disappointed by Lincoln's sluggish move toward emancipation and black citizenship, as well as his lenient reconstruction policy for the South. Speaking for many abolitionists, Frederick Douglass asserted that Lincoln's emancipation policy was "timid and short-sighted."[2] Secretary of the Treasury Salmon P. Chase fervently desired the presidency, and Radical Republicans frequently discussed his name for the Republican nomination, but in March 1864 Chase formally withdrew from the race.[3]

A movement for Gen. John C. Fremont, the radical who had headed the Republican ticket in 1856, also gained momentum. On May 31, a convention convened in Cleveland that nominated him on a platform pledged to restoration of the Union, a constitutional amendment to abolish slavery, and confiscation of rebel lands. Accepting the nomination, Fremont pledged to withdraw from the race if the Republican National Convention would nominate someone other than Lincoln. Union general Henry Wager Halleck described this "Ragtail" convention as "a mass of corruption and humbugs" whose "only object . . . was to be 'bought off.' No doubt they will sell out cheap, if either of the other parties wish to purchase. A sure opportunity for those who wish to own elephants!" Adam Badeau, a staff officer serving under Ulysses S. Grant, noted the "abuse" that Radicals heaped on Lincoln: "They repeat all that the Democrats said last year and were disloyal for saying."[4]

The Republican National Convention met at Baltimore on June 7, 1864, a week after the Cleveland convention. The convention nominated Lincoln and placed him on a platform pledging restoration of the Union and a constitutional amendment to abolish slavery. Despite Lincoln's perceived shortcomings, the country knew where he stood on the issues, which gave him a good deal of credibility among Republican voters. "Somehow the President has impressed the people at large with the conviction that they know where to find him," noted Francis Lieber. The convention dumped Vice President Hannibal Hamlin of Maine from the ticket in favor of Tennessee War Democrat Andrew Johnson. They also styled themselves the Union Party.[5] In making these decisions, Republican Party leaders hoped to appeal to northern Democrats as well as voters in the Border States. In many ways, the Baltimore convention produced a middle-of-the-road outcome: a candidate who had approached the slavery issue in a moderate way and a platform pledged to amending the Constitution, hardly a radical approach to permanent social change.[6] Eventually—on September 22, 1864—Fremont formally withdrew from the race and the Republican Party unified around Lincoln.[7]

The leading candidate for the Democratic nomination was Maj. Gen. George B. McClellan of New Jersey. McClellan had been a popular officer in the Army of the Potomac in the early months of the war, but disputes over military strategy as well as his inaction as commander of the army had caused President Lincoln to remove "Little Mac" from command in 1862. Most moderate Democrats supported McClellan's candidacy, while Peace Democrats longed for an antiwar nominee.

The Democratic National Convention was scheduled to meet at Chicago on July 4, but several Peace men convinced party leaders to postpone the convention until late August. With Grant stalled outside of Richmond and Sherman unable to capture Atlanta, opponents of McClellan's nomination believed a delay would help a Peace man win the top spot on the ticket. Most McClellan men, by contrast, believed that the convention should be held at once. Indecision and reliance on future military failures, in their view, could make the party appear disloyal and would not give party leaders enough time to organize and rouse the voters.[8] Nevertheless, when the convention finally did convene on August 29, McClellan won the nomination easily. Though disappointed, most members of the Peace wing accepted the choice as a "necessity," but they fought tooth and nail to select his running mate and to control the tenor of the platform.[9]

Some Democrats had hoped their party would offer a platform with virtually no substance on the issues as a way to unify all wings of the party.[10] But "the Vallandigham spirit" was "rampant" at the convention, and moderates sensed that Vallandigham's influence "will give trouble." Indeed, Vallandigham's influence made an indelible mark upon the platform. The first resolution pledged the fidelity of the party to the Constitution and Union. The second—one of the most notorious planks in all of U.S. history—declared "that after four years of failure to restore the Union by the experiment of war, during which . . . the Constitution itself has been disregarded in every part," a cessation of hostilities and other means must be used to bring about a reunion of the states. The third plank denounced military interference in elections. The fourth and fifth planks again castigated the Lincoln administration for violating the constitutional rights of the people and the states. And, finally, the sixth plank pledged the sympathy, care, and protection of the Democratic Party to the soldiers and sailors of the Union.[11]

Moderate Democrats were sorely disappointed with the platform. Congressman Samuel S. Cox of Ohio "clasped his hands in his lap and dropped his head, a picture of despair" while August Belmont, the party's national chairman, "also looked profoundly sad." An Iowa Republican in Chicago was appalled by what he witnessed. "The speeches were bold & seditious," he declared. "The Platform hostile to war, & therefore hostile to the Union."[12]

The Peace Democrats scored another huge victory in the selection of the vice-presidential nominee, Congressman George H. Pendleton of Ohio. Pendleton had been a favorite for the position for some time, and some believed that, as a westerner, he would balance the ticket and placate the desires of many midwestern Copperheads. Still, moderate Democrats feared that having Pendleton's name on the ticket would hurt the party on election day. He "will be a heavy load," wrote one Cincinnati Democrat, "but McC can carry it out here."[13]

The platform and vice-presidential nominee proved dissatisfying to Democrats throughout the North. "The nomination of M'Clellan was the inspiration of popular feeling," wrote former president James Buchanan. But "the platform is rather muddy. Peace would be a great blessing; but it would cost too dear at the expense of the Union." Another Democrat noted that the platform was a "wet blanket" that dissatisfied "a large number of *our friends,* and disappoint[ed] thousands of wavering Republicans who were ready and anxious to come over to us." Others believed that the Peace platform had galvanized Republicans against the traitors in the rear. "The Republicans gather heart, resume the aggressive, & are confident enough to bet on the result," wrote one dismayed Democrat. Indeed, many Republicans had been hoping for such results from the convention. Writing in August, Francis Lieber noted that "Lincoln's ice is melting away. Perhaps a very mean nomination at Chicago will give us a lift." After the convention, Lieber exulted "that the disgraceful, servile, lickspittle platform makes the re-election of Mr L. possible, and his re-election I suppose is now necessary for the National Cause."[14]

Knowing that the platform would be unacceptable to many northerners, moderate Democrats argued that it ought to be construed as a call for negotiations to restore peace on the basis of reunion. They looked to the general to write a letter of acceptance that would so interpret the infamous Peace plank. Others, too, hoped that McClellan would issue an Andrew Jackson–like letter of acceptance—one that pledged that the Union must be preserved. "The People are waiting for his letter they expect & wish something different from the platform," wrote one anxious Democrat. "Thousand[s] want an excuse to vote for him, [but] under the platform they say they cannot."[15]

On September 8, McClellan issued his letter accepting the nomination. In it, he declared that "the Union must be preserved at all hazards" and that, while peace was desirable, it would not be lasting unless the Union was preserved first. Thus, McClellan firmly placed himself on a war footing, privately noting that "the peace men are the only ones who squirm" and that "all the good men are delighted" with the letter. Indeed, McClellan strongly hoped to distance himself from the Peace wing of his party. He "wish[ed] they had kept Vallandigham down south when they had him there!" and asserted that the Peace Democrats— "these fools"—would "ruin the country," but "I won't help them."[16]

Moderate Democrats exulted in the letter. "McClellan's prospects are brightening since his letter of acceptance," wrote one relieved Democrat. "Without that letter, I doubt if he would have carried a state in the Union." Meanwhile, party chairman August Belmont opined: "If we carry the election at all it will be owing entirely to the stand which the General has taken."[17] Leaders like Belmont also believed that McClellan and his letter would help win the votes of Union soldiers. Prior to the nomination, Democratic financier Samuel L. M. Barlow had informed the editor of the *New York World* that "no one but McClellan can control any large portion of the army vote in the field and at home. . . . With any other man, we utterly lose the army vote."[18] Some Democrats rightly feared that their party's position on the soldier suffrage issue would alienate Democratic soldiers and that the army would only vote for the party that had supported their right to vote. In choosing McClellan, northern Democrats found a presidential candidate who had been loved by soldiers from both parties, and they hoped that this affection would be enough to win some of their votes on election day.[19]

Moderate Democrats exacted a pledge from Pendleton to remain silent during the campaign, but this move, in conjunction with McClellan's letter of acceptance, infuriated the Peace wing of the party. Copperhead William B. Reed of Philadelphia expressed his sense of dismay and betrayal. He blasted the moderate wing of the party for turning against the platform. "Depend on it," wrote Reed, "this will be a fatal mistake." Reed insisted that only a Peace message would carry the election, and he castigated the *New York World* for praising Sherman's "supposed victory" in Atlanta. Reed conceded that McClellan would never campaign as a Peace man, but he wished that, "for his own sake that he will utterly abstain from saying one word in favor of ulterior war." Besides, Reed maintained, it was not fair that McClellan should single-handedly try to change the work of the convention and the meaning of the platform: "It will not look like fair play. It is hoisting one flag to get us under your guns—and then running up another." But in election season, "the main point" was expediency—winning the most votes and preventing the most defections. Reed believed this goal would be accomplished by a strong and unified Peace message. Despondently, he concluded, "I am so utterly hopeless of the future except on the basis of two recognized confederacies that my counsel may be of no value."[20]

Ultimately, battlefield victories and losses determined the outcome of the election more than anything else. When Grant was stalled outside of Richmond and Sherman outside of Atlanta during the summer of 1864, Democratic prospects looked promising. It was during this time that Lincoln penned his famous memorandum concerning his probable failure of reelection.[21] Sherman's taking of Atlanta on September 1, Sheridan's string of victories in the Shenandoah Valley, and Farragut's capture of Mobile Bay drastically changed Lincoln's political fortunes.

UNION SOLDIERS AND THE PRESIDENTIAL ELECTION OF 1864

Union soldiers watched intently as both parties jockeyed for their votes, but by 1864 many soldiers had grown weary of their political leaders. Many soldiers expressed disillusionment with the candidates and with politics in general in the months leading up to the election. Many doubted whether they would bother to vote at all. "I hardly think that Abraham Lincoln will be reelected the people are rather getting down on him," wrote one Vermont soldier on August 28. "For my part I dont care who is elected President if this war can be settled soon as possible but I dont see possible chances of settling under Lincoln's administration." An Illinois soldier, who could not vote because his state did not enfranchise soldiers, wrote his mother on election day, "I would not vote for McClellan for I think him a traitor and I'll be dambed if I would vote for Lincoln."[22]

These sentiments seem to have been expressed most often by Democratic soldiers who supported the Republican ticket during the war. "If I vote at all I shall vote most of the Republican ticket," wrote one soldier to his Democratic family on November 8, 1864. It is significant that even by election day he had not decided whether or how he would vote. A surgeon from Pennsylvania informed his mother that "politics are commencing to run quite high, but as for myself, not proposing to vote, I interest myself very little. Moreover, I really don't know whom I would vote for." Similarly, a New York artillerist wrote to his wife on September 29, 1864: "You wanted to no who I was going to vote for. Most any body! I can't vote for old Abe. Tho, I think he will be elected. I can't go Maclelland, no way. The platform is made of copper, and I am no copperhead. So, I wont vote at all." In Atlanta this soldier observed that many southern women supported McClellan for president, "and for that verry reason I think the army should go for old Abe." So he decided to vote for Lincoln. "I can't support any copperhead candidate. I can't fite for the Union and vote against it. A house divided against it self can not stand. I go for the Union strart through. This is no time for party spirit to show it self. I am a Democrat, but I say hoora for old Abe and down with cesion." This soldier concluded that "the quickest way to end the rebellion is to elect Abe."[23]

This soldier touched on a sentiment that got to the motivation of many soldiers on election day. They voted for the candidate they believed would end the war quickly and honorably. "The Soldiers are all tierd of this war," wrote Michigan soldier Mack Ewing to his wife, Nan, in September 1864. "They are all (or the majority of them) are hurrahing for McLellon. they think if he is president that the war will stop." For himself, Ewing had "not made up my mind yet who to hurrah for. but I bet I am for the man that makes peace the Soonest." Surprisingly, Ewing was even willing to support Peace Democrats like Clement Vallandigham if they could make "an honorable peace" that would last. Thus, "if McLellon can compromise on honorable terms and make a lasting peace I say hurrah for McLelond for with old Abe there is compromise only to free the nigers and Nan I tell you that a niger is honestly looked on with more honor and esteemed higher and treated better by our rooling authorities than the Union Soldiers are." Ewing was particularly upset that "this war has become a niger war instead of a union war," but as long as it was a war for emancipation, he concluded: "lett the niger help fight for his freedom and Shear the hard Ships of the Army." Ewing was willing to help free the slaves, but he would not consent to be considered their inferior. And when peace came, he wanted to "lett the niger go to gina."[24]

One would not suspect that this soldier was an antebellum Republican, nor that he voted for Lincoln just two months after writing this letter, but he was and he did. Upon receiving this letter, his wife responded that she did not want him "to turn butter nut." He replied that he "almost begin to think that I cood not be a Republican any longer but I have made up my mind that Old Abe is the man for president any how." McClellan was losing support among the soldiers because of the Democratic platform, he said, and has "lost thousands of friends [in the army] which old Abe will find." Ewing now declared himself "tru blue" and "for old Abe."[25]

Mack Ewing's sentiments do not match the standard narrative of soldiers who voted for Lincoln. He had been a Republican prior to the war and had a Republican wife at home, yet two months before the election he sounded ready even to support a Copperhead like Clement Vallandigham. It took a stinging rebuke from his wife to convince him to vote for Lincoln. Usually historians have seen the opposite effect—that soldiers in the field reminded their friends and relatives at home to vote "loyally." But, in fact, there was no linear progression in soldiers' political sentiments. They wavered and ebbed. Their feelings about the war improved in times of success and dipped when things were going badly. And some, like Mack Ewing, had a loving spouse at home to guide them back into the Republican fold.

Ewing was not the only Republican to waver in his support of Lincoln. Soldiers' feelings about politics often changed with the fortunes of war. One New

York soldier—who had voted for Lincoln in 1860—declared in March 1864 that "the soldiers almost *all* are in favor (as myself) of Lincoln['s] re-election as it will dash the last hope of the rebels to earth." But the summer campaigning in Virginia took a toll on this soldier. By August he was so discouraged that he was "ready to *vote* for *any* man that will put an end (or try to) to this awful butchery." He despondently told his wife that he could not support either presidential candidate: "At this day McClellan is fast gaining ground & supporters in the army & will receive a very large vote if he is held up as a candidate but I shall never vote for him at least I *think not*," he wrote. Yet if Lincoln was reelected, "it will be prolonged struggle & *bloody too.*" He thus concluded that he did "not know who I shall vote for & I do not care whether I vote at all." Fortunately, the war took a turn for the better between August and November. By election day, he had changed his mind again and settled on Lincoln as the best man to bring the war to a close.[26] Like others around him, he had been lifted from the doldrums of summer by the Union military successes of the autumn of 1864.

Soldiers noticed this pattern among their comrades. One Boston man serving in Florida wrote in August 1864, "The democratic feeling is quite strong in the Western Army, and if we gain no great military success before November, I think McClellan will give Lincoln a close run; Abraham's popularity has gone up and down more than once before now, though I cannot see that he is now more unpopular than after the proclamation and Fredericksburg." He concluded, "I have no doubt his stock will rise before he leaves office, but whether in time to carry the election is perhaps doubtful."[27] In a similar vein, a Democratic officer from Pennsylvania recognized that Union victories might turn the election against his candidate. On August 25, 1864, he confidently told his brother that so long as the Democrats did not nominate "an unconditional peace man," "the election will go against the administration" because the "President is not popular. He is despised, I believe, or held in very slight esteem by his own party and nearly everybody else. Nothing can save him, but the idea that his election is necessary to prevent the South from dictating their own terms." A week later, on August 31, this soldier noted his "delight" at the nomination of McClellan, as well as the prospects for McClellan's election: "If some great and decisive result is not attained by our armies in a month he will be elected, which will be a glorious event. If some great and decisive result should be attained we can afford to see him defeated, but I cannot see hope of such a change in military operations and fortunes as to reverse the tide of public sentiment which appears to be setting in very strongly against the Rail Splitter."[28] Within hours, of course, the fall of Atlanta changed everything. An abolitionist serving with the Fifth Iowa Cavalry under Sherman described the army's reaction to the Union advances. "The news of Sheridan's victory is quite cheering," he wrote in his diary. "This, the taking of Atlanta and the successes at Mobile, will have a great influence on the elections. McClellan will get but few votes in the army of the west."[29]

The connection between Union victories and army support for Lincoln impressed one Maryland Republican so much that he reiterated three separate times in his memoirs that it was the fall of Atlanta and Sheridan's triumph in the Shenandoah Valley that turned the soldier vote to Lincoln. Writing after the war, he recalled the period shortly after the Democratic Convention in late August: "I regret to say that Genl. Mac was very popular, notwithstanding his unsuccessful campaign against Richmond, Va. But soon the clouds began to break away. On the third of September it was officially announced to us that Genl. Sherman had captured Atlanta, Ga. This news gave cause to the most hearty cheering possible." Indeed, it was the Union victories in the field that "turned" public opinion among the troops so that "McClellan began to lose support and Lincoln in a corresponding manner to gain favor." And they supported Lincoln because his "policy we knew to be Union, or War."[30]

Like those who voted for Lincoln, soldiers who supported McClellan did so because they believed he would bring a speedy and honorable conclusion to the war and secure the reunion of the states.[31] If McClellan was elected, one Massachusetts soldier told his wife, "I think the war will be over putey quick but if . . . Old Abe gets elected the war will last 4 [more] years."[32] A New York soldier believed "Gen McClellan will end it sooner and without embittering the two parties so much that they could never live happily together again." Similarly, a Pennsylvania soldier told his cousin that the general "is the only one that can settle the war. I hope you will not forget to put in a vote for little Mc and the union."[33] Soldiers like these likely believed that if Lincoln won the election it would galvanize the Confederates and prolong the war.

Soldiers who voted for McClellan saw themselves as Unionists, but they rejected the abolitionism of the Republican Party.[34] One Wisconsin soldier who knew he was voting against his father, brothers, and a majority of the army voted for McClellan because Mac was "best fitted to bring about an honorable Peace, and the Union as it was before the war."[35] A Michigan soldier who told his mother shortly after the Emancipation Proclamation was issued that he was thinking about deserting felt no better about fighting for emancipation by the autumn of 1864. "I am tired of seeing *White* men Slaughtered to Free the Negro," he wrote her. His experiences in the South made him conclude "that the Negro is on the whole better off in the state of servitude than [in the] begarly freedom to which he will inevitably fall if freed.... [I]t appears to be their highest ambition to lie in the Sun and hunt.... [I]t takes the greatest patience to get along with them." A Brooklyn soldier who supported McClellan noted the negative economic consequences of emancipation: "If the negroes are freed what are we to do with them. They will be the means of throwing the whites out of employment." The Irish, he predicted, would incite war in the North if they had to compete with blacks for jobs. Moreover, he believed that African Americans were lazy. "Whenever we want them to work we are compelled to send a guard after them," he wrote to his sister. "Mary Emma I do not like niggers no matter what you may say in their favor." Democratic soldiers' views of race permeated their criticism of their political opponents. One Pennsylvania cavalryman expressed his opposition to emancipation by criticizing those "Dam Degreaded Wreches" up North who called McClellan "a trator to his Country.... [Y]ou can tell all them Dam Sap headed nigrow Hug[g]ers up thear that i am a full Blooded McClelon man And Sow is Every good union soldier that Belongs to the Armey of the Potomac that is fighting for His Distracted Country."[36]

In like manner, not all soldiers who voted for Lincoln supported emancipation. We have already seen Mack Ewing's tepid support for emancipation. Other Lincoln voters felt the same. "I'm no abolitionist and if I had a vote and McClellan stood on a good old democratic platform I would vote for him, but as things are at present, if I had that vote it should be cast for Lincoln," wrote one Pennsylvanian stationed near Petersburg. "McClellan, standing alone or in connection with any good man, would gain the day, but as he stands in connection with the *traitor* Pendleton he must fail." Another Pennsylvanian who considered himself a "full Bloom" Republican admitted that "there are some things I do not like about Lincoln, one of them is why he does not exchange all the White Prisoners and let the Colored ones go if the south will not exchange them. I do not believe in having White Soldiers suffer to save a few Negroes."[37] Similarly, a Minnesota artillerist declared himself for Lincoln but against emancipation. "And whether slavery be right or wrong I dont believe in carrying on a bloody war for years for the sole object of Abolishing slavery. . . . [W]henever [the South] can be made or Per[s]uaded to lay down their Arms & Return to their Allegiance the war should end but not before."[38] Following the election, one soldier, who appears to have supported Lincoln, cursed abolitionists like Wendell Phillips for wanting "to make a nigger better than a white man."[39]

Soldiers could be practical abolitionists and even support Lincoln's reelection without really believing slavery morally wrong.[40] One former Wisconsin soldier believed that Lincoln's reelection would signal "Power at the North" to the rebels, and he longed for the South to be brought back to the Union. Still, he wrote: "I care not for Slavery. Although I do think Slavery was the Cause of all this Bloodshed. Some have told me that I fought for the Nigger. *No Never.* I fought to help put down the Rebellion and if by so doing I did help to Free the Nigger I am not to blame. I believe in Weakening the Rebels in every way we can and if it can be done best by taking there Property I say take it be it Nigger or be it Mules."[41] These were not the views of a man who had come to endorse emancipation as a moral issue, but simply as a practical war measure—one that would help bring success to the army.

Many Democrats who voted for Lincoln in 1864 saw their Republican vote as a one-time act. "No man who has served in this war, and whose love of country is stronger than his partizan prejudices can support the Chicago platform, or train under the Captains who made it," wrote Lt. Col. Theodore S. Bowers of Gen. Ulysses S. Grant's staff. "Whilst Gen. Rawlins and many other prominent Democrats of my acquaintance do not endorse all the policies of the present administration, yet they all give it their support as the best thing that can be done under the circumstances. As matters now stand, the Administration represents the friends of the country, and the Chicago party its enemies. Hence no man who wants to do right can hesitate which he will support." The army, Bowers continued, "spits upon [McClellan's] platform, and dispises the trickery and fraud of his letter of acceptance. It is a deliberate attempt to ride his horse to catch honest war Democrats on his letter and peace men on his platform. . . . I have a warm affection for the old Democratic party, but you, nor I, nor our patriotic friends can act with it until it is purified of the disloyal element that now controls it."[42] These are not the words of someone who was converted into one of the "life-long Republicans" of Jennifer Weber's account. Democrats like this one did not agree with all of Lincoln's policies, but they voted for him because they believed his election was the only way to save the Union.

Some soldiers saw themselves as choosing between the lesser of two evils. After mailing home his ballot for Lincoln, one New York soldier remarked that he had no respect for either presidential candidate. Old Abe needed "a new set of brains" while McClellan had too many private interests to be trusted. The only reason he voted for Lincoln was because the war had to be fought and won, and he believed Lincoln would do that. Charles Francis Adams received a telling letter from his son who was serving in the Fifth Massachusetts Cavalry: "Soldiers don't vote for individuals; they don't vote for the war; they have but one desire and that is to vote against those who delay the progress of the war at home; they want to vote down the copperheads." According to Adams Jr., soldiers decided how to vote based not on what they were *for*, but what they were *against*. "Look at the soldiers vote and that will show you what we think of your peace men," one Maine soldier told his wife, again implying that many voted against rather than for something. After commenting that he disliked both gubernatorial candidates in New York, but that he disliked the Republican "still more," Marsena Rudolph Patrick, the provost marshal general of the Army of the Potomac, commented: "It is a choice of evils—I vote for McClellan because I cannot vote for Lincoln."[43] Similarly, a War Democrat from New York decided to split his ticket, which was a rare occurrence in nineteenth-century elections. He feared Peace Democrats, especially those that tried to portray themselves as supportive of the war. "I voted the Republican State ticket and if Gen McClellan had not been on the other should have voted for Lincoln as the less of *two evils*."[44]

This last soldier's fear of Peace Democrats captured the essence of the view of most Democrats in the army who could not bring themselves to vote for McClellan. "I am afraid of Pendleton," he wrote. "I could respect him I think if he came out plain and plump a peace on any terms man but he is two faced[.] I think as much of McClellan as anyone can & would trust him with everything but many a night I have laid awake thinking if he should die, what would happen[;] still I voted for him."[45]

But the thought of a Peace Democrat on the ticket was more than most soldiers could bear. Prior to the Chicago Convention, one Ohio colonel warned Congressman Samuel S. Cox not to allow the Peace wing of the party to dominate the convention. "I believe War is at present necessary to preserve the Union," he wrote, "not war against the Institutions, or for the *subjugation or extermination* of the people of the South, but war for the overthrow of the Rebel government." This colonel would not vote for a ticket that was compromised by antiwar sentiment. "In the true American sense I am a *Democrat*," he proclaimed. But if his party leaders did not act the part of a loyal opposition, "I may not *vote* with the Democratic party."[46]

Many other Democratic soldiers felt alike. "The peace plank in the platform renders it untenable," observed one Republican soldier. "Army officers heretofore strong for McClellan say they cannot vote for an 'immediate cessation of hostilities.'" Similarly, a Rhode Island soldier noted in September that "six months ago a grait many of the soldiers would have voted for [McClellan] but he wont get as many now old abe is the man to finish this thing up." A New Yorker who voted for the general noted that "McClellan would have got A greate many more votes in the army if he had not been in with pendleton[.] the soldiers dont like pendleton." A soldier in the Regular Army summed up what must have been the sentiments of many Democratic soldiers in a letter to his sweetheart: "you think perhaps I am a McClellan man yes I would rather fol[l]ow him than any man on earth for I know him to pos[s]ess the true principle of the Soldier and a man, but I could not vote for him[.] [I]t is the wrong party that comes in to power with him if he is elected."[47]

Some soldiers were willing to overlook the Peace plank in the platform if the Democratic Party would offer relief for the suffering and inconveniences they faced at the front. These soldiers were weary of the war and the Lincoln administration's handling of it. "I wish the Chicago convention or some other would have the effect of reducing the prices of Sutler's goods," wrote one New York soldier. He also remarked that his pay was seven months late and that a "new administration might do better by us." Another soldier noted that the troops "do not like [Lincoln] at all. He gives us very little to eat three hard tack and a pint of Coffee for breakfast, Three Hard Tack and a piece of Salt Horse for dinner, Hard tack and Coffee for supper. It is very hard for any kind of men to live on that." Others believed that McClellan would not provide the soldiers with "shoddy" equipment. Some Republicans feared the effects of these issues on the army vote. The soldiers "are much dissatisfied because they have received no pay, [and] they fear that they will not be paid at the end of their term of service," wrote one worried Republican to an Illinois congressman. "Unless something is done soon to counteract this evil, I fear that our candidate for President will lose many votes."[48]

Many Democrats in the field also complained that Republicans at home did not understand what they were calling for when they urged the Lincoln administration forward until a peace was won. "'A vigorous prosecution of the war' sounds well to talk, it reads well in newspapers, and makes a good platform for political campaigns. But my God! do people know what it means? I do. It means every week or two to take out a few thousand men and butt them against the mud walls that surround Richmond, then march back to camp with from five to fifteen hundred [fewer] men than we went out with! . . . I am not in favor of withdrawing our armies and giving up everything, but think every honorable means that can be used to put an end to the war should be, and soon, too."[49]

Because of the suffering they had endured, Democratic soldiers and conservative Lincoln men resented those at home who denounced anti-abolition soldiers as disloyal. A Kentucky soldier told his sister in August 1864: "All men opposed to Father Abraham's way of doing buisiness [*sic*] are not in favor of Jeff Davis' way—nor Vallandigham's. And all men that dislike the *service*, are not *cowards*, no, not even all that get out by dishonorable trickery." In July, this soldier had said he would not vote for Lincoln "or anybody else." By October, he appeared to come out in favor of the incumbent, but he still would not allow his sister to call McClellan a traitor. "Loyal men are in favor of McClellan and Slavery—who are willing to prove their loyalty by facing the enemy upon the Battle field." It was a truer loyalty to enlist in the cause of the Union and oppose emancipation than to stay at home campaigning for Lincoln and abolition, he cautioned. "So I will request you not to make any more charges like those contained in your last to the Genl. of 'Ignorance, Treason, & Cowardice.'"[50]

Most Democrats in the army probably opposed both the Peace men of their party and the abolitionists of the other. The colonel of the Third New York Cavalry expressed the hope that "the Woods & Vallandighams" would be "entirely ignored" at the Chicago Convention. If these Peace men were ostracized "and Little Mac is nominated I think without doubt these rottens will be ousted," he wrote, referring to the Lincoln administration. "God grant that such will be the case[.] they have been permitted to fritter away the Blood & Treasure of the Nation too long already[.] it would be a sorry day that reelected the present dynasty."[51] An Indiana Democrat said he could endorse neither Vallandigham nor Lincoln: "I am a Douglas Democrat," he wrote in mid-1864 (three years after Douglas's death), "& will never vote for the mongrel, kinky headed abolitionists. I detest them." Another Democratic soldier, who believed party politics had a corrosive effect on the war effort, wrote: "I think the Peace Democracy are a despicable set, equally as bad as the worst abolitionist."[52]

VOTER TURNOUT IN THE ELECTIONS OF 1864

Because so many soldiers expressed feelings of disdain toward politics and the presidential election, or uncertainty over whom to trust and vote for, voter turnout in the elections of 1864 ought to be examined. The sample of regiments in table 1 represents all of the military units for which both election returns and complete morning reports for election day could be located. The sample reveals an estimated voter turnout of about 80 percent among the troops (although the actual voter turnout was likely lower, as explained below). This level of voter participation was typical for mid-nineteenth-century elections, but it is nevertheless telling that about 20 percent of the soldiers eligible to vote chose not to vote on election day. After all, voters at home might have to travel some distance to cast their ballots, but voters in the field had only to walk down their company street.[53] When the voter turnout from this sample is factored into the percentage of votes cast for President Lincoln, somewhere between 50 and 60 percent of the eligible soldier voters voted for Lincoln, substantially lower than the 78 percent figure generally stated.

The most obvious explanation for soldiers not voting would be troop movements and skirmishes. One election commissioner from Pennsylvania collected all of his returns except those of one battery "who moved last night or this morning." Some army officers were aware that this might be a problem, however, and planned accordingly. In order to see to a free and expedient election, the officers of the Fifth Corps, for example, prohibited drills on election day and requested all commanders "to take measures to enable their men to vote early and as promptly as possible." Evidence suggests that troop movements had a minimal effect on the soldier vote.[54]

Another reason that some soldiers did not vote might be that soldiers had not made themselves eligible to vote according to provisions in the laws that enfranchised them. The Pennsylvania statute, for example, required a ten-cent tax to be assessed in order for soldiers to be eligible to vote. It appears that many soldiers did not pay this tax in time for the state election in October. "The election passed off quietly, a very small vote being polled in consequence of not having tax receipts," wrote one Pennsylvania election commissioner to a Republican newspaper. This was "a matter that should not be again omitted by the friends of the soldier. With proper exertion a vote twice as large may be obtained [in November]." Similarly, a Pennsylvania soldier wrote home two weeks before the

October election: "For me to vote here 'twill be necessary for a receipt from the collector to be sent to me. It will be too late, I suppose, for the first election unless already done. But I should like to have things done for the Presidential." Fortunately, this soldier learned a few days later that his "officers had made arrangements for having those entitled to vote, assessed, etc., according to some order issued by the War Department."[55]

Testimony about the army's general attitude toward politics reveals that many soldiers may have been less concerned about voting than has generally been presumed. "I note all you say of politics, but in the army we take but little interest except earnestly to wish the election was over," wrote Gen. George Gordon Meade to his wife. "Until it is, nothing else will be thought of and no proper thought given to the war." Similarly, a Democrat from New York remarked that "politics don't trouble us much." And a soldier who came from a Democratic family but supported the Republican ticket while in the army wrote home to his father that soldiers "have little opportunity of studying politics, and also have so much else to think of as to have little inclination for it."[56] Thus, while many political issues were substantively relevant to the troops, the soldiers were often too busy to think about the issues, or simply did not have the information on hand with which to take educated positions.[57] As if to underscore the disinterestedness of some soldiers, one Pennsylvania cavalryman recorded in his diary on election day: "Laying in camp today nothing of importance."[58]

Election commissioners visiting the troops also got the impression that politics was not as important to many of the boys in blue as has generally been assumed. One commissioner was perceived as "rather disgusted with the result of his mission" because "very few of the soldiers had qualified themselves to vote and altogether appeared quite indifferent. He seemed to think the soldiers' vote would be very insignificant." Pennsylvania commissioner David McKelvy recorded a similar observation in the journal he kept while canvassing the troops: "The other officers were perfectly indifferent as to the election, and it was with some difficulty that they were urged in opening the polls yesterday and with more difficulty that they were to-day urged into the task of finishing out the forms. . . . They considered it just so much work put on them for nothing." After the state election in October, McKelvy determined that "getting the vote was a thankless job" and that he did not wish to serve again as an election commissioner for the presidential election.[59]

Documentary evidence from the field also suggests that some soldiers—

particularly Democrats—had a real indifference or aversion to participating in elections. The Eighteenth Indiana Light Artillery held a mock election to gauge the sense of the regiment on the upcoming election. According to one participant, there were only five votes in the Eighth Battery, four for Lincoln and one for McClellan. Of more interest are the ones who did not vote: "There were seven or eight of the eighth Battery who are regular butternuts in principle and refused to vote."[60] A New York soldier noted that "several refused to vote" in his regiment.[61] Another New Yorker said that few in his company supported McClellan: "only 3 out of about 50 so far and they are not decided and I think will not vote at all." A Massachusetts Democrat noted that his battery went for Lincoln, "but a great many of the McClellan men did not vote. They are of the weak kneed kind."[62] A soldier in the Ninety-Ninth Ohio Infantry wrote home that "the butternuts are ashamed to vote in the army."[63] A Kentuckian noted: "There were 448 men in the Regiment, some being too young, & others refusing to vote. The most of those who refused to vote were McClellan men."[64] Indeed, as one Illinois soldier found in his regiment: "There is several of the Democrats in our company that say they will not support Mac if he runs on the platform that they nominated him and some say they wont if old Pemberton [Pendleton] sticks to him."[65] This sentiment was widely held. As one New York soldier wrote, "Indeed, Pendleton being on the same ticket with McClellan almost deterred me from voting at all, and I know has taken hundreds of votes from him in the army."[66]

Corp. George M. Buck of the Twentieth Michigan Volunteers reported to General McClellan that intimidation and coercion led to a low voter turnout among the Democrats in his regiment: "It may surprise you that this army that owes so much to your creative genius and superior generalship should vote as it did," he wrote to the general shortly after the election, "but you little know how many and great were the difficulties that beset every soldier who dared speak one word in your favor." The power of the military was used "without stint." Noncommissioned officers and privates were "offered promotion if they would vote for Lincoln," Buck wrote, while Democrats were reduced "to the ranks or a 'place in the front during every engagement' if they chose to vote for you." He continued: "Everything that unscrupulous brutal power could do was done to induce or compel the soldiers to vote for Lincoln or at least to withhold their votes from you." Getting to the point, he knew of "hundreds" of soldiers "who voted for Lincoln under protest and hundreds more of your most ardent admirers who did not vote at all." As evidence, Buck pointed out that his regiment cast only 188 votes in the election even though more than 300 men in the regiment were qualified to vote. "Every one not voting would, if allowed the expression of his free will, have voted for you."[67]

Some Democrats passively supported Lincoln's reelection because they believed it was the best thing for the country, even if they could not bring themselves to vote for the president. One Democratic sailor from Connecticut—who almost certainly did not vote in the election—was disgusted by the positions that his party was taking during the campaign. He thus articulated a belief that Lincoln should be reelected, but he expressed this sentiment in practical, not ideological terms. "Think it bad Buisness to swap Horses while crossing the stream," he wrote in his diary. "The Republicans have had their whack at the Trough, and now to have to fat up the Democrats, the War would be good for another Year or two." But if Lincoln stayed at the helm, "six months had ought to finish it up." When word reached him that Lincoln had been reelected, he wrote tellingly, "I am glad of it, but I am not celebrating any."[68] A Maryland volunteer similarly noted after the election, "My Democratic chum said that he did not vote at all, and that he is very glad that President Lincoln was reelected."[69]

The range of sentiments exhibited by Union soldiers is both extensive and remarkable. Even many soldiers who voted for Lincoln expressed serious doubts as to his qualifications. Perhaps even more striking is that some 20 percent of the men endangering their lives for the Union were not motivated enough to get out of their tents to cast a vote for president in an election that ensured the downfall of both slavery and the Confederacy.

It seems that the current historiography overstates the level of attachment between Union soldiers and the Republican Party.[70] Many of the soldiers who voted for Lincoln did so out of disgust for the party that had deemed their work in the field a "failure" rather than out of support and admiration for Republican war aims. One way to measure the partisan attachment of Union soldiers to the Republican and Democratic Parties is by considering how soldiers acted in other elections close to, but not on the same day as, the presidential election.

Tables 2 and 3 compare the results of several state and congressional elections with the votes of those states in the presidential election. These state and congressional elections were held in the weeks just prior to the presidential election. As can be seen, there were drastic increases in the voter turnout among the soldiers in the November presidential election when compared with the September and October elections (with the exception of the Republican soldier vote in Maryland, which was an election in which voters had two days to cast their ballots). On average, the home votes of both parties increased by less than 9 percent from the state to the presidential election, whereas the Republican army vote increased almost 40 percent, and the Democratic army vote increased by nearly 100 percent. Tables 4 and 5 reveal that soldiers who voted for president and Congress on the same day also had a marked increase in turnout when voting for president (meaning that they "scratched" the names of congressional candidates from their tickets).

One explanation for the greater increase in turnout among the troops is that the voters at home were more tied to their political parties than were the soldiers in the field. The troops were more concerned with electing a commander in chief who would lead them to victory than they were with the two parties' positions on most of the political issues of the day. Electing the right president was the most important choice they would have to make—and for most soldiers, was the only one worth voting for. Despite General McClellan's letter of acceptance in which he pledged to prosecute the war until victory was won, many soldiers had reason to believe that if McClellan was elected, then all of their efforts in the field would come to naught. This belief was enough to convince more Republican soldiers to vote in November than in September and October, to get some Democrats to vote for Abraham Lincoln, and to keep other Democrats from voting at all. It also helps explain why so few Democratic soldiers voted in the state and congressional elections. Most Democratic soldiers, by 1864, had come to doubt their party's loyalty. They could not vote for Democratic congressmen and state leaders. But many could still vote for McClellan because they believed he would fight to restore the Union (as it was). As one soldier explained, "I don't suppose for a moment that *any soldier* would go home and vote a *Copperhead ticket*, and on the other hand *I* wouldn't vote a *republican* ticket just merely because it *was* republican but I should most assuredly vote for the Union, and those that would maintain it, let the *principle* appear under any name whatsoever."[71]

Scholars who have used the soldier vote to support various conclusions about the army have almost invariably ignored the soldiers' votes in the nonpresidential elections of 1864. By 1864, it seems that Republicans had maintained the support of their partisan friends in blue (the Republican Party did win a large majority of the soldier vote in September and October, too), whereas Democratic soldiers had lost confidence in both parties altogether. One New York soldier who cast his ballot for McClellan came to the sad conclusion that both parties were "equally corrupt, and equally far from my views in their extreme doctrines."[72] This soldier, like many of his comrades, believed he had to choose between the lesser of two evils. Some Democratic soldiers turned to Lincoln to finish out the war; some, like this one, voted for their party's candidate; and some opted to abstain from the franchise.

INTIMIDATION AT THE POLLS

Lincoln professed to want free elections in the field. "I want to get all the votes I can of course," Lincoln told Pennsylvania's election commissioners in October 1864, "but play fair gentlemen, play fair. Leave the soldiers entirely free to vote as they think best."[73] Nevertheless, Democrats—both at home and at the front—complained that it was difficult to vote the Democratic ticket in the field. Indeed, Richard Franklin Bensel writes that military camps during the Civil War "ranked among the less democratic polling places in American history."[74] As noted in chapter 2, at least one Democratic soldier was court-martialed earlier in 1864 for distributing Democratic campaign literature in camp.[75] Another soldier complained that his regiment received only Republican newspapers and that "some other regiments had no opportunity to vote any but the Republican ticket."[76] When Pvt. Rufus P. Miller of the Seventy-Fifth Ohio Volunteers found that there were no Democratic ballots in his camp, he angrily exclaimed, "I'd rather vote for Jeff. Davis than Abe. Lincoln. By God, them's my sentiments." He was court-martialed for the offense.[77] A New York soldier groused that "such mean, contemptible favoritism or partisanship" was "shown for Lincoln, by many officers in the army, representatives of the Sanitary and Christian Commissions, etc." that "hundreds of soldiers have been literally proscribed from voting for McClellan by their officers, and they have been obliged to get McClellan ballots from other sources."[78]

Officers could hold significant sway over their men during election season. A witness in a contested congressional election testified that one Democratic soldier "had several fall-outs with some of the boys in the army and with an officer about politics" and that "they insisted on him voting the republican ticket."[79] More striking is what took place in the Thirty-Fourth Kentucky Infantry, a regiment that had a strong Democratic majority among the enlisted men. The regiment's colonel, William Y. Dillard, was a Republican who could not attain a promotion to brigadier general because state leaders opposed him politically. A fellow officer and friend of Dillard's reported to vice-presidential candidate Andrew Johnson that the colonel was "using his influence to have them [his regiment] sent to the *front*—that they may learn what the Chicago party! means."[80] Indeed, Democratic soldiers feared that Republican officers would use their influence to suppress Democratic voters. An Ohio soldier believed "the majority of the Regt. will go for McClelland if they have a fair vote." But many, of course, doubted there would be fairness.[81]

Some Union officers appear to have played tricks on Democratic soldiers to keep them from voting. One Confederate prisoner of war overheard two New York enlisted men discussing their inability to vote even though they were legally old enough: "One said he wished he was at home to vote for McClellan; the other said he tried to vote for McClellan but they found out how he intended to vote and because he was under twenty-one when he enlisted, told him they reckoned he didn't have a vote."[82] Other soldiers believed they were court-martialed for partisan reasons even when there was nothing overtly political about the charges brought against them. One deserter who was confined to the guardhouse believed that the announcement of his verdict was being postponed until after the presidential election so that "Little Mack would loose a vote."[83]

Unlike the experiences of these Democratic soldiers, it was quite easy to cast a Republican ballot in the field. Prior to the presidential election, a group of Confederates captured four Union soldiers. The rebels took their prisoners' uniforms, as well as their Republican ballots, and confidently marched to the polls. Dressed in Union blue, they cast the ballots without being administered any loyalty oath or having their qualifications questioned—"for of course no one could object to us after voting for Lincoln."[84] Minors were also known to vote in the field in 1864 (which means that the actual voter turnout is probably lower than the estimate in table 1).[85]

Some Democratic soldiers were court-martialed for uttering political sentiments around the time of the election. Pvt. Richard B. Lynch of the Twelfth Pennsylvania Cavalry was arrested at a Baltimore tavern for drinking to the health of Stonewall Jackson and for "publicly aver[ring] that he was not in the Army as a soldier but as a Politician for McClellan." He was acquitted of the first charge (toasting the deceased rebel general) but convicted of the second (except for the words "for McClellan") and was sentenced to lose ten dollars pay for two months. Pvt. James S. Deck of the U.S. Signal Corps was arrested and court-martialed for saying he would desert and leave the country if Lincoln was reelected.[86] Lt. Edward B. Austin of the Fiftieth New York Engineers was court-martialed and dismissed from the service in September 1864 for saying that he would "stamp" Lincoln "finer than hell" and that, "If by giving my vote for Abe Lincoln I could save the Government I'll be God damned if I would give it."[87] Missouri artillerist Henry Ballma was court-martialed for saying, "Abraham Lincoln is a Damn'd son of a bitch, and those that voted for him were sons of bitches," on the day after the election. After his conviction, Ballma petitioned the court for clemency, claiming that he "never held any malice against, the President" and that "members of my company, knowing that I was a Democrat, tried to get me to express myself, by running Gen. McClellan down, but they done so when I was under the influence of liquor." The fact that he had been provoked did not sway the court. Ballma served one month in prison at hard labor and paid a twenty-dollar fine.[88] Political provocation, like that aimed at Ballma, sometimes led to violent interactions in the field. After a series of arguments about politics, one Missouri Republican threatened to "shoot the shit" out of his "Secessionist and Copperhead" lieutenant.[89]

On at least a few occasions, Democratic politicians and electioneers were threatened and driven from military camps. Ohio congressman Samuel "Sunset" Cox complained that "the camps [were] closed to us" and "the Barracks [were] used to keep us out & Republicans in." "The soldiers were hungry for our tickets," he exclaimed, "& the cry was for more, when the officers ordered us out! This in Columbus—a *free* state! Do you wonder how I am beaten. We left tickets there, when ordered out, but they were at once destroyed."[90]

Partisan soldiers took pride in this sort of behavior. One soldier told his aunt that "I am going to do all I can for Abe." He described two Democrats who came into his camp "peddling McClellan tickets" but explained that they probably would not be back. "We all took tickets and when they had given the boys all [of the] tickets they were talking to us telling us what a good man McClellan is. We let them talk as long as we could stand it and then we burnt the tickets and told them iff they did not get out of ther[e] in less than 5 minutes we would ride them out on a rail."[91] Years after the election a Pennsylvania officer recalled the treatment that his regiment gave to Democratic election commissioners: "Many of their ballots and other papers mysteriously disappeared, as well as they themselves, temporarily."[92]

Democratic soldiers claimed to be discriminated against because of their political convictions. Democrats in Philadelphia learned from their election commissioners that "Democrats were threatened to be sent to the front if they voted." Testimony from soldiers corroborates this account. One soldier noted that his regiment was canvassed "to see how many would vote for Lincoln if they got a chance to go home."[93] In such cases, soldiers were forced to decide if they would lie to receive a furlough or stick by their principles and their guns in the field. One New Hampshire Democrat informed his brother that "soldiers shall come home to vote & I shall be black as the D— to accomplish my ends."[94] Of course, soldiers who lied to get furloughs would either have to vote for Lincoln or be found out at the polls since Civil War–era ballots were printed by the parties on distinctively colored paper. On election-day eve, one New Jersey soldier angrily informed a friend how furloughs for voting had been determined: "The men who would vote the McClellan ticket were kept here and only Old A.'s men was sent to their states to vote. All of the McClellan men were kept here. I suppose I might have gotten home if I would have said I should vote for A. But never. I would sooner stay here for another year than to come home and vote for him."[95] Soldiers like this one refused to trade their vote for a furlough if doing so meant voting for Lincoln.

Republican leaders in the state and national capitals did not hide the partisanship behind their furlough decisions. "It is of the utmost importance, that our troops in the field who are entitled to vote . . . should have a short furlough to allow them to return home to vote," wrote the governor of Delaware to Secretary of War Edwin M. Stanton (Delaware had not permitted its soldiers to vote in the field). "Without the vote of our troops in the field it will be utterly impossible to carry our State, and the election of U.S. Senator, Representative to Congress[,] and Emancipation in Delaware, depend upon the result."[96] Doctors in the Union armies also were known to recommend extending furloughs for sick or wounded soldiers so that they could stay home to vote in the presidential election. "His vote will be of as much or more value in the Presidential Election, in this State," wrote one physician of an Indiana soldier, "than the service he might otherwise render the government, I think."[97]

Assistant Secretary of War Charles A. Dana remembered years later that the War Department was "busy in . . . arranging for soldiers to go home to vote, and also for the taking of ballots in the army." The War Department's interest in the election was "almost painful," according to Dana. "All the power and influence of the War Department, then something enormous from the vast expenditure and extensive relations of the war, was employed to secure the re-election of Mr. Lincoln."[98]

As the presidential election was approaching, the Union high command clamped down on anti-Lincoln and anti-emancipation soldiers, just as it had done in early 1863. Writing from New York, Sen. Edwin D. Morgan alerted Secretary of War Edwin M. Stanton to a scheme in which the McClellan campaign was seeking to get "the principal officers in the Army committed to McClellan with [the] expectation of getting the soldiers votes." Generals Hooker, Rosecrans, Heintzelman, and Scott were among those the McClellan campaign hoped to woo. "You will perhaps know all about the political preferences of the Generals whose names I have given," wrote Morgan, "and will know how to apply the remedy better than I do."[99]

The remedy included dismissing Democratic officers from the service. In June 1864, Stanton dismissed three officers from West Point, including superintendent Alexander H. Bowman, for committing "the heinous crime," as George B. McClellan put it, "of inviting so great a reprobate as myself to the Point" to give an address.[100] An officer stationed in Harrisburg, Pennsylvania, faced a "temporary abdication" for getting drunk and using "pretty rough language about the President" in July.[101] That same month the provost marshal of western Pennsylvania was removed from his position after he angered the local Republican press by seeking to limit their government contracts.[102] Lt. Cincinnatus Condict of the Twelfth Kentucky Cavalry was dismissed in August for tendering his resignation in "hostility to the Government which he had sworn to support."[103] In September, Lt. Abraham C. Merritt of the signal corps was dismissed for being a "worthless officer, and of doubtful loyalty." In September and October, Capt. Joseph R. Folwell of the 102nd Ohio Volunteers and Lt. Col. Edward Thorn of the Forty-Fifth U.S.C.T. were dismissed for violating the Fifth Article of War. Several white officers in black regiments were also dismissed for criticizing the conduct of black troops. Shortly after the presidential election, Lt. John E. Gharrett of the First U.S. Colored Heavy Artillery and Lt. Peter Gordon of the Sixteenth U.S.C.T. were both dismissed for attempting to resign because they lacked confidence in the black soldiers they were supposed to be leading.[104]

At least one dismissal targeted a large number of Democrats at once. When Senator Morgan informed Stanton that there were a number of quartermaster clerks who endorsed McClellan's election, Stanton dismissed twenty of them. When one of the clerks protested to the secretary of war, an unsympathetic Stanton replied, "When a young man receives his pay from an administration and spends his evenings denouncing it in offensive terms, he cannot be surprised if the administration prefers a friend on the job."[105]

One officer—who had recently been promoted to colonel—complained that his presence in Chicago during the Democratic Convention led to a reduction of rank. "Spies were in the Convention to report all officers in attendance upon it, or in the city at the time," he wrote. "I fell under their notice, and received an order revoking my commission as Col., reducing me to a Captaincy, and ordering me to report to Memphis for duty." Since his "offence" was "of purely a political character," he determined that he had no choice but to resign his commission. He knew five other officers at his post who had been "relieved . . . the same day that I was," and complained that there were "daily" orders "discharging all employees that will not vote for Lincoln."[106]

After resigning, this officer returned home to Indiana to campaign for McClellan. "My home has no horrors for me, and I shall gladly terminate a service that requires the uniform of the Army to be prostituted to the badge of political servitude," he wrote. "I cannot, will not, wear it longer with that as the bribe. Some of those lacking back-bone and nerve will probably succumb—but all *true men* will stand by their principles."[107]

In some cases, Stanton targeted Democrats but tried to conceal the partisanship behind his orders. In September 1864, an army surgeon informed McClellan that a Major Johnson (probably from Ohio) had been "summarily dismissed without a hearing" as part of Stanton's effort of "removing Officers who are suspected of opposition." McClellan's correspondent feared that Stanton was taking such actions before the election in order "to officer the Army as to bring the control of the officers over the men into action to influence their votes."[108] In like manner, Provost Marshal General of the Army of the Potomac Marsena Rudolph Patrick wrote caustically in his diary, "Capt. [Alfred] Ransom has been 'dismissed the Service for conduct unbecoming an Officer and Gentleman'— probably for throwing a Pitcher at the head of a person who told him, that any man who would vote for McClellan was a Traitor."[109]

Democrats in the army recognized what was happening. One complained that officers "known to be a friend of the Genl's" were "under espionage." Another claimed to be "surrounded with spies and informers," by which he meant Republicans.[110] Following Stanton's dismissal of the leadership at West Point, a Vermont soldier wrote that he was "puzzle[d]" by Stanton's "bitter" and "rab-bid" behavior and thought Lincoln "ought not to alow it."[111] Others feared that things would only get worse once Lincoln had secured his reelection. Provost Marshal General Patrick informed artillerist Charles Wainwright "that there was positively a long list of officers in the War Department whom Stanton had determined to decapitate so soon as he was sure of his re-election (Lincoln's election being really Stanton's); fifty of the number are in the Army of the Potomac."[112]

Such protests were not confined to Democratic officers. One officer who cast his lot with Lincoln noted the injustices that Democratic soldiers endured during the campaign. "It is indeed not difficult to get material for a grumble," he wrote in October 1864, "if one will but look about in this world."

> You see I can't be enthusiastic about such a government as Lincoln's, when I see, under my nose, the petty tyranny and persecution they practise against subordinate officers. Now there is Colonel Collis, a petty, scheming political officer; he sends letters to newspapers and despatches to Mr. Stanton about the enthusiasm for Lincoln in the army, etc., etc. Nothing is said to him; *that* is all right; he has an opinion, as he ought to have. *But* there is a Lieutenant-Colonel McMahon, lately Adjutant-General of the 6th Corps, an excellent soldier, whose brother fell at the head of a charge at Cool Arbor, and who himself had been in all the battles: *he* is a McClellan man, as was natural of one of General Sedgewick's Staff. He talks very openly and strongly about his side, as he has a right to do. What is the consequence? He is, without any warning, mustered out of the service! That is to say, a soldier who don't agree with the Administration must be got rid of; it is nothing in his favor that he has exposed his life in twenty different actions. You would scarcely credit the number of such cases as this, cases of petty spite, fitting rather to a bad-tempered child than to a great and dignified cabinet member. They suffer chances of victory to pass, rather than take voters from states.[113]

Such an obvious and ubiquitous double standard in which Republican soldiers could speak freely and Democratic ones were summarily punished caused this Lincoln man to lose some faith in his leaders in Washington. It also, most certainly, kept some Democratic soldiers from voting for McClellan. Democratic officers tended to keep quiet during the election, fearing that they might receive Stanton's remedy. In a "confidential" letter in August 1864, Col. Durbin Ward of the Seventeenth Ohio Infantry informed his correspondent that he was "driven to be cautious" because "publicly" speaking his political opinions "might cost me my commission."[114]

Democratic soldiers faced other types of intimidation and unequal treatment during election season as well.[115] Soldiers convalescing at the Satterlee Hospital in Philadelphia were not allowed to attend a Democratic meeting in October 1864.[116] Soldiers who attended a McClellan meeting near West Point were "confined in the guard house on their return, & as a punishment for holding the opinions of white men are now digging a drain for the Supt's water closet." Soldiers who attended Lincoln meetings, however, received no such punishment.[117] Evidence suggests that there was a great amount of pressure, and even coercion, for soldiers to toe the Republican Party line. As one Democratic artillerist noted just before the election, "if I was a civillian I would say what I thought about it but at present I think it better to keep silent."[118]

Some of the harshest and most partisan restrictions on voting were in Union controlled Tennessee. There, military governor and Republican vice-presidential candidate Andrew Johnson required a test-oath of voters that essentially branded all opposition to his ticket as disloyal. After swearing to support and defend the Constitution, a voter had to swear that he was "an active friend of the Government of the United States, and the enemy of the so-called Confederate States," that "I ardently desire" the defeat of the rebels, that "I sincerely rejoice" in Union victories, and that "I will heartily aid and assist the loyal people in *whatever measures may be adopted for the attainment of these ends*" (emphasis added). Striking directly at the heart of the Democratic platform, the oath taker further had to state "that I will cordially oppose all armistices or negotiations for peace with rebels in arms" until the U.S. government had reestablished its authority throughout the land. An oath like this—which was a requirement to vote in Tennessee—incontrovertibly branded support for the Democratic Party or opposition to emancipation as treason.[119]

One Kentucky soldier stationed in Tennessee complained to his sweetheart, "You have heard of the disfranchisement of *All* citizens of Tenn. who refused to vote the Lincoln ticket, making no difference, whatever, whether Loyal or not. Is this patriotism on the part of Lincoln & Johnson? Is this civil liberty?"[120] Johnson's politicized oath was a tangible and logical outcome of the Republican conception of loyalty that had taken root in the North during the war. Opponents of the president and his policies might lose their political rights because political opposition was treason.

Indeed, one New Jersey official who had recently visited Nashville, Tennessee, predicted that "no effort—even to intimidation or compulsion—will be spared by the Authorities to force the soldiers in this Department to vote for Lincoln & Johnson." He observed that any "McClellan man" among the troops was a "marked man"—denounced as a traitor and "persecuted in every way a petty but bitter tyranny can devise." He witnessed one New Jersey Democrat whose colonel reported him to the provost marshal, saying he was a "traitor and secessionist" who "ought to be hung." He claimed to know of another soldier "who proclaimed his determination to vote for McClellan" was "public[ly] *whipped*, on trumped up and trivial charges."[121]

Despite all this, some Democratic soldiers took great offense when demeaned for their party loyalties. "A captain the other day said if any person was not an abolitionist he was a copperhead," wrote one Democratic soldier. "I denied it." The captain then said he would try to get his men to vote for Lincoln. "I then said I would try to get my Company to vote for little Mac 'if this be treason, hang me.'" In like manner, an Ohio soldier was peeved by how "fast" the Republicans called Democrats "copperheads[,] for I am a democrat & a soldier to[o.] I would shoot the first man that would call me a copperhead." After declaring himself for McClellan, a Pennsylvania soldier criticized those that called the General a "tra[i]ter": "if A man tells me that I Wil nock him down or kill my self tr[y]ing to."[122] Democrats in the army, after all, bled and died the same as Republicans. Considering them disloyal exposed a peculiar contradiction in the Republicans' wartime definition of loyalty. If one had to adhere to Republican war aims, such as emancipation, to be loyal, then an anti-emancipation soldier could be considered disloyal, even as he risked his life for the nation.

CONCLUSION

It took some mettle to be a Democrat in the army in 1864. One Democratic soldier recalled in later years that many soldiers "believed McClellan to be the man for the place and voted for him. Lincoln, however, was elected and his history shows was for the best of our country. Yet we always admired General George B. McClellan. This was our first vote and the proudest of our life. It took some nerve at that time to be a Democrat."[123] That many soldiers, like this one, realized later in life that Lincoln was the best man for the job does not necessarily mean that most of the soldiers felt so confidently in 1864. Over time, the martyred president assumed a status of national deity. At the time of the election, however, the consensus was not as certain. Many Americans who never would have voted for Lincoln in 1860 or 1864 came to appreciate his greatness in the years after the war. "After all, I would not vote for him at the election," wrote one Democratic soldier in April 1865, "but I am glad that he was re-elected and am more glad to think he lived to know Richmond had been taken. He visited the Rebel City and sat on old Jeff's chair. Just as he was about to close the war, he has been cut down by the hand of a villain—a traitor who cried out after the fatal shot was fired that the South was revenged."[124] This soldier opposed Lincoln politically during the war and voted against him in 1864, but in the wake of his assassination felt a profound respect for the martyred president, feelings he had never held for Lincoln while he was alive.[125]

If, in fact, veterans did vote overwhelmingly Republican after the war, then their postwar party affiliation may have been based on postwar issues and not on a conversion to the war policies of the Republican Party in 1864. Party identification for many soldiers was still grounded more in the social and cultural variables of antebellum civilian life than in a changing of ideology during military experience.

Soldiers who supported McClellan for president did so because they believed he was the best candidate to reunite the nation and bring the war to a speedy close. These fighting men in blue are perhaps the most understudied political constituency of the Civil War era, yet their existence reveals a great deal about Civil War politics in general, and the treason and loyalty issues in particular. Northern voters who supported McClellan were castigated as traitors by the Republican majority. It should have been difficult to rationalize such accusations against those who were fighting and dying on the battlefield—yet the accusation of disloyalty was still sometimes made against these soldiers. That roughly 20 percent of the Union army did not vote for the "loyal" ticket, and another 20 percent voted against it, reveals that not all soldiers had adopted the Republicans' broadened and politicized definitions of loyalty and treason. It also reveals that those Democrats in the army who voted the Democratic ticket did not consider their party's goals as inconsistent with patriotism and Unionism. That many likely supported McClellan but could not bring themselves to vote for him (thus abstaining from the franchise) reveals that many Democrats in the army believed that their party's convention and platform did not represent their true feelings on the war. But neither of these groups would succumb to the pressure to vote Republican just to appear "loyal."

The low turnout for McClellan among the troops and the even lower turnout in the earlier state and congressional elections are indicative of a lack of faith of Democratic soldiers in the Democratic Party and platform in 1864. While many soldiers loved George McClellan as a general, they frequently commented on their dislike of "the company he kept." Many soldiers simply could not support McClellan's running mate, George H. Pendleton, who was among the numerous northern politicians who had branded the war a failure. It is likely that many Democratic soldiers consciously abstained from voting rather than endorse a platform that denounced their efforts on the battlefield. In doing so they renounced both the "peace" platform of the Democrats and the "abolitionist" platform of the Republicans. One Democrat in the army told his father: "As to Geo. B. McClellan, I like him well enough. But if his platform is a peace platform, I think that he will stand a poor show. But if it is a war platform, he will stand some chance and I would vote for him if I had the chance. But if he is a peace man, I would not vote for him. . . . Now I don't want you to think I am an Abe Lincoln man because I have been one of his soldiers or that I am a Republican, for I am not. But I am a Democrat and a war Democrat, too."[126] Democratic soldiers like this one would not vote for a ticket that they believed would undermine their efforts in the field, but they also would not vote Republican. Other Democrats wished that they could vote for a straight War Democrat ticket. At least one soldier wished he could vote for McClellan for president and Andrew Johnson, Lincoln's running mate, for vice president.[127]

Like other voters, soldiers felt the highs and lows of the national mood.[128] Prior to the capture of Atlanta, many Union soldiers felt disheartened about the war and the election. In the midst of the bloody and very costly Petersburg campaign, a young Oliver Wendell Holmes Jr. informed his parents: "I think the Army feels better than it might but there[']s no use in disguising that the feeling for McClellan has grown this campaign." In order to counteract the growing discontentment among the troops, Holmes "hope[d] for success strongly before the end of the summer."[129] Indeed, that success eventually arrived. After the fall of Atlanta and the historic national mood shift, many soldiers, like many other northern voters, rejected the Democratic candidate in favor of the Union ticket. The election of 1864 came during a momentous high, which helps explain the election day result among the troops, just as it explains Lincoln's victory as a whole. It is quite possible that many northern soldiers chose to vote for Lincoln only after the fall of Atlanta on September 1. On August 26, 1864, one officer stationed outside of Petersburg remarked to a friend that "almost every man has something to say against Lincoln & his *administration*. The McClellan & Peace Party are a long way ahead & if no other change takes place Mr. Lincoln will move out in due time."[130] But a gigantic change did take place. "Since the fall of Atlanty and Early's defeat our boys have seam to have woken up from their slumber," wrote one Wisconsin volunteer joyfully. "It did look as though the men did not cair what did become of the Country in case they cood onley get out of the armey, but now they are awaik & wide awaik and think so much of that pease party as they did."[131] If these soldiers' observations were correct, then perhaps it was the fall of Atlanta, more than any political issue, that turned the bulk of the army's support to Lincoln.

Indeed, during the summer of 1864 many soldiers doubted whether they would bother to vote in November. It was the boost in morale that came as a result of the victories in Atlanta, Mobile Bay, and the Shenandoah Valley that secured the soldier vote for Lincoln; it was not an overarching change in ideology or political sentiment. Nor was it a wholesale acceptance of emancipation as a moral goal, but, at most, as a practical war measure.

Union soldiers, like many northern voters, wavered in their political allegiances in the months and even days leading up to the election. "Never in my recollection have there been so many votes changed to the very day of polling, as in the last Presidential election," observed Francis Lieber, "and, probably, never before in the whole history of Civil Liberty." The issues at stake in the election transcended usual party squabbles, and many Democrats who had been "staggered" by the Chicago Platform voted against their party. It took them "some time to break loose," Lieber surmised, but on election day they did. Fremont men, too, realized they had to support the president, and many citizens who disliked Lincoln as a man also voted for him as the only viable Union choice.[132] On November 8, 1864, a large mass of people who typically would never vote as a bloc did so for the sake of defeating the rebellion.

5

"NOT FIT TO BE A CITIZEN"

The Disfranchisement of Deserters in the Postwar Period

IN MANY WAYS, the debate over permitting soldiers to vote during the Civil War prepared the nation for the debates over black suffrage and woman suffrage that would come in the early postwar years. In the course of the soldier vote debate, state legislatures and constitutional conventions argued about the meaning of citizenship and the rights that belonged to those who bore arms. Though military experience had been tied to suffrage on many occasions since the time of the Revolution, never before had so many states at one time brought these issues to the fore.[1] Historians who view the soldier vote only as a "lesser effect" of the war are missing some of the tangible significance of this understudied aspect of the Civil War.[2]

The patriotic rhetoric surrounding soldier suffrage, combined with the bravery of nearly two hundred thousand black men in blue, unleashed a set of forces that, in the words of one historian, "made the political and civil rights of blacks central to Reconstruction politics."[3] Opponents of emancipation clearly realized the logical outcome of Lincoln's decision to permit black men to serve as soldiers. A blacksmith with the Seventeenth Pennsylvania Cavalry confided in his diary in 1863 that the "confounded Africa of America decent will be the ruination of our Country." The Lincoln administration was "not satisfide with setting them free, but they must mak[e] soldiers out of them, and the next will be giving them a vote." And after they can "vote then the wite man will have to nock under the sweat sented nager."[4]

Unlike this cavalryman, some observers welcomed this logical outcome of black soldiering. When a Pennsylvania election commissioner reached the headquarters of Benjamin F. Butler, a radical Union general stationed in Virginia, in October 1864, he noted that Butler "had a large number of smoked yankees in his Dept. and wanted to know if we desired lists of them."[5] Butler, who would soon become a strong advocate for black suffrage, understood that black citizens of Pennsylvania ought to be allowed to vote even though their state constitution limited the franchise to white males. These ideas were certainly not lost on the black soldiers themselves. One African American from Philadelphia left his razor at the barbershop to shoulder a musket, seeking to fight for "the proper enjoyment of the rights of citizenship." Another black Pennsylvanian wondered from his camp near Richmond, "I cannot see why we should still be kept from exercising the full rights of citizenship" when we "are called upon to lay down our lives."[6]

Lincoln also came to understand that black suffrage was the logical outcome of his policy to free the slaves and make them soldiers. Indeed, in his last public address, Lincoln declared that he would support conferring the elective franchise on "the colored man" who was either "very intelligent" or to "those who serve our cause as soldiers."[7] If a person shared in the responsibility of citizenship by fighting for the nation, then he deserved to exercise the privileges of citizenship as well. Standing below the White House portico that night, John Wilkes Booth angrily declared, "That means nigger citizenship, now, by God, I'll put him through."[8] Lincoln, in a very real sense, died because of the connection he was making between military service, the franchise, and citizenship.

Lincoln had long connected military service with the right to vote. As early as 1836, as a candidate for the Illinois state legislature, he had publicly declared: "I go for all sharing the privileges of the government, who assist in bearing its burthens. Consequently I go for admitting all whites to the right of suffrage, who pay taxes or bear arms (by no means excluding females.)"[9] Thirty years later, those sentiments could be applied to African American males. Indeed, the ideological and political forces set loose by the great debate over permitting soldiers to vote during the Civil War found their fruition in the Fourteenth and Fifteenth Amendments to the Constitution.

The logic of permitting soldiers to vote—and of allowing black men to serve as soldiers—naturally led to the conclusion that black men who took up arms ought to be given the ballot. The Louisiana Constitution of 1864 permitted the state legislature to adopt legislation enfranchising any citizen of the United States who served in the military, paid taxes, or exhibited "intellectual fitness." George S. Denison wrote to Salmon P. Chase in October 1864 suggesting that these provisions were "a great step in the right direction" because under them "colored persons would be regarded as citizens." As such, "Equal suffrage can now be extended to the black man, whenever public opinion justifies it."[10] Thus, the arguments formulated and accepted in the soldier suffrage debate during the Civil War contributed, at least initially, to the Fifteenth Amendment's declaration six years later that the right of suffrage could not be denied on account of race.

Of course, if soldiers deserved the right to vote, then those who shirked their duty during the Civil War ought to lose that sacred privilege. "A man that will desert his country in this trying hour is not fit to be a citizen of the United States," wrote one Pennsylvania soldier to his sweetheart in 1863.[11] In the postwar period, Republicans throughout the nation embraced this viewpoint and sought to deprive deserters and draft dodgers of the rights of U.S. citizenship. Republicans viewed such legislation as an act of justice, believing that it was unfair for deserters to cancel out the votes of loyal citizens. Critics of this disfranchising legislation, by contrast, saw it as a partisan move to decrease the number of Democratic voters in the postwar period, just as they had seen soldier suffrage legislation as a partisan mechanism for increasing the number of Republican voters during the war.

CONGRESSIONAL DISFRANCHISEMENT OF DESERTERS

Throughout the war, Republicans sought to punish disloyalty wherever it was found—North and South, East and West. As the war was coming to a close, they moved to punish Union soldiers who had not adhered to the highest standards of loyalty. If a fighting soldier deserved to have the full rights of citizenship, a shirker had forfeited those rights. A school principal in Luzerne County, Pennsylvania, urged Lincoln in February 1865: "So many of those who are disloyal to the government are running away to avoid the draft, that I deem it *absolutely necessary* to have a law passed in Congress, forever disfranchising all such persons. This, in my humble opinion would effectually stop the exodus. I am only a common man, but I know it is my privilege to address the President. I hope you will consider this and suggest the idea at least to some members of Congress."[12]

This school principal apparently did not know that Congress had been debating the topic for more than a year and was on the cusp of enacting such legislation. In March 1864, Sen. Henry Wilson, a Radical Republican from Massachusetts, introduced a bill in the Senate that would deny the "rights of citizenship of the United States" to any deserter who did not return to the service within sixty days. It declared that "all deserters from said armies who have deserted beyond the limits of the United States" and who shall not return to the army

> shall be deemed and taken to have voluntarily relinquished and forfeited their rights of citizenship of the United States, and their rights to become citizens thereof, and such deserters shall thereafter be incapable of holding any office of trust or profit under the United States, or of exercising any rights of citizens of the United States.

The bill also required the president to "immediately" issue a proclamation stating that he would pardon any deserters who returned to fulfill their terms of service. Wilson argued that the bill would induce tens of thousands of soldiers to return to the ranks.[13]

In January and February 1865, the House and Senate debated separate bills to revise the federal conscription law. Each bill contained decitizenizing language similar to Wilson's earlier proposal (although these new bills now punished all deserters who did not return, not only those who fled the country). The debate in the Senate centered on several questions: Could Congress constitutionally require the president to issue a proclamation pardoning deserters? Would deserters be pardoned for other offenses they had possibly committed prior to deserting? Would permitting deserters to return with impunity demoralize those who had never deserted the Union army? Would deserters be inferior soldiers? And was this provision an ex post facto law? Democrat Thomas Hendricks of Indiana stood in opposition to the bill because it would now punish drafted men who did not report (under the 1863 conscription act they were classified as deserters). Hendricks conceded that "denial of the right of suffrage and the right to hold offices" in the government were "penalties known very well to the criminal laws of the country," but he maintained that it would be "a horrible thing to deprive a man of his citizenship, of that which is his pride and honor, from the mere fact that he has been unable to report upon the day specified after being notified that he has been drafted." Hendricks maintained that "the punishment is severe enough. It extends now from the denial of pay up to death; . . . Why add this other? It cannot do any good."[14] Hendricks's concerns fell on deaf ears, for few U.S. senators would have sympathy for draft dodgers. The bill passed within moments of his speech.

The debate in the House of Representatives was much more bitter. The bill's manager, Robert C. Schenck of Ohio, was a former Union general who had ruthlessly crushed dissent in Baltimore earlier in the war and had defeated Clement L. Vallandigham in his bid for reelection to Congress in October 1862. Schenck used the decitizenizing provisions of the bill to impugn the loyalty of the Democratic Party.[15]

Democrats opposed Schenck's bill for a number of political and constitutional reasons. Dwight Townsend of New York claimed that the bill could penalize pacifists or refugees from the South who, prior to heading north, had taken an oath not to take up arms against the Confederacy. If they were drafted and were unable to hire a substitute, they would either have to violate their honor or the law. Moreover, Townsend argued that the law "is one of the steps toward a consolidated Government [and] a violation of republican principle."[16]

Francis Kernan of New York pointed out that the bill provided no tribunal to determine that a deserter had lost his citizenship. James Wilson, an Iowa Republican, replied: "If one of these persons should return and should attempt to exercise the rights of a citizen, and he should be prevented from the exercise of those rights, then he can bring the question into the civil courts for determination." Robert Mallory, a Kentucky Unionist, suggested that the provision should be amended to apply only to "convicted" deserters, but Wilson opposed that change as well. If a deserter was "prevented from voting by challenge," Wilson argued, "then he has the right to go to the courts to have the question decided. . . . This will place him exactly in the same condition as to the right of suffrage as an alien, a person of foreign birth, presenting a vote. His vote may be challenged on the ground that he is not naturalized, and the judges of election may refuse his vote. He then has his remedy against the judges of election; so would a man under this section."[17]

The debate over this provision quickly turned ugly. Robert Schenck persistently tried to end debate and bring the bill up for a vote, while Democrats protested what they perceived as accusations of disloyalty from Schenck. "This bill and the debate under it have brought into issue the question of the loyalty of members upon this floor," argued Democrat John Winthrop Chanler of New York. Dwight Townsend declared that Schenck "has chosen to dispute my loyalty, and to class me as sympathizing with deserters," continuing: "I consider the remarks of the gentleman as not only an imputation on my position as a loyal citizen of the United States, but as an infamous accusation against the party to which I have the honor to belong." The Speaker of the House called Townsend to order, but Schenck retorted: "Let him go on." Townsend continued: "The attempt, therefore, of the gentleman to classify me as aiding or sympathizing with deserters, or at any rate as inferior in loyalty to the gentleman from Ohio, I treat with contempt and hurl back with scorn."[18]

Schenck replied that he had "said nothing about disloyalty," but if the Democrats voted in a way that "sympathize[d] with the man who has abandoned his country, its cause and its flag," then the Democrats' actions spoke for themselves. Schenck proceeded to criticize Democrats who claimed to support the war but never voted for legislation that would help to win it. "I know what too often is the worth of these professions, thrown out in general terms, of devotion to the country and its flag—professions unsustained by official acts when votes come to be given which will show whether such professions are founded upon actual conviction." Just as had been the case throughout much of the war, Democrats' opposition to a patriotic war measure made them appear to be in league with the rebels. The bill ultimately passed the House 83 to 46 with 53 members not voting.[19]

A conference committee of the two houses hammered out the differences between the two bills, and President Lincoln signed it into law on March 3, 1865.[20] In the law, Congress declared that deserters and draft dodgers

> shall be deemed and taken to have voluntarily relinquished and forfeited their rights of citizenship, and their rights to become citizens; and such deserters shall be forever incapable of holding any office of trust or profit under the United States, or exercising any rights of citizens thereof.

The law "authorized and required" President Lincoln to issue a public proclamation that any deserters who returned to the ranks within sixty days would be pardoned.[21] These restrictions were more severe than the provisions later ratified as part of the Fourteenth Amendment disqualifying former rebels from holding office in the United States. "There can be no penalty too great," argued Charles Sumner, "for the conspirators, who organized this great crime and let slip the dogs of war."[22] It seemed that Union deserters and draft dodgers were equal in disloyalty to the rebels of the South. On March 11, 1865—eight days after he signed the law disfranchising deserters—Abraham Lincoln issued a proclamation promising pardon to any deserter who returned to his regiment by May 10, 1865.[23]

Several aspects of this congressional debate over stripping deserters of citizenship are worthy of note. First, Congress denied deserters the rights of U.S. citizenship without explicitly declaring what those rights were.[24] Congress's action in this regard corresponded with traditional nineteenth-century rights rhetoric in America. Historian William E. Nelson argues that "the most common characteristic" of "citizens' rights rhetoric" during the Civil War era "was its vagueness and imprecision. Users of the rhetoric made it clear that citizens possessed rights guaranteed by the Constitution, but they never specified the precise content of those rights."[25] Even when the rights of U.S. citizenship were more precisely defined by the courts in the postwar period, as they were in the *Slaughterhouse Cases* (1873), they were defined quite narrowly.[26] In the 1870s, the woman suffrage movement would claim that the right to vote was a fundamental right of citizenship, but they lost that argument in numerous venues throughout the nation, culminating in the Supreme Court's decision in *Minor v. Happersett* (1875).[27]

The woman suffragists could have pointed to the deserter debate in Congress for evidence of their claim that voting was an inherent right of U.S. citizenship.[28] Congress was implicitly defining citizenship more broadly than it realized when it denied the "rights of citizenship" to deserters. After all, several congressmen specifically spoke of deserters losing their right to vote under this legislation. In truth, it was remarkable that congressmen should speak this way since Congress had no jurisdiction over the right to vote. Under the Constitution, the states determined who was eligible to vote. As such, suffrage may have been a right of state citizenship, but it was not an inherent right of U.S. citizenship. When congressmen implied that deserters would lose their right to vote, Congress was essentially equating the rights and privileges of state and federal citizenship. Moreover, Congress would have to rely on the states to enforce a federal law. It is little wonder that Representative Townsend of New York perceived the act as tending to consolidate the states under a stronger central government.

Second, Republicans refused to require conviction in a civil or military court before a deserter lost his citizenship rights. Instead, if a suspected deserter was refused his rights, then he could sue to prove his innocence and vindicate his reputation. In this way, Congress's deserter law dovetailed with other wartime legislation that disfranchised citizens who could not take oaths of past and future loyalty in good conscience. Throughout the war, Congress and the states had enacted legislation and loyalty oaths that disfranchised suspected traitors, in essence punishing disloyal citizens while bypassing the time, expense, and uncertainty involved in prosecuting treason trials.[29] In the same way, deserters would now be punished without a trial. Some deserters might choose not to attempt to vote rather than go through the embarrassment of having their vote rejected and the expense of attempting to vindicate themselves in court. Thus, deserters would be punished through the legislative process and at the polls rather than in the courts.

Third, the debate over disfranchising deserters put Democrats on the rhetorical defensive. In opposing the measure, Democrats opened themselves up to charges of disloyalty, just as they had on numerous other occasions during the Civil War. Democratic leaders almost always found themselves on the unpopular side of the debate when it came to the soldiers. They opposed the right of soldiers to vote and they defended the rights of deserters. Republicans, meanwhile, continued to articulate the belief that those whose loyalty was doubtful did not deserve the political and constitutional rights of citizenship. In defending those of dubious loyalty, the Democrats revealed what many observers believed to be their own disloyalty.

DISFRANCHISEMENT AT THE STATE LEVEL

Ironically, Congress left state authorities with the task of defining "the rights" of U.S. citizenship because the states would choose how to enforce the 1865 law. In fact, as the congressional debate revealed, the decision of who would be disfranchised would ultimately be made by local election officials. Michigan's attorney general received letters from local election supervisors asking how the law affected Michigan elections. The attorney general replied in an official opinion that the disfranchisement of deserters was an "irresistible" consequence of the federal law. If soldiers forfeited their "rights of citizenship" by deserting, then they "are not electors, under the Constitution and laws of this State, or entitled to hold any office of trust or profit under the same; and, consequently, cannot vote at our elections, or be eligible to such offices." The rationale was perfectly logical: "A voice in government and official incumbency are too clearly among the peculiar rights of citizenship to admit of argument; and, therefore, citizenship, together with the privileges named, being forfeited, *the right of voting is necessarily forfeited also.*"[30] Some state adjutant generals printed long reports that included the law, Lincoln's proclamation, and lists of deserters, draft dodgers, and bounty jumpers. Indiana's list, for example, was eighty-five pages long.[31] But these lists gave no instructions. The implication was simply that the persons listed would be barred from voting. Despite the fact that "the rights of citizenship" had never been legally defined, many Americans intuitively believed that suffrage was included. One Republican editor in central Pennsylvania praised Congress for ensuring "that no deserter who abandoned the cause of his country to the fury of traitors will be allowed to vote at Pennsylvania elections."[32]

Of course, from this perspective, loss of citizenship was much more lenient than the traditional punishments for desertion. "Certainly, the penalties imposed by said act of Congress are not as severe as those authorized to be inflicted in many other instances, for a violation of military laws or orders, some of which even authorize the instant killing of the offender," wrote the attorney general of Michigan. "The life of the nation being at stake, it is but the highest dictate of a sound and sagacious patriotism, to employ in its defense every means sanctioned by the usages of civilized warfare; and the penalties of the act of Congress . . . cannot be said to be inconsistent with them." Congress, in his view, possessed the constitutional power to prescribe a penalty for desertion; and those who deserted their country's cause ought to be grateful that they only lost their political rights and not their lives.[33]

Still, this act of Congress was an unquestionably broad exercise of power. It was one thing for Congress to disqualify American citizens from holding federal office; it was quite another thing to bar them from voting—a right that was traditionally defined, regulated, and enforced at the state level. As one angry Democrat from Wisconsin proclaimed, the ballot box "is not the gift of the Federal Constitution" and "the people of no state of this Union, are indebted to the Federal Constitution for the privileges of the ballot box."[34] Moreover, as Michigan's attorney general correctly noted, the law stripped deserters of their rights without any trial or conviction in court: "The forfeitures contemplated by this act of Congress, evidently do not depend upon the judgment or decree of any Court, rendered upon a trial and conviction; but are absolute, made so by the very terms of the act itself, and may be taken advantage of collaterally, a prior conviction being unnecessary."[35]

While some states, like Michigan, barred deserters from voting under the federal law, other states passed their own laws disfranchising deserters. New Hampshire, New York, Pennsylvania, Vermont, and Wisconsin enacted such measures in 1866 and 1867. Deserters from Wisconsin were also denied stays of proceedings in civil actions, a legal courtesy that previously had been granted to all soldiers.[36] In Ohio, draft dodgers were imprisoned at hard labor for up to six months, and lost the right to vote, to be a juror or witness in court, and to serve in civil office.[37] In 1867, Michigan exempted all soldiers from paying a state poll tax provided the soldier "shall never have been a deserter."[38]

Northern Republicans generally supported legislation disfranchising deserters. As governor of Maine in 1866, Joshua Lawrence Chamberlain, the hero of Little Round Top, argued that deserters and draft dodgers were traitors who should not be permitted to vote:

> There were among the true men who served in the war some nineteen hundred deserters—a very small per centage, but still too many. There were also some, of whom it is disagreeable to speak, who fled from the call of duty and took refuge within foreign borders to escape the draft. In our recent State election large numbers of these two classes appeared at the polls and cast their votes. Whether it is just to the soldier who offered his life for this imperilled country that his voice should be silenced by the equal vote of one who denounced and defied his country, whether it is sound policy to permit acts so unworthy of a citizen to go unrebuked, and treason so overt to escape odium, is for you and the people to say. Doubtless we can out-vote such an element, but still it is a grave question whether the traitor and deserter deserve an equal share with the loyal defender in the privileges and protection of the restored country.[39]

Chamberlain's argument echoed Robert C. Schenck's. The man who deserted the army was as morally guilty as the traitor. Although Maine never adopted the disfranchising legislation that Chamberlain requested, state election judges in Maine prohibited deserters from voting under the federal law.[40]

Northern Democrats, by contrast, roundly opposed the legislation. The debate over a state disfranchising law in the Pennsylvania legislature quickly degenerated into an ugly partisan fight over disloyalty during the Civil War, just as it had in the U.S. House of Representatives. In between the partisan jabs and personal insults, the legislators managed to discuss some of the actual aspects of the bill. One Pennsylvania Democrat proposed amending the bill so that it would not disfranchise those who had lost their citizenship under the federal law, but rather deserters who had been convicted by court-martial. He said that this was to "make this act conform to the decisions of the courts" in Pennsylvania and other states (discussed below), but the assembly rejected his proposal by a party vote. Another Democrat caustically proposed amending the title of the bill to be "An act to repeal the first section of the third article of the Constitution of Pennsylvania [granting suffrage], and abolish the right of trial by jury." One Republican responded to the Democratic proposals by accusing the Democrats of opposing the measure so that they could "gobble up every deserter's vote that may be offered at the polls."[41]

Several states debated whether to incorporate disfranchising provisions into their state constitutions. State legislatures that debated such provisions tended to support them, while state constitutional conventions routinely rejected such proposals. In 1867, the Kansas state legislature adopted a proposed constitutional amendment that would disfranchise all Union soldiers who had received a dishonorable discharge unless they were reinstated in the military, as well as all Kansans who had voluntarily borne arms in support of the rebellion. In November 1867, Kansas voters ratified the proposed amendment by a vote of 16,860 to 12,165, although, according to one state historian, "for years thereafter scarcely a session of the legislature was held in which there was not a bill, or at least a petition, asking for the removal of these political disabilities from some of the persons who had fallen under the ban." The state supreme court upheld the provision in 1894, saying that "the people in their organic law may . . . determine who shall participate in the government." This, the court claimed, is "a power universally and necessarily exercised by the framers of every constitution." The clause remained part of the Kansas constitution until 1974.[42]

In Ohio, black suffrage and the disfranchisement of deserters merged into a single campaign issue. After several failed attempts, the Republican legislature in Ohio adopted a proposed constitutional amendment in April 1867 that would enfranchise African Americans and disfranchise deserters. Radical Republicans had hoped simply to strike the word "white" from the suffrage clause of the state constitution, but they could not convince enough conservative Republicans to vote with them. In order to win over conservative Republican support, the Radicals amended the proposal to not only enfranchise black men but also to disfranchise deserters from the Union army. According to one historian, "conservative Unionists were ready to vote for negro suffrage, provided they could at the same time, disfranchise as many Peace Democrats as possible." Cynical observers believed the object of the proposed amendment was to disfranchise members of the political opposition, while Republicans claimed that the bill would ensure a free and fair franchise. "Shall 'skedadlers' from the draft, Knights of the Golden Circle, rebels and enemies of the country be permitted to vote," asked one Ohio Republican, "while those who fought in defense of the government are denied the right."[43]

The debate in the Ohio legislature became something of a rumpus. Several Republican legislators attempted to resign their seats rather than vote on the proposal to enfranchise blacks and disfranchise deserters. The legislature also voted on measures to permit women to vote (rejected 35 to 53), to disfranchise all Union soldiers, and to disfranchise all persons who had voted for Clement Vallandigham in 1863. Newspapers nationwide reported that five Democrats resigned their seats in protest of the latter proposal.[44]

Strangely enough, after the amendment had passed the legislature, Republicans throughout the state were hesitant to endorse it. They now feared that it would anger white voters, driving large numbers away from the party while actually enfranchising only a negligible number of African American men. Republicans therefore downplayed the importance of the amendment. Granting the vote to black men, one Ohio Republican assured the voters, had "nothing to do with social position or relations." Meanwhile, Democrats race-baited the electorate, claiming that "Ohio shall become a negro colony, controlled by Negro votes." The Democratic message carried the day, and the voters of Ohio rejected the amendment in October 1867, casting fewer than 46 percent of their votes in its favor.[45]

While state legislatures were willing to disfranchise deserters by statutory law and proposed constitutional amendments, state constitutional conventions were hesitant to write such provisions into their states' fundamental laws. In 1867, Michigan's constitutional convention debated disfranchising all future deserters, but the proposition was overwhelmingly rejected for several reasons. First, many delegates doubted that this sort of crime and punishment should be included in the state's organic law. Others did not believe a local board of elections should become the judge of whether a crime had occurred. "In such a case a man is condemned without the formalities and safeguards of a trial," declared one member of the convention in opposition to the measure. The punishment for a crime without the benefit of a trial, according to another delegate, deprived alleged deserters of due process rights. Still others claimed that youthful, inexperienced soldiers sometimes deserted without understanding the full consequences of their actions. And not only cowards deserted, either. "Many times some of our best soldiers, under trying circumstances, have been guilty of desertion," stated one delegate. "Many such have afterwards nobly redeemed their characters, when they have again gone upon the field, after the offense had been pardoned or the punishment mitigated. They have in many cases redeemed their characters by the sacrifice of their lives." Finally, because this provision would deal only with future desertions, such a punishment now might hamper future efforts at recruitment. There was no necessity, in the view of the convention, to adopt such a provision in these current times of peace.[46]

At New York's constitutional convention of 1867–68, a Union army veteran introduced a provision that would disfranchise Civil War deserters as well as those who had voluntarily rebelled against the United States. "I believe that by adopting this amendment we shall say that we believe citizenship is a sacred thing," he argued, "and th[at] there is a difference between a loyal man and the man who is not loyal, that there is a difference between the man who stood faithfully in the battle front and the man who deserted his colors." Others concurred, arguing that citizenship required persons to have "character," "integrity," and other virtues. "Any man who will not stand by his government in the ordinary exercise of the duties of citizenship, at a time of trial," argued one delegate, "is not entitled to the highest prerogative that government can give." Another delegate maintained that the deserter "occupies a position far more detestable than an open enemy" because he "carries within his traitorous heart the evils of misplaced confidence." He continued:

> Shall we say that the coward who skulks at the approach of war, the traitor who steals the guise of a friend, and with a heart blacker than a spy conveys vital information to the enemy, the voluntary rebel who stabs at the life of the nation, are to be clothed with citizenship and the elective franchise in this great and patriotic State? . . . These deserters are criminals, vagabonds and bounty jumpers, and cowards, who have not the loyalty, integrity, courage or manhood to protect, preserve or defend the government or its flag, and for these reasons should be excluded from the ballot-box, that great fountain of purity and preservation.

The point was clear. Deserters were "not fitted to exercise the elective franchise" and "unfit to enjoy the privileges of citizenship, unfit recipients of that power." Even more, permitting them to vote would "degrade American citizenship."[47]

While such rhetoric had gained significant traction during the war years, the delegates were hesitant to write such ideas into New York's organic law. A bipartisan group of delegates defeated the proposal. Some argued that it would punish men more than two years after the close of the war, which was particularly egregious since many deserters had been impressionable young men who had acted impulsively on the advice of a parent or a Copperhead newspaper. What was needed now was "kindness," "forgiveness" and "reconciliation," not vengeance. Others contended that such a provision would hurt New York's economy by essentially forcing many workers to leave the state. Still others believed that this was merely a "partisan" measure intended to hurt the Democratic Party. More importantly, several delegates pointed out that the measure had no enforcement mechanism. It would be inadequate, argued one delegate, to rely on muster rolls to determine who was disfranchised. "I do not believe that those rolls would do justice to the men whose names are marked upon them as deserters." Moreover, it would be impractical to have the inspectors of election hear challenges and witnesses at the polls.[48]

The issue of disfranchising deserters periodically came up in political debates and elections in the ensuing years. When, for example, Democrat Hugh H. Moore won election to the New York state senate in 1873, his Republican challenger, Walter S. Pinckney, contested the election on the basis of alleged irregularities at the polls. Part of the challenge also consisted in accusations that Moore had deserted during the Civil War and that the act of Congress disfranchised him and barred him from holding office. One witness claimed that Moore "has not voted in this city for some time, until the last election, when he was nominated for state senator, and when he did not dare to keep back from the polls for fear of some reason being asked why he did not vote." Moore held onto his seat. When the state published an official biography of each member of the legislature, it stated: "In the late war for the defense of the Union, Senator Moore bore his part manfully." Moore had served in several engagements in the 133rd New York Infantry. "His army history is unique in one respect, he never actually enlisted. Having a brother in the One Hundred and Thirty-third regiment, he ran away from home, being at the time a mere lad, and joined that command without going through the form of enlisting."[49]

Over time, the states slackened how stringently they enforced the state and federal statutes. In 1868, for example, Wisconsin gave accused deserters additional opportunities to prove their innocence. That same year the state legislature rejected a proposal to repeal the state's disfranchising law, but a strongly worded minority report from the Assembly's judiciary committee, which called the law "sensational" and "buncombe," set the stage for the law's repeal the following year. The minority report argued that no legislative power—"State or national"—could change the qualifications for voting; only the people could do that through constitutional revision. As such state and federal laws unjustly and unconstitutionally deprived voters of their rights without due process of law. While this view was in the minority in 1868, it became the majority opinion the following year. The Wisconsin legislature repealed the state's disfranchising law on March 10, 1869.[50] Other states simply stopped enforcing the laws once they had been struck down in the state judiciaries.

DISFRANCHISEMENT AND THE COURTS

The disfranchising law of Congress quickly came under the scrutiny of several state courts. Critics of the law claimed that it was an ex post facto law; that it altered the rules of evidence by requiring insufficient proof of guilt; that it permitted Congress "to regulate the right of suffrage in the states, or to impair it"; and that it violated the Bill of Rights by inflicting penalties on citizens "before and without a trial and conviction by due process of law."[51]

On October 10, 1865, one Henry Reily of Franklin County, Pennsylvania, attempted to vote in the state elections, but his ballot was refused by the judge of the election, Benjamin Huber, who claimed that Reily was a deserter. Reily had been drafted on July 19, 1864, but had never reported to the provost marshal; nor was he ever mustered into the Union army. He thus was listed as a deserter in official army records.[52]

The case first came before Judge Alexander King in Franklin County. King, a Republican, had already declared the law of Congress unconstitutional in another case because, he claimed, it punished citizens and took away their fundamental rights without a conviction in court. "These fundamental principles of civil liberty cannot be overlooked or disregarded by the courts, to which we all look for protection without seriously imperilling the safety of the people," King declared. "It is a thousand times better," he continued, for one candidate to lose an election than that he should win "by trampling under foot the sacred right" because "no man shall be condemned without any opportunity of being heard in his own defense." Using this rationale, King ruled in favor of Reily, the deserter, and ordered Huber to pay Reily one dollar in damages plus court costs. Huber appealed the decision to the state supreme court and asked that the monetary judgments against him be revoked.[53]

The opinion of the Supreme Court of Pennsylvania was handed down by future U.S. Supreme Court justice William Strong. The court held that this act of Congress was not an ex post facto law because the deserter continued in his absence both before and after the act was passed. "Its operation is entirely prospective," wrote Strong. "If a drafted man owes service to the Federal Government, every new refusal to render the service may be regarded as a violation of public duty, a public offence for which Congress may impose a penalty." The court also held that Congress was not regulating the right of suffrage within the states, but simply depriving the offender of the opportunity to vote. "I cannot doubt," wrote Strong, "that as a penalty for crime against the General Government, Congress may impose upon the criminal forfeiture of his citizenship of the United States. Disfranchisement of a citizen as a punishment for crime is no unusual punishment." If a state only permitted U.S. citizens to vote, then the law necessarily disfranchised them. But that conferral of suffrage was done by the state constitution and not by the law of Congress. The federal law therefore did not supersede the state constitutions; if the states wished to permit deserters— non-U.S. citizens—to vote, they could do so.[54]

The most important part of Strong's opinion had to do with the enforcement of the act. Strong held that the act must be read within the context of other federal laws that pertained to the raising of troops. Congress had already passed laws permitting deserters and draft dodgers to be tried and punished in military courts. Within this context, Strong held that the act of March 3, 1865, "has the single object of increasing the penalties" of offenders who had already been convicted by courts-martial. "For the conviction and sentence of such a court there can be no substitute. They alone establish the guilt of the accused, and fasten upon him the legal consequences." The court thus upheld the act of Congress, but in this case ruled in favor of the deserter because he had never been convicted by courts-martial.[55]

Strong's analysis either misread, ignored, or was unaware of Congress's intent. The Republican majority in Congress had clearly intended for deserters to lose the right to vote without a prior conviction, but the state judges responded in a way that would protect the rights of state citizens and ensure due process. More importantly, Strong's opinion may have been a judicial attempt to limit a broad and ambiguous legislative act rather than declare it unconstitutional.[56] Despite its misreading of the statute, *Huber v. Reily* became an important precedent for other courts to follow. Indeed, courts in Maine, New York, and New Hampshire relied on the Pennsylvania precedent, declaring that deserters could only lose their citizenship rights if they had been convicted in a military court.[57] The Supreme Court of the United States also upheld this interpretation of the law in 1885, declaring that Strong's interpretation of the statute "has been uniformly held by the civil courts as well as by the military authorities."[58] When Congress revised the statute in the 1940s (discussed below), Strong's interpretation—that deserters needed to be convicted before they could lose their citizenship—was explicitly incorporated into the statutory law.

The 1866 Pennsylvania law disfranchising deserters came under the scrutiny of the courts the following year. Gov. Andrew G. Curtin had waited to sign the bill while *Huber v. Reily* was still pending before the state supreme court. Curtin and Pennsylvania attorney general William M. Meredith were reported to have some doubts as to the state law's constitutionality.[59] Curtin may also have been hesitant to sign the law since it was widely perceived as partisan. "This measure," according to historian William Blair, "was intended to give every possible advantage to the Republican Party" in the 1866 gubernatorial race.[60]

In order to enforce the statute, the state legislature requested a descriptive list of deserters from the Office of the Provost Marshal General, in Washington, D.C. This enormous 274-page document contained physical descriptions of Pennsylvania's thirty thousand deserters, as well as information regarding their residence, occupation, and the facts of their desertion. Election officials at polling places throughout the state could use the list to keep deserters from voting.[61]

On October 9, 1866, Edward McCafferty attempted to vote in Huntington County, Pennsylvania, but his vote was rejected by the election judges in his township since he had never reported for duty when he was drafted in May 1864. McCafferty sued but lost in a trial court; he appealed his case to the state supreme court.[62]

Writing again for the court, William Strong held the Pennsylvania disfranchising law unconstitutional. According to the state constitution, "In elections by the citizens, every white freeman of the age of twenty-one years, having resided in this state one year, and in the election district where he offers to vote ten days immediately preceding such election, and within two years paid a state or county tax, which shall have been assessed at least ten days before the election, shall enjoy the rights of an elector." This constitutional provision, according to Strong, clearly conferred the right to vote upon McCafferty. Moreover, McCafferty had never been convicted by courts-martial, so he never lost his U.S. citizenship.[63]

Strong next took careful aim at the Pennsylvania law. In *Huber,* Strong had determined that the federal law required conviction by courts-martial in order for a deserter to lose his citizenship. The Pennsylvania statute, by contrast, merely required copies of muster rolls and other military records to prove the fact of desertion. "The act thus denies the rights of an elector to all who under the Act of Congress have been registered as deserters from the military service of the United States, even though they have not been tried, convicted and sentenced for the offence. It attempts to disfranchise those who are enfranchised by the fundamental law of the Commonwealth, and it enacts what shall be the evidence of disfranchisement." If the legislature could come up with a new qualification for voting, its

> power is superior to the organic law of the state, and the legislature, instead of being controlled by it, may mould the Constitution at their pleasure. Such is not the law. A right conferred by the Constitution is beyond the reach of legislative interference. If it were not so, there would be nothing stable; there would be no security for any right. It is in the nature of a constitutional grant of power or of privileges that it cannot be taken away by any authority known to the government. . . . It has always been understood that the legislature has no power to confer the elective franchise upon other classes than those to whom it is given by the [state] Constitution, for the description of those entitled is regarded as excluding all others.

Strong therefore struck down the state law as an unconstitutional grasp of power. The state constitution's broad description of who possessed the right to vote meant "therefore the right of suffrage is with us indefeasible."[64]

Justice Daniel Agnew, a Republican, wrote a lengthy dissent, which was joined by his fellow Republican John M. Read. Agnew argued that the state legislature could take away a citizen's status as "freeman" as a penalty for offenses and that the person would thus lose his right to vote. Agnew pointed out that the state constitution required freemen to be trained and armed and ready to defend the commonwealth. If one thus deserted or failed to report, he was not living up to the expectations that the constitution placed upon him. Moreover, the state legislature had previously disfranchised those who corrupted the election process by betting on elections, treating, or through bribes. "The ground is that these offences strike at the purity and freedom of elections, destroy their equality, and sap the very foundation of our entire political system by corrupting the persons who vote." Agnew then presented a "mountain of authority" to "prove that a voluntary deserter from his public duty relinquishes his privilege as a freeman—that he who refuses to defend his country when in peril, and by his desertion discovers his want of 'interest with and attachment to the community,' whose offence strikes at the very foundation of free government, is one who has no right to affect the interests of that community by his voice or his vote." He is "craven" and "no longer a freeman, but a 'recreant,' who is unfit to govern those whom he deserted in the hour of their peril." If Congress had a right to decitizenize deserters (which the court had conceded in *Huber*), then a state "has the clear right to adopt and to apply that disfranchisement to his condition as a citizen of the state." And the legislature could determine that this "forfeiture is triable by the election board."[65]

Agnew argued that the federal government could use conscription to raise and maintain armies.[66] "From the power to draft follows of necessity the power to declare a penalty for disobedience," Agnew reasoned. "The power existing, the extent of the penalty is within the discretion of the law-making power, whether it be to forfeiture of life or property, or the loss of citizenship." Still, Agnew argued that stripping a deserter of his citizenship rights was not a punishment in the ordinary sense of the word and therefore did not require conviction in court. Rather, it was the declaration of a status—a qualification for voting—just as race, age, and residence were. As such, conviction in a civil court or by courts-martial was not necessary to prove one's status. The election judges were competent to inquire into a voter's citizenship, just as they could determine his race or his age. "The right of citizenship," wrote Agnew, "is simply political, a mere condition or *status* of the individual. It is not sufficient to tell us that conviction of desertion is necessary before the political *status* can be known." The status of citizen was not a "natural right" that was beyond the reach of the government. Citizenship could be "surrendered" if the citizen violated certain laws. Striking at Strong's opinions in both *Huber* and *McCafferty,* Agnew concluded: "And Congress having declared it without reference to any conviction, it will not do to say it can be shown only by a conviction."[67]

The March 3, 1865, law of Congress remained on the books well into the twentieth century. Congress codified the law as part of the *Revised Statutes of the United States* in 1874.[68] In 1912, Congress amended the provision to apply only to desertion in wartime.[69] Congress again codified these provisions as part of the Nationality Act of 1940. Under the 1940 act, noncitizen deserters and draft dodgers who were convicted by courts-martial became "ineligible to become a citizen of the United States" and "forever incapable of holding any office of trust or of profit under the United States, or of exercising any rights of citizens thereof." A citizen or national who deserted from the military in wartime and was convicted by courts-martial "shall lose his nationality."[70] This revision of the 1865 law incorporated two key changes regarding citizens' rights. First, in accordance with the prevailing interpretation of the measure, the statute now explicitly required conviction by courts-martial. Second, citizens would now lose their "nationality" rather than their "rights of citizenship." It had never been quite clear whether a deserter lost his citizenship under the 1865 act or just his rights of citizenship. Political commentators in the early twentieth century differed on this point. But the 1940 act clarified the ambiguity. Now deserters would lose their nationality— their citizenship—as a result of their crime.[71]

During World War II, the War Department requested Congress to amend the Nationality Act to deprive deserters of their citizenship only if they were dishonorably discharged following a conviction by court-martial. Under this revision, if the military reinstated the deserter, his "nationality or citizenship or civil or political rights" would be restored.[72] As such, the law would now encourage deserters to rejoin the army, just as its 1865 predecessor had done. Moreover, as Justice Felix Frankfurter would later point out, "The obvious purpose of the 1944 amendment, requiring dishonorable discharge as a condition precedent to expatriation, was to correct the situation in which an individual who had been convicted of desertion, and who had thus lost his citizenship, was kept on duty to fight and sometimes die 'for his country which disowns him.'"[73]

The Nationality Act of 1940 and its 1944 revision came under the scrutiny of the Supreme Court of the United States as a result of an obscure World War II desertion case. In May 1944, Pvt. Albert Trop, a twenty-year-old Ohioan who was stationed with the American army in Morocco, was serving time in a military stockade for some "breach of discipline." On May 22 he and a companion escaped from the stockade and headed for Rabat, but after a day's journey they decided to turn around and head back to the base. Trop testified: "We had decided to return to the stockade. The going was tough. We had no money to speak of, and at the time we were on foot and we were getting cold and hungry." They were picked up by an Army truck and taken back to the stockade. Shortly thereafter Trop was court-martialed and sentenced to hard labor for three years, loss of all pay, and dishonorable discharge.[74]

In 1952, Trop applied to the State Department for a passport, but his request was denied on the ground that he had lost his citizenship as a result of his dishonorable discharge. A U.S. district court and the U.S. Court of Appeals for the Second Circuit both upheld the State Department's decision. Trop then appealed his case to the Supreme Court.

Writing for a 5–4 majority, Chief Justice Earl Warren struck down the law as a violation of the Eighth Amendment's prohibition on cruel and unusual punishments. Warren pointed out that the law was "based directly on a Civil War statute, which provided that a deserter would lose his 'rights of citizenship.'" He immediately added: "The meaning of this phrase was not clear."[75]

Warren criticized the federal statute, saying that it placed the rights of citizenship in the hands of the military because military authorities could exercise "complete discretion" over who was dishonorably discharged or who was reinstated. The military thus "becomes the arbiter of citizenship" and "has been given the power to grant or withhold citizenship." He further argued that Congress could not deprive Americans of their citizenship and that doing so constituted a cruel and unusual punishment. "As long as a person does not voluntarily renounce or abandon his citizenship," wrote Warren, "and this petitioner had done neither, I believe his fundamental right of citizenship is secure." Warren conceded that since wartime desertion was punishable by death, "there can be no argument that the penalty of denationalization is excessive in relation to the gravity of the crime," yet he proceeded to argue that the punishment was more cruel than execution because it violated "the dignity of man." "Fines, imprisonment and even execution may be imposed depending upon the enormity of the crime," wrote Warren, "but any technique outside the bounds of these traditional penalties is constitutionally suspect." As such, Warren argued that the Court must determine whether denationalization of a citizen was "within the limits of civilized standards."[76]

Warren concluded that the federal law violated the civilized standards laid out in the Eighth Amendment because the statute inflicted "the total destruction of the individual's status in organized society." He continued:

It is a form of punishment more primitive than torture, for it destroys for the individual the political existence that was centuries in the development. The punishment strips the citizen of his status in the national and international political community. His very existence is at the sufferance of the country in which he happens to find himself. . . . This punishment is offensive to the cardinal principles for which the Constitution stands. It subjects the individual to a fate of ever-increasing fear and distress. He knows not what discriminations may be established against him, what proscriptions may be directed against him, and when and for what cause his existence in his native land may be terminated. He may be subject to banishment, a fate universally decried by civilized people. He is stateless, a condition deplored in the international community of democracies.

Relying on foreign standards of justice, Warren pointed out that only two other nations—the Philippines and Turkey—denationalized soldiers for desertion. "The civilized nations of the world are in virtual unanimity that statelessness is not to be imposed as punishment for crime." Warren concluded: "In this country the Eighth Amendment forbids this to be done."[77]

In a concurring opinion, Justice William J. Brennan argued that denationalization would have terrible psychological effects upon deserters. "Expatriation, in this respect, constitutes an especially demoralizing sanction," argued Brennan. "The uncertainty, and the consequent psychological hurt, which must accompany one who becomes an outcast in his own land must be reckoned a substantial factor in the [Court's] ultimate judgment." Rather than trying to rehabilitate deserters, Brennan argued that this law was based on "retribution," "rough justice," and "naked vengeance." He continued: "I can think of no more certain way in which to make a man in whom, perhaps, rest the seeds of serious antisocial behavior more likely to pursue further a career of unlawful activity than to place on him the stigma of the derelict, uncertain of many of his basic rights." Ultimately, Brennan concluded that Congress had exceeded its constitutional authority in depriving deserters of their rights of citizenship.[78]

Writing in dissent, Justice Felix Frankfurter held that the 1865 law of Congress, as incorporated into the Nationalization Act of 1940, was a reasonable piece of legislation and that the Court should refrain from imposing its own views of public policy upon the American public. A foremost advocate for judicial humility, Frankfurter wrote that "self-restraint is of the essence in the observance of the judicial oath, for the Constitution has not authorized the judges to sit in judgment on the wisdom of what Congress and the Executive Branch do." According to Frankfurter, Congress may determine that "stern measures—what to some may seem overly stern—are needed" to protect the nation, and it is not the duty of the judiciary to strike down the law simply because a majority of the justices disagree with the policy.[79]

Frankfurter criticized the hysteria that he perceived in the majority and concurring opinions. A deserter who lost his citizenship would be treated as an alien, and aliens were generally treated quite well in the United States. The denationalized deserter, therefore, "need not be in constant fear lest some dire and unforeseen fate be imposed on him by arbitrary governmental action— certainly not 'while this Court sits.' . . . The multitudinous decisions of this Court protective of the rights of aliens bear weighty testimony. And the assumption that brutal treatment is the inevitable lot of denationalized persons found in other countries is a slender basis on which to strike down an Act of Congress otherwise amply sustainable."[80]

Finally, Frankfurter contended that denationalization was "not 'punishment' in any valid constitutional sense" but rather was part of Congress's constitutional obligation to regulate the military. But even if it were a punishment, Frankfurter maintained that calling it "cruel and unusual" would "stretch that concept beyond the breaking point." He continued:

> It seems scarcely arguable that loss of citizenship is within the Eighth Amendment's prohibition because disproportionate to an offense that is capital and has been so from the first year of Independence. Is constitutional dialectic so empty of reason that it can be seriously urged that loss of citizenship is a fate worse than death? The seriousness of abandoning one's country when it is in the grip of mortal conflict precludes denial to Congress of the power to terminate citizenship here, unless that power is to be denied to Congress under any circumstance. . . . In this country, desertion has been punishable by loss of at least the "rights of citizenship" since 1865.

If Congress can take away citizenship for other reasons—such as marrying a foreigner or voting in a foreign election—then this law could hardly be considered a cruel and unusual punishment.[81]

Strangely enough, this 1957 Supreme Court decision, which was rooted in a Civil War–era statute, set early parameters for future debates in the United States over the "living Constitution." Chief Justice Warren couched his opinion in familiar language of judicial restraint and adherence to the Constitution, arguing that he was "oath-bound to defend the Constitution" and to exercise "judgment" rather than rely "upon personal preferences."[82] But there was other language in his opinion that revealed his true objectives. "The provisions of the Constitution are not time-worn adages or hollow shibboleths," he wrote. "They are vital, living principles that authorize and limit governmental powers in our Nation." The language of the Eighth Amendment was not "static" or "precise." Rather, "The Amendment must draw its meaning from the evolving standards of decency that mark the progress of a maturing society."[83] This phraseology has become a key point of contention in the battle over how the Supreme Court should interpret the Constitution. Indeed, in the past fifty years, the Court has cited the language of "evolving standards of decency" in some forty cases, the most important of which pertain to the death penalty.[84] Warren's reliance on foreign law to strike down the denationalization of deserters was another harbinger of other legal debates to come.

EPILOGUE

"A VOTE IN THE DEMOCRACY FOR WHICH THEY ARE FIGHTING AND DYING"

THE SOLDIER VOTE was one of the most politically significant issues of the Civil War, yet it has received little scholarly attention over the past 150 years. The only book-length study on the subject is Josiah Benton's 1915 work, *Voting in the Field: A Forgotten Chapter of the Civil War.* Benton's statement that soldiers' voting "has passed without consideration, and with little notice, by the historians of that period" remains almost as true today as when he wrote it a century ago.[1]

Two reasons explain this oversight. First, the votes cast in the field by Union soldiers did not provide the margin of victory in the presidential election of 1864. Maryland's October 1864 referendum abolishing slavery was the most important election in which the soldier vote was truly decisive. Other than that, the soldier vote decided only a handful of minor state and congressional races.[2] Second, most historians have assumed that there were no issues worth investigating in the history of soldier suffrage legislation. The story seems straightforward: Republicans wanted soldiers to vote because they believed that most soldiers were Republicans and would vote for their party. Democrats opposed extending the franchise to soldiers in the field because they feared it would ensure Republican electoral success. The outcome was a virtual fait accompli. Writes James M. McPherson: "Having won the military victories that turned the war around, these citizens in uniform prepared to give 'Old Abe,' as they affectionately called their commander in chief, a thumping endorsement at the polls."[3] In like manner, Jennifer L. Weber argues that Union soldiers' support for Lincoln and the Republican Party never wavered, even in the dark days of August 1864. "When Lincoln's political fortunes stood at their lowest point," she writes, "his supporters in the ranks were a crucial source of political sustenance."[4]

What actually happened was far more nuanced and much more complex. Soldier support for Lincoln and emancipation was not nearly as "thumping" as McPherson, Weber, and other historians describe it. Prior to the fall of Atlanta in September 1864, many wondered whether they would bother to vote in the presidential election because they had significant doubts about both major parties and candidates. Even some Republican soldiers wavered in their support of the president during the summer of 1864. In the end, approximately 20 percent of the eligible voters in the field chose not to vote in the presidential election; an even greater percentage chose not to vote in the state and congressional elections that year. And more than 20 percent of the soldiers who voted cast their ballots for McClellan. Thus, more than 40 percent of the soldiers who were eligible to vote in 1864 did not vote for Lincoln's reelection. The war did not convert the mass of Union soldiers into lifelong Republicans; nor were the soldiers necessarily a source of "sustenance" for the Lincoln administration.[5]

Finally, the Union army saw a change in composition between April 1861 and November 1864. Lincoln's issuance of the Emancipation Proclamation pushed many Democrats out of the service in the winter and spring of 1863. As one Ohio soldier noted in May of that year, "what soldiers are left are true Blue[;] what few Butternuts we had have either disserted or resigned."[6] The exodus continued between November 1863 and November 1864, when thousands upon thousands of soldiers opted not to reenlist. George B. McClellan appears to have recognized some of the changes that had taken place in the army. Shortly before the presidential election, McClellan noted that he had received "many letters from privates & *ex*-soldiers—*all* right."[7] His emphasis on "*ex*" soldiers suggests that he believed many of his supporters had left the service by the fall of 1864. If the army lost many Democratic soldiers after their three-year terms of enlistment were up, it would make the case that the bulk of Democrats in the service converted to the Republican Party during the Civil War even less tenable.[8]

The scholarly neglect of the soldier vote of 1864 has also caused historians to underestimate the nature, complexity, and true significance of Lincoln's civil liberties policies during the Civil War. Lincoln's measures for dealing with anti-emancipation soldiers fit into the larger picture of how he and his subordinates often dealt with Democratic opposition at home. The military suppressed dozens of Democratic newspapers, causing many editors to silence or alter their anti-administration and anti-emancipation views.[9] In like manner, Lincoln, Secretary of War Edwin M. Stanton, and the Union high command punished anti-emancipation and anti-administration officers and enlisted men, thus working to silence their Democratic comrades and coerce acquiescence among the Union army as a whole. Lincoln's civil liberties policies were far more comprehensive than scholars have realized, touching Democratic dissent not only at home but also in the field.

And yet, if scholars focus only on the negative aspects of Lincoln's civil liberties policies—his suspension of the privilege of the writ of habeas corpus and his use of the military to arrest and try many American citizens (both civilian *and* soldier) for their Democratic views—we will miss a significant aspect of the civil liberties issue during the Civil War. Lincoln and his party accomplished a great feat for civil liberty when they enfranchised soldiers during the war. Indeed, the enfranchisement of so many soldiers and sailors during the war was an unprecedented expansion of civil liberty that should not be overlooked. Moreover, the policy of enfranchising soldiers is a crucial component of Lincoln's legacy in civil liberties matters, for it laid the groundwork for the Fourteenth and Fifteenth Amendments by affirming that the right to vote was at the core of what it meant to be a U.S. citizen.

SOLDIER SUFFRAGE FROM THE CIVIL WAR TO WORLD WAR II

In the years following the Civil War, members of both political parties moved to repeal their states' soldier suffrage laws. To a large extent the laws had been enacted to serve only a temporary purpose—to ensure that the citizen armies of the Civil War could vote. By 1915, when Josiah Benton wrote *Voting in the Field,* Benton counted only six states (Kansas, Maine, Michigan, Nevada, New York and Rhode Island) that still permitted soldiers to vote. Benton's interest in the Civil War soldier vote was "not only . . . historic" but also "sentimental." "I was a private in a Vermont regiment," he wrote fondly, "and cast my first vote for Lincoln in 1864."[10]

A few states, including Nevada, New Jersey, New York and Rhode Island, enfranchised servicemen during the Spanish-American War.[11] Soldiers from at least two states voted in the elections of 1916 from their outposts along the Mexican-American border.[12] The pace of enacting legislation increased during World War I. By 1918, eighteen states had adopted laws specifically permitting soldiers to vote away from home. Most of these absentee voting laws for the military were enacted in 1916 or 1917. A number of states at this time also had general absentee voting measures, which meant that twenty-eight states permitted soldiers to vote away from home during World War I.[13]

Collecting the soldiers' votes during World War I proved a difficult undertaking. Gen. John J. Pershing claimed that the soldiers could not vote overseas "without seriously interfering with the military efficiency of our fighting forces." In 1918, the *New York Times* reported that the War Department was preparing "a formal recommendation against any attempt to record the soldier vote in France for elections held during the war" because "no practical method of taking votes of members of the expeditionary forces could be devised." The Associated Press also found that New York soldiers displayed "little interest" in elections during the war.[14]

By the 1940s, nearly every state had an absentee-balloting measure, but no one had yet devised an effective way to collect the votes of American servicemen who were serving throughout the world. Writing in 1945, one political scientist captured the scene:

> Judging from pressure-group activities, congressional hearings, and the general political demands of the public, the people by 1942 expected service personnel to be given the privilege of voting. The magnitude of the problem of placing a ballot in the hands of every qualified elector in the service seemed astronomical. By November, 1942, American service personnel had spread to the four corners of the earth. Not to mention the uncertainty of the overseas mails, it appeared a physical impossibility to have several million men and women vote through a maze of forty-five (in 1942) absentee-voters' laws when these persons were scattered among all allied fronts.

Compounding these difficulties, each state had its own requirements for marking and collecting ballots, men of various states were mixed into single military units, state laws varied widely as to in which elections (state, local, federal, primaries, etc.) soldiers could vote, and it would be nearly impossible for each state to send commissioners to visit every military installation, ship, and encampment to collect the ballots of their state's soldiers.[15]

To overcome these obstacles, Congress enacted a law on September 16, 1942, allowing all voters who were serving in the U.S. military to request a "war ballot" that would be prepared by each state's secretary of state. The law also exempted voters in the field from state poll taxes. Southern Democrats opposed the measure because of its potential to broaden the franchise. Calling it "a monstrosity, shoved through in the name of the American soldier, who did not ask for it," Rep. John Rankin of Mississippi declared: "It is part of a long-range communistic program to change our way of life and to take the control out of the hands of the white Americans in the various states and turn them over to certain irresponsible elements." Civil rights activists, by contrast, saw the soldier vote as an opportunity to fulfill the Thirteenth, Fourteenth, and Fifteenth Amendments. Edgar G. Brown, the director of the National Negro Council, noted on September 2, 1942, that "the 400,000 Negro soldiers from poll-tax states will have an opportunity to participate for the first time . . . and have a vote in the democracy for which they are fighting and dying."[16]

Despite this optimism, the election results, according to one contemporary account, "were extremely disappointing." Only 137,686 soldiers applied for federal "war ballots" and of that number, only 28,051 sent their ballots home in time to be counted in the election of 1942. The Census Bureau attributed the low voter turnout to four things: first, that the law was passed within two months of the election, which made it too difficult for some states to comply with the act; second, that some soldiers might have bypassed the federal law and voted under their states' provisions; third, that it was an off-year election and that general elections in the South generally drew little enthusiasm (it was the primary that counted most); and fourth, that the soldiers did not have enough time to request and then return their ballots. Thus, only one-half of 1 percent of America's 5.5 million soldiers and sailors voted under Congress's election law of 1942.[17]

Pressure began to mount to make sure that men and women in the service would be given the right to vote in the presidential election of 1944. Bills were introduced in both houses of Congress in 1943 to streamline the voting process by creating a bipartisan War Ballot Commission to distribute ballots. Under these proposals, soldiers would no longer be required to request a ballot, and state-required poll taxes would continue to be set aside. In truth, President Franklin D. Roosevelt had come to believe that the soldier vote was essential to him winning an unprecedented fourth term. Voters at home were evenly divided. "If the Presidential election were held at this time," reported George Gallup in December 1943, "the outcome would, therefore, be determined by the soldier vote." But Roosevelt had reason to feel confident. A Gallup Poll revealed that he would win more than 60 percent of the soldiers' votes.[18]

Northern Democrats generally supported the legislation on the basis that citizen-soldiers deserved the rights of democracy. "Millions of our fellow-citizens have entered the armed forces and are engaged throughout the world in the bitter struggle to defend the institutions of democracy," argued Sen. Theodore Francis Green, a Rhode Island Democrat. Republicans and southern Democrats, by contrast, opposed the measures because they would violate states' rights and enfranchise black soldiers. Some opponents claimed that such proposals were an unconstitutional grasp of federal power over the state-centered right of suffrage; others countered that expansive federal power like this was constitutional as a war measure. In the House, Democrat John Rankin of Mississippi called the bill "just the beginning of a scheme to abolish state governments." Unlike during the Civil War, Republicans were now willing to join with southern Democrats to disfranchise the soldiers in order to win elections. "Even if the President makes an issue of Republican opposition to the federal ballot," declared Sen. Robert Taft of Ohio, "the votes on that issue are negligible compared to the number of real votes the President will get if the federal ballot is adopted."[19]

Supporters of the bill argued that the government owed it to the soldiers since most World War II soldiers had been conscripted into the army. They were citizens who had been forced to leave "their desks, homes, farms, factories, and businesses to answer the call to arms." The government therefore was obligated "to create an effective machinery to protect those in the armed forces from the loss of their important political right of voting, which has been taken away from them by the Congress, either as a result of their having been drafted or of the acceptance of their voluntary service." Stated one of the Senate bill's sponsors: "The Federal Government has, by drafting these men, taken away from them the opportunity of complying with the registration laws of the states. Therefore, they have disenfranchised these soldiers and sailors. . . . We are simply trying to restore to them a right which we have taken away."[20]

Republican opponents of the law now borrowed the excuses that the Democratic Party had offered in the 1860s. Sen. Styles Bridges of New Hampshire claimed that soldiers could become the victims of coercion:

Any bill which is passed by the Senate with my vote must have very definite safeguards against the young men and women of our armed forces being intimidated to vote for their Commander-in-Chief. By "intimidation," I mean physical intimidation, or intimidation by propaganda spread by the O.W.I.

[Office of War Information], or any other agency. We must be convinced that they who are giving so freely of their lives will not be herded to the polls, so to speak, in the manner used by Boss Hague or Boss Kelly.

Still others claimed that the soldiers did not want the ballot, that they would be corrupted by politics, or that they were uninformed on the issues. Sen. Hugh A. Butler of Nebraska claimed that the soldiers were more interested "in getting a sufficient amount of supplies to finish the war quickly and then to get home and vote" than to be given the ballot in the field. Georgia Democrat John S. Gibson even suggested that the soldiers would rather give up their right to vote than risk opening up the door to election frauds.[21]

In many ways, the debate over permitting soldiers to vote in the 1940s was a continuation of debates over civil rights and racial equality that had begun in the 1860s. One Tennessee Democrat in the House of Representatives accused a New York congressman of using the proposed legislation "to bring about social equality of the races in the South. . . . This is the most important battle that has been made since the Civil War for the preservation of states' rights in the South. . . . We do not intend to let this administration tell us to change our racial problem in the South." If they did not get their way, several southern Democrats even threatened to bolt the party and form a third party so that the presidential election would be thrown into the House.[22]

As the debate intensified, Roosevelt urged the passage of the legislation in a message to Congress on January 25, 1944. The president called for stronger federal control over the election process, saying that state-centered approaches to absentee voting were "a fraud on the soldiers and sailors now training and fighting for us and our sacred rights." One historian describes the greeting Roosevelt's message received in Congress:

Republicans in the House booed as they heard Roosevelt's message read into the record and hooted when they heard him describe himself as an "interested citizen." In the Senate, Rufus Holman (R-OR) suggested that Roosevelt withdraw as a candidate so that the debate on the bill could come to an end. . . . "It is only natural," said [Ohio senator Robert A.] Taft, "that men who have the responsibilities which they have are convinced that their continuance in office is essential to the welfare of the country."

Ultimately, Roosevelt was not able to get the bill that he wanted. States' rights Democrats joined with Republicans to defeat the proposals that would have given more power over the franchise to the federal government. Instead, a conference committee of both houses passed a compromise bill in March 1944 that permitted soldiers to vote either the federal "war ballot" or under the state absentee voting laws. Roosevelt refused to sign the law. On March 31, 1944, he sent a message to Congress saying that he would permit the bill "to become law without my signature. The bill is, in my judgment, wholly inadequate to assure to servicemen and women as far as is practically feasible the same opportunity which they would have to vote if they were at home." Rather than act decisively by enacting strong federal controls over the election process, Roosevelt lamented that the bill "might be fairly called a standing invitation to the several States to make it practicable for their citizens to vote."[23]

Despite this legislative defeat, Roosevelt won an unprecedented fourth term in the election of 1944. The military vote made up 5.6 percent of the total votes cast. Almost 4.5 million servicemen and servicewomen requested ballots. The states deemed about 100,000 of these requests as invalid and sent out 4.2 million ballots to the field (meaning that nearly 200,000 requests went unfulfilled). Of those 4.2 million ballots, only 2.8 million were returned to the states (the states then rejected about 100,000 of the ballots). Thus, out of the approximately 9 million eligible voters in the field, about 30 percent successfully voted.[24]

The battle over enfranchising members of the armed forces during World War II ignited a brief interest in the soldier vote of the Civil War. Several scholars penned accounts that were sympathetic to the Republican cause of enfranchising soldiers during the Civil War. The October 1944 issue of *New York History* carried two articles on the subject. Oscar O. Winther argued that voting in the field was "managed calmly and expeditiously" and that the election of 1864 was not a controlled "bayonet vote." William M. Burcher offered a narrative history of soldier suffrage in New York from the American Revolution to World War II, concluding that soldiers in 1944 would likely receive ample opportunity to vote under New York's statute (New York's governor, Thomas E. Dewey, the Republican nominee for president, had opted not to permit soldiers and sailors from New York to use the "federal ballot" that had been enacted by Congress earlier that year). And Lynwood G. Downs's 1945 narrative of Minnesota's political struggle to enfranchise the troops concluded that "Minnesota has reason to be proud of its record in granting to its volunteers in the Civil War the right of suffrage."[25]

Writing as a graduate student in 1944, Frank L. Klement took the opposite position, describing Civil War–era Republican efforts to enfranchise Wisconsin troops as a brazenly partisan scheme to win elections. "In control of the state legislature, the Republican Party was in a position to pull rabbits out of the hat if need be," wrote Klement. "The party politicians visualized a controlled soldiers' vote . . . as a medium which would enable Republicanism to keep the stage and the state's governmental machinery. If soldiers were allowed to vote in the field, under the supervision of their Republican regimental officers . . . it would be possible to develop a vote reserve that could save the day for straggling administration candidates."[26]

Wisconsin Democrats, in Klement's account, "were political realists" who "viewed Republican strategy as the product of selfishness," but they were unable to defeat the Republican majorities and lost the debate in both houses of the legislature by strict party lines. Within weeks, the "Republican experiment proved its worth." In November 1862, the votes of soldiers prevented the Democratic Party from winning control of the state house and "reversed the verdict in countless local contests." Following the election, Republicans worked hard to keep Democrats from receiving commissions in the army so that only Republicans would oversee future elections. To fortify their strength even further, the Republicans amended the law after the 1862 election to allow soldiers to vote in elections for state judges—this, while the state supreme court was hearing a case on the validity of the law that had emerged out of the 1862 elections. The members of the supreme court—some of whom were up for reelection—could not overcome their partisan impulses, and they upheld the law despite its questionable constitutional validity. "It would have been political suicide for Chief Justice [Luther S.] Dixon to betray the party which had adopted him and to invalidate the soldiers' vote act," wrote Klement. The "controlled soldiers' vote scheme" again "paid dividends" for the Republicans in 1863 as "the soldiers' votes crushed Democratic hopes and reversed the decision of the Wisconsin citizenry." According to Klement, permitting soldiers to vote was a "bit of political magic" that saved the Republican Party in Wisconsin during its "darkest hours."[27] Frank Klement's first published scholarly article—a harsh and cynical critique of the Republican Party during the Civil War—portended the revisionist scholarship that would become his legacy over the next forty years.[28]

Finally, in "Voters in Blue: The Citizen Soldiers of the Civil War," T. Harry Williams painted a picture of the Union army as an ideological entity that constantly debated political and military issues. "These men were politicians and voters in civilian life," wrote Williams, "and they did not shed their political ideas or ambitions when they donned a uniform." Such a vigorously democratic army frequently seemed to verge on mutiny. "Worse than that, there seemed at times a possibility that the citizen army would become so entangled in partisanship and so impressed with the correctness of its political notions that it would seek to impose its will upon the country by force or threat of force, thus subverting democratic government." Williams concluded by suggesting that some Republicans "feared a revolutionary movement to overthrow their power, particularly one headed by the army," but no such threat ever materialized.[29]

Published in the *Mississippi Valley Historical Review* in 1944, Williams's interpretation was forty years ahead of its time. Reid Mitchell accurately notes that scholars of the World War II generation—most notably Bell Irvin Wiley—generally eschewed ideology and politics in their analyses of Civil War soldiers' motivation for enlisting and fighting. "It seems to be the case that scholarship on the soldier can be divided into that written by the World War II generation and that by the Vietnam War generation," writes Mitchell.[30] Williams's essay—written amid the political debate over enfranchising American troops during World War II—was an exception to this generation of scholarship. More importantly, Williams pointed in the direction that Civil War scholarship would begin to turn in the 1980s and 1990s. In short, it took the historical profession a half century to catch up.

THE SOLDIER VOTE IN THE TWENTY-FIRST CENTURY

Today, absentee voting is an ordinary part of the electoral process in the United States. In fact, at least one state requires all votes to be cast by mail.[31] As a consequence, most twenty-first-century Americans tend not to think much about the "army vote." It is generally assumed that any soldier, sailor, marine, or member of the Air Force or Coast Guard can vote if he or she so desires.

But it is not always easy for army personnel to get their ballots counted at home. Prior to the presidential election of 2000, a bipartisan majority in the House of Representatives passed a bill that would have permitted soldiers to vote at army bases, but President Bill Clinton urged the Democratic leadership in the Senate not to act quickly on the measure. "It may have been a productive partisan political maneuver, but it was terrible policy when Senate Democratic Leader Tom Daschle tried to block passage of a bill designed to accommodate voting by the U.S. military," opined the *Florida Times Union* (Jacksonville). "Three weeks before the Nov. 7 election, [the] bill sailed through the House with widespread, bipartisan support. But now the Clinton administration is asking Senate Democrats to oppose the bill—and Daschle has put a 'hold' on it, a tactic designed to kill it."[32] Such a move, suggested one conservative columnist in the *Wall Street Journal*, demonstrated that the Democrats were "hostile to the rights of soldiers to vote."[33]

Military votes were part of the controversy in the presidential election of 2000. Florida law required military votes to have a military or foreign postmark to "be considered valid." The state required the postmarks to ensure that the ballots had not been cast after election day. For some reason—and without the knowledge of the servicemen and servicewomen—the military's mail service had not placed a postmark on a number of absentee ballots. They therefore could not be counted under Florida law.[34]

During the recount debacle, the Democratic candidate for president, Vice President Al Gore, sent lawyers to Florida to challenge the military ballots in court in an attempt to have them thrown out. Ironically, the controversy saw each party flip-flop on its traditional political and constitutional positions. The Republicans, who typically advocate strict construction of the Constitution and adherence to the text of the law, called for the ballots to be counted regardless of their deficiencies. Meanwhile, the Democrats, who typically support a broadening of the franchise and the extension of political and civil rights, asked the courts to throw out the ballots.

Republicans capitalized on the situation and used it to criticize Democrats as hostile to the troops. "The vice president's lawyers have gone to war, in my judgment, against the men and women who serve in our armed forces," declared one Montana Republican. "The man who would be their commander in chief is fighting to take away the votes from the people he would command."[35] Within the context of the contested election of 2000, Bill Clinton's opposition to permitting the troops to vote at military bases appeared to some as a conspiracy to disenfranchise the troops. The *Florida Times Union* noted that President Clinton's and Senator Daschle's move to block the bill that would have permitted soldiers to vote at military bases "could be a coincidence or it might be part of a larger Democratic effort to suppress the military vote in the aftermath of an election in which ballots cast by service personnel probably cost them the presidency." Vice President Gore's lawyers were attempting to disqualify military ballots in Florida based "on the most obscure of technicalities," while, "paradoxically, their activists in the streets are chanting slogans about counting all votes and making every vote count." The editors concluded: "The Democrats' risky scheme, in other words, is to win this election by disqualifying military votes and then not to make it any easier for members of the armed service to vote in the future."[36]

Debate over what to do with the military ballots engulfed certain parts of the nation. The *Virginian-Pilot* (Norfolk), which circulates in a heavily military area, carried a series of letters to the editor on the subject. Several writers criticized the paper for remaining "silent" while "the Gore-at-any-cost power brokers targeted military absentee ballots, systematically disenfranchising our military personnel." Meanwhile, a Vietnam veteran claimed to be "a bit miffed at Bush Inc. supporters wrapping themselves in the flag in a high state of dudgeon over the Democrats' initial rejection of Florida absentee military ballots lacking postmarks, claiming that the Democrats are anti-military." Florida law, this writer pointed out, "specifically states that absentee ballots must be postmarked, and there is no exception for military ballots." As such, the Democratic Party ought not to be blamed if they were thrown out.[37]

Still, this controversy placed many Democrats on the defensive. Syndicated columnist Molly Ivins, writing as "an admittedly partisan Democrat," criticized her own party for "pulling such revolting maneuvers as signing onto a lawsuit to throw out military ballots, whilst publicly maintaining that every vote should count."[38] In December 2000, the Florida Supreme Court and a federal appeals court held that the ballots could count. Vice President Gore's lawyers contemplated appealing the decision to the U.S. Supreme Court.[39] "Ultimately," wrote legal scholar Alan M. Dershowitz, "bipartisan sympathy, led by Sen. Bob Dole and Sen. Joseph Lieberman [the Democratic candidate for vice president], for members of the military prevented any serious challenge to these ballots from taking place."[40]

Military votes have continued to be an issue since the election of 2000. Servicemen and servicewomen have been able to vote under the Uniformed and Overseas Citizens Absentee Voting Act of 1986, but voter turnout under this act has generally been quite low. Only 22 percent of the nearly 2.6 million eligible military voters voted in the off-year elections of 2006, compared to 41 percent of the voting-age population at home. In the presidential election of 2008, 30 percent of military voters cast a vote, compared to 62 percent at home.[41]

In the wake of such appallingly low numbers, lawmakers in Washington moved to find better ways to ensure that those on the front lines would be able to exercise the full rights of citizenship. In 2009, Congress passed—with overwhelmingly bipartisan support—the Military and Overseas Voter Empowerment Act (MOVE Act). The law requires states to send absentee ballots to servicemen and servicewomen at least forty-five days before a federal election, and it requires the states to provide electronic delivery of blank absentee ballots. The MOVE Act also requires the Department of Defense to establish voter assistance offices on all military bases and to use expedited mail when returning military ballots. These provisions are intended to ensure that military voters have ample time to request, receive, and return absentee ballots. Sen. Charles Schumer (D-NY), one of the authors of the law, stated that the MOVE Act would "bring[ ] overseas voting into the 21st century."[42]

Despite these steps forward, failure on the part of several states and the Department of Justice to implement the provisions of the law led to low voter turnout among the armed services in the 2010 off-year election. One study of nearly 2 million military voters from twenty-four states found that only 4.6 percent were able to request, receive, and return their ballots in time to be counted in the election. In this sample of 2 million military voters, 310,625 requested a ballot, 95,535 returned their ballot (a 30.8 percent return rate), and 5,648 were rejected (5.9 percent). Thus, only 89,887 of some 2 million eligible voters actually voted in the election.[43]

Advocates for reforming the absentee balloting process today describe the low voter turnout among the troops in much the same way as Republicans did in the 1860s:

Military voters have long been disenfranchised—both at the state and federal level—by a voting process that fails to recognize the unique challenges created by a military voter's transitory existence or the delays associated with delivering an absentee ballot to a war zone halfway around the world. Given these soldiers' daily sacrifices and their willingness to defend this nation's freedom, it is incumbent on Americans to remedy this problem and provide U.S. soldiers with the same rights they are being asked to protect.

Unfortunately, most Americans today do not realize that so many men and women in the service are practically disenfranchised by the friction and abrasion of war and by states that do not send out ballots in time to be cast. Until something changes to simplify the voting process, and to ensure that members of the armed forces are given ample time to request, receive, fill out, and return their ballots, "military personnel will continue to be the largest group of disenfranchised voters in the United States."[44]

APPENDIX

In *The March to the Sea and Beyond,* Joseph T. Glatthaar states that only 6.5 percent of the Union soldiers chose to reenlist.[1] Glatthaar appears to have calculated this statistic by multiplying the total number of men who reenlisted between November 1863 and November 1864 (136,507) by 100 and dividing that number by the total number of men who enlisted under Lincoln's calls for troops from April 1861 to April 1864 (2,100,951). Glatthaar does not account for the fact that many of these men would have been ineligible to reenlist in 1863–64 (such as the men who enlisted for three months after Lincoln's April 1861 call for troops). Nor does he account for men who had died or been discharged.

In *For Cause and Comrades,* by contrast, James M. McPherson states that "136,000 veterans reenlisted—more than half of those whose terms expired in 1864." What caused so many men to reenlist? "The persistence of ideological convictions and a determination to finish the job were crucial factors for many soldiers," writes McPherson. "Unit pride and loyalty" also "prompted many three-year veterans in Union regiments to reenlist in 1864."[2] The problem with McPherson's calculation is that he underestimates the number of soldiers who were eligible to reenlist. He refers to those "whose terms expired in 1864"—but more than just these soldiers were eligible. The *Final Report of the Provost Marshal General* (1866) lays out the criteria for who was eligible to reenlist: "three-years men still in service, having less than one year longer to serve, and . . . men enlisted for nine (9) months or less, who had less than three (3) months to serve."[3] McPherson's calculation thus appears to exclude all men whose terms of service expired in 1863 and 1865, although his footnotes do not reveal his sources nor exactly how he determined the "more than half" figure.

The actual number is significantly less than McPherson's estimate and probably about double Glatthaar's. The *Annual Report of the Secretary of War* (1865) states that 136,507 soldiers reenlisted between November 1, 1863, and November 1, 1864.[4] As previously stated, soldiers who had enlisted for three years and had one year or less remaining in their enlistment were eligible to reenlist, as were soldiers who had enlisted for nine months or less and who had less than three months remaining in their enlistment. The following table, which is derived from page 160 of part 1 of the *Final Report of the Provost Marshal General* (1866), details how many soldiers were called into the service and which ones were eligible for reenlistment between November 1, 1863, and November 1, 1864.

DATE OF CALL OR PROCLAMATION	NUMBER CALLED FOR	PERIOD OF SERVICE	TOTAL NUMBER OBTAINED	ELIGIBLE TO REENLIST?
April 15, 1861	75,000	3 months	93,326	No
May/July 1861	582,748	3 years	714,231	Yes
May/June 1862	N/A	3 months	15,007	No
July 2, 1862	300,000	3 years	431,958	Yes
August 4, 1862	300,000	9 months	87,588	No
June 15, 1863	100,000	6 months	16,361	Yes
Oct. 1863/Feb. 1864	500,000	3 years	374,807	No
March 14, 1864	200,000	3 years	284,021	No
April 23, 1864	85,000	100 days	83,652	No
July 18, 1864	500,000	1, 2, or 3 years	384,882	No
December 19, 1864	300,000	1, 2, or 3 years	204,568	No
Totals:	2,942,748	—	2,690,401	—

While the *Final Report* states that the May and July 1861 calls were for three-years' men, thirty-eight New York regiments and a handful of regiments from other states mustered in for two years. These regiments would not have been eligible to reenlist between November 1863 and November 1864. In order to account for these regiments, I deduct 50,000 from the 714,231 men obtained during the summer 1861 calls. Thus, approximately 1,112,550 enlisted men would have been eligible to reenlist between November 1863 and November 1864, provided they were alive and had not deserted or been discharged. Determining the number of men who had died or been discharged requires a few additional statistics and calculations.

Up through the April 1864 call for troops, 1,905,030 men had enlisted for some duration. (This number excludes 93,326 who enlisted under Lincoln's April 1861 call for 75,000 troops as well as the three-months' men who enlisted under the calls of May and June 1862, and the nine-months' men who enlisted under the August 1862 call.)

By July 1864, 175,879 Union soldiers had died in battle or as a result of disease.[5] According to the Provost Marshal General's *Final Report,* Union volunteers were discharged for disability at a rate of 78.81 per 1,000.[6] Thus, of the 1,112,550 volunteers who were eligible to reenlist, approximately 87,680 would have been discharged for disease or disability.

Determining an estimate of the number of deaths among those who were eligible to reenlist can be accomplished by simple apportionment:

$$\frac{1,112,550}{1,905,030} = \frac{x}{175,879} \quad x = 102,715 \text{ deaths}$$

The estimated number of soldiers who died (102,715) and were discharged (87,680) must be deducted from the number who were eligible to reenlist (1,112,550). This leaves 922,155 soldiers who were alive and eligible to reenlist between November 1, 1863, and November 1, 1864. Deserters have not been excluded from this estimation since they presumably demonstrated their views about reenlistment with their feet.

The final calculation determines an estimated reenlistment rate:

$$\frac{136,507}{922,155} = \frac{x}{100} \quad x = 14.8\%$$

TABLES

TABLE 1. Estimated voter turnout for the presidential election in a sample of Union regiments

Total votes cast for Lincoln in sample	6,510
Total votes cast for McClellan in sample	2,629
Total votes in sample	9,139
Total present Nov. 8	13,849
Estimated eligible voters (80.8%)	11,484
Estimated voter turnout (%)	79.6
% of eligible soldiers who voted for Lincoln	56.7
% of eligible soldiers who voted for McClellan	22.9

EXPLANATION OF METHODOLOGY BEHIND TABLE 1

Table 1 contains statistics for all of the regiments for which I could determine the total votes cast as well as the total number of men present on election day. The regiments included in this sample are the 16th Maine Volunteers; the 9th, 11th, and 12th New Hampshire Volunteers; the 57th, 69th, 84th, 88th, 91st, 97th, 99th, 100th, 107th, 110th, 116th, 118th, 140th, 150th, 190th, 203rd, 208th, 209th, and 211th Pennsylvania Volunteers; and the 6th, 11th, 17th, 20th, 23rd, 30th, 32nd, 37th, 42nd, and 43rd Wisconsin Volunteers. These regiments gave a slightly lower percentage of their vote to Lincoln (71 percent) compared with the average for the Union army as a whole (78 percent).

I used statistics regarding the age of Union troops from Benjamin A. Gould, *Investigations in the Military and Anthropological Statistics of American Soldiers* (New York: Hurd and Houghton, 1869), page 87, to estimate the number of soldiers who were old enough to vote in November 1864. In a sample of soldiers from the army, Gould estimates the age breakdown in the Union army in July 1864 as follows:

16 to 19 years old	116,440
20 years old	80,590
21 and older	681,970

In order to determine how many men were of voting age on election day in 1864 (roughly eighteen weeks after the sample), I took the total number of 20-year-olds (80,590) and multiplied it by .35 (to account for the time between the sample and the election) and added that number (28,207) to the total of men who were already 21 (681,970), giving me an estimated 710,177 men who were of voting age in November 1864. I divided that number by the total number of men present in Gould's sample (879,000) to estimate that 80.8 percent of the men were eligible voters.

Six of the regiments in the sample produced a voter turnout of more than 100 percent (the 140th, 208th, and 211th Pennsylvania, the 11th New Hampshire, and the 20th and 32nd Wisconsin), ranging from 104 to 115 percent. I thus adjusted the number of eligible voters in each of those regiments to bring the voter turnout in all six regiments down to 96 percent, which was the voter turnout in the next highest regiment (the 209th Pennsylvania).

TABLE 2. Comparison of soldiers' votes in the presidential and other 1864 elections (% of increase in parentheses)

	R-HOME	R-ARMY	R-TOTAL	D-HOME	D-ARMY	D-TOTAL
Ohio election for secretary of state						
Oct. 1864	204,459	32,751	237,210	177,840	4,599	182,439
Nov. 1864 pres. election	224,008 (9.6)	41,646 (27.2)	265,654 (12.0)	195,811 (10.1)	9,788 (112.8)	205,599 (12.7)
Ohio congressional elections						
Oct. 1864	210,708	28,878	239,586	171,855	6,981	178,836
Nov. 1864 pres. election	224,008 (6.3)	41,646 (44.2)	265,654 (10.9)	195,811 (13.9)	9,788 (40.2)	205,599 (15.0)

TABLE 2 *(continued)*

	R-HOME	R-ARMY	R-TOTAL	D-HOME	D-ARMY	D-TOTAL
		Pennsylvania congressional elections				
Oct. 1864	247,423	17,888	265,311	244,919	5,232	250,151
Nov. 1864 pres. election	269,679 (9.0)	26,712 (49.3)	296,391 (11.7)	263,967 (7.8)	12,349 (136.0)	276,316 (10.5)
		Maine gubernatorial elections				
Sept. 1864	62,529	3,054	65,583	46,287	116	46,403
Nov. 1864 pres. election	63,631 (1.8)	4,174 (36.7)	67,805 (3.4)	46,250 (-0.1)	828 (613.8)	47,078 (1.5)
		Maine congressional elections				
Sept. 1864	62,212	3,099	65,311	46,417	72	46,489
Nov. 1864 pres. election	63,631 (2.3)	4,174 (34.7)	67,805 (3.8)	46,250 (-0.4)	828 (1050.0)	47,078 (1.3)
		Maryland constitutional referendum (two days of voting in October)				
Oct. 1864	27,541	2,633	30,174	29,536	263	29,799
Nov. 1864 pres. election	37,353 (35.6)	2,800 (6.3)	40,153 (33.1)	32,418 (9.8)	321 (22.1)	32,739 (9.9)
		Total of all state elections in this sample compared to the presidential election				
State & cong.	814,872	88,303	903,175	716,854	17,263	734,117
Sum of votes in pres. election from previous six examples	882,310 (8.3)	121,152 (37.2)	1,003,462 (11.1)	780,507 (8.9)	33,902 (96.4)	814,409 (10.9)

Note: After several years of searching, I have been unable to find official election returns from the 1864 congressional elections in Pennsylvania. The *Tribune Almanac and Political Register for 1865* lists the soldier vote as 7,635 Republican and 2,500 Democrat, but it does not include every congressional district. Benton's *Voting in the Field* puts the number at 17,888 Republican and 12,656 Democrat. While the *Tribune Almanac* is generally the most reliable source for election statistics in the nineteenth century, in this instance I believe it underestimates the actual vote. The other election returns in this table are taken from official reports published by each respective state.

TABLE 3. Maine regiments in the elections of 1864

REGIMENT	GUB. ELECTION, SEPT. 1864		PRES. ELECTION, NOV. 1864	
	Republican	Democrat	Lincoln	McClellan
1st Infantry, Veterans	—	—	155	39
8th Infantry	133	3	179	15
9th Infantry	173	1	293	47
12th Infantry	122	6	108	26
13th Infantry	85	5	190	20
14th Infantry	26	0	44	13
15th Infantry	40	4	130	53
16th Infantry	114	1	152	61
17th Infantry	200	2	201	47
19th Infantry	107	0	129	31
20th Infantry	139	2	138	13
29th Infantry	138	3	175	40
30th Infantry	156	7	184	26
31st Infantry	56	6	108	20
32nd Infantry	54	0	68	31
1st Battery	—	—	32	31
2nd Battery	21	0	90	14
3rd Battery	73	4	77	5
4th Battery	46	11	59	34
5th Battery	33	0	36	8
6th Battery	59	0	58	3
7th Battery	60	0	78	90
1st Cavalry	243	7	289	46
2nd Cavalry	277	2	273	1
Detachment at Cavalry Depot	54	8	59	8
1st Cavalry at Hospital	65	2	65	2
1st Heavy Artillery	132	5	149	23
2nd Battalion of Heavy Artillery	57	0	71	0
Base Hospital	36	3	44	0
Sickles Hospital	13	1	19	3
Camp Distribution	37	2	106	25

TABLE 3 *(continued)*

REGIMENT	GUB. ELECTION, SEPT. 1864		PRES. ELECTION, NOV. 1864	
	Republican	Democrat	Lincoln	McClellan
Campbell Hospital	14	1	24	5
Detachment at New Orleans	51	1	52	1
2nd and 5th Corps Hospital	73	3	78	3
Maine Agency in D.C.	64	5	93	7
Lincoln Hospital	11	0	35	9
City Point Hospital	29	6	33	7
Camp Stoneman	13	2	—	—
Ft. Washington	50	13	—	—
Soldiers at Annapolis	—	—	32	2
Co. A, Coast Guard	—	—	47	17
Detach at Pt. Lookout	—	—	21	2
Total	3,054	116	4,174	828

Note: This table illustrates that, for the most part, the same soldiers were given the opportunity to vote in both the state and national elections. The increased voter turnout, therefore, cannot be explained by an increased opportunity of soldiers to vote in November.

TABLE 4. Comparison of soldiers' votes in congressional elections held on the same day as the presidential election (% of increase in parentheses)

	R-HOME	R-ARMY	R-TOTAL	D-HOME	D-ARMY	D-TOTAL
	Iowa congressional election					
Cong. election	72,263	16,410	88,673	47,883	1,463	49,346
Pres. election	71,765	17,310	89,075	47,675	1,921	49,596
	(-0.7)	(5.5)	(0.5)	(-0.4)	(31.3)	(0.5)
	Wisconsin congressional election					
Cong. election	57,492	9,125	66,617	55,941	1,709	57,650
Pres. election	68,216	11,372	79,588	62,590	2,428	65,018
	(18.7)	(24.6)	(19.5)	(11.9)	(42.1)	(12.8)

TABLE 5. Soldier vote in Michigan's November 8, 1864, elections

	R-HOME	R-ARMY	R-TOTAL	D-HOME	D-ARMY	D-TOTAL
Congressional	82,145	8,907	91,052	70,839	1,945	72,784
Gubernatorial	81,744	9,612	91,356	71,301	2,992	74,293
Presidential	75,950	9,402	85,352	64,411	2,959	67,370

Note: For the sake of thoroughness, Michigan's gubernatorial, congressional, and presidential election statistics are included here. In the presidential election, seventeen counties did not return their ballot results in time and were therefore not counted in the election, which explains the low turnout in the "home vote" in that election. Nevertheless, these elections show a marked increase in the soldier vote from the congressional election to the gubernatorial and presidential elections, signifying that the soldiers were more willing to support Democrats running for the presidency and other executive offices than for other positions.

SOURCES FOR TABLES

Annual Report of the Secretary of State to the Governor of the State of Ohio, for the Year 1864. Columbus: Richard Nevins, 1865.

Dubin, Michael J. *United States Congressional Elections, 1788–1997: The Official Results of the Elections of the 1st through 105th Congresses.* Jefferson, N.C.: McFarland, 1998.

Lord, William Blair, and Henry M. Parkhurst, eds. *The Debates of the Constitutional Convention of the State of Maryland.* 3 vols. Annapolis: Richard P. Bayly, 1864, 3:1925–26.

Maine Legislative Manual, 1865. Augusta: Stevens and Sayward, 1865.

Message of the Governor of Wisconsin, Together with the Annual Reports, of the Officers of the State, for the Year, A.D. 1865. Madison, William J. Park, 1866.

O.R. ser. 1, vol. 42, pt. 3, pp. 560–78.

RG-19, Records of the Department of Military and Veterans Affairs (Morning Reports). Pennsylvania State Archives, Harrisburg.

RG 94, Records of the Adjutant General's Office. Entry 115 (Book Records of Volunteer Union Organizations, Morning Reports). National Archives and Records Administration, Washington, D.C.

Tribune Almanac and Political Register for 1865. New York: Tribune Association, 1865.

NOTES

ABBREVIATIONS

CCHS   Chester County Historical Society, West Chester, Pa.

CG   *Congressional Globe.*

CMSR   Compiled Military Service Records, RG 94, Records of the Adjutant General's Office, National Archives and Records Administration, Washington, D.C.

Court-Martial Case file   General Court-Martial Case Files, Record Group 153, Records of the Office of the Judge Advocate General (Army), National Archives and Records Administration, Washington, D.C. (Each case file includes an alphanumeric case number.)

CWH   *Civil War History.*

CWL   Roy P. Basler et al., eds., *The Collected Works of Abraham Lincoln.* 9 vols. New Brunswick, N.J.: Rutgers University Press, 1953–55.

CWMC   Civil War Miscellaneous Collection, U.S. Army Military History Institute, Carlisle, Pa.

GLI   Gilder Lehrman Institute of American History, New York, N.Y.

HL   The Huntington, San Marino, Calif.

HSDC   Historical Society of Dauphin County, Harrisburg, Pa.

HSP   Historical Society of Pennsylvania, Philadelphia.

LC   Manuscript Division, Library of Congress, Washington, D.C.

Lincoln Papers   Abraham Lincoln Papers, Manuscript Division, Library of Congress, Washington, D.C. (American Memory).

MHI   U.S. Army Military History Institute, Carlisle, Pa. (excluding collections from the Civil War Miscellaneous Collection).

NARA   National Archives and Records Administration, Washington, D.C.

NYHS   New-York Historical Society, New York.

O.R.   *War of the Rebellion: A Compilation of the Official Records of the Union and Confederate Armies.* 128 vols. Washington, D.C.: Government Printing Office, 1880–1901.

PHMC   Pennsylvania State Archives, Harrisburg.

Stat.   *The Public Statutes at Large of the United States of America* (Each citation is preceded by a volume number and followed by page numbers.)

U.S.   *United States Reports* (Each citation is preceded by a volume number and followed by page numbers.)

INTRODUCTION

1. Abraham Lincoln to George G. Meade, March 9, 1864, in *CWL*, 7:233.

2. Allan Nevins, ed., *A Diary of Battle: The Personal Journals of Colonel Charles S. Wainwright* (New York: Harcourt, Brace and World, 1962), 328.

3. See, for example, William A. Wallace, *Reasons of Hon. Wm. A. Wallace, of Clearfield, For His Vote on Amendments to the Constitution* (n.p., 1864); and Alexander H. Bailey, *Allowing Soldiers to Vote. Mr. Bailey's Speech on the Bill to Extend the Elective Franchise to the Soldiers of this State in the Service of the United States. In Senate, April 1, 1863* (n.p., 1863).

4. Jean H. Baker, *Affairs of Party: The Political Culture of Northern Democrats in the Mid-Nineteenth Century* (Ithaca, N.Y.: Cornell University Press, 1983; repr., New York: Fordham University Press, 1998), 52; Harold M. Hyman, *A More Perfect Union: The Impact of the Civil War and Reconstruction on the Constitution* (New York: Knopf, 1973), 279; James M. McPherson, *For Cause and Comrades: Why Men Fought in the Civil War* (New York: Oxford University Press, 1997), 129; Jennifer L. Weber, *Copperheads: The Rise and Fall of Lincoln's Opponents in the North* (New York: Oxford University Press, 2006), 2. See also Frank J. Williams, *Judging Lincoln* (Carbondale: Southern Illinois University Press, 2002), chap. 6. Similar but more nuanced accounts have been told by political scientist Joseph Allen Frank and historians William C. Davis and Steven J. Ramold. See William C. Davis, *Lincoln's Men: How President Lincoln Became Father to an Army and a Nation* (New York: Free Press, 1999); Steven J. Ramold, *Across the Divide: Union Soldiers View the Northern Home Front* (New York: New York University Press, 2013), 143–67; and Joseph Allen Frank, *With Ballot and Bayonet: The Political Socialization of American Civil War Soldiers* (Athens: University of Georgia Press, 1998).

5. Chandra Manning, *What This Cruel War Was Over: Soldiers, Slavery, and the Civil War* (New York: Random House, 2007), 12–13, 43, 45. For a helpful recent analysis of the spectrum of Union soldiers' views toward emancipation, see Ramold, *Across the Divide*, 55–86.

6. James M. McPherson, *Ordeal by Fire*, 3 vols. (New York: McGraw-Hill, 1982), 2:457.

7. John Berry to Samuel L. M. Barlow, August 27, September 3, 11, 22, October 10, and November 4, 1864, all in Samuel L. M. Barlow Papers, HL.

8. By the midpoint of the war, most War Democrats had forsaken their party and joined with the Republicans—many even came to support the Republicans' policies of emancipation, conscription, and suspension of the writ of habeas corpus. See Joel H. Silbey, *A Respectable Minority: The Democratic Party in the Civil War Era, 1860–1868* (New York: W. W. Norton, 1977), 56–59, 92–93.

9. What I am calling the "moderate" wing of the Democratic Party could be likened to the faction that Joel H. Silbey calls the "Legitimists." See ibid., 96–99. These were Democrats who clung to the long-standing traditions of the Democratic Party as a positive force in American politics. They saw their party as the only national institution that could save the Union from the divisiveness of the sectional Republican Party. Moreover, they believed that the Union should be restored, but they believed that Lincoln's policies for restoring the Union were doing more to ensure disunion than to bring about reunion.

10. Upon visiting America in the 1830s, Alexis de Tocqueville observed a phenomenon that he called the "tyranny of the majority." Tocqueville claimed that the majority in a democratic society stifles political dissent to the point that members of the minority become too afraid to voice their opinions. "I know of no country where there is less independence of thought and real freedom of debate than in America," he wrote. According to Tocqueville, the majority shames the minority, forcing

it to "bend"—like a branch—until finally a person who expresses a dissenting position "withdraw[s] into silence as if he felt ashamed at having spoken the truth." Members of the minority thus feel ostracized and different; they hide in the shadows and refuse to make their opinions known. See Alexis de Tocqueville, *Democracy in America*, trans. Gerald E. Bevan (New York: Penguin, 2003), 297–99.

11. See *Revised Regulations for the Army of the United States, 1861* (Philadelphia: J. G. L. Brown, 1861), 500, 508.

12. Thomas W. Bennett to Laz Noble, February 7, 1863, Civil War Collection: Regimental Correspondence, reel 71, Indiana State Archives, Indianapolis. As will be seen in chapter 2, Colonel Bennett served on a board of examiners to rid disloyal officers from the army in the early months of 1863.

13. Alexander Keyssar, *The Right to Vote: The Contested History of Democracy in the United States* (New York: Basic, 2000), 104.

14. The connection between loyalty and Republican war aims was perhaps most clearly evident in Gen. Milo S. Hascall's General Orders No. 9, which he issued in Indiana in April 1863. Equating the government with the Lincoln administration, Hascall declared that "he who is factiously and actively opposed to the war policy of the Administration is as much opposed to his Government." Opposition to the Republican war policies of emancipation and conscription, in Hascall's view, was treason. See "General Orders No. 9," April 15, 1863, in *O.R.*, ser. 2, vol. 5, p. 485.

15. Durbin Ward to Samuel S. Cox, August 2, 1864, Samuel S. Cox Papers, Brown University.

16. Quoted in Dennis W. Brandt, *From Home Guards to Heroes: The 87th Pennsylvania and Its Civil War Community* (Columbia: University of Missouri Press, 2006), 167.

17. Arthur Bestor, "The American Civil War as a Constitutional Crisis," *American Historical Review* 69 (January 1964): 327–52.

18. On this point, see Gary W. Gallagher, *The Union War* (Cambridge: Harvard University Press, 2011).

19. Readers interested in learning more about Tom Lowry's Index Project should consult his website, www.theindexproject.com/.

20. Joseph T. Glatthaar, *Soldiering in the Army of Northern Virginia: A Statistical Portrait of the Troops Who Served under Robert E. Lee* (Chapel Hill: University of North Carolina Press, 2011), xiii–xiv.

21. Joseph T. Glatthaar, *The March to the Sea and Beyond: Sherman's Troops in the Savannah and Carolinas Campaigns* (New York: New York University Press, 1985), xiii.

CHAPTER ONE

1. Quoted in David Herbert Donald, *Lincoln* (New York: Simon and Schuster, 1995), 280.

2. H. A. Weaver to Andrew G. Curtin, April 16, 1861, and John M. Read to Curtin, April 17, 1861, both in RG 19 (Records of the Department of Military and Veterans Affairs), Series 19.29 (General Correspondence, 1793–1935), PHMC.

3. Fisher, diary entry for April 18, 1861, in Jonathan W. White, ed., *A Philadelphia Perspective: The Civil War Diary of Sidney George Fisher* (New York: Fordham University Press, 2007), 84.

4. Orville Hickman Browning to Abraham Lincoln, April 22, 1861, and James R. Doolittle to Lincoln, Lincoln Papers. See also Hickman to Lincoln, April 18, 1861, and the article on "Patriotism" in the Democratic *Harrisburg Patriot and Union*, April 24, 1861. James M. McPherson estimates that

40 percent of Union soldiers came from Democratic backgrounds and 10 percent came from Border States. See McPherson, *For Cause and Comrades: Why Men Fought in the Civil War* (New York: Oxford University Press, 1997), 121.

5. Adam I. P. Smith, *No Party Now: Politics in the Civil War North* (New York: Oxford University Press, 2006), chap. 2; Jonathan W. White, "Citizens and Soldiers: Party Competition and the Debate in Pennsylvania over Permitting Soldiers to Vote, 1861–64," *American Nineteenth Century History* 5 (Summer 2004): 49; Melinda Lawson, *Patriot Fires: Forging a New American Nationalism in the Civil War North* (Lawrence: University Press of Kansas, 2002), 79–82. On Lincoln's larger effort to forge a new, permanent Union Party, see Michael F. Holt, "Abraham Lincoln and the Politics of Union," in *Political Parties and American Political Development from the Age of Jackson to the Age of Lincoln* (Baton Rouge: Louisiana State University Press, 1992), 323–53.

6. Again, some had held this position from the very beginning, but this contingent within the party grew after the first year of the war, especially at times when Union military fortunes were at a low point. See Joel H. Silbey, *A Respectable Minority: The Democratic Party in the Civil War Era, 1860–1868* (New York: W. W. Norton, 1977), 99–101.

7. August Belmont to Samuel L. M. Barlow, August 24, 1862, Barlow Papers.

8. T. J. Barnett to Barlow, May 16 and 18, and July 2, 1863, Barlow Papers.

9. William M. Burcher, "A History of Soldier Voting in the State of New York," *New York History* 25 (October 1944): 459; Pennsylvania, *An Act to Enable the Militia or Volunteers of this State, When in the Military Service of the United States or of this State, to Exercise the Rights of Election,* act of March 29, 1813, in *Acts of the General Assembly of the Commonwealth of Pennsylvania* (Philadelphia: John Bloren, 1813), 213; Pennsylvania, *An Act Relating to Elections of this Commonwealth,* act of July 2, 1839, in *Laws of the General Assembly of the Commonwealth of Pennsylvania* (Harrisburg: Packer, Barrett and Paree, 1839), 528–29; Josiah Benton, *Voting in the Field: A Forgotten Chapter of the Civil War* (Boston: Plimpton Press, 1915), 269–70; David Grimsted, *American Mobbing, 1828–1861: Toward Civil War* (New York: Oxford University Press, 1998), 212.

10. George Bergner, ed., *The Legislative Record: Containing the Debates and Proceedings of the Pennsylvania Legislature for the Session of 1864* (Harrisburg: "Telegraph" Steam Book and Job Office, 1864), 505–9, 1025; *Lebanon Advertiser,* November 6, 1861.

11. Sidney George Fisher, diary entry for November 10, 1861, in Jonathan W. White, ed., *A Philadelphia Perspective: The Civil War Diary of Sidney George Fisher* (New York: Fordham University Press, 2007), 121.

12. *Commonwealth v. Kunzmann,* 41 Pennsylvania Reports 440 (1862).

13. *Philadelphia Bulletin,* October 1861, quoted in Jennifer Ruth Horner, "Blood and Ballots: Military Voting and Political Communication in the Union Army during the United States Civil War, 1861–1865" (Ph.D. diss., University of Pennsylvania, 2006), 168.

14. Pennsylvania's 1813 voting law had been adopted under the state constitution of 1790. In 1838, the state ratified a new constitution. The following year, the Pennsylvania legislature enacted a new election law, incorporating much of the 1813 soldier vote law. But there were important differences between the 1790 and 1838 constitutions that the lawmakers did not take into account when they rewrote the state's election law in 1839. For example, the state constitution of 1790 had not required residence or election districts, but both were required under the constitution of 1838. Woodward focused on these different qualifications for suffrage in the Pennsylvania constitutions of 1790 and 1838 because the legislators who wrote the voting act of 1839 had failed to take into account the

qualifications for suffrage in the new constitution that had not appeared in the constitution of 1790. According to Woodward, the legislators had been negligent in hastily patterning the act of 1839 after that of 1813.

15. *Chase v. Miller,* 41 Pennsylvania Reports 418–26 (1862).

16. Ibid.

17. *Ewing v. Thompson,* 43 Pennsylvania Reports 372 (1862), and *Ewing v. Filley* et al., 43 Pennsylvania Reports 384 (1862). For the opinions of the lower court, see *Thompson v. Ewing,* 1 Brewster's Reports 67 (1861–62), and *Stevenson v. Lawrence,* 1 Brewster's Reports 126 (1861–62).

18. *Harrisburg Patriot and Union,* May 24, 1862; *Wilkes-Barre Luzerne Union,* May 28, 1862; *Lebanon Advertiser,* May 28, 1862.

19. Several Republican newspapers reprinted a perfunctory article from Harrisburg's Republican *Telegraph.* See, for example, *Huntington Globe,* May 22, 1862, and *Pittsburgh Daily Gazette and Advertiser,* May 24, 1862. At least one Republican paper praised Woodward's opinion. John W. Forney's *Philadelphia Press,* May 23, 1862, stated that the "wisdom of the decision . . . will be acknowledged by every thinking person, and by none sooner or readier than by the patriotic officers and soldiers, whom it at first blush appears to deprive temporarily of the elective franchise," because soldiers could recognize the dangers of holding elections in camp where they would subvert discipline and good order among the troops.

20. Hubert H. Wubben, *Civil War Iowa and the Copperhead Movement* (Ames: Iowa State University Press, 1980), 33, 58, 88; Benton, *Voting in the Field,* 41–52, 250–53.

21. Benton, *Voting in the Field,* 53–66; Frank L. Klement, "The Soldier Vote in Wisconsin during the Civil War," *Wisconsin Magazine of History* 28 (September 1944): 37–47; Lynwood G. Downs, "The Soldier Vote and Minnesota Politics, 1862–65," *Minnesota History* 26 (September 1945): 187–200; Walter N. Trennery, "Votes for Minnesota's Civil War Soldiers," *Minnesota History* 36 (March 1959): 167–70.

22. William Lewis Young, "Soldier Voting in Ohio during the Civil War" (master's thesis, Ohio State University, 1948), 4–7.

23. A Republican attempt to enfranchise Delaware soldiers in February 1862 was defeated by the Democratic majority in that state. See Benton, *Voting in the Field,* 266–67.

24. Mark E. Neely Jr. argues that the Democrats misread the results of the elections of 1862. The northern public was not becoming antiwar, as the Democrats believed; northerners were tired of losing the war. See Mark E. Neely Jr., "The Constitution and Civil Liberties under Lincoln," in Eric Foner, ed., *Our Lincoln: New Perspectives on Lincoln and His World* (New York: W. W. Norton, 2008), 48–49.

25. A few Republican leaders recognized the importance of the soldier vote to Republican electoral victories prior to the elections of 1862. See, for example, Morton S. Wilkinson et al. to Lincoln, October 7, 1862, Lincoln Papers.

26. Amasa McCoy to Curtin, January 3, 1863, Slifer-Dill Papers, Dickinson College Archives.

27. William Henry Walling to Sisters, November 6, 1862, Walling Letters, CWMC.

28. William H. West to Lincoln, October 20, 1862, Lincoln Papers.

29. Abraham Lincoln to Carl Schurz, November 10, 1862, in *CWL,* 5:493–95.

30. James S. Brisbin to Simon Cameron, October 25, 1862, quoted in William Blair, "We Are Coming, Father Abraham—Eventually: The Problem of Northern Nationalism in the Pennsylvania Recruiting Drives of 1862," in Joan E. Cashin, ed., *The War Was You and Me: Civilians in the American Civil War* (Princeton: Princeton University Press, 2002), 188.

31. George Templeton Strong, diary entry for November 5, 1862, in Allan Nevins and Milton Halsey Thomas, eds., *The Diary of George Templeton Strong,* 4 vols. (New York: Macmillan, 1952), 3:272.

32. J. Glancy Jones to Charles J. Biddle, August 10, 1863, Biddle Family Papers, HSP.

33. Daniel Coit Gilman to Lieber, February 26, 1863, Lieber Papers.

34. Mark E. Neely Jr., *The Fate of Liberty: Abraham Lincoln and Civil Liberties* (New York: Oxford University Press, 1991), 57–58.

35. Arnold M. Shankman, "Soldier Votes and Clement L. Vallandigham in the 1863 Ohio Gubernatorial Election," *Ohio History* 82 (Winter/Spring 1973): 101.

36. *Legislative Record (1864),* 1026. These ideas were internalized by many Democrats. See, for example, J. Stable to Jeremiah S. Black, September 23, 1863, Jeremiah S. Black Papers, LC.

37. A Wisconsin state senator quoted in Klement, "Soldier Vote in Wisconsin," 40.

38. William A. Wallace, *Reasons of Hon. Wm. A. Wallace, of Clearfield, For His Vote on Amendments to the Constitution* (n.p., 1864), 2–4, 6–7.

39. Charles Z. Lincoln, ed., *State of New York: Messages from the Governors* (Albany: J. B. Lyon, 1909), 5:508–12.

40. Wallace, *Reasons,* 3–4, 6, 8.

41. *New York World,* April 17, 1863, quoted in Horner, "Blood and Ballots," 180; William Blair Lord and Henry M. Parkhurst, eds., *The Debates of the Constitutional Convention of the State of Maryland* (Annapolis: Richard P. Bayly, 1864), 2:1280–81.

42. Letter to the editor, *New York Times,* April 19, 1864.

43. In an attempt to win back support of the soldiers, some northern Democrats proposed paying Union soldiers in gold rather than paper money, but such a policy would have bankrupted the U.S. treasury. See Mark E. Neely Jr., *The Union Divided: Party Conflict in the Civil War North* (Cambridge: Harvard University Press, 2002), 136.

44. Jennie Cleland to J. W. Cleland, July 13, 1863, collection of the author.

45. Alexander H. Bailey, *Allowing Soldiers to Vote. Mr. Bailey's Speech on the Bill to Extend the Elective Franchise to the Soldiers of this State in the Service of the United States. In Senate, April 1, 1863* (n.p., 1863), 1.

46. *Salem (N.J.) National Standard,* August 24, 1864, quoted in Horner, "Blood and Ballots," 166.

47. Lord and Parkhurst, eds., *Debates,* 2:1282–85.

48. Pennsylvania General Assembly, *Journal of the House of Representatives of the Commonwealth of Pennsylvania, of the Session Begun at Harrisburg, on the Fifth Day of January, 1864* (Harrisburg: Singerly and Myers, 1864), 95. The resolution was adopted by a vote of 84 to 3, with 13 legislators not voting. A majority of the Democratic members clearly felt compelled to vote for the resolution.

49. Samuel Gramly Diary, entries for July 31 and August 3, 1864, Accession MSVF XXX-0055U, Penn State University Archives, Special Collections Department, University Libraries, Pennsylvania State University.

50. Louis A. Meier, ed., "The Diaries of Hiram Corson, M.D.: Civil War Years, 1862–1865," *Bulletin of the Historical Society of Montgomery County, Pennsylvania* 33 (Fall 2002): 250.

51. For in-depth discussions of the legislative processes by which the states enfranchised their soldiers, the court challenges these laws faced, and the mechanisms for voting that these laws created, see Benton, *Voting in the Field;* T. Harry Williams, "Voters in Blue: The Citizen Soldiers of the Civil War," *Mississippi Valley Historical Review* 31 (September 1944): 187–204; Frank L. Klement, "The Soldier Vote in Wisconsin during the Civil War," *Wisconsin Magazine of History* 28 (September 1944):

37–47; Oscar O. Winther, "The Soldier Vote in the Election of 1864," *New York History* 25 (October 1944): 440–58; Lynwood G. Downs, "The Soldier Vote and Minnesota Politics, 1862–65," *Minnesota History* 26 (September 1945): 187–210; Walter N. Trennery, "Votes for Minnesota's Civil War Soldiers," *Minnesota History* 36 (March 1959): 167–72; Arnold Shankman, "Soldier Votes and Clement L. Vallandigham in the 1863 Ohio Gubernatorial Election," *Ohio History* 82 (Winter/Spring 1973): 88–104; Samuel T. McSeveney, "Winning the Vote for the Connecticut Soldiers in the Field, 1862–1864: A Research Note and Historiographical Comment," *Connecticut History* 26 (November 1985): 115–25; Samuel T. McSeveney, "Re-electing Lincoln: The Union Party Campaign and the Military Vote in Connecticut," *CWH* 32 (June 1986): 139–58; Jonathan W. White, "Canvassing the Troops: The Federal Government and the Soldiers' Right to Vote," *CWH* 50 (September 2004): 290–316; White, "Citizens and Soldiers," 47–70.

By gubernatorial proclamation, Republican vice-presidential candidate Andrew Johnson also permitted Union soldiers from Tennessee to vote. See Leroy P. Graf et al., eds., *The Papers of Andrew Johnson: Volume 7, 1864–1865* (Knoxville: University of Tennessee Press, 1986), 205.

52. Benton, *Voting in the Field,* 135.

53. Thaddeus Stevens to Henry L. Dawes, October 23, 1862, in Beverly Wilson Palmer, and Holly Byers Ochoa, eds., *The Selected Papers of Thaddeus Stevens,* 2 vols. (Pittsburgh: University of Pittsburgh Press, 1997), 1:325.

54. Edward McPherson to Thaddeus Stevens, October 31, 1862, ibid., 326. Stevens introduced a soldier voting bill in Congress that would have implemented some of these ideas, but it was never put to a vote. See H.R. 9, 38th Cong., 1st sess.

55. William Parker Cutler, diary entry for January 21, 1863, in Allan G. Bogue, ed., "William Parker Cutler's Congressional Diary of 1862–63," *CWH* 33 (December 1987): 323.

56. *An Act to enable the People of Nevada to form a Constitution and State Government, and for the Admission of such State into the Union on an equal Footing with the original States,* act of March 21, 1864, in 13 Stat. 30.

57. U.S. Constitution, art. 4, sec. 3 (1787).

58. Rob. Kellogg to Father, March 19, 1863, in Nina Silber and Mary Beth Sievers, eds., *Yankee Correspondence: Civil War Letters between New England Soldiers and the Home Front* (Charlottesville: University Press of Virginia, 1996), 118. Connecticut politicians also complained about the preferences given to Republican soldiers. See William Church to Alexander Long, April 12, 1863, Alexander Long Papers, Cincinnati Historical Society. For further discussion of the role of the federal government over soldier suffrage, see chapter 4, as well as White, "Canvassing the Troops."

59. Frank L. Klement, *The Limits of Dissent: Clement L. Vallandigham and the Civil War* (Lexington: University Press of Kentucky, 1970), 186; Christopher Dell, *Lincoln and the War Democrats: The Grand Erosion of the Conservative Tradition* (Rutherford, N.J.: Fairleigh Dickinson University Press, 1975), 243–45.

60. James M. McPherson, *For Cause and Comrades: Why Men Fought in the Civil War* (New York: Oxford University Press, 1997), 146.

61. Andrew Evans to Sam Evans, June 27, 1863, in Robert F. Engs and Corey M. Brooks, eds., *Their Patriotic Duty: The Civil War Letters of the Evans Family of Brown County, Ohio* (New York: Fordham University Press, 2007), 162.

62. Albert Castel, *Tom Taylor's Civil War* (Lawrence: University Press of Kansas, 2000), 48, 79, 189. This soldier had very harsh words to say about Lincoln and ultimately chose not to vote in the

presidential election of 1864. By April 1865, however, he finally recognized Lincoln's greatness. See ibid., 160–73, 192, 217–18. For more discussion of Democratic soldiers choosing not to vote in the presidential election of 1864, see chapter 4.

63. For a brief overview of Brough's political affiliation, see Chandra Manning, *What This Cruel War Was Over: Soldiers, Slavery, and the Civil War* (New York: Random House, 2007), 266–67n24.

64. Luke Lyman to Parents, May 15, 1863, Lyman Family Papers, CWMC.

65. Burke A. Hinsdale, ed., *The Works of James Abram Garfield*, 2 vols. (Boston: James R. Osgood and Co., 1882), 2:700.

66. Ironically, Curtin and other future Republicans had enthusiastically supported President Polk's nomination of Woodward to the Supreme Court of the United States in 1845. See undated memorial to the U.S. Senate, signed by A. G. Curtin and others, in RG 46, Records of the U.S. Senate, Committee Papers, Committee on the Judiciary (SEN 29B-A4), NARA.

67. Blair, "We Are Coming, Father Abraham—Eventually," 183.

68. See Alexander K. McClure, *Old Time Notes of Pennsylvania*, 2 vols. (Philadelphia: John C. Winston, 1905), 2:53–55; McClure, *Lincoln and Men of War Times* (1892; repr., Philadelphia: Rolley and Reynolds, 1962), 231–32; *Chicago Tribune*, June 23, 1863; Lincoln to Curtin, April 13, 1863, and Curtin to Lincoln, April 14, 1863, Simon Cameron to Lincoln, September 18, 1863, all in Lincoln Papers; Curtin, "Farewell Message to the Assembly of 1863," in *Pennsylvania Archives*, 130 vols. (Harrisburg: William Stanley Ray, 1902), ser. 4, vol. 8, p. 501; John S. Richards to Simon Cameron, June 2, 1863, and L. W. Hall to Simon Cameron, September 17, 1863, both in Cameron Papers, HSDC; Simon Cameron to C. A. Walborn, June 2, 1863, Autograph Collection, HSP; Erwin Stanley Bradley, *The Triumph of Militant Republicanism: A Study of Pennsylvania and Presidential Politics 1860–1872* (Philadelphia: University of Pennsylvania Press, 1964), 166–67; C. W. Ashcino[?] to Edward McPherson, September 29, 1863; Annie to Edward McPherson, August 6, 1863, both in Edward McPherson Papers, LC; Simon Cameron to C. A. Walborn, June 2, 1863, Society Small Collection, HSP; Simon Cameron to Samuel Calvin, September 24, 1863, Samuel Calvin Papers, HSP; M. H. Cobb to Simon Cameron, June 10, 1863, J. K. Moorhead to Simon Cameron, June 20, 1863, R. G. White to Simon Cameron, September 18, 1863, Judge D. Krause[?] to Simon Cameron, September 26, 1863, Salmon P. Chase to Simon Cameron, September 23, 1863, and Samuel Calvin to Simon Cameron, all in Cameron Papers, LC.

69. Warren J. Woodward to Charles R. Buckalew, March 1863, Buckalew Papers, LC; *Doylestown Democrat*, April 21, July 21 and 28, 1863; Warren J. Woodward to Lewis S. Coryell, April 6, 1863, Lewis S. Coryell Papers, HSP; George H. Bowman to Jeremiah S. Black, March 6, 1863, Jeremiah S. Black Papers, LC; Adam J. Glossbrenner to James Buchanan, June 4, 1863, Buchanan Papers, HSP.

70. *Pittsburgh Daily Commercial*, September 17, 1863.

71. George A. Woodward to T. J. Bigham, September 23, 1863, in *Soldiers Read!! Citizens Read!!! Address of the Democratic State Central Committee. Letter of Major Geo. A. Woodward. Letter of Judge Woodward* (Philadelphia: Age Office, 1863), 7–8.

72. Ibid.

73. T. J. Bigham to George W. Woodward, September 30, 1863, in *Pittsburgh Daily Commercial*, October 1, 1863. Bigham and Woodward appear to have had at least a slight acquaintance before the war. In the 1850s, they served together on a committee of the Pennsylvania Agricultural Society. See the first and second *Annual Report of the Transactions of the Pennsylvania State Agricultural Society* (Harrisburg: A. Boyd Hamilton, 1854–55), 1:101, 2:8.

74. George W. Woodward to Eli Slifer, October 28, 1861, Slifer-Dill Papers. For another example of Woodward taking pride in his son's promotion, see Woodward to Edwin M. Stanton, September 16, 1866, Stanton Papers.

75. McClure, *Old Time Notes,* 2:61. Some Republicans claimed that having two sons in the army did not prove Woodward's loyalty. See *Wellsboro Agitator,* September 2, 1863.

76. *Philadelphia Inquirer,* August 27, 1863; *Philadelphia Press,* August 27, 1863.

77. *Pittsburgh Daily Commercial,* October 7, 1863.

78. Woodward to Jeremiah S. Black, December 10, 1863, in White, ed., "Pennsylvania Judge," 215; George W. Woodward, *Speech of George W. Woodward, at the Great Union Meeting, Held December 13, 1860, in Independence Square, Philadelphia* (Philadelphia: Ringwalt and Brown, 1860), 3–4; *Mifflinburg Telegraph,* October 8, 1863. For some of the pamphlets that selectively quoted Woodward's speech, see William A. Cook, *Hon. Geo. W. Woodward and the Gubernatorial Contest in Pennsylvania. Review of his Speech in Independence Square, Philadelphia, December 13, 1860. A True Exposition of His Principles and Purposes* ([Washington, D.C.]: Chronicle Print, 1863); *Democratic Opinions on Slavery! 1776–1863* (n.p., [1863]); *The Views of Judge Woodward and Bishop Hopkins on Negro Slavery at the South: Illustrated from the Journal of a Residence on a Georgian Plantation* (Philadelphia, 1863); *Opinions of a Man Who Wishes to be Governor of Pennsylvania: Extracts from a Speech of Judge Woodward, delivered on Thursday, December 13, 1860, at Independence Square, Philadelphia* (Philadelphia: C. Sherman Son and Co., 1863); *A Picture of Slavery, Drawn from the Decisions of Southern Courts* (Philadelphia: Crissy and Markley, 1863); and *Woodward in 1860 & 1863* (Philadelphia: Crissy and Markley, 1863).

79. *Pittsburgh Daily Commercial,* September 23, 1863.

80. George B. McClellan to Charles J. Biddle, October 12, 1863, in Stephen W. Sears, ed., *The Civil War Papers of George B. McClellan: Selected Correspondence, 1860–1865* (New York: Ticknor and Fields, 1989), 558–59; *Philadelphia Inquirer,* October 13, 1863; *New York Times,* October 13 and November 19, 1863. See also Biddle to McClellan, September 2, 1863; Biddle to Woodward, September 30, 1863; and Biddle to Andrew Porter, October 2, 1863, all in Biddle Family Papers; Joseph Chambers McKibben to Barlow, October 1, 1864, and David H. Williams to Samuel L. M. Barlow, September 29, 1863, both in Samuel L. M. Barlow Papers, HL.

81. Diary entry for October 13, 1863, in Adam Guroski, *Diary,* 3 vols. (1862–66; repr., New York: Burt Franklin, 1968), 2:344; George P. Smith to Edwin M. Stanton, October 13, 1863, Edwin M. Stanton Papers, LC; *Chicago Tribune,* October 23, 1863. See also William E. Chandler, *The Soldier's Right to Vote: Who Opposes It? Who Favors It? Or, The Record of the M'Clellan Copperheads Against Allowing the Soldier Who Fights, the Right to Vote While Fighting* (Washington, D.C.: Lemuel Towers, 1864), 8–9.

82. Samuel W. Pennypacker to Aunt, October 18, 1863, Pennypacker Mills, County of Montgomery, Schwenksville, Pa.

83. George G. Meade to wife, August 31, 1863, in George Gordon Meade, ed., *The Life and Letters of George Gordon Meade, Major-General United States Army,* 2 vols. (New York: Scribner's, 1913), 2:145; *New York Tribune,* August 31, 1863; *Union County Star and Lewisburg Chronicle,* September 4, 1863.

84. *Mifflinburg Telegraph,* October 8, 1863; *Union County Star and Lewisburg Chronicle,* August 18, 28, September 1, 4, 1863.

85. Thaddeus Stevens, "Speech on State Elections," September 17[?], 1863, in Beverly Wilson Palmer and Holly Byers Ochoa, eds., *The Selected Papers of Thaddeus Stevens,* 2 vols. (Pittsburgh: Uni-

versity of Pittsburgh Press, 1997), 1:408. The Republican press also portrayed Judge Lowrie as anti-soldier, even telling an anecdote that Judge Lowrie had turned several "noble-hearted soldiers" away from his door when they asked him for something to eat. According to the story, Lowrie shouted that he "*would prefer* GIVING BREAD TO REBELS, RATHER THAN UNION SOLDIERS!" The truth was that Lowrie actually had a son in the Union army. Like Woodward, Lowrie took great pride in his son's service. See *Mifflinburg Telegraph,* October 8, 1863; Walter H. Lowrie to Robert Patterson, April 20, 1861, in Nathaniel P. Banks Papers, LC.

86. Fitz-John Porter to Biddle, September 24, 1863, Biddle Family Papers.

87. McClure, *Old Time Notes,* 2:57.

88. See, for example, *Union County Star and Lewisburg Chronicle,* September 8, 1863; *Philadelphia Daily Evening Bulletin,* October 12, 1863; or the resolutions adopted by various Pennsylvania units in *Philadelphia Inquirer,* October 1, 1863, and *Wellsboro Agitator,* September 30, 1863. See also Timothy J. Orr, "'A Viler Enemy in Our Rear': Pennsylvania Soldiers Confront the North's Antiwar Movement," in Aaron Sheehan-Dean, ed., *The View from the Ground: Experiences of Civil War Soldiers* (Lexington: University of Kentucky Press, 2007), 171–98.

89. Lemuel D. Dobbs, quoted in Joseph Gibbs, *Three Years in the Bloody Eleventh: The Campaigns of a Pennsylvania Reserves Regiment* (University Park: Pennsylvania State University Press, 2002), 232.

90. J. Hoffman to Eli Slifer, August 1863, Slifer-Dill Papers. See also H. J. Stable to Jeremiah S. Black, September 23, 1863, Black Papers, LC; George W. Hamersly to Thaddeus Stevens, September 29, 1863, Thaddeus Stevens Papers, LC.

91. James Chatham to Eli Slifer, October 2, 1863; see also Adam Grittinger to Eli Slifer, September 1, 1863, and William Griffith to Alexander Fry, October 6, 1863, all in Slifer-Dill Papers; see also R. G. White to Simon Cameron, September 18, 1863, and C. S. Minor to Simon Cameron, September 23, 1863, both in Cameron Papers, LC; T. Good to Simon Cameron, September 25, 1863, Cameron Papers, HSDC; and C. W. Ashcino[?] to McPherson, September 29, 1863, McPherson Papers.

92. Curtin to Lincoln, September 17, 1863, Lincoln Papers.

93. Stanton to Generals Couch, Brooks, and Cadwalader, October 8, 1863, and [Stanton] to Sir, September 28, 1863, all in Stanton Papers. Other departments of the government also granted leaves of absence to allow Pennsylvanians to return home to vote. See, for example, Salmon P. Chase to Edward McPherson, October 5, 1863, McPherson Papers.

94. Jack Willoughby to Daul, September 12 and 26, 1863, James Randolph Simpson and George Simpson Papers, CWMC.

95. Hiram Corson, diary entry for October 11, 1863, in Louis A. Meier, ed., "The Diaries of Hiram Corson, M.D.: Civil War Years, 1862–1865," *Bulletin of the Historical Society of Montgomery County* 33 (Fall 2002): 232.

96. William C. Duncan to Eli Slifer, September 18 and 21, 1863, W. G. Herrold to Eli Slifer, September 23, 1863, all in Slifer-Dill Papers.

97. Henry G. Conser to Curtin, October 6, 1863, RG 19, Series 19.29, PHMC; Samuel P. Bates, *History of Pennsylvania Volunteers, 1861–5,* 5 vols. (Harrisburg: B. Singerly, 1869–71), 4:584.

98. Adam Grittinger to Eli Slifer, September 1, 1863, Slifer-Dill Papers.

99. John W. Bailey, diary entry for September 29, 1863, John W. Bailey Diary, Harrisburg Civil War Round Table Collection, MHI; William Griffith to Alexander Fry, October 6, 1863, Slifer-Dill Papers.

100. J. Hoffman to Eli Slifer, August 1863, Slifer-Dill Papers.

101. William C. Duncan to Eli Slifer, October 1, 1863, Slifer-Dill Papers. See also [Edwin M. Stanton] to Sir, September 28, 1863, and Stanton to Generals Couch, Brooks, and Cadwalader, October 8, 1863, all in Stanton Papers.

102. Hugh McAllister to James A. Beaver, September 10 and 12, 1863, James A. Beaver Papers, 1855–1914 (bulk 1881–1896), Accession 1941-000H, Historical Collections and Labor Archives, Special Collections Department, University Libraries, Pennsylvania State University. For more information on this regiment and its interactions with voters at home, see Carol A. Reardon, "'We Are All in This War': The 148th Pennsylvania and Home Front Dissension in Centre County during the Civil War," in Paul A. Cimbala and Randall M. Miller, eds., *Union Soldiers and the Northern Home Front: Wartime Experiences, Postwar Adjustments* (New York: Fordham University Press, 2002), 3–29.

103. James A. Beaver to Mother, September 18, 1863, and Beaver to My Dear Friend, September 7, 1863, both in James A. Beaver Papers (MG-389), PHMC.

104. William Williams, quoted in Reardon, "148th Pennsylvania," 26.

105. *Bellefonte Democratic Watchman,* November 13, 1863. See also J. D. Shugert to Charles J. Biddle, October 16, 1863, Biddle Family Papers.

106. Moreover, many soldiers had been addressed by the governor in large ceremonies before marching off to war. The governor's speaking ability was second to none. Before hearing Curtin speak, in August 1863, General Meade expected to "be overwhelmed with his eloquence and perhaps dumfounded." Other soldiers had similar experiences with the governor. Thus, it did not take much to convince the troops that Curtin was worthy of reelection. See Meade to wife, August 27, 1863, in Meade, *Life and Letters,* 2:145; and M. H. Richards to Sophie, September 16, 1862, Richards Family Papers, CWMC. On Curtin as a friend to the soldiers, see Allan L. Bevan to Sister, August 11, 1863, Bevan Letters, and Jacob B. Dannaker to Father, August 30, 1863, Dannaker Letters, both in CWMC; and Jacob Heffelfinger diary entries for October 8–14, 1863, Jacob Heffelfinger Diaries, *Civil War Times Illustrated* Collection, MHI.

107. Jacob Swartzlander to Cousin Han, October 24, 1863, Hanna Eliza Delp Collection, CWMC.

108. Cyrus W. Beamenderfer to Daniel Musser, October 24, 1863, Daniel Musser Papers (MG-95), PHMC. Drafts of two editorials, two pro-McClellan song sheets, and personal letters from 1863 and 1864 that exude his support for McClellan are also in the Musser Papers.

Soldiers did not like it when politicians at home voted against supplies or rights for the troops. In November 1862, an Illinois soldier noted, "I find that all the officers in the field with whom I have conversed since the late elections, regardless of their own political antecedents, *damn* all northern democrats who stay at home, vote against us and strive to rob us of our political rights." See George T. Allen to Lyman Trumbull, November 12, 1862, Lyman Trumbull Papers, LC.

109. W. H. Dieffenbach to Friend, September 27, 1863, James Randolph Simpson and George Simpson Papers, CWMC.

110. See, for example, Edwin Z. Judson to Curtin, October 1, 1863, Charles Parham to Curtin, October 7, 1863, John Ely to Curtin, October 17, 1863, Joseph E. Cramer to Curtin, October 20, 1863, all in RG 19 (Records of the Department of Military and Veterans Affairs), Series 19.29 (General Correspondence, 1793–1935), PHMC.

111. *Chambersburg Franklin Repository,* October 7, 1863, quoted in Arnold Shankman, "For the Union As It Was and the Constitution As It Is: A Copperhead Views the Civil War," in James I. Robertson Jr. and Richard M. McCurry, eds., *Rank and File: Civil War Essays in Honor of Bell Irvin Wiley* (San Rafael, Calif.: Presidio Press, 1976), 105.

112. James Brediu [?] to Charles J. Biddle, October 16, 1863, Biddle Family Papers.

113. J. N. Baldwin to Manton Marble, October 14, 1863, Manton Marble Papers, LC.

114. *Tribune Almanac and Political Register for 1864* (New York: Tribune Association, 1864), 69.

115. Daniel Garrison Brinton to Pap, August 20, 1863, Daniel Garrison Brinton Letters, CCHS.

116. James Bell to E. C. Williams, October 23, 1863, collection of the author.

117. For a recent analysis of Union soldiers' opposition to Copperheads, see Steven J. Ramold, *Across the Divide: Union Soldiers View the Northern Home Front* (New York: New York University Press, 2013), 115–42. Ramold similarly contends that in the election of 1864, Union soldiers voted *against* McClellan and the Peace Democrats. See ibid., 160–62.

Soldiers who supported Woodward believed that his election would be a "rebuke" to the radicals of the Republican Party—in other words, they opposed the extreme of the other party. See, for example, Alfred B. McCalmont, *Extracts from Letters Written By Alfred B. McCalmont* ([Franklin, Pa.]: Privately printed, 1908), 63.

118. Hermon Clarke to Father, December 7, 1863, in Harry F. Jackson and Thomas F. O'Donnell, eds., *Back Home in Oneida: Hermon Clarke and His Letters* (Syracuse: Syracuse University Press, 1965), 116–17.

In some cases, the soldiers voted Democratic because they perceived the Republican candidate as anti-soldier. Wrote one New York soldier of his state's November 1862 gubernatorial election: "A test-vote was taken on election day in our Regiment to try the relative strength of Seymour and Wadsworth. 168 votes were polled, of which Wadsworth received only 52. This was not so much because Seymour or his principles were popular, as for the reason that Wadsworth, long before his nomination for Governor of New-York, was generally known to the army as rather the leader of a clique so obnoxious to the soldier, which was loud and virulent in its abuse of McClellan. The feeling was rather McClellan versus Fremont, than Seymour versus Wadsworth." See William Chittenden Lusk, ed., *War Letters of William Thompson Lusk* (New York: privately printed, 1911), 224–25. Seymour's vetoing of a bill to enfranchise New York soldiers in 1863 likely turned many enlisted men against him.

CHAPTER TWO

1. Bruce Tap, *Over Lincoln's Shoulder: The Committee on the Conduct of the War* (Lawrence: University Press of Kansas, 1998), 55–79; *CG*, 37th Cong., 2nd sess., p. 130; *Philadelphia North American and United States Gazette*, February 11, 1862; Harry C. Blair and Rebecca Tarshis, *The Life of Colonel Edward D. Baker, Lincoln's Constant Ally* (Portland: Oregon Historical Society, 1960), 171; Charles Sumner to Ralph Waldo Emerson, June 18, 1864, in Beverly Wilson Palmer, ed., *The Selected Letters of Charles Sumner*, 2 vols. (Boston: Northeastern University Press, 1990), 2:245. See also T. Harry Williams, "The Committee on the Conduct of the War: An Experiment in Civilian Control," in *The Selected Essays of T. Harry Williams* (Baton Rouge: Louisiana State University Press, 1983), 15–30.

2. The Fifth Article of War prohibited soldiers from using "contemptuous or disrespectful words" against the president, vice president, Congress, or governor and legislature of any state in which they were quartered. See *Revised Regulations for the Army of the United States, 1861* (Philadelphia: J. G. L. Brown, 1861), 500.

3. *An Act to Define the Pay and Emoluments of Certain Officers of the Army, and for Other Purposes,* act of July 17, 1862, in 12 Stat. 596.

4. Ira Berlin, "Who Freed the Slaves? Emancipation and Its Meaning," in David W. Blight and Brooks D. Simpson, eds., *Union & Emancipation: Essays on Politics and Race in the Civil War Era* (Kent, Ohio: Kent State University Press, 1997), 105–21; Barbara J. Fields, "Who Freed the Slaves?" in Geoffrey C. Ward, comp., *The Civil War* (New York: Alfred A. Knopf, 1990), 179.

5. James B. Swan, *Chicago's Irish Legion: The 90th Illinois Volunteers in the Civil War* (Carbondale: Southern Illinois University Press, 2009), 59–63.

6. Court-Martial Case file OO-727.

7. Sam Farnum to Frank, May 13, 1864, War Letters, 1861–1865, NYHS.

8. D. L. Seymour to Joseph Hooker, February 17, 1863, in CMSR for Allen M. Seymour.

9. Statement of Ambrose Burnside, May 11, 1863, in *The Trial of Hon. Clement L. Vallandigham, by a Military Commission: And the Proceedings under His Application for a Writ of Habeas Corpus in the Circuit Court of the United States for the Southern District of Ohio* (Cincinnati: Rickey and Carroll, 1863), 40–41.

10. *CG*, 38th Cong., 1st sess., p. 1539. Writing of Democrats in the army, the Washington correspondent for the *New York Tribune* opined in December 1862: "The shooting of a half dozen imbeciles and semi-traitors, whose shoulders glisten with silver stars, would save streams of precious plebian blood." Quoted in T. Harry Williams, "Voters in Blue: The Citizen Soldiers of the Civil War," *Mississippi Valley Historical Review* 31 (September 1944): 190.

11. Stephen W. Sears, *George B. McClellan: The Young Napoleon* (New York: Ticknor and Fields, 1988), 324–27; McClellan to Mary Ellen McClellan, September 25, 1862, and to Lincoln, October 7, 1862, both in Stephen W. Sears, ed., *The Civil War Papers of George B. McClellan: Selected Correspondence, 1860–1865* (New York: Ticknor and Fields, 1989), 481, 493–94.

12. John Hay, diary entry for September 26, 1862, in Michael Burlingame and John R. Turner Ettlinger, eds., *Inside Lincoln's White House: The Complete Civil War Diary of John Hay* (Carbondale: Southern Illinois University Press, 1997), 41; Michael Burlingame, ed., *Lincoln's Journalist: John Hay's Anonymous Writings for the Press, 1860–1864* (Carbondale: Southern Illinois University Press, 1998), 317–18. Rumors swirling around Washington held that Secretary of War Edwin Stanton hoped to see Key hanged. See Virginia Jeans Laas, ed., *Wartime Washington: The Civil War Letters of Elizabeth Blair Lee* (Urbana: University of Illinois Press, 1991), 190, 259.

13. Ibid; *CWL*, 5:442–43, 508–9. David Herbert Donald quotes Lincoln as having said of Key's dismissal, "I wanted an example." See David Herbert Donald, *Lincoln* (New York: Simon and Schuster, 1995), 387.

14. Salmon P. Chase to William Starke Rosecrans, October 25, 1862, in John Niven et al., eds., *The Salmon P. Chase Papers*, 5 vols. (Kent, Ohio: Kent State University Press, 1993–98), 3:305.

15. David Brion Davis and Steven Mintz, eds., *A Boisterous Sea of Liberty: A Documentary History of America from Discovery through the Civil War* (New York: Oxford University Press, 1998), 518.

16. Thomas P. Lowry, *Utterly Worthless: One Thousand Delinquent Union Officers Unworthy of a Court-Martial* (Lexington, Ky.: n.p., 2010), 49.

17. Quoted in Stephen E. Towne, "Detectives, Secret Agents, and Spies: Army Intelligence and the Defeat of Secret Conspiracy in the Old Northwest during the Civil War," unpublished book manuscript in the possession of the author. For further discussion of these sorts of boards of examiners, see Timothy J. Orr, "'All Manner of Schemes and Rascalities': The Politics of Promotion in the Union Army," in Andrew L. Slap and Michael Thomas Smith, eds., *This Distracted and Anarchical People: New Answers for Old Questions about the Civil War Era North* (New York: Fordham University Press, 2013), 87–89.

18. Quoted in Steven J. Ramold, *Across the Divide: Union Soldiers View the Northern Home Front* (New York: New York University Press, 2013), 144–45.

19. Following the war, Whiting sought vindication through a military trial, but he was found guilty of violating the Fifth Article of War and conduct unbecoming an officer and gentleman. He then petitioned President Andrew Johnson for reinstatement. The lenient Democrat restored Whiting's rank on May 19, 1866. Thomas M. O'Brien and Oliver Diefendorf, *General Orders of the War Department, Embracing the Years 1861, 1862, and 1863*, 2 vols. (New York: Derby and Miller, 1864), 2:588; Court-Martial Case file MM-3652; *Congressional Serial Set*, 45th Cong., 2nd sess., Sen. Report 220, and 49th Cong., 1st sess., House Report 3181.

In 1879, a court of inquiry exonerated Haller, holding that he had been wrongfully dismissed during the Civil War. See C. H. Wells to Edwin M. Stanton, March 3, 1863, copy in Robert C. Schenck Papers, Box 2.2, University Archives, Miami University of Ohio, Miami; *The Dismissal of Major Granville O. Haller of the Regular Army, of the United States by Order of the Secretary of War* (Paterson, N.J.: Daily Guardian, 1863); House Rep. 375, 45th Cong., 2nd sess.; Sen. Rep. 860, 47th Cong., 3rd sess.; Theodore N. Haller, "Life and Public Services of Colonel Granville O. Haller: Soldier, Citizen and Pioneer," *Washington Historian* 1 (April 1900): 106.

20. John S. Williams to Laz Noble, January 13, 1863, and Oliver P. Morton to Edwin M. Stanton, January 30, 1863, both in Civil War Collection: Regimental Correspondence, reel 64, Indiana State Archives, Indianapolis; *Report of the Adjutant General of the State of Indiana*, 8 vols. (Indianapolis: Alexander H. Conner, 1868–69), 2:589, 591.

21. Whitlaw Reid, *Ohio in the War: Her Statesmen, and Generals, and Soldiers*, 2 vols. (Columbus, Ohio: Eclectic Pub. Co., 1893), 496; O'Brien and Diefendorf, *General Orders*, 20, 45; *Testimony Taken by the Joint Select Committee to Inquire into the Conditions of Affairs in the Late Insurrectionary States*, 13 vols. (Washington, D.C.: Government Printing Office, 1872), 2:801–9; Roger D. Hunt, *Colonels in Blue: Michigan, Ohio and West Virginia: A Civil War Biographical Dictionary* (Jefferson, N.C.: McFarland, 2011), 61–62.

22. *Report of the Adjutant General of Indiana*, 1:69, 3:87–88. An undated memo on State of Indiana Executive Department letterhead points out that Howard had been overheard "*railing* against the Prests Proclamation—denouncing the war as an 'abolition war to free the niggers,'" and that he refused to support his regiment's pro-emancipation resolutions during the spring of 1863. Photocopies supplied by Stephen E. Towne. See chapter 3 for further discussion of regimental resolutions.

23. Jean Powers Soman and Frank L. Byrne, eds., *A Jewish Colonel in the Civil War: Marcus M. Spiegel of the Ohio Volunteers* (Kent, Ohio: Kent State University Press, 1985), 303; Reid, *Ohio in the War*, 2:116; CMSR for DeSilva.

24. Joseph Allen Frank, *With Ballot and Bayonet: The Political Socialization of American Civil War Soldiers* (Athens: University of Georgia Press, 1998), 134.

25. McConnell was apparently permitted to resign so that his dismissal was wiped from the record. See *New York Times*, December 28, 1863; Lowry, *Utterly Worthless*, 60.

26. Christian G. Samito, *Becoming American under Fire: Irish Americans, African Americans, and the Politics of Citizenship during the Civil War Era* (Ithaca: Cornell University Press, 2009), 247n72; Joseph T. Wilson, *The Black Phalanx: A History of the Negro Soldiers of the United States in the Wars of 1775–1812, 1861–'65* (Hartford: American Publishing Co., 1890), 295.

27. See Alfred H. Jones to Lincoln, September 18, 1863, Andrew G. Curtin to Lincoln, August 10, 1863, James K. Moorhead to Lincoln, August 8, 1863, James Gill and M. B. Soury to Lincoln, August

12, 1863, Montgomery Blair to Lincoln, August 5 and 11, 1863, George G. Meade to Lincoln, September 25, 1863, Simon Cameron to Lincoln, August 10, 1863, and Edgar Cowan to Lincoln, September 22, 1863, all in Lincoln Papers. For the quote, see John S. Cosgrove to Alexander Montgomery, October 17, 1863, ibid.

28. Thaddeus Stevens to Edwin M. Stanton, December 15, 1863, Lincoln Papers.

29. Charles Garretson to Lincoln, April 14, 1864, Lincoln Papers; Guy V. Henry, *Military Record of Civilian Appointments in the United States Army,* 2 vols. (New York: Carleton, 1869–73), 1:318.

30. John Y. Simon et al., eds., *The Papers of Ulysses S. Grant,* 31 vols. (Carbondale: Southern Illinois University Press, 1967–2009), 7:528–29. In the postwar period, Warner served as the Democratic mayor of Peoria. See *Prominent Democrats of Illinois* (Chicago: Democrat Publishing Co., 1899), 144.

31. O'Brien and Diefendorf, *General Orders of the War Department,* 2:97–98.

32. Ibid.

33. John Smith to E. O. C. Ord, January 25, 1867, in CMSR for John M. Garland.

34. David Hunter to Lincoln, April 25, 1863, in *O.R.,* ser. 1, vol. 14, pp. 447–48. Lincoln did not directly respond to this letter, but five days later he refused to dismiss an anti-emancipation officer whom Hunter had wanted dishonorably dismissed because, he said, the order of dismissal did not provide satisfactory evidence to support the allegation (see the case of David Schaad in chapter 3). A month later, Hunter again asked Lincoln for the power to raise black regiments, but this time he did not ask for the power to arrest disloyal officers. See Hunter to Lincoln, May 22, 1863, Lincoln Papers. Lincoln may have doubted Hunter's ability to make prudent judgments. He replied that he did not have time "to answer at length" Hunter's letter. See Lincoln to Hunter, June 9, 1863, in *CWL,* 6:256. Soon thereafter Lincoln removed Hunter from command of the Department of the South.

35. John McNab to Franklin Pierce, May 3, 1862, Pierce Papers, LC. Lincoln permitted McNab to have a hearing before a court of inquiry in 1861, but the date of McNab's letter to Pierce suggests that he was not exonerated. See *CWL,* 4:480, 5:11.

36. John R. Brown to Lyman Trumbull, September 1863, Lyman Trumbull Papers, LC. Maj. Alexander Montgomery, discussed above, also professed not to know the reason for his dismissal. See Richard Henry Lee to Fendal, August 13, 1863, collection of the author.

37. Isaac D. Sailer to Simon Cameron, September 20, 1864, Simon Cameron Papers, LC.

38. For an excellent discussion of courts-martial procedures in the Union army, see Lorien Foote, *The Gentlemen and the Roughs: Violence, Honor, and Manhood in the Union Army* (New York: New York University Press, 2010), 10–15. It should be noted that all but one of the cases discussed in this book were general, not regimental, courts-martial.

39. Court-Martial Case file NN-856 (John McClelland).

40. Court-Martial Case file MM-988; Simon, *Papers of Grant,* 9:584.

41. Court-Martial Case file NN-438; Harriet Stevens, ed., *The Graybeards: The Letters of Major Lyman Allen, of the 37th Regiment Iowa Volunteer Infantry* (Iowa City: Camp Pope Bookshop, 1998), 13, 108–10.

42. Court-Martial Case file MM-429. Wagner was also charged with encouraging his men to disobey orders.

43. Court-Martial Case file LL-810.

44. Court-Martial Case file NN-500; Charles Steck to Robert C. Schenck, April 28, June 5, and August 12, 1863, W. L. Marshall to Schenck, June 11, 1863, and A. Schoepf to Schenck, August 14, 1863, all in RG 393, Part 1, Entry 2343 (Middle Department, General Records, Correspondence, Letters

Received, 1863–1866), box 3. A second charge incorporated several other crimes regarding financial matters, some of which Steck was found guilty of having committed.

45. Ibid.

46. Court-Martial Case file LL-327.

47. Court-Martial Case files LL-299 and NN-3825. Woodward was also convicted of neglect of his hospital duties.

48. RG 153, Entry 18, case 4.

49. Court-Martial Case file LL-101.

50. Cyrus F. Boyd, diary entry for March 9, 1863, in Mildred Throne, ed., *The Civil War Diary of Cyrus F. Boyd, Fifteenth Iowa Infantry, 1861–1863* (Iowa City: State Historical Society of Iowa, 1953), 133–34.

51. Court-Martial Case file NN-393. For a similar case involving a soldier from New Mexico, see Pvt. Michael McElroy's case in Court-Martial Case file LL-439.

52. Court-Martial Case file OO-102.

53. Court-Martial Case file NN-2879.

54. Court-Martial Case file LL-447. On occasion, officers who were dismissed for speaking disloyally had their punishments overturned because of technicalities in the record. See, for example, Court-Martial Case files NN-481 (Assistant Surgeon Fred A. Schell, Seventy-First Indiana Volunteers) and NN-3853 (Lt. J. Campbell Fortune, First Mississippi Marine Brigade). Lincoln also vacated some sentences of dismissal because of technicalities. Capt. William Woodbury of the Second Minnesota Volunteers was sentenced to be dismissed for using "disloyal," anti-emancipation language in December 1862, but Lincoln commuted his sentence because the primary witness against Woodbury had, without any apparent reason, waited five months to report the offense. See Court-Martial Case file MM-378. According to historian Lorien Foote, it was common for soldiers to be reinstated because of technicalities in the proceedings against them. See Foote, *Gentlemen and the Roughs*, 15.

55. Court-Martial Case file MM-0683. For another case of insubordination in which an Iowa soldier refused orders and yelled that he would rather be in prison "than serve in this God damned Lincoln war," see RG 153, Entry 18, case 34 (Alfred R. Long, Eighth Iowa Cavalry).

56. See Court-Martial Case files LL-1650 (Thomas Richardson, Sixth California Volunteers), LL-1739 (Alfred Lambert, First Missouri Militia), LL-3334 (Capt. John Mansfield, Second Wisconsin Infantry), and NN-2196 (Thomas C. Mitchell, Fifty-Second Enrolled Missouri Militia). For other cases of soldiers who were court-martialed for cursing the federal government or for cheering for the rebels, see Court-Martial Case files LL-2780 (Thomas Johnson, Second California Cavalry), MM-1690 (Thomas Hughes, First Nevada Volunteers), and RG 153, Entry 18, case 56 (Henry W. Hills, Eleventh Kansas Cavalry).

57. Court-Martial Case file KK-319 (emphasis added).

58. Court-Martial Case files NN-433 and MM-1367.

59. William Berdine to Lincoln, March 2 and April 8, 1863, and Moses Wisewell to Lincoln, March 3, 1863, all in Lincoln Papers.

60. *CWL*, 6:126, 165.

61. Court-Martial Case file OO-727. Mathey's defense claimed that the charges had been instigated by one of the witnesses to prevent Mathey from being promoted to major. For Kimball's antebellum political background, see John A. Garraty and Mark C. Carnes, eds., *American National Biography*, 24 vols. (New York: Oxford University Press, 1999), 12:678–80. For other cases from the election of 1864, see chapter 4.

62. See, for example, Court-Martial Case files KK-702 (Commissary Sergeant Frederick Williamson, Fifth Pennsylvania Cavalry), LL-1010 (Sgt. Jacob J. Crook, Forty-Seventh Illinois Infantry), NN-477 (Seth Laird, Fourteenth Ohio Battery), OO-481 (Christian Cook, Sixteenth Kansas Cavalry). In some instances, soldiers were acquitted of speaking treasonably (in opposition to Lincoln and his policies) but were convicted and punished for other offenses. See, for example, Court-Martial Case files KK-370 (Benjamin B. Smith, Seventh Kentucky Cavalry), LL-1397 (Lt. John S. Obenender, Ninety-Sixth Pennsylvania Infantry), LL-1647 (Capt. William Stone, 118th Ohio Infantry), MM-369 (Lt. Samuel Montgomery, Eighteenth Pennsylvania Cavalry), MM-404 (Alexander Gartley, Ninety-First Indiana Infantry), MM-429 (Lt. Johnson Vaughan, Fifth Indiana Cavalry), and NN-499 (Capt. Alexander V. Smith, Lafayette [Pennsylvania] Cavalry).

63. John W. Chase to brother, June 26, 1864, in John S. Collier and Bonnie B. Collier, eds., *Yours for the Union: The Civil War Letters of John W. Chase, First Massachusetts Light Artillery* (New York: Fordham University Press, 2004), 345.

64. For example, Col. Wellington H. Ent of the Sixth Pennsylvania Reserves refused to criticize Lincoln's policies during the war but became a vocal Democratic speaker afterward. See Richard A. Sauers and Peter Tomasak, *The Fishing Creek Confederacy: A Story of Civil War Draft Resistance* (Columbia: University of Missouri Press, 2012), 133.

65. Frank, *With Ballot and Bayonet*, 139.

66. John H. Riggs to father, January 2, 1863, quoted in Nina Silber and Mary Beth Sievers, eds., *Yankee Correspondence: Civil War Letters between New England Soldiers and the Home Front* (Charlottesville: University Press of Virginia, 1996), 73.

67. Charles J. Biddle to Lewis Coryell, April 21, 1862, Lewis Coryell Papers, HSP; Samuel P. Bates, *History of Pennsylvania Volunteers, 1861–5*, 5 vols. (Harrisburg: B. Singerly, 1869–71), 1:923.

68. Court-Martial Case of Newton B. Spencer, *Civil War Times Illustrated* Collection, MHI.

69. Court-Martial Case file LL-93. In some newspaper cases, politics lay just below the surface. Pvt. Thomas Leak of the Eighty-Third Ohio Infantry was found guilty of conduct prejudicial to good order and military discipline for writing a letter to the editor of the *Missouri Democrat* in which he complained about the food and conditions at the military hospital where he was convalescing. See Court-Martial Case file NN-438.

70. Court-Martial Case file LL-348.

71. Copies of the general orders stating the facts of Gillespie's case are in KK-730, LL-185 and MM-6; the actual case file is in MM-11.

72. Letter of Isaac J. Wistar, September 1, 1861, in Isaac J. Wistar Civil War Collection, Wistar Institute Archives, University of Pennsylvania, Philadelphia.

73. Charles J. Biddle to Isaac J. Wistar, January 7, 1863, copies in both the Wistar Collection and the Biddle Family Papers, HSP.

74. Isaac J. Wistar, *Autobiography of Isaac Jones Wistar, 1827–1905: Half a Century in War and Peace* (1914; repr., New York: Harper and Brothers, 1937), 420.

75. Swan, *Chicago's Irish Legion*, 62–63.

76. Court-Martial Case file LL-348.

77. George Breck to Ellen, February 8, 1863, and November 15, 1864, in Blake McKelvey, ed., *Rochester in the Civil War* (Rochester, N.Y.: Rochester Historical Society, 1944), 122, 143–44.

78. Court-Martial Case file LL-1359.

79. See, for example, Frank, *With Ballot and Bayonet*, 129–33; Richard F. Whiteside to John Painter, January 31, 1863, in Court-Martial Case file NN-821; John Tillson to Lyman Trumbull, No-

vember 7, 1862, Trumbull Papers. For an instance of a promotion being traded for an officer delivering his enlisted men's votes, see Richard Franklin Bensel, *The American Ballot Box in the Mid-Nineteenth Century* (New York: Cambridge University Press, 2004), 268–69. When seeking promotion, many soldiers touted their affiliation with the Republican Party and their hatred for Copperheads. See, for example, Elias S. Dennis to Lyman Trumbull, January 17, 1863, Trumbull Papers; and "A Republican" to Oliver P. Morton, February 11, 1863, in Civil War Collection: Regimental Correspondence, reel 13, Indiana State Archives, Indianapolis.

80. Henry L. Abbott to Mamma, May 7(?), 1863, in Robert Garth Scott, ed., *Fallen Leaves: The Civil War Letters of Major Henry Livermore Abbott* (Kent, Ohio: Kent State University Press, 1991), 178.

81. W. W. H. Davis to Coryell, January 10, 1864, Coryell Papers. Like many other Democrats in the army, Davis chose not to reenlist when his term expired in September 1864. See Bates, *History of Pennsylvania Volunteers*, 3:744. For a discussion of Davis's views of black soldiers, see Gary W. Gallagher, *The Union War* (Cambridge: Harvard University Press, 2011), 112. The Republican newspaper in Davis's hometown chastised him for his anti-emancipation views. "Shame on Col. Davis! that he should permit his paper to be used to discourage volunteering, thus obliging our brave boys in front of the enemy to bear their hard burthens single-handed," it wrote, referring to Democratic opposition to the enlistment of black soldiers. "If the war is merely 'to crush out slavery with the musket,' as the [*Doylestown*] *Democrat* says it is, then, to be consistent, Col. Davis ought to resign his commission in the army and come home. Why should he continue to draw his sword in a war which is waged solely for the benefit of the negro? This question instinctively flies to the lips of thousands of people in Bucks county." See *Bucks County Intelligencer* (Doylestown, Pa.), October 27, 1863.

82. Alfred B. McCalmont, *Extracts from Letters Written by Alfred B. McCalmont* ([Franklin, Pa.]: Privately printed, 1908), 58, 60–61, 63–67, 71–72, 86–87, 98. For discussion of an officer who was denied promotion three times because of his "interest in Genl. McClellan and Govr. [Horatio] Seymour [of New York]," see James O. Miller to Nellie McClellan, September 1, 1864, McClellan Papers, LC.

83. C. Knight Aldrich, ed., *Quest for a Star: The Civil War Letters and Diaries of Colonel Francis T. Sherman of the 88th Illinois* (Knoxville: University of Tennessee Press, 1999), 31–37, 68.

84. Ibid., 71.

85. Ibid., 43–44. Lt. Col. Loren Kent of the Twenty-Ninth Illinois Volunteers recommended Col. Michael K. Lawler of the Eighteenth Illinois Infantry for promotion. After praising Lawler's skill as an officer, Kent wrote: "If the President is disposed to promote solely on political grounds Col Lawler will remain without the '*Star*' as he advances no claim in that way. His aim is to be what he is a true officer and soldier." But Kent believed that Lincoln would be wise to consider a solid officer like Lawler. "By attending to the claims of such men instead of *Political gamesters,* our cause will in the future meet with fewer reverses." See Loren Kent to Lyman Trumbull, January 14, 1864, Trumbull Papers. Kent's argument was persuasive; Lawler received a promotion to brigadier general in April 1863.

86. Isham Nicholas Haynie to Lyman Trumbull, December 10, 1862, Trumbull Papers; Ezra J. Warner, *Generals in Blue: Lives of Union Commanders* (Baton Rouge: Louisiana State University Press, 1964), 222–23; Simon, *Papers of Grant,* 7:538. Officially, Haynie cited illness in his family as his reason for resigning.

87. Roger D. Hunt, *Colonels in Blue: Union Army Colonels of the Civil War: The New England States* (Atglen, Pa.: Schiffer Military History, 2001), 92.

88. Michael F. Holt, "Abraham Lincoln and the Politics of Union," in *Political Parties and American Political Development from the Age of Jackson to the Age of Lincoln* (Baton Rouge: Louisiana State

University Press, 1992), 341–42. For an officer who noticed the postelection sacking of officers, see McCalmont, *Extracts*, 64–65.

In the postwar period, Alfred Pleasonton claimed that he had been offered command of the Army of the Potomac if he would support emancipation and Lincoln's reelection, which he refused to do. "I wasn't like Grant," he said. "I refused to pay the price." See William B. Styple, ed., *Generals in Bronze: Interviewing the Commanders of the Civil War* (Kearny, N.J.: Belle Grove, 2005), 126. Gen. William B. Franklin's family made a similar claim after the war. See John Merryman Franklin, *Recollections of My Life* (Baltimore: Reese Press, 1973), 82–83. Of course, these stories may be anomalous (or perhaps untrue). David Work argues that antebellum party affiliation did not have a major effect on Lincoln's decisions regarding the promotion of senior officers. See David Work, *Lincoln's Political Generals* (Champaign: University of Illinois Press, 2009), 9–10, 15–20.

On party affiliation hindering the promotion of junior officers, see Mary R. Dearing, *Veterans in Politics: The Story of the G.A.R.* (Baton Rouge: Louisiana State University Press, 1959), 7–13, 22; Orr, "All Manner of Schemes and Rascalities," 81–103. Orr demonstrates persuasively that political favoritism was a two-way street, with both parties favoring promotions for their party faithful over members of the other party.

89. Harry F. Jackson and Thomas F. O'Donnell, eds., *Back Home in Oneida: Hermon Clarke and His Letters* (Syracuse: Syracuse University Press, 1965), 47.

90. Quoted in Allen C. Guelzo, *Lincoln's Emancipation Proclamation: The End of Slavery in America* (New York: Simon and Schuster, 2004), 169.

91. See Williams, "Voters in Blue," 193; Benjamin P. Thomas and Harold Hyman, *Stanton: The Life and Times of Lincoln's Secretary of War* (New York: Knopf, 1962), 259–62. According to Bruce Tap, members of the committee sought to destroy the political and military prospects of Democratic officers. See, for example, Tap's discussion of McClellan in *Over Lincoln's Shoulder*, 156–57.

92. Court-Martial Case file LL-587.

93. Isaac M. Keller to Joseph Holt, September 14, 1863, ibid. Republicans swept the elections in Sandusky. See Christine Dee, ed., *Ohio's War: The Civil War in Documents* (Athens: Ohio University Press, 2006), 154–56. For discussion of a Democratic editor from Pennsylvania who enlisted in the emergency troops during the Gettysburg invasion and then deserted, see Thomas M. Conprofist [?] to A. L. Russell, August 10, 1863, RG 19 (Records of the Department of the Military), Subgroup: Office of the Adjutant General, Series 19.29 (General Correspondence), PHMC.

94. Thomas P. Lowry, *Don't Shoot That Boy: Abraham Lincoln and Military Justice* (Mason City, Iowa: Savas, 1999), 60–61.

95. Court-Martial Case file KK-371

96. Lowry, *Don't Shoot That Boy*, 46; Court-Martial Case files MM-1213 (Capt. William Millar, Twenty-Fifth Missouri Volunteers) and MM-3418 (Capt. William Morrow, 187th Ohio Volunteers). For two Illinois soldiers who were punished for trying to sell a black woman into slavery, see Court-Martial Case file MM-586 (L. S. Ward and A. T. Wilson, Fifteenth Illinois Cavalry).

97. Assisting in the returning of fugitive slaves also violated a new article of war adopted by Congress in March 1862.

98. Bradford Verter, "Disconsolations of a Jersey Muskrat: The Civil War Letters of Symmes H. Stillwell," *Princeton University Library Chronicle* 58 (Winter 1997): 259. For an Indiana cavalryman who was court-martialed for driving contrabands from his camp at gunpoint, see Court-Martial Case file NN-2879 (Daniel Rutherford, Tenth Indiana Cavalry). In other instances, white soldiers abused

and mistreated southern slaves. See, for example, Court-Martial Case file KK-666 (John Kain, New York Volunteer Engineers); Glenn David Brasher, *The Peninsula Campaign and the Necessity of Emancipation: African Americans and the Fight for Freedom* (Chapel Hill: University of North Carolina Press, 2012), 140–41; and Jacqueline Glass Campbell, *When Sherman Marched North from the Sea: Resistance on the Confederate Home Front* (Chapel Hill: University of North Carolina Press, 2003), 45–49. For cases in which white officers mistreated black soldiers, see William A. Dobak, *Freedom by the Sword: The U.S. Colored Troops, 1862–1867* (Washington, D.C.: Center of Military History, 2011), 113–16; and Christian G. Samito, *Becoming American under Fire: Irish Americans, African Americans, and the Politics of Citizenship during the Civil War Era* (Ithaca: Cornell University Press, 2009), 55–56, 69–70, 85, 89. For other instances of violence against black soldiers and refugees, see Joseph T. Glatthaar, *The March to the Sea and Beyond: Sherman's Troops in the Savannah and Carolinas Campaigns* (New York: New York University Press, 1985), 54–58. On the relationship between black soldiers and their white officers, see Joseph T. Glatthaar, *Forged in Battle: The Civil War Alliance of Black Soldiers and White Officers* (New York: Free Press, 1990).

99. Edwin S. Redkey, ed., *A Grand Army of Black Men: Letters from African-American Soldiers in the Union Army, 1861–1865* (New York: Cambridge University Press, 1992), 38–39.

100. Kentucky's population also had strong ties to both North and South, which made it difficult for the state to choose sides. See Mary Scrugham, *The Peaceable Americans of 1860–1861: A Study in Public Opinion* (New York: Columbia University Press, 1921), 105–25; and Elizabeth D. Leonard, *Lincoln's Forgotten Ally: Judge Advocate General Joseph Holt of Kentucky* (Chapel Hill: University of North Carolina Press, 2011), 134–53.

101. Lincoln, "Message to Congress in Special Session," July 4, 1861, in *CWL*, 4:428–41. This view had been articulated earlier in the spring by other northern Republicans. See, for example, *Philadelphia Inquirer*, May 8, 1861; and *Pittsburgh Daily Commercial*, October 9, 10, 13, 1863. Some Democrats also took this position. See *Harrisburg Patriot and Union*, April 20, 1861, which argued that "armed neutrality is only another name for armed resistance."

102. Hambleton Tapp, "Incidents in the Life of Frank Wolford, Colonel of the First Kentucky Union Cavalry," *Filson Club Historical Quarterly* 10 (April 1936): 82–99; *CG*, 38th Cong., 2nd sess., p. 74.

103. Albert G. Hodges to Lincoln, May 10, 1864, and E. W. Hawkins to Lincoln, June 5, 1864, both in Lincoln Papers. Testimony describing Wolford's speech is available in his CMSR.

104. John David Smith and William Cooper, Jr., eds., *A Union Woman in Civil War Kentucky: The Diary of Frances Peter* (Lexington: University Press of Kentucky, 2000), 195–202.

105. Simon, *Papers of Grant*, 10:548.

106. Ibid., 548–49; E. Merton Coulter, *The Civil War and Readjustment in Kentucky* (Chapel Hill: University of North Carolina Press, 1926), 199–200; Tapp, "Incidents," 93; *New York Times*, April 1, 1864. A draft of the charges and specifications against Wolford is available in his CMSR. The case was called "The President of the United States against Col. Frank Wolford."

107. Lincoln, "Proclamation Suspending Writ of Habeas Corpus," July 5, 1864, in *CWL*, 7:425–27.

108. Tapp, "Incidents," 92–93; Lincoln, parole for Frank Wolford, July 7, 1864, Lincoln, parole and discharge for Frank Wolford, July 17, 1864, Lincoln to James Speed, July 17, 1864, Lincoln to Frank Wolford, July 17, 1864, all in Lincoln Papers.

109. Wolford to Lincoln, July 30, 1864, Lincoln Papers.

110. Tapp, "Incidents," 94–95; Coulter, *Civil War and Readjustment,* 204–7; Richard T. Jacob to Lincoln, December 26, 1864, Lincoln Papers.

111. Robert J. Breckinridge to Lincoln, November 16, 1864, Lincoln Papers.

112. *Congressional Serial Set,* 38th Cong., 2nd sess., Sen. Exec. Doc. No. 16, pp. 4–5. From prison, Wolford protested that he had not been informed of the reasons for his arrest. See Wolford to Captain Dickson, December 19, 1864, in Wolford's CMSR.

113. *CG,* 38th Cong., 2nd sess., pp. 63, 73–77, 532; *O.R.,* ser. 2, vol. 8, p. 23; Tapp, "Incidents," 94–95.

114. See Lincoln to Ulysses S. Grant, August 9, 1863, in *CWL,* 6:374–75; see also Lincoln to Charles D. Robinson, August 17, 1864, in *CWL,* 7:499–502.

115. Lincoln to James C. Conkling, August 26, 1863, in *CWL,* 6:406–10.

116. In the postwar period, friendship with Wolford was still deemed a mark of disloyalty. See William Stewart to James Speed, February 26, 1866, RG 60 (General Records of the Department of Justice), Entry 9 (Letters Received by the Attorney General, 1809–1870), Attorney General's Office Box 1, National Archives at College Park). Meanwhile, Democrats held Wolford up as a martyr who "was thrown into a bastile for criticizing Lincoln's despotism." See *The Old Guard* 2 (October 1864), 234–35.

CHAPTER THREE

1. John Beatty, *Memoirs of a Volunteer, 1861–1863* (1879; repr., New York: W. W. Norton, 1946), 168–69; Frank L. Klement, *Dark Lanterns: Secret Political Societies, Conspiracies, and Treason Trials in the Civil War* (Baton Rouge: Louisiana State University Press, 1984), 157–58; G. R. Tredway, *Democratic Opposition to the Lincoln Administration in Indiana* (Indianapolis: Indiana Historical Bureau, 1973), 101; S. F. Horrall, *History of the Forty-Second Indiana Volunteer Infantry* (Chicago: Privately printed, 1892), 184–85.

2. Court-Martial Case file NN-472. For another soldier who was court-martialed for claiming that the Emancipation Proclamation was unconstitutional and that Lincoln had violated his oath of office, see LL-1010.

3. In one unusual instance, a military court chose not to punish an officer who resigned because he disagreed with the changing nature of the war. Gen. George H. Thomas—a hard-nosed Virginian in the Union army—approved of the court's decision but wrote: "Lieutenant Logan can congratulate himself upon the mildness of the sentence awarded, as the reasons offered by him in tendering his resignation would have justified the Court in prescribing a much more severe punishment. It is hoped that hereafter his conduct may be not only more military but more manly." See Court-Martial Case file LL-2263.

4. John Y. Simon et al., eds., *The Papers of Ulysses S. Grant,* 31 vols. (Carbondale: Southern Illinois University Press, 1967–2009), 7:536–37.

5. Ibid; CMSR for James McDaniel.

6. Court-Martial Case file MM-901.

7. Ibid.

8. Court-Martial Case file MM-744. On January 1, 1863, Smith said "that his sympathies were with the South—that he was opposed to the Emancipation Proclamation of the President—That he was tired of the service, and would quit it, and that he would take one half of his Brother's Company and go into the Southern Army." His letter of resignation made no mention of emancipation, however.

9. Court-Martial Case file LL-811.

10. Court-Martial Case file KK-590.

11. Ibid. Howard, in fact, had written prior to the trial: "Lieut. Nichols affects to be influenced by the war policy of the Government with which he has nothing whatever to do. He avows open disloyalty and it is recommended to remove his uniform & put him across the lines with a certificate of his dishonorable discharge."

12. Ibid.

13. Ibid.

14. Ibid.

15. Ibid.

16. John Day Smith, *The History of the Nineteenth Regiment of Maine Volunteer Infantry, 1862–1865* (Minneapolis: Great Western Printing, 1909), 42; Steven J. Ramold, *Across the Divide: Union Soldiers View the Northern Home Front* (New York: New York University Press, 2013), 82.

17. Robert A. Constable to Franz Sigel, January 9, 1863, in CMSR for Robert A. Constable; Roger D. Hunt, *Colonels in Blue: Michigan, Ohio and West Virginia: A Civil War Biographical Dictionary* (Jefferson, N.C.: McFarland, 2011), 40; Stephen W. Sears, *Chancellorsville* (Boston: Houghton Mifflin, 1996), 13. Sears states that Constable was dismissed "for disloyalty," but Constable's CMSR seems to indicate otherwise.

18. Hubert H. Wubben, *Civil War Iowa and the Copperhead Movement* (Ames: Iowa State University Press, 1980), 102–3.

19. Beardsley had said, "we have no government that we are fighting for—no government; Congress is a mean, abolition faction; the Constitution is broken—we have no Constitution; the abolitionists of the North brought on this war; the Republicans are abolitionists," as well as that he "would rather fight under Lee than under an abolition leader." In his resignation, Beardsley cited "important individual interests" and that he knew that his superior officers preferred another, lower-ranking officer to command the Ninth New York Cavalry. Eric J. Wittenberg shows how Beardsley's superior officers eagerly accepted his resignation so that he could be replaced by a more competent officer. See Roger D. Hunt, *Colonels in Blue: Union Army Colonels of the Civil War: New York* (Atglen, Pa.: Schiffer Military History, 2003), 42; and Eric J. Wittenberg, *The Union Cavalry Comes of Age: Hartwood Church to Brandy Station, 1863* (Washington, D.C.: Brassey's, 2003), 28–30.

20. Christopher Dell, *Lincoln and the War Democrats: The Grand Erosion of the Conservative Tradition* (Rutherford, N.J.: Fairleigh Dickinson University Press, 1975), 244; Whitelaw Reid, *Ohio in the War: Her Statesmen, Her Generals, and Soldiers,* 2 vols. (Columbus, Ohio: Eclectic Pub. Co., 1893), 2:546. Groom had been court-martialed earlier for releasing a slave catcher as well as using vulgar language about sleeping with prostitutes. See Court-Martial Case file NN-3790.

21. Lewis Hanback to Hettie, October 8, 1864, Lewis Hanback Letters, The Filson.

22. Henry P. Hubbell to Brother, January 26, 1863, Hubbell Family Papers, Special Collections, Firestone Library, Princeton University.

23. Hubbell to Brother, June 2, July 9, and October 23, 1863, Hubbell Family Papers.

24. Stephen Whitney to Barlow, January 24 and August 16, 1863, Barlow Papers.

25. James B. Swan, *Chicago's Irish Legion: The 90th Illinois Volunteers in the Civil War* (Carbondale: Southern Illinois University Press, 2009), 57.

26. Roger D. Hunt, *Colonels in Blue: Union Army Colonels of the Civil War: The Mid-Atlantic States: Pennsylvania, New Jersey, Maryland, Delaware, and the District of Columbia* (Mechanicsburg,

Pa.: Stackpole, 2007), 93; Dona Bayard Sauerburger and Thomas Lucas Bayard, eds., *I Seat Myself to Write You a Few Lines: Civil War and Homestead Letters from Thomas Lucas and Family* (Bowie, Md.: Heritage, 2002), 123. Jones's CMSR does not give any indication of why he resigned.

27. Lewis Collins and Richard H. Collins, *Collins' Historical Sketches of Kentucky: History of Kentucky*, rev. ed., 2 vols. (Covington: Collins & Co., 1878), 1:118; Helyn W. Tomlinson, ed., *"Dear Friends": The Civil War Letters and Diary of Charles Edwin Cort* (N.p., 1962), 45. The general commanding recommended that Cochran's resignation be accepted because "He has served well and faithfully and has good grounds for asking to retire." See Thomas Speed, R. M. Kelly, and Alfred Pirtle, *The Union Regiments of Kentucky* (Louisville: Courier-Journal Job Printing Co., 1897), 419. The actual letter is available in Cochran's CMSR.

28. Richard M. Goldwaite to Ellie, December 17, 1862, January 24, 1863, February 4, 1863, all in Marti Skipper and Jane Taylor, eds., *A Handful of Providence: The Civil War Letters of Lt. Richard Goldwaite, New York Volunteers, and Ellen Goldwaite* (Jefferson, N.C.: McFarland, 2004), 173, 185–88.

Other Democrats, like Goldwaite, chose not to reenlist when their regiments mustered out in the spring of 1863. Col. Levi Maish of the 130th Pennsylvania Infantry, for example, mustered out with his regiment in May 1863 and went home to study law. He eventually served as a Democrat in the Pennsylvania state legislature and the U.S. House of Representatives. See Hunt, *Colonels in Blue: The Mid-Atlantic States,* 109.

In like manner, Lt. Charles Brockway of the Forty-Third Pennsylvania Volunteers, a prominent Democrat from Columbia County, was reputed to have been the first enlistee from his county in 1861. By August 1864, according to historians Richard A. Sauers and Peter Tomasak, he "was becoming disillusioned with the abolitionist goals of the war and was thinking about resigning." Brockway chose not to resign; instead he mustered out in October 1864, rather than reenlist. See Richard A. Sauers and Peter Tomasek, *The Fishing Creek Confederacy: A Story of Civil War Draft Resistance* (Columbia: University of Missouri Press, 2012), 47; Samuel P. Bates, *History of Pennsylvania Volunteers, 1861–5,* 5 vols. (Harrisburg: B. Singerly, 1869–71), 1:996; and J. H. Battle, ed., *History of Columbia and Montour Counties, Pennsylvania* (Chicago: A. Warner, 1887), 125.

29. This statistic is based on a count of the men who mustered out between June and August 1864 in New York State Adjutant General Office, *Annual Report of the Adjutant-General of the State of New York,* 43 vols. (Albany: James B. Lyon, 1893–1905), 32:1205–1382.

30. James A. Bayard to Thomas F. Bayard, January 23, 1863, Thomas F. Bayard Papers, LC.

31. David Acheson to Father, March 8, 1863, in Sara Gould Walters, ed., *Inscription at Gettysburg: In Memoriam to Captain David Acheson, Company C, 140th Pennsylvania Volunteers* (Gettysburg, Pa.: Thomas, 1991), 66.

32. Chandra Manning, *What This Cruel War Was Over: Soldiers, Slavery, and the Civil War* (New York: Random House, 2007), 86–89. Contrary to Manning's description, soldiers in the Army of the Potomac also described low morale in early 1863. One, for example, wrote on February 4, 1863, "The changes in the army and the recent operations have produced a very marked dissatisfaction. There is but one opinion in regard to the [Lincoln] Administration, and it is very freely expressed. The directing power, wherever it may be, is ridiculously incompetent." See Alfred B. McCalmont, *Extracts from Letters Written by Alfred B. McCalmont* (Franklin, Pa.: Privately printed, 1908), 36. Eric J. Wittenberg has also found a good deal of demoralization among the Army of the Potomac's cavalry units in January 1863. See Wittenberg, *The Union Cavalry Comes of Age: Hartwood Church to Brandy Station, 1863* (Washington, D.C.: Brassey's, 2003), 9–13.

Ella Lonn's classic study listed nine reasons that soldiers deserted, none of which directly implicated emancipation, although a few of them could be interpreted as being tangentially related to slavery. See Ella Lonn, *Desertion during the Civil War* (Gloucester, Mass.: American Historical Association, 1928), chap. 9. More recently, scholars have focused on how community pressures influenced decisions to desert. See, for example, Judith Lee Hallock, "The Role of the Community in Civil War Desertion," *CWH* 29 (June 1983): 123–34. Joan E. Cashin and Steven J. Ramold offer nuanced and deeply researched interpretations of Union soldiers and desertion, both of which take into account soldiers' views of emancipation. See Joan E. Cashin, "Deserters, Civilians, and Draft Resistance in the North," in Cashin, ed., *The War Was You and Me: Civilians in the American Civil War* (Princeton: Princeton University Press, 2002), 262–85; and Steven J. Ramold, *Baring the Iron Hand: Discipline in the Union Army* (DeKalb: Northern Illinois University Press, 2010), chap. 6.

33. Lincoln to Erastus Corning and others, June 12, 1863, in *CWL*, 6:266. Corning replied that Vallandigham had done no such thing—that Vallandigham had always encouraged his audiences to obey the law but to vote Lincoln and the Republicans out of office. Such language amounted to political speech, argued Corning, not treason.

34. Matthew Birchard and others to Lincoln, July 1, 1863, in Frank Moore, ed., *Rebellion Record: A Diary of American Events*, 12 vols. (New York: G. P. Putnam, 1861–68), 7:379.

35. Lincoln to Corning, June 12, 1863, in *CWL*, 6:266.

36. Thomas W. Bennett to Laz Noble, February 7, 1863, in Civil War Collection: Regimental Correspondence, reel 71, Indiana State Archives, Indianapolis.

37. Jonathan W. White, ed., "The Civil War Disloyalty Trial of John O'Connell," *Ohio Valley History* 9 (Spring 2009): 2–20. For an instance in which a private citizen was arrested and then tried in a civil court for writing a letter to a soldier that encouraged desertion, see Stephen E. Towne, "Detectives, Secret Agents, and Spies: Army Intelligence and the Defeat of Secret Conspiracy in the Old Northwest during the Civil War," unpublished book manuscript in the possession of the author.

38. Court-Martial Case files KK-158 (Pvt. James Rariden of the Twenty-Seventh Illinois, who claimed to be a member of the Knights of the Golden Circle and sought to induce one of his comrades to desert with him), LL-1083 (Pvt. William H. Hensen of the Eleventh Missouri), LL-1481 (Pvt. John McCaslin of the 104th New York), LL-1611 (Pvt. Daniel Lenhart of the Eightieth Ohio), LL-1724 (Pvt. Joseph Crostlow of the Fiftieth Indiana), MM-935 (Pvt. Arthur Sissel of the Seventy-Seventh Ohio), NN-416 (Pvt. Otho Darr of the Fourteenth Pennsylvania Cavalry), NN-1161 (Pvt. Chauncey Worline of the Eighty-Eighth Ohio), and NN-2707 (Pvt. William Johnson of the Seventy-Third Illinois). In some of these cases, the soldier deserted because of the influence of Copperheads; in other cases, they had already deserted and were persuaded by Copperheads to remain at home. In each case, the soldier was convicted, and they received a wide variety of punishments, including one who was publicly reprimanded and another who was branded with the letter "D."

39. Court-Martial Case file MM-132. Enlisted men also came to recognize the ill effects of Copperheads who "worked assiduously to thin our ranks by encouraging desertion." See, for example, the letter of Pvt. George W. Bollinger of the Second Ohio Infantry in Richard A. Baumgartner, ed., *The Bully Boys: In Camp and Combat with the 2nd Ohio Volunteer Infantry Regiment, 1861–1864* (Huntington, W.V.: Blue Acorn Press, 2011), 377.

40. Court-Martial Case file NN-393.

41. Court-Martial Case file NN-3466. In some cases, soldiers were suspected of having deserted out of opposition to emancipation, but such motivation was not proved at their court-martial. See, for example, the case of Pvt. Thaddeus Heselp in LL-156.

42. Quoted in Alan A. Siegel, *Beneath the Starry Flag: New Jersey's Civil War Experience* (New Brunswick, N.J.: Rutgers University Press, 2001), 93. See also Steven J. Ramold, *Across the Divide: Union Soldiers View the Northern Home Front* (New York: New York University Press, 2013), 79–80.

43. Both New York soldiers quoted in Merle Curti, *The Roots of American Loyalty* (New York: Columbia University Press, 1946), 160.

44. Benjamin F. Stalder to Parents, November 11, 1862, Benjamin F. Stalder Papers, CWMC. After being court-martialed for going absent without leave, Stalder returned to his regiment. A year later, he reenlisted. See CMSR for Benjamin F. Stalder, Sixty-Third Ohio Infantry (serving with the Third Michigan Light Artillery). An abstract of the charges from Stalder's court-martial record is in his CMSR, not in RG 153.

45. Court-Martial Case file MM-404.

46. George G. Sinclair to Francis Sinclair, January 6 and 27, 1863, George G. Sinclair Papers, CWMC; CMSR for George G. Sinclair, Eighty-Ninth Illinois Infantry.

47. A Soldier in the Twelfth Vermont Militia to R. W. Southgate, January 18, 1863, in David Brion Davis and Steven Mintz, eds., *A Boisterous Sea of Liberty: A Documentary History of America from Discovery through the Civil War* (New York: Oxford University Press, 1998), 525. According to an officer in the 154th New York in March 1863: "Some regiments went so far as to declare that they would never go into another fight with the rebels, that thare was no use trying any more for we could never subdue them by force, that it was nothing but a damned nigger war, and that the sooner it was settled on some terms the better." Quoted in Mark H. Dunkelman, "Through White Eyes: The 154th New York Volunteers and African-Americans in the Civil War," *Journal of Negro History* 85 (Summer 2000): 99.

48. Edgar Richmond to Isaac Van Ness, January 28, 1863, in Susan T. Puck, ed., *Sacrifice at Vicksburg: Letters from the Front* (Shippensburg, Pa.: Burd Street Press, 1997), 47.

49. Hicken, *Illinois,* 140.

50. Two months before the regiment was disbanded, Maj. Gen. Ulysses S. Grant dismissed eight officers from the regiment on various charges of fraud, incompetence, cowardice, encouraging desertion, and disloyalty. Lt. James Evans, for example, a former Democratic newspaper editor, was dismissed for "inciting dissatisfaction among the men of his regiment, and speaking in an improper manner of the war and President." Grant was careful to state in this February 1863 order that the regiment as a whole was exonerated "from all suspicions of disloyalty." By April 1863, however, the regiment had displayed enough disloyalty to be disbanded, with the exception of Co. K, which was transferred to the Eleventh Illinois. Of the regiment's 348 deserters, only one came from Co. K. See Allen C. Guelzo, "Defending Emancipation: Abraham Lincoln and the Conkling Letter, 1863," *CWH* 48 (December 2002): 318; T. M. Eddy, *Patriotism of Illinois,* 2 vols.(Chicago: Clarke and Co., 1866), 2:396; Simon, *Papers of Grant,* 7:270–73. For a more sympathetic view of the regiment, see George E. Parks, "One Story of the 109th Illinois Volunteer Infantry Regiment," *Journal of the Illinois State Historical Society* 56 (Summer 1963): 282–97.

51. Edwin Weller to Father, January 17, 1863, in William Walton, ed., *A Civil War Courtship: The Letters of Edwin Weller from Antietam to Atlanta* (New York: Doubleday, 1980), 21–22.

52. Augustus Abend [Auburne] to Barlow, January 17, 1863, Barlow Papers.

53. Onley Andrus to Mary, January 24, 1863, in Fred Albert Shannon, ed., *The Civil War Letters of Sergeant Onley Andrus* (Urbana: University of Illinois Press, 1947), 46. Nine men from the Sixty-Sixth Indiana also deserted together in January 1863. See Ramold, *Baring the Iron Hand,* 231. And historian Allen C. Guelzo also describes mass disaffection among the troops following the issuance of the final

Emancipation Proclamation. See Allen C. Guelzo, *Lincoln's Emancipation Proclamation: The End of Slavery in America* (New York: Simon and Schuster, 2004), 187–88.

Some soldiers deserted out of opposition to the use of black troops. After noting that two men from his regiment and nine from the Seventy-Ninth Indiana had deserted on February 24, 1863, one Kentucky soldier wrote that "desertions were now becoming so frequent that my worst fears seemed to have a good opportunity of being realized. Many of our Regiment had threatened it since the passage of the Negro Soldier Law and I feared that when a break should be made that a great many would leave." See Kenneth W. Noe, ed., *A Southern Boy in Blue: The Memoir of Marcus Woodcock, 9th Kentucky Infantry (U.S.A)* (Knoxville: University of Tennessee Press, 1996), 149.

54. Court-Martial Case file LL-552.

55. Ibid.

56. Ibid.

57. Court-Martial Case file NN-125.

58. David Acheson to Father, February 7, 1863, in Sara Gould Walters, *Inscription at Gettysburg: In Memoriam to Captain David Acheson, Company C, 140th Pennsylvania Volunteers* (Gettysburg, Pa.: Thomas, 1991), 59. Acheson contrasted these views with those of a "good soldier": "A good soldier will say (I heard them) he is tired of the war (when he is asked) but he will not say anything in that line until asked."

59. T. Harry Williams, "Voters in Blue: The Citizen Soldiers of the Civil War," *Mississippi Valley Historical Review* 31 (September 1944): 200.

60. Joseph Allen Frank, *With Ballot and Bayonet: The Political Socialization of American Civil War Soldiers* (Athens: University of Georgia Press, 1998), 139. Frank cites James P. Banta, diary entry for January 2, 1863, in Banta Manuscripts, Lilly Library, Indiana University, Bloomington. The Lilly Library kindly provided me with a photograph of the entry, from which I quote.

61. Quoted in Towne, "Detectives, Secret Agents, and Spies." Long speeches in camp could be an effective way to win enlisted men over to support for emancipation. An Ohio soldier observed the lieutenant governor of Indiana making "a speech to the 38th, 42d and 88th Indiana regiments. . . . He told them who the Copperheads were. . . . He was death to Copperheads." Quoted in Richard A. Baumgartner, ed., *The Bully Boys: In Camp and Combat with the 2nd Ohio Volunteer Infantry Regiment, 1861–1864* (Huntington, W.V.: Blue Acorn Press, 2011), 374. But soldiers did not always react favorably to such speeches. One New York soldier complained about having to listen to a two-hour anti-Copperhead speech given in his camp. "After we broke ranks the boys gave cheers for the N.Y. Democracy & yelled out 'damn the Abolition Sons of B—,'" he wrote with disgust. See Augustus Abend [Auburne] to Barlow, February 24, 1863, Barlow Papers.

62. Court-Martial Case file MM-1007; *Report of the Adjutant General of the State of Indiana*, 8 vols. (Indianapolis: Alexander H. Conner, 1868–69), 8:771. Kritzer's CMSR indicates that he deserted on November 12, 1862, January 3 and 31, February 3, October 28, and November 1, 1863. One notation in his file said that he "Will desert whenever he can." Kritzer died in a military hospital on February 11, 1864, "under sentence of G. Court Martial."

63. Court-Martial Case file LL-595.

64. William H. Hastings, ed., *Letters from a Sharpshooter: The Civil War Letters of Private William B. Greene, Co. G, 2nd United States Sharpshooters (Berdan's), Army of the Potomac, 1861–1865* (Belleville, Wisc.: Historic Publications, 1993), 19, 115, 126–29, 153–57, 166–74, 184, 188, 227, 248–52, 257–69.

65. Brig. Gen. W. E. Jones to Robert E. Lee, January 26, 1863, and Lee to Jones, February 2, 1863, both in *O.R.*, ser. 1, vol. 25, pt. 2, pp. 605–6.

66. Quoted in Victor Hicken, *Illinois in the Civil War,* 2nd ed. (Urbana: University of Illinois Press, 1991), 128.

67. For examples of Union soldiers who joined the rebels or were accused of deserting to the enemy, see Thomas P. Lowry, *Don't Shoot That Boy: Abraham Lincoln and Military Justice* (Mason City, Iowa: Savas, 1999), 115–16, 122; Frank, *Ballot and Bayonet,* 137; Court-Martial Case files KK-120 (Patrick Divine, Second District of Columbia Volunteers), LL-2677 (Chester B. Wall, First Mississippi Mounted Rifles), MM-1019 (John Kestison, Eleventh Illinois Cavalry), NN-393 (Barnabas Carter, Ninety-First Ohio Volunteers), NN-3800 (Frederick Hill, Thirteenth Illinois Infantry), OO-102 (Joseph Daganfield, Fifty-Fifth Pennsylvania Volunteers); Robert I. Alotta, *Civil War Justice: Union Army Executions under Lincoln* (Shippensburg, Pa.: White Mane, 1989), 102, 149–51; Darius J. Safford to sister, December 17, 1864, in Jeffrey D. Marshall, ed., *A War of the People: Vermont Civil War Letters* (Hanover, N.H.: University Press of New England, 1999), 280; Joseph Gould, *The Story of the Forty-Eighth [Pennsylvania Infantry]* (Philadelphia: Alfred M. Slocum, 1908), 277–78; and Lonn, *Desertion during the Civil War,* chap. 13.

68. Kathryn W. Lerch, "Prosecuting Citizens, Rebels & Spies: The 8th New York Heavy Artillery in Maryland, 1862–1864," *Maryland Historical Magazine* 94 (Summer 1999): 140–41. Haring received a "lenient" sixth-month sentence because of several letters received by the military testifying to Haring's loyalty prior to his enlistment. Brig. Gen. W. W. Morris wrote incredulously on Haring's case file: "There does not appear to be any evidence except the statement appended to the proceedings which are not sworn to [and] consequently not evidence of the prisoner's 'loyalty and devotion to the Government which he exhibited under trying circumstances before his entry into the United States Service.'" See Court-Martial Case file LL-607.

Others were also court-martialed for threatening to desert to the enemy. Pvt. William Smith of the Fifth Illinois Cavalry claimed that he had been in the rebel service previously and that he would desert the U.S. service to rejoin the Confederates. He was convicted and sentenced "to be stripped of his uniform in the presence of his Regiment, and to be drummed out of his camp, and to be imprisoned for the term of eight years . . . with the loss of all pay and allowances that are now due him, or that may become due him as a soldier," but the sentence was mitigated to dishonorable discharge and loss of all pay. See Court-Martial Case file LL-2677.

69. Lowry, *Don't Shoot That Boy,* 114.

70. Benjamin A. Gould, *Investigations in the Military and Anthropological Statistics of American Soldiers* (New York: Hurd and Houghton, 1869), 594.

71. William Starke Rosecrans to Henry W. Halleck, February 17, 1863, *O.R.*, ser. 1, vol. 23, pt. 2, p. 75.

72. Lowry, *Don't Shoot That Boy,* 258–62.

73. Benjamin F. Butler, *Butler's Book: Autobiography and Personal Reminiscences of Major-General Benjamin F. Butler* (Boston: A. M. Thayer and Co., 1892), 296.

74. Lowry, *Don't Shoot That Boy,* 257–63.

75. Court-Martial Case file NN-670; G. W. Lewis, *Campaigns of the 124th Regiment Ohio Volunteer Infantry* (Akron: Werner, 1894), 239. According to the court-martial records, Andrus served in Co. I under the alias Harvey Anderson. His regimental history contains no soldier named "Andrus," but it does list an "Anderson" in Co. D with no first name, no muster in date, and no "remarks" on his military service.

76. Lowry, *Don't Shoot That Boy,* 90; Thomas M. O'Brien and Oliver Diefendorf, *General Orders of the War Department, Embracing the Years 1861, 1862, & 1863,* 2 vols. (New York: Derby and Miller, 1864), 2:328–29. From his CMSR, it appears that Clifton may have escaped from imprisonment in July 1863. It is unclear whether he was actually executed.

77. Webb to mother, March 6, 1863, in Benson Bobrick, *Testament: A Soldier's Story of the Civil War* (New York: Simon and Schuster, 2003), 226–27.

78. William McKnight to wife, January 24, 1863, in Donald C. Maness and H. Jason Combs, eds., *Do They Miss Me at Home?: The Civil War Letters of William McKnight, Seventh Ohio Volunteer Cavalry* (Athens: Ohio University Press, 2010), 46.

79. George Gordon Meade, *The Life and Letters of General George Gordon Meade,* 2 vols. (New York: Scribner, 1913), 2:146.

80. Baldwin to Sis, April 24, 1863, in J. Ferrell Colton and Antoinette G. Smith, eds., *Column South: With the Fifteenth Pennsylvania Cavalry from Antietam to the Capture of Jefferson Davis* (Flagstaff: Colton, 1960), 60.

81. Court-Martial Case file NN-821 (Richard F. Whiteside, Sixty-First Illinois) (emphasis added).

82. Court-Martial Case file LL-733.

83. Court-Martial Case file MM-774; Lincoln, "Proclamation Granting Amnesty to Soldiers Absent without Leave," March 10, 1863, in *CWL,* 6:132–33. For other, similar cases, see Court-Martial Case files NN-56 (H. J. Frost, Tenth U.S. Infantry) and NN-1760 (John Cargill, Third Potomac Home Brigade).

84. Court-Martial Case file MM-1312.

85. Court-Martial Case file MM-787; *CWL,* 6:475, 488; Jonathan Birch to Lincoln, September 22, 1863, and enclosed petition, Lincoln Papers; Jesse W. Weik, "A Law Student's Recollection of Abraham Lincoln," *Outlook,* February 11, 1911, p. 313.

86. Nor did all soldiers who loathed emancipation threaten to desert. For example, one soldier wrote in his diary on January 2, 1863: "We today got the Proclamation, 'All slaves shall be and are hereafter free.' . . . Now you see by the Proclamation that we are fighting, not for the Union but for the *nigger.* I however am *not* fighting for the nigger. I fight because having once gone into it, I will not back out." See Stephen W. Sears, ed., *On Campaign with the Army of the Potomac: The Civil War Journal of Theodore Ayrault Dodge* (New York: Cooper Square Press, 2001), 138.

87. B. Theodore Parks to Col. Henry C. Eyer, September 11, 1861, and January 31, 1863, and Parks to mother, September 15, 1864, B. Theodore Parks Papers, CWMC; Samuel P. Bates, *History of Pennsylvania Volunteers, 1861–5,* 5 vols. (Harrisburg: B. Singerly, 1869–71), 4:570.

88. Andrus to Mary, November 22, 1862, and March 4, 1864, in Shannon, ed., *Onley Andrus,* 28, 75.

89. Stillwell to mother, December 5, 1862, March 8, April 16, November 24, 1863, and August 5, September 7, 1864, Civil War Papers of Symmes H. Stillwell, Rare Books and Special Collections, Firestone Library, Princeton University. For another Republican soldier who acted violently against southern blacks and who said that he would not reenlist because he opposed fighting in a war to free the slaves, see the Benjamin B. Brock Letters (Collection C00239), Michigan State University Archives, East Lansing. See, in particular, Brock's letters of February 3, March 9 and 12, April 6, and September 3, 1863, and March 14 and April 14, 1864. And for other soldiers who had been abolitionists when they enlisted but who rejected abolitionism during the war, see Joseph T. Glatthaar, *The March to the Sea and Beyond: Sherman's Troops in the Savannah and Carolinas Campaigns* (New York: New York University Press, 1985), 40, 55.

90. See the appendix.

91. Quoted in Siegel, *Beneath the Starry Flag,* 92; William S. Stryker, *Record of Officers and Men of New Jersey in the Civil War, 1861–1865,* 2 vols. (Trenton: J. L. Murphy, 1876), 1:947.

92. George D. Williams to Harry, March 24, June 20, and August 18, 1864, Henry S. Jay Papers, CWMC.

93. Allan G. Bogue, ed., "William Parker Cutler's Congressional Diary of 1862–63," *CWH* 33 (December 1987): 323–29.

94. Noe, ed., *Southern Boy in Blue,* 152–53.

95. Mary E. Kellogg, ed., *Army Life of an Illinois Soldier: Including a Day-by-Day Record of Sherman's March to the Sea* (1906; repr., Carbondale: Southern Illinois University Press, 1996), 153–54.

In February 1863, Union generals Stephen A. Hurlbut and Jeremiah C. Sullivan banned the *Chicago Times* from their military districts, but Gen. Ulysses S. Grant revoked the order since it did not have authority from Washington, D.C. See Simon, *Papers of Grant,* 7:316–19.

96. Kellogg, ed., *Army Life of an Illinois Soldier,* 153–54.

97. Charles A. Partridge, ed., *History of the Ninety-Sixth Regiment Illinois Volunteer Infantry* (Chicago: Brown, Pettibone and Co., 1887), 101. See also Mark E. Neely Jr., "The Civil War and the Two-Party System," in James M. McPherson, ed., *We Cannot Escape History: Lincoln and the Last Best Hope of Earth* (Urbana: University of Illinois Press, 1995), 97–101.

98. Mark E. Neely Jr., *The Union Divided: Party Conflict in the Civil War North* (Cambridge: Harvard University Press, 2002), 42–45; Timothy J. Orr, "'A Viler Enemy in Our Rear': Pennsylvania Soldiers Confront the North's Antiwar Movement," in Aaron Sheehan-Dean, ed., *The View from the Ground: Experiences of Civil War Soldiers* (Lexington: University of Kentucky Press, 2007), 171–98.

99. Neely, *Union Divided,* 42–47.

100. James Anderson to C. N. Lamison, April 18, 1863, in Court-Martial Case file LL-552. Anderson's sentence was overturned on a technicality and he maintained his commission.

101. *Proceedings of the Officers and Soldiers of the Indiana Regiments in the Army of the Cumberland, on the Memorial and Resolutions to the Indiana Legislature* (Indianapolis: Joseph J. Bingham, 1863), 30.

102. Court-Martial Case file NN-472.

103. Court-Martial Case file MM-448.

104. Lincoln to David Hunter, April 30, 1863, and Endorsement on the Case of David Schaad, April 30, 1863, both in Lincoln Papers.

105. Court-Martial Case file MM-448.

106. Ibid; Bates, *History of Pennsylvania Volunteers,* 4:1243. In a similar case, Jacob Crook of the Forty-Seventh Illinois Infantry was court-martialed for speaking out against his regiment's resolutions, but the court decided not to attach criminality to his words because several witnesses testified about Crook's loyal military service. See Court-Martial Case file LL-1010.

107. Hubert H. Wubben, *Civil War Iowa and the Copperhead Movement* (Ames: Iowa State University Press, 1980), 97–98.

108. Richard E. Matthews, *The 149th Pennsylvania Volunteer Infantry Unit in the Civil War* (Jefferson, N.C.: McFarland, 1994), 51–52, 112–14. For information on deserters from this regiment in February 1863, see Robert M. Sandow, *Deserter Country: Civil War Opposition in the Pennsylvania Appalachians* (New York: Fordham University Press, 2009), 129.

On some occasions, officers opposed their regiment's resolutions because the language in them had been moderated too much in order to receive the assent of the regiment. See Sears, ed., *On Campaign,* 186–88.

109. Frank, *Ballot and Bayonet,* 139.

110. Cyrus F. Boyd, diary entry for March 6, 1863, in Mildred Throne, ed., *The Civil War Diary of Cyrus F. Boyd, Fifteenth Iowa Infantry, 1861–1863* (Iowa City: State Historical Society of Iowa, 1953), 132.

111. Ibid.

112. Partridge, ed., *Ninety-Sixth Illinois,* 102–3.

113. Mary R. Dearing, *Veterans in Politics: The Story of the G.A.R.* (Baton Rouge: Louisiana State University Press, 1959), 22. In like manner, Frank L. Klement writes, "All petitions were quite alike in form and meaning, indicating that some master hand had pulled the strings." See Klement, *The Copperheads in the Middle West* (Chicago: University of Chicago Press, 1960), 215.

To be sure, some of the resolutions, such as those of the 140th Pennsylvania Infantry, are clearly documented as having been written at the regimental level. See Walters, ed., *Inscription at Gettysburg,* 66–77. Political scientist Joseph Allen Frank writes, "Officers indoctrinated their men by distributing political tracts and by drafting resolutions supporting candidates or the Emancipation Proclamation." See Frank, *With Ballot and Bayonet,* 139. Some men believed that their officers wrote these resolutions because they were "fishing for a Brigadier Generalship, and this I suspect is a fine new bait." See Sears, ed., *On Campaign,* 186.

114. Lorna Lutes Sylvester, ed., "The Civil War Letters of Charles Harding Cox," *Indiana Magazine of History* 68 (March 1972): 51n34.

115. W. H. H. Terrell to John T. Wilder, January 24, 1863, quoted in Kenneth M. Stampp, *Indiana Politics during the Civil War* (Bloomington: Indiana University Press, 1949), 173–74; Klement, *Copperheads in the Middle West,* 215; Calvin Fletcher, diary entries for February 3 and 12, 1863, both in Gayle Thornbrough and Paula Corpuz, eds., *The Diary of Calvin Fletcher,* 9 vols. (Indianapolis: Indiana Historical Society, 1972–1983), 8:39, 50. I thank Stephen E. Towne for providing me with a photocopy of Terrell's letter.

116. Thomas E. Rodgers, "Republicans and Drifters: Political Affiliation and Union Army Volunteers in West-Central Indiana," *Indiana Magazine of History* 92 (December 1996): 342.

117. Simpson S. Hamrick to A. D. Hamrick, January 14, 1862, typescript, Simpson S. Hamrick, Civil War Letters, Putnam County Library, photocopy generously supplied by Thomas E. Rodgers.

118. Quoted in James M. McPherson, *Tried by War: Abraham Lincoln as Commander in Chief* (New York: Penguin, 2009), 157.

119. On the impact of the Emancipation Proclamation, see Harold Holzer, *Emancipating Lincoln: The Proclamation in Text, Context, and Memory* (Cambridge: Harvard University Press, 2012).

120. As will be seen in chapter 5, Republicans in the postwar period generally believed that most deserters were Democrats.

CHAPTER FOUR

An earlier version of this chapter appeared in Andrew L. Slap and Michael Thomas Smith, eds., *This Distracted and Anarchical People: New Answers for Old Questions about the Civil War–Era North* (New York: Fordham University Press, 2013). It is reproduced with permission.

1. Samuel L. M. Barlow to George B. McClellan, September 23, 1864, George B. McClellan, Sr., Papers, LC; William Cassidy to Barlow, September 21, 1864, Samuel L. M. Barlow Papers, HL.

2. Frederick Douglass quoted in Larry E. Nelson, "Black Leaders and the Presidential Election of 1864," *Journal of Negro History* 63 (January 1978): 47.

3. John Niven, *Salmon P. Chase: A Biography* (New York: Oxford University Press, 1995), 343–64.

4. Nelson, "Black Leaders," 48; Halleck to Francis Lieber, June 2, 1864, Francis Lieber Papers, HL; Adam Badeau to Harry, August 8, 1864, Adam Badeau Papers, Special Collections, Firestone Library, Princeton University.

5. For the sake of simplicity, I use the term "Republican Party" rather than "Union Party" in this chapter. I do so while recognizing that several scholars argue that the Union Party label was more than a simple nominal change. See, for example, Michael F. Holt, *Political Parties and American Political Development from the Age of Jackson to the Age of Lincoln* (Baton Rouge: Louisiana State University Press, 1992), 323–53; Adam I. P. Smith, *No Party Now: Politics in the Civil War North* (New York: Oxford University Press, 2006).

While I view the Republicans' decision to change their party name as more of a cosmetic than a substantive change, I concur with Adam I. P. Smith and Gary W. Gallagher, that "Union" was the central issue in the election—particularly for the soldiers. Unlike James M. McPherson and Chandra Manning, who see the soldier vote in the election of 1864 as indicative of soldier support for emancipation, I see the soldiers' support of Lincoln as a statement of their views on reunion. Other leading scholars have held similar views. For example, in *The Union War*, Gallagher argues that "continuation of a war to save the Union," and not emancipation, "was the primary issue" in the election of 1864. He continues, "Although some have placed emancipation at the heart of the presidential election of 1864, soldiers' comments left no doubt that saving the nation, to use General Rosecrans's language, easily trumped killing slavery as a motivation to vote for the Union ticket of Lincoln and Andrew Johnson." Similarly, Smith argues that the "Union Party appeal also helped to consolidate the support of soldiers for Abraham Lincoln." According to Smith, "The conflation of party and nation [both under the banner of Union] meant that only the election of a Union Party candidate could be considered by the troops guarding the polls to be a loyal, and therefore acceptable outcome." Moreover, Smith argues, the experience of fighting for the Union was "among the most important reasons for the support Lincoln received from the army." See Gary W. Gallagher, *The Union War* (Cambridge, Mass.: Harvard University Press, 2011), 78, 106; Smith, *No Party Now*, 99, 156–57.

6. Francis Lieber to Henry W. Halleck, January 16, 1864, Lieber Papers; William Frank Zornow, "The Union Party Convention at Baltimore in 1864," *Maryland Historical Magazine* 45 (September 1950): 176–200; Don E. Fehrenbacher, "The Making of a Myth: Lincoln and the Vice-Presidential Nomination in 1864," *CWH* 41 (December 1995): 273–90.

7. Nelson, "Black Leaders," 49–52; John F. Woods to Sister, June 19, 1864, Woods Family Collection (MG-188), PHMC; Tom Chaffin, *Pathfinder: John Charles Fremont and the Course of American Empire* (New York: Hill and Wang, 2002), 475; John Adam Kasson to Thomas Haines Dudley, October 2, 1864, Thomas Haines Dudley Papers, HL; Montgomery Blair to Barlow, May 1, 11, and 27, 1864, Barlow Papers.

8. See David H. Williams to Barlow, June 23, 1864, and James F. Noble to Samuel S. Cox, November 22, 1863, both in Barlow Papers. Some of McClellan's friends believed that delaying the convention would also help him, but this was largely a movement on behalf of the Peace wing of the party.

See John Van Schaick Lansing Pruyn to Barlow, June 18 and 25, 1864, August Belmont to Barlow, June 15, 1864, Fernando Wood to Barlow, June 15, 1864, George Washington Cass to Barlow, May 7, 1864, all in Barlow Papers; Stephen W. Sears, *George B. McClellan: The Young Napoleon* (New York: Ticknor and Fields, 1988), 368–69; and Mark E. Neely Jr., *The Union Divided: Party Conflict in the Civil War North* (Cambridge: Harvard University Press, 2002), 118–40).

9. Badeau to Harry, August 29, 1864, Badeau Papers; Samuel S. Cox to Barlow, November 21, 1863, A. Banning Norton to Barlow, June 22, 1864, Washington McLean to Barlow, August 29, 1864, Thomas Marshall Key to Barlow, August 24, 1864, David H. Williams to Barlow, August 22, 1864, and Manton Marble to Barlow, August 29 and 30, 1864, all in Barlow Papers; Jonah D. Hoover to Franklin Pierce, February 16, 1864, Franklin Pierce Papers, LC.

10. Toward the middle of the political spectrum were Conservative Unionists—mainly former Whigs opposed to emancipation, presidential suspension of the writ of habeas corpus, and other Republican war measures. These politicians hoped to join with moderate Democrats to defeat Lincoln and "the Military-Abolition party." Conservative Unionists had been organizing in various ways since 1862. On December 24, 1863, the national committee of the Conservative Union Party met at Philadelphia, where it nominated George McClellan for president, and a former Whig governor of Tennessee, William B. Campbell, for vice president. The Conservative Unionist platform criticized Lincoln for disregarding the Constitution and trampling on the rights of American citizens. It called on voters to replace him with a president who would be able to make peace and terms of reunion with the South, guaranteeing all constitutional rights to all Americans. Taking an early position, the Conservative Unionists hoped that Democrats would follow their lead and adopt their candidates and platform.

If the Conservative Unionists believed they would be able to unite with the Democrats to form an anti-Lincoln, anti-abolition coalition, they would be sorely disappointed. The resolutions adopted by the Conservative Unionists were read, amid much cheering and fanfare, at the Democratic National Convention, but that show of support was a mere facade. The Democratic Party—still reeling from its defeats in the 1863 gubernatorial elections—had not yet found its footing, and was more divided than ever. Rather than settle on the fairly moderate platform and nominations of the Conservative Unionists, the Democratic Party embarked on yet another divisive, extreme, and self-destructive national convention. See William C. Harris, "Conservative Unionists and the Presidential Election of 1864," *CWH* 38 (December 1992): 298–318; quotation from 301; and James H. Goodsell, ed., *Official Proceedings of the Democratic National Convention, Held in 1864 at Chicago* (Chicago: Times Steam Book and Job Printing House, 1864), 20–21.

11. James F. Noble to Samuel S. Cox, November 22, 1863, Belmont to Barlow, August 29, 1864, both in Barlow Papers; Goodsell, ed., *Official Proceedings*, 27.

12. Sears, *McClellan*, 373; John Adam Kasson to Thomas Haines Dudley, October 2, 1864, Dudley Papers.

13. Thomas Marshall Key to Barlow, August 24, 1864, Barlow Papers. For background on Pendleton, see Thomas S. Mach, *"Gentleman George" Hunt Pendleton: Party Politics and Ideological Identity in Nineteenth-Century America* (Kent, Ohio: Kent State University Press, 2007).

14. James Buchanan to Lewis S. Coryell, September 6, 1864, Lewis S. Coryell Papers, HSP; Daniel Devlin to Barlow, September 1, 1864, William Cassidy to Barlow, September 5, 1864, Theodore Romeyn to Barlow, August 31, 1864, all in Barlow Papers; Lieber to Halleck, August 21 and September 9, 1864, Lieber Papers; J. F. Rathbone to Marble, November 4, 1864, Manton Marble Papers, LC; S. Miller to General, September 24, 1864, McClellan, Papers.

15. Amasa J. Parker to Barlow, September 5, 1864, Daniel Devlin to Barlow, September 1, 1864, Andrew Morris to Barlow, September 2, 1864, James Robb to Barlow, September 3, 1864, all in Barlow Papers.

16. During the campaign, some Republicans charged McClellan with being "the leader of the Confederate forces," and rumors circulated throughout the North that he had offered his services to the Confederate government. But these rumors could not have been further from the truth. Mc-Clellan heartily wanted Union victories in the field and reunion of the states (although he did not consider abolition of slavery a prerequisite for reunion); he celebrated Sherman's capture of Atlanta, and he noted that his letter of acceptance "will be acceptable to all true patriots, & will only drive off the real adherents of Jeff Davis this side of the line." See George B. McClellan to Democratic National Committee, September 8, 1864, to Mary Ellen McClellan, September 9, 1864, to Samuel L. M. Barlow, June 17, 1864, to William C. Prime, August 10, 1864, to William H. Aspinwall, September 6, 1864, to William T. Sherman, September 26, 1864, and to Charles A. Whittier, September 27, 1864, all in Stephen W. Sears, ed., *The Civil War Papers of George B. McClellan: Selected Correspondence, 1860–1865* (New York: Ticknor and Fields, 1989), 578, 586, 594–97, 604–5; Abram J. Dittenhoefer, *How We Elected Lincoln: Personal Recollections* (1916; repr., Philadelphia: University of Pennsylvania Press, 2005), 93; Halleck to Lieber, September 12, 1864, Lieber Papers; Clement Hoffman to Mother, April 16, 1864, Clement Hoffman Letters, Harrisburg Civil War Round Table Collection, MHI; Stephen W. Sears, "McClellan and the Peace Plank of 1864: A Reappraisal," *CWH* 36 (April 1990): 57–64; and Stephen W. Sears, *George B. McClellan: The Young Napoleon* (New York: Ticknor and Fields, 1988), 361–62.

17. William H. Clement to Barlow, September 16, 1864, Barlow Papers; Belmont to Marble, September 13, 1864, Marble Papers.

18. Samuel L. M. Barlow to Marble, August 21, 1864, Marble Papers. Despite many Democrats' general aversion to the war, party leaders sought to make their candidates appear supportive of both the war effort and the troops by "getting up a '*war*' record for Pendleton for the army," as well as "good McClellan military documents." See Geo. W. A. to Manton Marble, September 27, 1864, Marble Papers.

19. Barlow to Marble, August 21, 1864, Marble Papers.

20. William B. Reed to Barlow, September 4, 22 and 30, 1864, Barlow Papers. Joel H. Silbey argues that Peace men, those he terms Purists, were more concerned with maintaining party principles than winning electoral victories. See Joel H. Silbey, *A Respectable Minority: The Democratic Party in the Civil War Era* (New York: W. W. Norton, 1977), 105–12. Letters like these from Reed, however, reveal that Peace men believed that their principles were the only ones that could carry the presidential election.

21. Abraham Lincoln, "Memorandum Concerning His Probable Failure of Re-election," August 23, 1864, in *CWL,* 7:514; Halleck to Lieber, September 2, 1864, Lieber Papers.

22. Napoleon Bonaparte Hudson to Nathaniel, August 28, 1864, Hudson Letters, and Frederic Henry Kellogg to Mother, November 8, 1864, Kellogg Letters, both in CWMC.

23. Harvey Reid to Father, November 8, 1864, in Frank L. Byrne, ed., *Uncommon Soldiers: Harvey Reid and the 22nd Wisconsin March with Sherman* (Knoxville: University of Tennessee Press, 2001), 198; Daniel G. Brinton to mother, September 12, 1864, Daniel G. Brinton Letters, CCHS; Leaner E. Davis to Wife, September 29 and October 21, 1864, Davis Letters, CWMC.

24. Henry McKendree "Mack" Ewing to Nan Ewing, September 6, 1864, Archives of Michigan (available through seekingmichigan.org).

25. Mack to Nan, September 25, 1865, ibid. For Ewing's Republican politics during the election of 1860, see William H. Arthur to Mack, October 21, 1860.

Another soldier noted shortly after the Chicago Convention that "The McClellan men here are not so boisterous as they were a few weeks since." See Edmund Raus, ed., "'Dear Brother Isaac . . .': Letters from George Edgcomb, 15th New York Engineers," *Military Images* 8 (May–June 1987): 15. Other Republican soldiers made similar observations. See Christian Brun, ed., "A Palace Guard View of Lincoln: The Civil War Letters of John H. Fleming," *Soundings: Collections of the University [of California at Santa Barbara] Library* 3 (December 1971): 35–36; Andrew Knox to Sarah Knox [wife], September 10, 1864 (GLC03523.20.16), GLI; and Joseph T. Glatthaar, *The March to the Sea and Beyond: Sherman's Troops in the Savannah and Carolinas Campaigns* (New York: New York University Press, 1985), 46, 48.

26. John F. L. Hartwell to wife, March 14, August 2, and August 14, 1864, in Ann Hartwell Britton, and Thomas J. Reed, eds., *To My Beloved Wife and Boy at Home: The Letters and Diaries of Orderly Sergeant John F. L. Hartwell* (Madison, N.J.: Fairleigh Dickinson University Press, 1997), 206, 264–65, 270, 308. For another Republican who turned against Lincoln, see Joseph M. Overfield, ed., *The Civil War Letters of Private George Parks, Co. C, 24th New York Cavalry Volunteers* (Buffalo: Gallagher Printing, 1992).

27. John C. Gray, Jr., to John C. Ropes, August 21, 1864, in Worthington Chauncey Ford, ed., *War Letters, 1862–1865, of John Chipman Gray and John Codman Ropes* (Boston: Houghton Mifflin, 1927), 376. This soldier supported Lincoln but wavered slightly before the fall of Atlanta, writing that if the Democrats nominated Maj. Gen. John A. Dix, "I should vote for him myself but I do not believe there is much chance of his being nominated." See Gray to mother, September 1, 1864, ibid., 393.

28. Alfred B. McCalmont, *Extracts from Letters Written by Alfred B. McCalmont* ([Franklin, Pa.]: Privately printed, 1908), 95–96. For a Democratic soldier who, in August 1864, believed that Mc-Clellan would win a majority of the soldier vote, see William H. Hastings, ed., *Letters from a Sharp-shooter: The Civil War Letters of Private William B. Greene, Co. G, 2nd United States Sharpshooters (Berdan's), Army of the Potomac, 1861–1865* (Belleville, Wisc.: Historic Publications, 1993), 249, 252.

29. John Quincy Adams Campbell, diary entry for September 23, 1864, in Mark Grimsley and Todd D. Miller, eds., *The Union Must Stand: The Civil War Diary of John Quincy Adams Campbell, Fifth Iowa Volunteer Infantry* (Knoxville: University of Tennessee Press, 2000), 183.

30. Barbara Schilling Everstine, ed., *My Three Years in the Volunteer Army of the United States of America, from August 12th, 1862, to June 10th, 1865: Edw. Schilling, Co. F, Fourth Md. Vol. Infty.* (N.p., 1985), 85, 87, 94. In another section of the memoir, he wrote: "I regret to state that Little Mac (as he is familiarly called) was for a time very popular, but Genl. Sherman's capture of Atlanta, Ga. and Genl. Sheridan's brilliant victories in the Shenandoah Valley, Va. soon turned the peoples['] and Soldiers['] mind[.] Mac was denounced[;] the Chicago platform declared a traitors['] document[; and] Mac's most earnest supporters dropped off and and [*sic*] fell in with the Lincoln men." See ibid., 94.

31. Historian Reid Mitchell argues that many soldiers would not vote for the Democratic platform because "abandoning the war meant making a mockery of their sacrifices." When the soldiers cast their ballots "overwhelmingly for Abraham Lincoln and the Republican party in the 1864 election—[they] voted, indeed, for the continuance of the war." See Reid Mitchell, *The Vacant Chair: The Northern Soldier Leaves Home* (New York: Oxford University Press, 1993), 158–59. For such views of a Lincoln supporter, see George R. Agassiz, ed., *Meade's Headquarters 1863–1865: Letters of Colonel Theodore Lyman from Wilderness to Appomattox* (Boston: Atlantic Monthly Press, 1922), 245, 259–60.

32. Samuel Brooks to Wife, November 4, 1864, Brooks Letters, CWMC. See also Carl Uterhard to Mother, September 5, 1864, Christopher Monn to Brother et al., December 9, 1863, Christian Bonsel

to Parents et al., January 29, 1865, and G. W. Schwarting to Brother, August 15, 1864, all in Walter D. Kamphoefner and Wolfgang Helbich, eds., *Germans in the Civil War: The Letters They Wrote Home* (Chapel Hill: University of North Carolina Press, 2006), 172, 273, 330, 443; H. J. H. Thompson to wife, March 27 and November 27, 1864, quoted in John G. Barrett, *The Civil War in North Carolina* (Chapel Hill: University of North Carolina Press, 1963), 226; Isaac E. Blauvelt to Hannah Speaker, November 21, 1864, in Charles E. Finsley, ed., *Hannah's Letters: Civil War Letters of Isaac E. Blauvelt, Friends and Other Suitors* (Dallas: Kings Creek Press, 1997), 60–61.

33. John Berry to Samuel L. M. Barlow, September 3, 1864, Barlow Papers; Daniel Helker to George Miller, November 2, 1864, George Miller Collection, MHI; see also John Borry to Daniel Musser, September 12, 1864, Daniel Musser Papers (MG-95), PHMC.

34. Unlike some of their civilian brethren at home, Democratic soldiers wanted victories in the field. See, for example, Lewis to Harry, September 3, 1864, Henry S. Jay Papers, CWMC; John Berry to Barlow, August 27, 1864, Barlow Papers; Symmes Stillwell to Mother, December 3, 1864, and September 7, 1864, Civil War Papers of Symmes H. Stillwell, Rare Books and Special Collections, Firestone Library, Princeton University. On the importance of "Union" to northern soldiers, see Gallagher, *The Union War*.

35. Martin G. Ellison to Parent and Sister, October 1, 1864, Martin G. Ellison Papers, Research Center, Wisconsin Veterans Museum, Madison. (I thank Abbie Norderhaug for providing me with photocopies of the Ellison Papers.) See also George F. Morse to Father, November 6, 1864, Morse Letters, CWMC; Charles A. Coward to Father, January 25, 1863, Coward Letters, CWMC; John Berry to Barlow, August 27, 1864, Barlow Papers.

36. John Morton to mother, January 13, 1863 and August 31, 1864, Morton Letters, and Morris W. Chalmers to sister, September 26, 1864 and October 27, 1864, Chalmers Letters, both in CWMC; Charles Henry Morgan to Susannah Miller, September 23, 1864, CCHS.

37. John S. McVey to Horace Subers, October 15, 1864, McVey Letters, and Thomas C. Bowman to Sister, October 20, 1864, Bowman Letters, both in CWMC.

38. Brigham Foster to wife, November 9, 1864, Foster Letters, CWMC. This soldier also believed that the southern people would never be willing to end the war while Lincoln was president and his emancipation policy was the law of the land.

39. Jacob B. Dannaker to Mother, December 28, 1864, Dannaker Letters, CWMC.

40. Gary W. Gallagher, *The Union War* (Cambridge: Harvard University Press, 2011), 101–8. According to Glenn David Brasher, Union soldiers welcomed fugitive slaves into their camps to serve as labor forces so that the soldiers would not exhaust themselves doing fatigue duty. See Glenn David Brasher, *The Peninsula Campaign and the Necessity of Emancipation: African Americans and the Fight for Freedom* (Chapel Hill: University of North Carolina Press, 2012), 105, 108–11, 191–214.

41. Thomas Townsend to Mary, October 18, 1864, in Susan T. Puck, ed., *Sacrifice at Vicksburg: Letters from the Front* (Shippensburg, Pa.: Burd Street Press, 1997), 78.

42. T. S. Bowers to Isham N. Haynie, October 9, 1864, Isham N. Haynie Papers, Abraham Lincoln Presidential Library, Springfield, Ill. The recipient of this letter, Isham Haynie, was an officer in the Forty-Eighth Illinois who had resigned his commission in the spring of 1863 when the Republican-controlled Senate refused to confirm his promotion to brigadier general (see chapter 3). From the content of this letter, it appears that Haynie had declared his support for Lincoln in 1864.

43. Edward King Wightman to Brother, October 26, 1864, in Edward G. Longacre, ed., *From Antietam to Fort Fisher: The Civil War Letters of Edward King Wightman, 1862–1865* (Madison, N.J.:

Fairleigh Dickinson University Press, 1985), 212–13; Charles Francis Adams Jr. to Father, October 15, 1864, in Worthington Chauncey Ford, ed., *A Cycle of Adams Letters, 1861–1865,* 2 vols. (Boston: Houghton Mifflin, 1920), 2:204; Charles H. Smith to wife, October 20, 1864, Charles H. Smith Letters, CWMC; Patrick, diary entry for October 25, 1864, in Sparks, ed., *Diary,* 433. For a soldier who loathed both African Americans and Copperheads, see the letters of George W. Tillotson of the Eighty-Ninth New York Volunteers (GLC04558), GLI, selections of which are available in Robert E. Bonner, ed., *The Soldier's Pen: Firsthand Impressions of the Civil War* (New York: Hill and Wang, 2006).

44. John Berry to Samuel L. M. Barlow, November 4, 1864, Barlow Papers.

45. Ibid. This soldier's fear that McClellan might die in office was shared by others. Some northern voters even feared that the Peace men would assassinate McClellan so that Pendleton could assume the presidency. See S. Miller to General, September 24, 1864, McClellan Papers.

46. Durbin Ward to Samuel S. Cox, August 2, 1864, Samuel S. Cox Papers, Brown University. This soldier continued: "Lincoln is not at all my choice and it is difficult for me to conceive a contingency in which I shall vote for him. But still even a worse may be elected." He further argued that slavery could not be abolished by force, as Lincoln sought to do, but that if the Democrats put McClellan on a Peace platform, "you will ruin your Candidate by the load you will put on his back."

47. Adam Badeau to Harry, September 4, 1864, Badeau Papers; John Preston Campbell to Sister, September 11, 1864, Campbell Letters, Edward Cotter to Parents, November 15, 1864, Cotter Letters, and Samuel J. Marks to Carrie, October 1, 1864, Marks Letters, all in CWMC. In like manner, one soldier told his father, "I would be for Mc but [for] the man that is his vice and the platform." Instead, he supported Lincoln because "he is the very man to put down this rebellion and will do it and I am for him." See T. B. Adams to father, October 25, 1864, in Jean Anne W. Hudder, ed., *Dear Wife: Captain Joseph Adams' Letters to His Wife, Eliza Ann, 1861–1864* (s.l.: J. A. W. Hudder, 1985), 147.

48. Hermon Clarke to Father, September 11, 1864, and October 3, 1864, in Harry F. Jackson and Thomas F. O'Donnell, eds., *Back Home in Oneida: Hermon Clarke and His Letters* (Syracuse: Syracuse University Press, 1965), 161, 166; Morris W. Chalmers to Sister, October 27, 1864, Chalmers Letters, and George W. Lewis to Henry S. Jay, August 29 and September 3, 1864, Henry S. Jay Papers, both in CWMC; A. Beeler to Elihu Washburne, October 6, 1864, Elihu Washburne Papers, LC.

49. Hermon Clarke to Father, November 13, 1864, in Jackson and O'Donnell, eds., *Back Home,* 176–77.

50. Robert Winn to Sister, July 16, August 1, October 19, 21, and 26, 1864, Winn-Cook Family Papers, The Filson. Kentucky was the only state from which the soldiers gave a majority for McClellan.

51. George W. Lewis to Harry, August 29, 1864, Henry S. Jay Papers, CWMC.

52. William Allen Clark to Parents, June 5, 1864, in Margaret Black Tatum, ed., "'Please Send Stamps': The Civil War Letters of William Allen Clark, Part IV," *Indiana Magazine of History* 91 (December 1995); 420; Andrew Knox to Wife, February 22, 1863, Knox Letters, CWMC. See also George D. Williams to Henry S. Jay, March 24, June 20, and August 18, 1864, Henry S. Jay Papers, CWMC.

53. At least three writers have noted the low voter turnout among the troops. "Only 3,121 of approximately 15,000 Union soldiers [from Maryland] took advantage of this opportunity [to vote]," writes Jean H. Baker, "although certainly some soldiers received convenient furloughs and returned home to vote. The voting procedures in the field, which permitted officers to collect ballots, probably intimidated some Democrats from voting." See Jean H. Baker, *The Politics of Continuity: Maryland Political Parties from 1858 to 1870* (Baltimore: Johns Hopkins University Press, 1973), 131n59. Arnold M. Shankman points out that only about 30 percent of Ohio soldiers voted in the gubernatorial election

of 1863. See Arnold M. Shankman, "Soldier Votes and Clement L. Vallandigham in the 1863 Ohio Gubernatorial Election," *Ohio History* 82 (Winter/Spring 1973): 101. Josiah Benton attributed low voter turnout in the presidential election of 1864 to the difficulty of getting ballots to the soldiers in the field. See Benton, *Voting in the Field,* 315–22.

54. McKelvy, "Diary," 404; *O.R.,* ser. 1, vol. 42, pt. 3, 549. See also William H. Newlin, *A History of the Seventy-Third Regiment of Illinois Infantry Volunteers:* Published by the Authority of the Regimental Reunion Association of Survivors of the 73d Illinois Infantry Volunteers, 1890), 388; William C. Hacket to Wife, October 27, 1864, Hacket Letters, CWMC; E. P. Sturges to Folks, November 9, 1864, E. P. Sturges Correspondence, *Civil War Times Illustrated* Collection, MHI. For an instance in which a state's election commissioners could not reach several regiments, see Lynwood G. Downs, "The Soldier Vote and Minnesota Politics, 1862–65," *Minnesota History* 26 (September 1945): 205–9.

55. J. B. Wood, "Visit to the Army of Eastern Virginia and North Carolina," *West Chester Village Record,* October 25 1864; Kermit Molyneux Bird, ed. *Quill of the Wild Goose: The Civil War Letters and Diaries of Private Joel Molyneux, 141st P. V.* (Shippensburg, Pa.: Burd Street Press, 1996), 230, 235.

56. George Gordon Meade to wife, October 7, 1864, in George Gordon Meade, *The Life and Letters of George Gordon Meade,* 2 vols. (New York: Charles Scribner's Sons, 1913), 2:232, 239; Hermon Clarke to Brother, October 9, 1864, in Jackson and O'Donnell, eds., *Back Home,* 169; Jesse Brown to sister, October 23, 1864 (GLC03523.15.19), GLI; Edwin Weller to Nett, October 15, 1864, in William Walton, ed., *A Civil War Courtship: The Letters of Edwin Weller from Antietam to Atlanta* (New York: Doubleday, 1980), 115–16; Harvey Reid to Pa, September 19, 1863, in Byrne, ed., *Uncommon Soldiers,* 91. See also J. C. Hoadley, ed., *Memorial of Henry Sanford Gansevoort* (Boston: Franklin Press, 1875), 157–58, 173–74, 179–81, 188–89; and G. D. McCormick to Margaret Williams, September 28, 1864, Evan Williams Civil War Letters, Historical Collections and Labor Archives, Paterno Library, Pennsylvania State University.

57. This is not to imply that they were ideologically disinterested, as past scholars, such as Bell Irvin Wiley, describe them.

58. John W. Rowell, *Yankee Cavalrymen: Through the Civil War with the Ninth Pennsylvania Cavalry* (Knoxville: University of Tennessee Press, 1971), 196.

59. Meade, *Life and Letters,* 2:233–34; McKelvy, "Diary," 404, 410.

60. John H. Rippetoe to Mary J. Rippetoe, September 18, 1864, Rippetoe Letters, CWMC. This soldier was still proud of the vote in his unit, which must have gone overwhelmingly for Lincoln.

61. William D. Butler to James and the folks, October 26, 1864, War Letters 1861–65, NYHS. Again, in his regiment the majority also went for Lincoln.

62. Willie Root to Laura, October 16, 1864, Willie Root Diary and Letters, *Civil War Times Illustrated* Collection, 2nd ser., MHI; John W. Chase to Brother, November 12, 1864, in John S. Collier and Bonnie B. Collier, eds., *Yours for the Union: The Civil War Letters of John W. Chase, First Massachusetts Light Artillery* (New York: Fordham University Press, 2004), 376.

63. Jacob Early to Sarah and Minnie, November 8, 1864, in Robert A. Driver and Gloria S. Driver, eds., *Letters Home: The Personal Side of the American Civil War* (Roseburg, Ore.: Privately printed, 1992), 85.

64. Henry Clay Weaver to darling, November 10, 1864, in James M. Merrill and James F. Marshall, eds., "Georgia through Kentucky Eyes: Letters Written on Sherman's March to Atlanta," *Filson Club History Quarterly* 30 (October 1956): 338.

65. George Drake to Father, September 22, 1864, in Julia A. Drake, ed., *The Mail Goes Through or*

Civil War Letters of George Drake (San Angelo, Tex.: Anchor, 1964), 115. See also Bonner, ed., *Soldier's Pen,* 144.

66. Quoted in David E. Long, *The Jewel of Liberty: Abraham Lincoln's Reelection and the End of Slavery* (Mechanicsburg, Pa.: Stackpole, 1994), 232.

67. George M. Buck to McClellan, November 10, 1864, McClellan Papers.

68. Walter Jacobs, journal entries for September 24, October 26, and November 19, 1864, in Walter Jacobs Family Papers (MS0514), The Mariners' Museum Library, Paul and Rosemary Trible Library, Christopher Newport University, Newport News, Va. Other soldiers used the same metaphor of not wanting to swap horses while midstream. See, for example, Stewart Bennett and Barbara Tillery, eds., *The Struggle for the Life of the Republic: A Civil War Narrative by Brevet Major Charles Dana Miller, 76th Ohio Volunteer Infantry* (Kent, Ohio: Kent State University Press, 2004), 208–9.

69. Walter G. Dunn to Emma, November 19, 1864, in Judith A. Bailey and Robert I. Cottom, eds., *After Chancellorsville, Letters from the Heart: The Civil War Letters of Private Walter G. Dunn & Emma Randolph* (Baltimore: Maryland Historical Society, 1998), 138.

70. Partisan attachment may have also, at times, seemed less secure among Republican soldiers. One wounded cavalryman at a hospital in Philadelphia warned Pennsylvania's Republican governor that if the soldiers were not allowed to go home to vote (rather than vote at the hospital), many would refuse to vote at all, and he warned the governor that "some of the less intelligent even threaten to 'change their colors.'" See H. K. Smith to [Andrew G. Curtin], October 12, 1864, RG 19 (Records of the Department of the Military), Subgroup: Office of the Adjutant General, Series 19.29 (General Correspondence), PHMC. Other Republican soldiers threatened to vote against Lincoln for not being hawkish enough. See, for example, Lance Herdegen and Sherry Murphy, eds., *Four Years with the Iron Brigade: The Civil War Journals of William R. Ray, Co. F., Seventh Wisconsin Infantry* (Cambridge, Mass.: Da Capo Press, 2002), diary entries for August 31 and September 4, 6, 1864.

71. George W. Tillotson to Wife, November 21, 1863 (GLC04558.124), George W. Tillotson Papers, GLI.

72. Nevins, ed., *Diary of Battle,* 473.

73. Margaret McKelvy Bird and Daniel W. Crofts, eds., "Soldier Voting in 1864: The David McKelvy Diary," *Pennsylvania Magazine of History and Biography* 115 (July 1991): 393.

74. Richard Franklin Bensel, *The American Ballot Box in the Mid-Nineteenth Century* (New York: Cambridge University Press, 2004), 268.

75. See, for example, Court-Martial Case file LL-1359.

76. Hermon Clarke to Father, October 16 and 17, 1864, in Jackson and O'Donnell, eds., *Back Home,* 171, 173; Robert Emmet Doyle to Barlow, October 27, 1864, Barlow Papers; "From the Headquarters of the Army of the Potomac," September 22, 1864, Geo. W. A. to Mr. Croly, September 22 and 25, 1864, Horatio Seymour to August Belmont, September 26, 1864, Geo. W. A. to Marble, September 27 and October 2, 1864, all in Marble Papers; Wilhelm Mobus to Parents et al., November 4, 1864, in David L. Anderson, ed., "The Letters of 'Wilhelm Yank': Letters from a German Soldier in the Civil War," *Michigan Historical Review* 16 (Spring 1990): 81; Peter Curley to Andrew Curtin, October 11, 1864, Slifer-Dill Papers, Dickinson College.

77. Court-Martial Case file MM-1797. After finding that there were no Democratic ballots at his camp on election day, Private Miller went searching for some at another regimental camp. Upon returning, his comrades tore up his ballots and declared that anyone who voted for McClellan "was a traitor and a coward." At his trial, Miller informed the court that he had fought at fifteen of the sixteen battles in which his regiment had been engaged. The court found Miller guilty of having said

that he would rather vote for Jefferson Davis than Lincoln, but did not attach criminality to his words on account of how his comrades had provoked him.

78. George Breck to Ellen, October 23, 1864, in Blake McKelvey, ed., *Rochester in the Civil War* (Rochester, N.Y.: Rochester Historical Society, 1944), 141.

79. *Congressional Serial Set*, 39th Cong., 1st sess., House Misc. Doc. 117, p. 140.

80. Leonidas C. Houk to Andrew Johnson, October 31, 1864, in Leroy P. Graf et al., eds., *The Papers of Andrew Johnson: Volume 7, 1864–1865* (Knoxville: University of Tennessee Press, 1986), 262.

81. Gideon R. Viars to Mary Viars, September 21, 1864, Viars Family Papers, The Filson; "Kentucky Unionist" to August Belmont, September 27, 1864, Marble Papers.

82. Quoted in Jennifer Ruth Horner, "Blood and Ballots: Military Voting and Political Communication in the Union Army during the United States Civil War, 1861–1865" (Ph.D. diss., University of Pennsylvania, 2006), 206.

83. Quoted in Lowry, *Don't Shoot That Boy*, 137.

84. Harry Gilmor, *Four Years in the Saddle* (New York: Harper, 1866), 272–75.

85. For evidence of minors voting, see James G. Knight, "Some Experiences of a Soldier and Engineer," manuscript memoir dated 1890, James G. Knight Papers, Research Center, Wisconsin Veterans Museum, Madison; Susan Hinckley Bradley, ed., *A Soldier-Boy's Letters, 1862–1865* (Boston: Privately printed, 1905), 48; *Congressional Serial Set*, 38th Cong., 1st sess., House Report 66, pp. 1–2, 9, 12 (majority report), and 9, 14–15 (minority report); 38th Cong., 2nd sess., House Misc. Doc. 57, pp. 529–31, 534, 544–49; 39th Cong., 1st sess., House Report 88, p. 4; 39th Cong., 1st sess., House Misc. Doc. 9, pt. 3, pp. 92, 160; 39th Cong., 1st sess., House Misc. Doc. 92, pp. 1–3, 130–32, 142; 39th Cong., 1st sess., House Misc. Doc. 117, pp. 26–27, 31, 139–40. Not all minors who wanted to vote were successful. See, for example, James A. Thorson, ed., *Pontius Family Letters, 1861–1933* (Omaha, Neb.: Privately printed, 1999), 16–17. And some minors' votes were thrown out later during contested elections.

86. Court-Martial Case files LL-2615 and MM-2213.

87. RG 153, Entry 18, case 98. He was acquitted of saying the last statement.

88. Court-Martial Case file MM-1545.

89. Court-Martial File LL-2698. In this case, the Republican soldier was court-martialed for conduct prejudicial to good order and military discipline. He pleaded guilty but asked for clemency because of the provocation of the Democratic officer. He was sentenced to one year in prison at Alton, Illinois, and a fifty-dollar fine.

Fights could break out between soldiers of varying political persuasions. Writing in September 1864 from Atlanta, one Illinois soldier reported to his mother that he had "seen one fight on the subject [of politics] since I com[m]enced writing this letter." See George A. Hudson to mother, September 11, 1864, George A. Hudson Papers, LC. At a Confederate prison camp, one Democratic soldier noted that the Confederate guards held an election for the prisoners. The soldiers were given a sack of peas, which would serve as their ballots. McClellan voters would vote with a symbolic "white pea," while "those who wished to vote for Lincoln, the nigger President, could take . . . a black pea." The Lincoln men formed a large majority, "and some of them not being very liberal, they fell on the four poor McClellan men and beat them shamefully, and might have killed some of them; but a majority of us interfered, and stopped them." See Hugh Moore, "A Reminiscence of Confederate Prison Life," *Journal of the Illinois State Historical Society* 65 (Winter 1972): 457–58.

90. Samuel S. Cox to Marble, October 12, 1864, Marble Papers; Cox to Barlow, October 11, 1864, Barlow Papers; Cox to McClellan, October 11, 1864, McClellan Papers.

91. James S. Graham to Aunt Ellen, November 7, 1864, in William H. Bartlett, ed., *Aunt and the*

Soldier Boys (Santa Cruz, Calif.: Privately printed, 1973), 152. Democrats could also be guilty of such behavior. See Fitz-John Porter to Barlow, June 3, 1863, Barlow Papers. Republican soldiers from New York also believed they would be defrauded of their votes by unscrupulous state agents in Baltimore and Washington. See William P. Forman to Seward, October 28, 1864, Seward Papers; and Jonathan W. White, "Canvassing the Troops: The Federal Government and the Soldiers' Right to Vote," *CWH* 50 (September 2004): 303–9.

92. Quoted in Horner, "Blood and Ballots," 222–23. Ironically, this officer's battalion gave a majority for McClellan, but "the votes of the officers were almost unanimously for Lincoln." It thus may have been the officers in conjunction with several of the enlisted men who tormented the Democratic electioneers.

93. William B. Reed to Barlow, October 18, 1864, Barlow Papers; Nelson G. Huson to George T. Huson, August 14, 1864 (HM29119), HL. This sort of electioneering had occurred in previous elections as well. See Jonathan W. White, "Citizens and Soldiers: Party Competition and the Debate in Pennsylvania over Permitting Soldiers to Vote, 1861–64," *American Nineteenth Century History* 5 (Summer 2004): 57.

94. Hastings, ed., *Letters from a Sharpshooter,* 248. He likely either meant "Darkey" or "Devil."

95. John D. Cottrell to Maggie, November 7, 1864, in Richard M. Trimble, ed., *Brothers 'Til Death: The Civil War Letters of William, Thomas, and Maggie Jones, 1861–1865* (Macon, Ga.: Mercer University Press, 2000), 117.

96. William Cannon to Edwin M. Stanton, October 27, 1864, Edwin M. Stanton Papers, LC. See also the discussion of the 1863 Pennsylvania gubernatorial election in chapter 1.

97. Quoted in Horner, "Blood and Ballots," 192. See also Bensel, *American Ballot Box,* 266n118.

98. Charles A. Dana, *Recollections of the Civil War* (New York: Collier, 1963), 227.

99. E. D. Morgan to Stanton, September 15, 1864, Stanton Papers, LC.

100. George B. McClellan to Elizabeth B. McClellan, July 3, 1864, in Sears, ed., *Civil War Papers of George B. McClellan,* 581–82. Other officers and enlisted men who were arrested, court-martialed, and/or dismissed during the election season include Brig. Gen. James G. Spears, Col. Frank Wolford of the First Kentucky Cavalry, Pvt. Newton B. Spencer of the 179th New York Infantry, and Lt. Charles Steck of Pennsylvania Independent Battery A. For information on these soldiers, see chapters 2 and 3.

101. Alfred B. McCalmont, *Extracts from Letters Written by Alfred B. McCalmont* ([Franklin, Pa.]: Privately printed, 1908), 94.

102. Ibid., 88, 93–94; Robert M. Sandow, *Deserter Country: Civil War Opposition in the Pennsylvania Appalachians* (New York: Fordham University Press, 2009), 117–18.

103. Lowry, *Utterly Worthless,* 19. Condict's CMSR says "to protect" instead of "to support." Privately, Condict wrote that his dismissal was "unfortunate" but that his principles were "unchanged because I have never seen a reason to change them." Condict professed that his "love for my Country is still as strong as ever" but that the nation's "rulers have betrayed my confidence and outraged my notions of right thus paralyzing my energies and disqualifying me for effective service." Still, he would not turn against the Union, writing that he would "be crushed" before he would "lift a hand against my Country." Writing just before the presidential election, he concluded, "I still hope that Heaven may avert the dreadful calamities that threaten us as a nation." See Cincinnatus Condict to Uzal Condict, October 2, 1864, collection of the author.

104. Lowry, *Utterly Worthless,* 32, 34, 36, 63, 94, 105; *United States Service Magazine* 2 (October 1864): 398, 2 (November 1864): 496–97, and 2 (December 1864): 584. More cases are discussed in

chapter 2. Other white officers in black regiments kept these sorts of opinions to themselves. See, for example, Frank Levstik, ed., "The Civil War Diary of Colonel Albert Rogall," *Polish American Studies* 27 (Spring/Autumn 1970): 33–79.

105. Quoted in Benjamin P. Thomas and Harold M. Hyman, *Stanton: The Life and Times of Lincoln's Secretary of War* (New York: Alfred A. Knopf, 1962), 328.

106. John H. Ferry to McClellan, October 3, 1864, McClellan Papers.

107. Ibid.

108. Charles S. Tripler to McClellan, September 20, 1864, McClellan Papers.

109. Marsena Rudolph Patrick, diary entry for January 2, 1865, in David S. Sparks, ed., *Inside Lincoln's Army: The Diary of General Marsena Rudolph Patrick, Provost Marshal General, Army of the Potomac* (New York: Thomas Yoseloff, 1964), 455.

110. James O. Miller to Nellie McClellan, September 1, 1864, and Tripler to McClellan, September 20, 1864, both in McClellan Papers. See also Charles D. Deshler to McClellan, September 13, 1864, and George W. Morgan to McClellan, November 3, 1864, both in McClellan Papers.

111. Charles C. Morey to parents, July 8, 1864, Charles C. Morey Collection (GLC03523.18.18), GLI.

112. Allan Nevins, ed., *A Diary of Battle: The Personal Journals of Colonel Charles S. Wainwright* (New York: Harcourt, Brace and World, 1962), 480.

113. Agassiz, ed., *Meade's Headquarters*, 247–48.

114. Durbin Ward to Samuel S. Cox, August 2, 1864, Samuel S. Cox Papers, Brown University. Another officer wrote to his brother: "I do not say much about politics here. There never is much propriety in political discussions and wrangles." See Alfred B. McCalmont, *Extracts from Letters Written by Alfred B. McCalmont* ([Franklin, Pa.]: Privately printed, 1908), 86–87.

115. James O. Miller to Nellie McClellan, September 1, 1864, McClellan Papers; Sears, *McClellan*, 363–64, 382–83. Some soldiers feared that their mail was being opened, read, and censored by neighbors and the government. See Horner, "Blood and Ballots," 88, 96.

116. Cyrus W. Beamenderfer to Daniel Musser, October 31, 1864, Daniel Musser Papers (MG-95), PHMC.

117. Alanson Randol to Barlow, October 13, 1864, Barlow Papers. For an instance in which an anti-McClellan soldier received leniency from a court-martial when he was tried for swearing at a pro-McClellan soldier during the presidential campaign, see Lorien Foote, *The Gentlemen and the Roughs: Violence, Honor, and Manhood in the Union Army* (New York: New York University Press, 2010), 34–36.

118. Collier and Collier, eds., *Yours for the Union*, 363.

119. *The American Annual Cyclopaedia and Register of Important Events of the Year 1864*, 14 vols. (New York: D. Appleton, 1862–75), 764–65.

120. Merrill and Marshall, eds., "Georgia through Kentucky Eyes," 338. According to this soldier's letter, it is apparent that soldiers in Tennessee were able to vote for McClellan, but he recounted that one black man was not permitted to vote the Democratic ticket.

121. Charles D. Deshler to McClellan, September 13, 1864, McClellan Papers. For a New York captain who also called himself a "*marked* man," see Levi Beardsley to McClellan, October 11, 1864, ibid.

122. John Berry to Barlow, February 27, 1864, Barlow Papers; Jacob Weiker to Sister, April 29, 1863, Weiker Letters, CWMC; Francis M. Elliott to Sister, October 29, 1864, in Peter G. Boag, ed., "'Dear Friends': The Civil War Letters of Francis Marion Elliot, A Pennsylvania Country Boy," *Pitts-*

burgh History 72 (Holiday 1989): 196. See also Cyrus W. Beamenderfer to Daniel Musser, February 20 and July 13, 1864, Daniel Musser Papers (MG-95), PHMC.

123. Lewis G. Schmidt, *A Civil War History of the 147th Pennsylvania Regiment* (Allentown, Pa.: Lewis G. Schmidt, 2000), 1000.

124. John D. Cottrell to Maggie, April 24, 1865, in Trimble, ed., *Brothers 'Til Death*, 141.

125. Remarkably, some Union soldiers exulted in the death of their commander in chief, an action which violated the Fifth Article of War. Most soldiers who hated Lincoln were probably wise enough to keep their rejoicings to themselves. "Our tyrannical President Abraham Lincoln was shot in a theatre by a man by the name of Wilkes Booth," wrote one German soldier serving in a Pennsylvania regiment. "The whole country grieves at his death. Personally I am heartily pleased over it, yet for appearance sake I must make a long face over it." See Franz Schwenzer to Father-in-Law, July 4, 1865, translation in CWMC.

Not all soldiers were shrewd enough to conceal their true feelings. One private under Irvin McDowell's command in the Department of the Pacific was convicted of using "treasonable and mutinous language" when he declared that "Abraham Lincoln, was a long sided son of a bitch, and ought to be killed long ago." When brought before a court-martial, the soldier said he never used "profane or vulgar language" and that he "would not rejoice over the . . . assassination of a gentleman whom I highly respected." He had been a soldier in the regular army for ten years, he declared, and once was wounded in the head by a musket ball. The result was that whenever he was drunk he had no recollection of what he did: "I am Non Compos Mentis, and act in a strange and unaccountable manner." He claimed to have been intoxicated when the alleged incident occurred (this excuse was given by nearly every soldier court-martialed for exulting in Lincoln's death). He therefore asked for clemency, but instead he was convicted and sentenced to be shot. The commanding general, however, mitigated his sentence to hard labor for the duration of his term of service and the loss of all pay. See Court-Martial Case file MM-2771 (Pvt. James Walker, Eighth California Volunteers).

Other soldiers were also sentenced to death for celebratory language relating to the death of Lincoln. One veteran in Baltimore was charged with "conduct tending to excite and cause a mutiny" for "express[ing] pleasure at and approbation of the assassination and death of Abraham Lincoln" in the presence of many enlisted men. He was arrested and confined to the guard house, but escaped and was later picked up in town, where he was confined to the city jail. He pled "not guilty," claiming to be "drunk" and "crazy" during these various occurrences, but was convicted and sentenced to death. The commanding general mitigated his sentence to three years at hard labor with loss of pay. See Court-Martial Case file MM-2304 (Pvt. Charles Hodson, Second Veteran Reserve Corps).

In cases where the evidence was not sufficient to prove that a soldier had uttered treasonable words regarding the president's death, or where witnesses did not agree upon the facts, the prisoners were acquitted, or, if convicted, their sentences were overturned by the commanding general. See Court-Martial Case files MM-2190 (Barney Lowrie, Fifth New York Artillery), MM-2379 (Sgt. James Corner, Seventeenth U.S. Infantry), OO-1078 (Hanson Grey, Twelfth New Hampshire Volunteers), OO-1146 (Garnett Cole, First New Jersey Cavalry), and OO-1267 (Patrick Kelly, Fifteenth New York Heavy Artillery). Many were sentenced to hard labor for exulting in Lincoln's death; all were dishonorably discharged and lost any back and future pay due to them. See, for example, Court-Martial Case files MM-1936 (Elijah Chapman, Tenth Veteran Reserve Corps), MM-2047 (John Largest, Twenty-Fourth Michigan Infantry), MM-2093 (John Tillman, Tenth Veteran Reserve Corps), MM-2344 (James Flint, Thirty-Sixth Ohio Volunteers), and MM-2531 (John Nash, 142nd Indiana Infantry).

One Indiana soldier who proclaimed, "Abe Lincoln is dead. Hurrah for old Abe. Who cares a damn, let him go to hell," was found guilty by a court-martial and sentenced "to be paraded through the grounds" of the hospital where the offense had taken place, for two hours, with an escort of drums and fifes, and "with a placard on his back, with the following words written or printed plainly thereon: This man said 'Abe Lincoln is dead; who cares a damn, let him go to hell.'" See Court-Martial Case file MM-2547 (Alexander Cissell, Fifty-Second Indiana Infantry). One can only imagine the harsh response such a punishment elicited from his peers.

For other soldiers who were court-martialed and punished for exulting in Lincoln's assassination, see Court-Martial Case files MM-2011 (Sgt. Henry Brainard of the Ninety-Eighth New York Volunteers), MM-2384 (Pvt. William Hall of the 151st New York Volunteers), OO-771 (Corp. Andrew J. Russell of the Eighth Michigan Cavalry), OO-1076 (Lt. Col. Nicholash Dale of the Second Wisconsin Cavalry), and OO-1129 (Pvts. Jacob Campbell, Frank Allen and John Ryman of the Thirtieth Michigan Infantry).

126. Chester W. Shaw to Father and Mother, September 20, 1864, in Michael David Raya, ed., *Letters from the Front: Three Years in the Civil War* (Privately printed, 2001), 86.

127. Nevins, ed. *Diary of Battle, 476.* This soldier refused to vote for Horatio Seymour's reelection in New York in 1864, but he did end up voting for McClellan for president.

Adding Johnson to the ticket certainly persuaded some conservative soldiers to vote for Lincoln. A newspaper correspondent wrote to Andrew Johnson shortly before the election describing some of the Democrats in the army: "Several of the officers, however, will vote the Union ticket, on account of your name being on it, although they say they do not fully endorse Lincoln." See Benjamin C. Truman to Andrew Johnson, July 17, 1864, in Graf, *Papers of Andrew Johnson,* 7:37.

128. For an excellent discussion of the ebbs of flows of army morale, see James M. McPherson, *For Cause and Comrades: Why Men Fought in the Civil War* (New York: Oxford University Press, 1997), 155–62. See also Glatthaar, *March to the Sea and Beyond,* 43.

129. Oliver Wendell Holmes, Jr., to parents, June 24, 1864, in Mark DeWolfe Howe, ed., *Touched with Fire: The Civil War Letters and Diary of Oliver Wendell Holmes, Jr., 1861–1864* (1947; repr., New York: Da Capo Press, 1969), 150.

130. Pat to Harry, August 26, 1864, Henry S. Jay Papers, CWMC.

131. This soldier added in October: "I do not know anything new to write to you except that their is a great change hear in political matters the men are a getting their eyes open and can see wheir they are and they began to think that Linkon has done something after all, and they are redy to try him again is the talk of a great meny that 2 months ago was for McClenon body & sole." See Guy C. Taylor to wife, September 22 and October 14, 1864, both in Kevin Alderson and Patsy Alderson, *Letters Home to Sarah: The Civil War Letters of Guy C. Taylor, 36th Wisconsin Volunteers* (Madison: University of Wisconsin Press, 2012), 115, 130.

132. Memorandum on the Election of 1864, by Francis Lieber, on the back of Erastus Cornelius Benedict to Lieber, November 21, 1864.

CHAPTER FIVE

1. On the connection between military service and citizenship, see Ricardo A. Herrera, "Self-Government and the American Citizen as Soldier, 1775–1861," *Journal of Military History* 65 (January

2001): 21–52; Earl J. Hess, *Liberty, Virtue, and Progress: Northerners and Their War for the Union* (New York: New York University Press, 1988; repr., New York: Fordham University Press, 1997), chap. 4; Charles Royster, "'The Nature of Treason': Revolutionary Virtue and American Reactions to Benedict Arnold," *William and Mary Quarterly* 36 (April 1979): 165–66.

2. Alexander Keyssar, *The Right to Vote: The Contested History of Democracy in the United States* (New York: Basic, 2000), 104. Relying heavily on Keyssar's work, Mark A. Graber argues that scholars must pay more attention to expansions of suffrage, like the soldier vote, as evidence that civil liberties do not always narrow in times of war. See Mark A. Graber, "Voting Rights and Other 'Anomalies': Protecting and Expanding Civil Liberties in Wartime," in Thomas E. Baker and John F. Stack Jr., eds., *At War with Civil Rights and Civil Liberties* (Lanham, Md.: Rowman and Littlefield, 2006), 153–76.

3. Xi Wang, *The Trial of Democracy: Black Suffrage and Northern Republicans, 1860–1910* (Athens: University of Georgia Press, 1997), 11.

4. Andrew Irwin Diary, undated but probably May 1863, CCHS. Similarly, in July 1864, Harrisburg's leading Democratic paper declared that Democrats "do not fear the *white* soldiers' vote." See *Patriot and Union,* July 8, 1864.

5. Margaret McKelvy Bird and Daniel W. Crofts, eds., "Soldier Voting in 1864: The David McKelvy Diary," *Pennsylvania Magazine of History and Biography* 115 (July 1991): 396. For instances of black soldiers voting in the election of 1864, see Joseph P. Reidy, "The African American Struggle for Citizenship Rights in the Northern United States during the Civil War," in Susannah J. Ural, ed., *Civil War Citizens: Race, Ethnicity, and Identity in America's Bloodiest Conflict* (New York: New York University Press, 2010), 225.

6. J. H. Hall, Fifty-Fourth Massachusetts Infantry, Morris Island, S.C., August 3, 1864, in *Christian Recorder,* August 27, 1864, quoted in Edwin S. Redkey, ed., *A Grand Army of Black Men: Letters from African-American Soldiers in the Union Army, 1861–1865* (New York: Cambridge University Press, 1992), 205; Henry Carpenter Hoyle, Forty-Third US Colored Infantry, near Richmond, Va., February 18, 1865, in *Christian Recorder,* March 18, 1865, quoted ibid., 219. See also Virginia M. Adams, ed., *On the Altar of Freedom: A Black Soldier's Civil War Letters from the Front* (Amherst: University of Massachusetts Press, 1991), 21; Christian G. Samito, *Becoming American under Fire: Irish Americans, African Americans, and the Politics of Citizenship during the Civil War Era* (Ithaca: Cornell University Press, 2009), 5–6, 22–23, 26–102, 134–71; Joseph R. Fornieri, "Lincoln on Black Citizenship," in Paul D. Moreno and Johnathan O'Neill, eds., *Constitutionalism in the Approach and Aftermath of the Civil War* (New York: Fordham University Press, 2013), 55–80.

7. Lincoln, "Last Public Address," April 11, 1865, in *CWL,* 8:403. See also Lincoln to Michael Hahn, March 13, 1865, ibid., 7:243.

8. Quoted in James L. Swanson, *Manhunt: The 12-Day Chase for Lincoln's Killer* (New York: Morrow, 2006), 6.

9. Lincoln, "To the Editor of the *Sangamo Journal,*" June 13, 1836, *CWL,* 1:48.

10. George S. Denison to Salmon P. Chase, October 8, 1864, in *Sixth Report of Historical Manuscripts Commission: With Diary and Correspondence of Salmon P. Chase* (Washington, D.C.: Government Printing Office, 1902), 449–50. The idea that permitting soldiers to vote had implications for African Americans was spreading throughout the North. See, for example, F. W. Delang to Lincoln, September 14, 1864, Lincoln Papers.

11. William T. Shimp to Annie, September 1, 1863, William T. Shimp Papers, CWMC. Another soldier went so far as to say that any northerner who voted the Democratic ticket "is a traitor to his

God and his country and deserves no longer to be called a citizen of the U.S." See James S. Graham to Aunt Ellen, October 24, 1864, in William H. Bartlett, ed., *Aunt and the Soldier Boys* (Santa Cruz, Calif.: Privately printed, 1973), 151.

12. Abel Marcy to Abraham Lincoln, February 11, 1865, in RG 107 (Records of the Office of the Secretary of War), microfilm M221 (Letters Received by the Secretary of War: Main Series, 1801–1870), reel 272, NARA.

This idea also gained some adherents in the Confederacy. In March 1864, Georgia governor Joseph E. Brown proposed that the state enact legislation that would confiscate the property of deserters as well as "forever disfranchise and *decitizenize*" them. See Joseph E. Brown, *Message of His Excellency Joseph E. Brown, to the Extra Session of the Legislature, Convened March 10th, 1864* (Milledgeville: Boughton, Nisbet, Barnes and Moore, 1864), 7.

13. S. 175, 38th Cong., 1st sess.; *CG*, 38th Cong., 1st sess., pp. 1249–50.

14. S. 36, 38th Cong., 1st sess.; S. 408, 38th Cong., 2nd sess.; *CG*, 38th Cong., 1st sess., pp. 1249–50; 38th Cong., 2nd sess., pp. 642–43.

15. H.R. 678, 38th Cong., 2nd sess.; *CG*, 38th Cong., 1st sess., pp. 1155–57. Ironically, Schenck had been critical of Andrew Jackson's infringements of civil liberties during the War of 1812. See Matthew Warshauer, *Andrew Jackson and the Politics of Martial Law: Nationalism, Civil Liberties, and Partisanship* (Knoxville: University of Tennessee Press, 2006), 144–45.

16. *CG*, 38th Cong., 2nd sess., pp. 1155–57.

17. Ibid., 1155.

18. Ibid., 1156.

19. Ibid., 1155–61.

20. S. 36, 38th Cong., 1st sess. (includes the Report of the Committee of Conference).

21. *An Act to Amend the Several Acts Heretofore Passed to Provide for the Enrolling and Calling Out the National Forces, and for Other Purposes,* act of March 3, 1865, in 13 Stat. 490. At the same time, Congress rewarded people for their personal acts of loyalty. On March 3, 1865—the same day that the law stripping deserters of the rights of citizenship was enacted—Congress adopted two joint resolutions to the benefit of loyal soldiers and their families. The first encouraged government and private employers to give preference when hiring to soldiers who had been honorably discharged from the military "by reason of disability resulting from wounds or sickness incurred in the line of duty." The second offered freedom to the wives and children of former slaves who enlisted in the Union army. Congress also took measures to protect the graves of Union soldiers from desecration, and in July 1866, Congress granted to loyal Tennesseans the right to submit claims to the federal government for wartime losses. See *A Resolution to Encourage the Employment of Disabled and Discharged Soldiers,* and *A Resolution to Encourage Enlistments and to Promote the Efficiency of the Military Forces of the United States,* both adopted March 3, 1865, in 13 Stat. 571; *A Resolution Respecting the Burial of Soldiers Who Died in the Military Service of the United States during the Rebellion,* adopted April 13, 1866, in 14 Stat. 353; and *Joint Resolution to Extend the Provisions of the Act of July Fourth, Eighteen Hundred and Sixty-four, Limiting the Jurisdiction of the Court of Claims to the Loyal Citizens of Tennessee,* adopted July 28, 1866, in 14 Stat. 370–71.

22. *CG*, 37th Cong., 2nd sess., p. 2196.

23. Proclamation No. 27, in 14 Stat. 752. In 1867, Congress amended the law to exclude soldiers and sailors who deserted after April 19, 1867. See *An Act for the Relief of Certain Soldiers and Sailors therein Designated,* act of July 19, 1867, in 15 Stat. 14.

24. As will be seen below, it was also unclear whether deserters who were U.S. citizens actually lost their citizenship, or only lost their ability to exercise their rights of citizenship.

25. William E. Nelson, *The Fourteenth Amendment: From Political Principle to Judicial Doctrine* (Cambridge: Harvard University Press, 1988), 71. See also Samito, *Becoming American under Fire*, 1–3.

26. See *The* Slaughterhouse Cases, 83 U.S. 36 (1873); Rogers M. Smith, *Civic Ideals: Conflicting Visions of Citizenship in U.S. History* (New Haven: Yale University Press, 1997), 327–37.

27. *Minor v. Happersett*, 88 U.S. 162 (1875); Ann D. Gordon, *The Trial of Susan B. Anthony* (Washington, D.C.: Federal Judicial Center, 2005); Keyssar, *Right to Vote*, 172–221; Smith, *Civic Ideals*, 337–42.

28. In the midst of the debate over disfranchising deserters in New York, one Republican chided the Democrats for opposing the disfranchisement of deserters but not that of women and African Americans: "I understand the gentleman from Onondaga finds full authority to exclude a black man, and that he finds full authority to exclude women, and full authority to exclude any one he wants to exclude, but he cannot find any authority to exclude deserters or any other man whom he does not desire to exclude. He cannot find any way to exclude traitors, why? He does not wish to exclude them." See E. F. Underhill, comp., *Report of the Proceedings and Debates of the Constitutional Convention for the Revision of the Constitution of the State of New York, 1867–'68*, 5 vols. (Albany: Weed, Parsons & Co., 1868), 1:524.

29. See Jonathan W. White, "'To Aid Their Rebel Friends': Politics and Treason in the Civil War North" (Ph.D. diss., University of Maryland at College Park, 2008).

30. Albert Williams to George Richmond, October 18, 1866, in *Annual Report of the Attorney General of the State of Michigan for the Year 1866* (Lansing: John A. Kerr, 1866), 23–24.

31. *Report of the Adjutant General of the State of Indiana*, 8 vols. (Indianapolis: Alexander H. Conner, 1868–1869), 8:743–831.

32. *Harrisburg Telegraph* quoted in the *Bellefonte Central Press*, June 1, 1866.

33. Williams, *Annual Report*, 22.

34. *Journal of Proceedings of the Twentieth Annual Session of the Wisconsin Legislature, for the Year 1868* (Madison: Atwood and Rublee, 1868), 174.

35. Williams, *Annual Report*, 23.

36. New Hampshire, *An Act Concerning Deserters from the Military and Naval Service of the United States, and Avoiding the Draft into the Same*, act of July 7, 1866, in *Laws of the State of New-Hampshire, Passed June Session, 1866* (Concord: George E. Jenks, 1866), 3238–40; Pennsylvania, *A Further Supplement to the Election Laws of this Commonwealth*, act of June 4, 1866, in *Laws of the General Assembly of the State of Pennsylvania, Passed at the Session of 1866, in the Nineteenth Year of Independence* (Harrisburg: Singerly and Myers, 1866), 1107–9; Vermont, *An Act in Relation to the Qualifications of Voters*, act of November 8, 1866, in *Acts and Resolves Passed by the General Assembly of the State of Vermont, at the Annual Session, 1866* (Montpelier: Freeman Steam Printing Establishment, 1866), 32; Wisconsin, *An Act to Amend Chapter 7 of the Revised Statutes, Entitled, "Of General and Special Elections; of the Manner of Conducting the Same, and of the Canvass,"* act of March 26, 1866, in *General Laws Passed by the Legislature of Wisconsin, in the Year 1866, Together with Joint Resolutions and Memorials* (Madison: William J. Park, 1866), 32–33; Wisconsin, *An Act to Amend Chapter 32 of the General Laws of 1863, Entitled "An Act Relative to the Commencement and Prosecution of Civil Actions against Persons in the Military Service of the Country,"* act of April 7, 1865, in *General Laws Passed by the Legislature of Wisconsin, in the Year 1865, Together with Joint Resolutions and*

Memorials (Madison: William J. Park, 1865), 481–82; New York, *An Act to Provide for a Convention to Revise and Amend the Constitution,* act of March 29, 1867, in *Laws of the State of New York, Passed at the Ninetieth Session of the Legislature, Begun January First, and Ended April Twentieth, 1867, in the City of Albany* (Albany: Weare C. Little, 1867), 287. The New York law only applied to voters in an election to elect delegates to a state constitutional convention. New Hampshire deserters were also barred from holding office in the state.

37. Ohio, *To Punish Persons Who Leave Their Places of Residence for the Purpose of Avoiding Conscription,* act of March 29, 1865, in *General and Local Laws and Joint Resolutions Passed by the Fifty-Sixth General Assembly of the State of Ohio, at its Second Session, Begun and Held in the City of Columbus, January 3, 1865, and in the Sixty-Third Year of Said State* (Columbus: Richard Nevins, 1865), 68.

38. Michigan, *An Act to Exempt Soldiers, Sailors and Marines from the Payment of a Capitation or Poll Tax,* act of March 21, 1867, in *Acts of the Legislature of the State of Michigan, Passed at the Regular Session of 1867,* 2 vols. (Lansing: John A. Kerr, 1867), 1:101.

39. Joshua Lawrence Chamberlain, "Address to the Senate and House of Representatives," 1866, in *Resolves of the State of Maine, from 1866 to 1868, Inclusive* (Augusta: Owen and Nash, 1868), 143–44.

40. *State v. Symonds,* 57 Maine Reports 148 (1869).

41. George Bergner, ed., *The Legislative Record: Containing the Debates and Proceedings of the Pennsylvania Legislature for the Session of 1866* (Harrisburg: "Telegraph" Steam Book and Job Office, 1866), 485, 699, 701.

42. Kansas *Constitutional Convention* (Topeka: Imri Zumwalt, 1920), 627; Frank W. Blackmar, *Kansas: A Cyclopedia of State History, Embracing Events, Institutions, Industries, Counties, Cities, Towns, Prominent Persons, Etc.,* 2 vols. (Chicago: Standard, 1912), 1:405–6; *Boyd v. Mills* 53 Kansas Reports 603 (1894); Elwill M. Shanahan, *The Constitution of the State of Kansas with Amendments* (Topeka: Robert R. Sanders, 1973), 15–16; Kansas, *Senate Concurrent Resolution No. 77: A Proposition to Amend the Constitution of the State of Kansas by Revising Article 5, Relating to Suffrage,* adopted March 27, 1974, in *1974 Session Laws of Kansas* (Topeka: Robert R. Sanders, 1974), 1541–42. Dora L. Costa and Matthew E. Kahn incorrectly state that Kansas repealed this provision in 1874. See Dora L. Costa and Matthew E. Kahn, *Heroes and Cowards: The Social Face of War* (Princeton: Princeton University Press, 2008), 169. Other states, like Maryland and West Virginia, also disenfranchised Confederate soldiers in the early postwar period.

At the referendum on November 5, 1867, voters in Kansas rejected proposed constitutional amendments to enfranchise women (9,070 for and 19,857 against) and to enfranchise black men (10,483 for and 19,421 against). See Frank J. Ryan, *Constitution of the State of Kansas and Amendments and Proposed Amendments Submitted* (Topeka: Ferd Voiland Jr., 1946), 27.

43. Steven H. Steinglass and Gino J. Scarselli, *The Ohio Constitution: A Reference Guide* (Westport, Conn.: Greenwood, 2004), 354; George H. Porter, *Ohio Politics during the Civil War Period* (New York: Columbia University Press, 1911), 235–54; Republican legislator quoted in Robert D. Sawrey, *Dubious Victory: The Reconstruction Debate in Ohio* (Lexington: University Press of Kentucky, 1992), 103. It is worth pointing out that in these postwar debates Republicans often assumed that most deserters were Democrats.

44. Porter, *Ohio Politics,* 235–54; *Pittsfield (Mass.) Sun,* April 25, 1867; Sawrey, *Dubious Victory,* 101–4.

45. Sawrey, *Dubious Victory,* 104–19 (quotes from 109 and 113). Ohio's constitutional amendment would have disfranchised Union soldiers who had deserted after the surrender at Appomattox (about

one-quarter of Ohio's 27,000 Civil War deserters). Fearing that many of these "deserters" were loyal soldiers who might turn against the Republican Party should such a provision be enacted, Ohio Republicans sought help from Congress, which passed a law in July 1867 declaring that any soldier who deserted after April 19, 1865, would not be considered a deserter. See ibid., 105.

46. William Blair Lord and David Wolfe Brown, eds., *The Debates and Proceedings of the Constitutional Convention of the State of Michigan, Convened at the City of Lansing, Wednesday, May 15th, 1867*, 2 vols. (Lansing: John A. Kerr & Co., 1867), 2:776–79.

47. Underhill, comp., *Report of the Proceedings and Debates*, 1:519–22, 525.

48. Ibid., 519–27. Later in the debate the convention also rejected a proposal to permit the state legislature to disfranchise deserters. See ibid., 561–63.

49. "Senate Document No. 47," in *Documents of the Senate of the State of New York, Ninety-Eight Session—1875*, 6 vols. (Albany: Weed, Parsons and Co., 1875), 3:253–56; W. H. McElroy and Alex. McBride, *Life Sketches of Government Officers and Members of the Legislature of the State of New York for 1875* (Albany: Weed, Parsons and Co., 1875), 91–92. Moore's CMSR reveals that he enlisted in September 1862 when he was actually nineteen years old and that he deserted in September 1863. See CMSR for Hugh H. Moore, 113th New York Infantry.

50. Wisconsin, *An Act to Amend Chapter Sixty-Seven (67) of the General Laws of 1867, Entitled "An Act to Authorize the Secretary of State to Procure and Furnish to Clerks of County Boards of Supervisors Authenticated Lists of Deserters from the Military and Naval Service of the United States, and to Provide for their Distribution," and for Other Purposes in Connection with Men Charged with Desertion*, act of March 6, 1868, in *General Laws Passed by the Legislature of Wisconsin, in the Year 1868, Together with Joint Resolutions and Memorials* (Madison: Atwood and Rublee, 1868), 171–73; Wisconsin, *Assembly Journal (1868)*, 173–78; repealed on March 10, 1969, in *General Laws Passed by the Legislature of Wisconsin, in the Year 1869, Together with Joint Resolutions and Memorials* (Madison: Atwood and Rublee, 1869), 141.

51. *Huber v. Reily*, 53 Pennsylvania Reports 115 (1866).

52. Ibid.

53. *Lancaster Intelligencer*, January 31 and May 30, 1866.

54. *Huber v. Reily*, 53 Pennsylvania Reports 112–22.

55. Ibid. Chief Justice George W. Woodward concurred in the opinion, stating that he agreed with "most of [Strong's] reasonings" but that he believed the act was an ex post facto law. Justices John M. Read and Daniel Agnew dissented. Republicans throughout the state praised the state supreme court in anticipation of the decision, believing that the court would unequivocally uphold the law. "This decision will have a most healthful effect at a time when all State and national legislation looking to the punishment or disfranchisement of traitors and deserters is sought to be set at naught through the evil example of men high in power." *Harrisburg Telegraph* quoted in the *Bellefonte Central Press*, June 1, 1866.

56. Today, this sort of judicial action is known as the doctrine of constitutional doubt. According to this jurisprudential practice, a judge construes a statute of questionable constitutionality in a way that allows the judge to uphold the law rather than strike it down. As Justice Antonin Scalia of the U.S. Supreme Court explains: "The doctrine of constitutional doubt is meant to effectuate, not to subvert, congressional intent, by giving *ambiguous* provisions a meaning that will avoid constitutional peril, and that will conform with Congress's presumed intent not to enact measures of dubious validity." Quoted in Trevor W. Morrison, "Constitutional Avoidance in the Executive Branch," *Columbia*

Law Review 106 (October 2006): 1207n64. Scalia continues: "The doctrine of constitutional doubt does not require that the problem-avoiding construction be the preferable one—the one the Court would adopt in any event. Such a standard would deprive the doctrine of all function. 'Adopt the interpretation that avoids the constitutional doubt if that is the right one' produces precisely the same result as 'adopt the right interpretation.' Rather, the doctrine of constitutional doubt comes into play when the statute is 'susceptible of' the problem-avoiding interpretation—when that interpretation is reasonable, though not necessarily best." Quoted in Ernest A. Young, "Constitutional Avoidance, Resistance Norms, and the Preservation of Judicial Review," *Texas Law Review* 78 (1999–2000): 1578.

57. *Severance v. Healey,* 50 New Hampshire Reports 448 (1870); *State v. Symonds,* 57 Maine Reports 148 (1869); *Gotcheus v. Matheson,* 58 New York Reports 152 (1870).

In the spring and summer of 1865, at least eight soldiers or drafted men were disfranchised by courts-martial following conviction for desertion, although none of the cases cited the congressional law. These cases included three drafted men in Indiana, Joseph Kemper (OO-1348), Joel Morris (MM-2716), and Jeremiah Swails (MM-2716); a drafted man in Michigan named Joshua E. Parker (MM-3035); a drafted man in Illinois named William Gemmell (MM-3005); Pvt. Samuel Johnson of the Forty-Third Indiana Volunteers (OO-1118); Pvt. Henry Hogle of the Sixth Indiana Cavalry (OO-1046); and Pvt. John Simmons of the Sixteenth Illinois Cavalry (MM-2201). Upon reviewing the cases of Privates Simmons and Hogle, Brig. Gen. Richard W. Johnson disapproved of their disfranchisement saying it was "without authority of law." The generals who reviewed the other deserters' sentences allowed the punishments to stand. At least two other soldiers were disfranchised for committing other crimes. Corp. Abednego Stephens of the Twenty-Second Veteran Reserve Corps was disfranchised for larceny (OO-636), and Corp. Andrew J. Russell of the Eighth Michigan Cavalry was disfranchised for exulting in Lincoln's assassination (OO-771). As in the desertion cases, Brigadier General Johnson disapproved of Russell's disfranchisement.

58. *Kurtz v. Moffitt,* 115 U.S. 501 (1885).

59. *Lancaster Intelligencer,* May 30, 1866.

60. William Blair, "A Record of Pennsylvania Deserters," *Pennsylvania Magazine of History and Biography* 135 (October 2011): 537–38.

61. Ibid. The list of deserters from Pennsylvania included all deserters from all times, not simply those who did not return under the 1865 act. If Pennsylvania election officials sought to disfranchise all deserters on the list, then they may have exceeded the requirements of the federal law of 1865 as well as the state law of 1866.

The Wisconsin legislature also requested a similar list from the secretary of war. See Wisconsin, *An Act to Authorize the Secretary of State to Procure and Furnish to Clerks of County Boards of Supervisors Authenticated Lists of Deserters from the Military and Naval Service of the United States, and to Provide for their Distribution,* act of March 29, 1867, in *General Laws Passed by the Legislature of Wisconsin, in the Year 1866* (Madison: Wm. J. Park, 1866), 64–65.

62. *McCafferty v. Guyer,* 59 Pennsylvania Reports 109 (1868).

63. Ibid., 110–13.

64. Ibid.

65. Ibid., 113–19.

66. In November 1863, the Supreme Court of Pennsylvania held the federal conscription law unconstitutional. Following the election of 1863, in which Daniel Agnew defeated Chief Justice Walter H. Lowrie, the court reheard the case and reversed itself in January 1864. It is possible that in *Huber* the

justices hoped to avoid declaring another federal law unconstitutional. For the controversy over the Pennsylvania Supreme Court and conscription, see *Kneedler v. Lane,* 45 Pennsylvania Reports 238 (1863 and 1864); and Mark E. Neely Jr., *Lincoln and the Triumph of the Nation: Constitutional Conflict in the American Civil War* (Chapel Hill: University of North Carolina Press, 2011), 214–34.

67. *McCafferty v. Guyer,* 59 Pennsylvania Reports 121–28.

68. 18 Stat. 350.

69. 37 Stat. 356.

70. *The Nationality Act of 1940,* act of October 14, 1940, in 54 Stat. 1141–42, 1168–69. Supreme Court Justice Felix Frankfurter called the law "a direct descendant of a provision enacted during the Civil War." See *Trop v. Dulles,* 356 U.S. 116 (1957).

71. John P. Roche, "The Loss of American Nationality—The Development of Statutory Expatriation," *University of Pennsylvania Law Review* 99 (October 1950): 60–65.

72. Ibid., 117; *An Act to Amend the Nationality Act of 1940,* act of January 20, 1944, in 58 Stat. 4.

73. *Trop v. Dulles,* 356 U.S. 119 (1958).

74. Ibid., 87–88, 114.

75. Ibid., 89.

76. Ibid., 90–93, 99–100.

77. Ibid., 101–3.

78. Ibid., 105–14.

79. Ibid., 120–23.

80. Ibid., 127.

81. Ibid., 124–28.

82. For discussion of "judgment" and the importance of the judicial oath of office, see *Federalist* No. 78 and Chief Justice John Marshall's opinion in *Marbury v. Madison* (1803).

83. *Trop v. Dulles,* 356 U.S. 100–103.

84. I conducted a search on HeinOnline to attain these results.

EPILOGUE

1. Josiah Benton, *Voting in the Field: A Forgotten Chapter of the Civil War* (Boston: Plimpton Press, 1915), 3.

2. Soldiers' votes may also have provided Lincoln's margin of victory in New York in November 1864, but since their ballots were mailed home and counted with the "home vote," it is impossible to know for certain.

3. James M. McPherson, "War and Politics," in Geoffrey C. Ward et al., comp., *The Civil War* (New York: Knopf, 1990), 352–53.

4. Jennifer L. Weber, "All the President's Men: The Politicization of Union Soldiers and How They Saved Abraham Lincoln," in Orville Vernon Burton, Jerald Podair, and Jennifer L. Weber, eds., *The Struggle for Equality: Essays on Sectional Conflict, the Civil War, and the Long Reconstruction* (Charlottesville: University of Virginia Press, 2011), 76–77, 87–88.

5. The soldiers convalescing at Carver Hospital in Washington, D.C., voted 3–1 against Lincoln. Upon learning this fact, Lincoln remarked to his secretary of war: "That is hard on us. Stanton, they know us better than the others." Quoted in Benton, *Voting in the Field,* 322.

6. John Dow to Thomas (brother), May 30, 1863, Dow Family Papers, The Filson.

7. George B. McClellan to Manton Marble, September 17, 1864, Manton Marble Papers, LC. For some of the letters that McClellan received from former soldiers, see Isaac J. Wistar to McClellan, September 3, 1864, Ebenezer W. Peirce to McClellan, September 3, 1864, George A. Whitten to McClellan, September 7, 1864, Preston F. Smith to McClellan, September 8, 1864, R. E. Freeman to McClellan, September 9, 1864, John C. A. Stackhouse to McClellan, September 9, 1864, Frank Haines to McClellan, September 9, 1864, William J. Cork to McClellan, September 13, 1864, A. W. Burns to McClellan, September 17, 1864, S. Byron Scott to McClellan, September 23, 1864, Sidney Herbert to McClellan, September 29 and October 6, 1864, Richard C. Kendall to McClellan, October 3, 1864, John W. Mahan to McClellan, October 8, 1864, William H. Irwin to McClellan, October 12, 1864, Peter Baldy to McClellan, October 18, 1864, A. P. Martin to McClellan, October 20, 1864, Charles H. Pierson to McClellan, November 1, 1864, and C. H. Colgrove to McClellan, November 5, 1864, all in McClellan Papers. Some veterans also formed themselves into an organization called the McClellan Legion, which sought to rally former soldiers to support McClellan's candidacy.

8. More scholarly attention ought to be paid to reenlistment patterns in the Union armies. On the difficulty of determining why soldiers chose not to reenlist, see Earl J. Hess, *The Union Soldier in Battle: Enduring the Ordeal of Combat* (Lawrence: University Press of Kansas, 1997), 89.

9. For examples of anti-emancipation editors silencing their views, see Stephen E. Towne, "Killing the Serpent Speedily: Governor Morton, General Hascall, and the Suppression of the Democratic Press in Indiana, 1863," *Civil War History* 52 (April 2006): 51–53; Mark E. Neely Jr., "'Seeking a Cause of Difficulty with the Government': Reconsidering Freedom of Speech and Judicial Conflict under Lincoln," in *Lincoln's Legacy: Ethics and Politics*, ed. Phillip Shaw Paludan (Urbana: University of Illinois Press, 2008), 58.

10. Benton, *Voting in the Field*, 66, 72, 89, 107, 131, 156, 220–21, 314–15, 322.

11. Ibid., 156–57, 187–88, 280; P. Orman Ray, "Military Absent-Voting Laws," *American Political Science Review* 12 (August 1918): 462.

12. Lynwood G. Downs, "The Soldier Vote and Minnesota Politics, 1862–65," *Minnesota History* 26 (September 1945): 210; William M. Burcher, "A History of Soldier Voting in the State of New York," *New York History* 25 (October 1944): 468–69.

13. Ray, "Military Absent-Voting Laws," 461–62; Boyd A. Martin, "The Service Vote in the Elections of 1944," *American Political Science Review* 39 (August 1945): 723.

14. Pershing quoted in Jennifer Ruth Horner, "Blood and Ballots: Military Voting and Political Communication in the Union Army during the United States Civil War, 1861–1865" (Ph.D. diss., University of Pennsylvania, 2006), 246; *New York Times*, March 21, 1918, and November 4, 1917.

15. Martin, "Service Vote," 724.

16. Ibid., 725–26; Rankin and Brown quoted in Christopher DeRosa, "The Battle for Uniform Votes: The Politics of Soldier Voting in the Elections of 1944," in Edward G. Longacre and Theodore J. Zeman, eds., *Beyond Combat: Essays in Military History in Honor of Russell F. Weigley* (Philadelphia: American Philosophical Society, 2007), 130–31.

17. Martin, "Service Vote," 725–26.

18. Ibid., 720, 726–27; Gallup quoted in Horner, "Blood and Ballots," 249.

19. Martin, "Service Vote," 727–29; Green quoted in DeRosa, "Uniform Ballots," 134; Rankin quoted in Horner, "Blood and Ballots," 248, Taft on 251. The states' rights protest was not solely a southern protest; it was voiced by secretaries of state from states throughout the nation. See DeRosa, "Uniform Votes," 131–33.

20. Horner, "Blood and Ballots," 254–55; bill sponsor quoted in DeRosa, "Uniform Ballots," 136.

21. Horner, "Blood and Ballots," 253–60; Butler quoted in DeRosa, "Uniform Ballots," 135.

22. DeRosa, "Uniform Votes," 137; C. P. Trussell, "Senators Clash on Soldier Vote; Byrd Denounces Guffey's Charges," *New York Times,* December 8, 1943.

23. DeRosa, "Uniform Votes," 138–40; Franklin D. Roosevelt, "Statement of the President on Allowing Soldier Vote Bill to Become Law without His Signature," March 31, 1944, in Samuel I. Rosenman, comp., *The Public Papers and Addresses of Franklin D. Roosevelt, 1944–45 Volume: Victory and the Threshold of Peace* (New York: Harper and Brothers, 1950), 111.

24. DeRosa, "Uniform Votes," 145. For a full account of the balloting process, see ibid., 140–48.

25. Oscar O. Winther, "The Soldier Vote in the Election of 1864," *New York History* 25 (October 1944): 454, 452; Burcher, "History of Soldier Voting," 459–81; Downs, "The Soldier Vote and Minnesota Politics," 210.

26. Frank L. Klement, "The Soldier Vote in Wisconsin during the Civil War," *Wisconsin Magazine of History* 28 (September 1944): 37–38.

27. Ibid., 38–47.

28. For an account of Klement's serendipitous journey to studying Civil War politics and midwestern Copperheadism, see Steven K. Rogstad's introduction to Frank L. Klement, *Lincoln's Critics: The Copperheads of the North* (Shippensburg, Pa.: White Mane, 1999), xi–xxxvii.

29. T. Harry Williams, "Voters in Blue: The Citizen Soldiers of the Civil War," *Mississippi Valley Historical Review* 31 (September 1944), 187–88, 203.

30. Reid Mitchell, "'Not the General But the Soldier': The Study of Civil War Soldiers," in James M. McPherson and William J. Cooper Jr., eds., *Writing the Civil War: The Quest to Understand* (Columbia: University of South Carolina Press, 1998), 93.

31. In November 1998, Oregon voters approved Measure 60, which provided that all primary and general elections would be conducted by mail in accordance with *Oregon Revised Statutes* 254.462–254.482.

32. "Congress Muzzling the Military," *Florida Times Union* (Jacksonville), December 13, 2000 (accessed through ProQuest).

33. John Fund, "Absentee Ballots: Disenfranchising the U.S. Military," *Wall Street Journal,* November 24, 2000 (accessed through ProQuest).

34. Alan M. Dershowitz, *Supreme Injustice: How the High Court Hijacked Election 2000* (New York: Oxford University Press, 2001), 220n75.

35. Marc Racicot quoted in James W. Ceaser and Andrew E. Busch, *The Perfect Tie: The True Story of the 2000 Presidential Election* (Lanham, Md.: Rowman and Littlefield, 2001), 185–86.

36. "Congress Muzzling the Military" *Florida Times Union* (Jacksonville), December 13, 2000 (accessed through ProQuest).

37. "The Dilemma of Those Rejected Military Ballots," *Virginian-Pilot* (Norfolk), December 2, 2000 (accessed through ProQuest).

38. Molly Ivins, "Forgive, But Do Not Forget," *Austin American Statesman,* December 19, 2000 (accessed through ProQuest).

39. Bill Rankin, "11th Circuit Court: Atlanta Justices Uphold Overseas Ballots Arriving after Election Day," *Atlanta Constitution,* December 12, 2000; Vickie Chachere, "Bush Wins Cases on Florida Absentee Ballots, State Top Court Backs Judges," Associated Press, December 13, 2000 (accessed through ProQuest).

40. Dershowitz, *Supreme Injustice,* 220n75.

41. M. Eric Eversole and Hans A. von Spakovsky, *A President's Opportunity: Making Military Voters a Priority, Legal Memorandum No. 71* (Washington, D.C.: Center for Legal and Judicial Studies, Heritage Foundation, 2011), 2–3.

42. Ibid., 3–4.

43. Ibid.

44. Hans von Spakovsky and M. Eric Eversole, *America's Military Voters: Re-enfranchising the Disenfranchised, Legal Memorandum No. 45* (Washington, D.C.: Center for Legal and Judicial Studies, Heritage Foundation, 2010), 1.

APPENDIX

1. Joseph T. Glatthaar, *The March to the Sea and Beyond: Sherman's Troops in the Savannah and Carolinas Campaigns* (New York: New York University Press, 1985), 187.

2. James M. McPherson, *For Cause and Comrades: Why Men Fought in the Civil War* (New York: Oxford University Press, 1997), 173, 84.

3. *Final Report Made to the Secretary of War, by the Provost Marshal General* (1866), pt. 1, p. 57.

4. *Congressional Serial Set,* 38th Cong., 2nd sess., House Exec. Doc. 83, pp. 52, 55.

5. Benjamin A. Gould, *Investigations in the Military and Anthropological Statistics of American Soldiers* (New York: Hurd and Houghton, 1869), 10.

6. *Final Report Made to the Secretary of War, by the Provost Marshal General* (1866), pt. 1, p. 77.

BIBLIOGRAPHY

PRIMARY SOURCES

Archival and Manuscript Sources

Brown University, Special Collections, John Hay Library, Providence, R.I.
  Samuel S. Cox Papers

Bucknell University, Special Collections and University Archives, Lewisburg, Pa.
  Slifer-Walls Collection (Sheary Project)

Bucks County Historical Society, Spruance Library, Doylestown, Pa.
  John Charles Burrill Journal
  Civil War Papers
  General W. W. H. Davis Papers
  Doylestown Township History Collection
  Samuel Hart Collection
  Helen H. Hunt Collection

Chester County Historical Society, West Chester, Pa.
  Thomas S. Bell Civil War Letters
  Daniel G. Brinton Civil War Letters
  Joseph Darlington Civil War Letters
  William W. Heed Civil War Diaries
  Andrew Irwin Civil War Diaries
  Anna Lamborn Diaries
  Edward J. Marshall Diaries
  Charles Henry Morgan Civil War Letters
  Thomas Wood Diaries

Cincinnati Historical Society
  Alexander Long Papers

Collection of the Author
    Jennie Cleland to J. W. Cleland, July 13, 1863
    Richard Henry Lee to Fendal, August 13, 1863
    James Bell to E. C. Williams, October 23, 1863
    Cincinnatus Condict to Uzal Condict, October 2, 1864

Columbia University, Archives and Special Collections
    Belmont Family Papers

Dickinson College, Archives and Special Collections
    Joseph Cullen Ayer Papers
    John Hays Family Papers
    Horatio King Papers
    William Rawle Papers
    Slifer-Dill Papers
    Cornelius Vanderbilt Papers

Dauphin County Historical Society, Harrisburg, Pa.
    Simon Cameron Papers

The Filson Historical Society, Louisville, Ky.
    Bodley Family Papers
    Simon Boliver Buckner Papers
    John B. Bruner Papers
    Don Carlos Buell Papers
    Bullitt Family Papers—Oxmoor Collection
    Thomas Walker Bullitt Diary
    John Breckinridge Castleman Papers
    Corlis-Respess Family Papers
    Garrett Davis Papers
    Dawalt Family Papers
    Dow Family Papers
    Gregg Family Papers
    Grigsby Collection
    Haldeman Family Papers
    Lewis Hanback Letters
    William Jefferson Helsley Papers
    Martha Buford Jones Diaries
    Charles Lanman Collection
    William Nelson Papers
    David G. Peck Papers

James M. Porter Papers
Channing Richards Papers
James Speed Letters
William Tanner Papers
James A. Thomas Papers
Luther Thayer Thustin Papers
George W. Vanvalkenburgh Papers
Viars Family Papers
Winn-Cook Family Papers

Gilder Lehrman Institute of American History, New York, N.Y.
  Gilder Lehrman Collection
      Francis P. Blair Papers (GLC03209)
      William Brunt Collection (GLC07006)
      Collection of Civil War Letters from Various Soldiers and Civilians (GLC02197)
      Collection of Letters from Lincoln's Cabinet Members (GLC05603.01)
      Collection of Letters of the Presidents (GLC00529)
      Paul Sieman Forbes Letter (GLC08656)
      Gibson Collection of Civil War Soldiers Archives (GLC03523)
          Jesse Brown Collection (GLC03523.15)
          Andrew Knox Collection (GLC03523.20)
          Charles C. Morey Collection (GLC03523.18)
      Ethan A. Jenks Collection (GLC02750)
      Joseph Jones Collection (GLC02739)
      Lyman Family Letters (GLC03606)
      George B. McClellan Letter (GLC05041)
      Morris Family Letters (GLC06451)
      Levi W. Norton Collection (GLC09006)
      Henry C. Parrott Letters (GLC03858.02)
      John H. Powers Collection (GLC02181)
      William O. Stoddard Letter (GLC03192)
      George W. Tillotson Collection (GLC04558)
      Van Valkenburgh Family Papers (GLC00686)
      Samuel Watson Vannuys Collection (GLC07687)
      Charles E. Walbridge Collection (GLC04663)
      Almira Winchell Civil War Letters (GLC04706)
      Matthew Wood Collection (GLC02176)

Historical Society of Delaware, Wilmington
  Bayard Collection
  James A. Bayard Jr. Family Letters

William and Frank Brobson Papers
George Read Riddle Papers
William H. Ross Papers

Historical Society of Pennsylvania, Philadelphia
    Biddle Family Papers
    James Buchanan Papers
    Cadwalader Family Papers
    Salmon Chase Papers
    Chief Justices of the Supreme Court of Pennsylvania Papers
    Lewis S. Coryell Papers
    Ferdinand J. Dreer Autograph Collection
    Simon Gratz Collection
    Ellis Lewis Papers
    MacVeagh Family Papers
    Peter McCall Papers
    Society Miscellaneous Collection
    Society Small Collection
    Swank Manuscripts

Indiana State Archives, Indianapolis
    Civil War Collection: Regimental Correspondence

Library Company of Philadelphia
    McAllister Collection
    Reed Family Papers

Library of Congress, Manuscript Division, Washington, D.C.
    Nathaniel P. Banks Papers
    Edward Bates Papers
    Thomas F. Bayard Papers
    Jeremiah S. Black Papers
    Charles R. Buckalew Papers
    Simon Cameron Papers
    Alfred Carmon Papers
    Salmon P. Chase Papers
    John Covode Papers
    George A. Hudson Papers
    Reverdy Johnson Papers
    Abraham Lincoln Papers (American Memory)
    Manton Marble Papers

George B. McClellan Sr. Papers
Edward McPherson Papers
Franklin Pierce Papers
William H. Seward Papers
Horatio Seymour Papers
Edwin M. Stanton Papers
Thaddeus Stevens Papers
Lyman Trumbull Papers
Elihu B. Washburne Papers
Thurlow Weed Papers
Gideon Welles Papers

Abraham Lincoln Presidential Library, Springfield, Ill.
Isham N. Haynie Papers

London School of Economics, Special Collections, London
Emigrants' Letters
Mill-Taylor Collection

Luzerne County Historical Society, Wilkes-Barre, Pa.
George W. Woodward Papers
Woodward Family Papers
Hendrick B. Wright Papers

The Mariners' Museum Library, Paul and Rosemary Trible Library, Christopher Newport University, Newport News, Va.
Walter Jacobs Family Papers (MS0514)

Miami University of Ohio, University Archives, Miami, Ohio
Robert C. Schenck Papers

Michigan State Archives (available at seekingmichigan.org/)
Civil War Letters of Mack and Nan Ewing

Michigan State University Archives, East Lansing
Arnold Family Papers (C00227)
Albert W. Barber Letters (C00282)
Benjamin B. Brock Letters (Collection C00239)

National Archives and Records Administration, College Park, Md.
RG 60, General Records of the Department of Justice

National Archives and Records Administration, Washington, D.C.
    RG 46, Records of the United States Senate
    RG 94, Records of the Adjutant General's Office
    RG 107, Records of the Office of the Secretary of War
    RG 153, Records of the Office of the Judge Advocate General (Army)
    RG 393, Records of United States Army Continental Commands

New York Historical Society
    Helen Fairchild Collection of Horatio Seymour Papers
    Miscellaneous Manuscript Collection
    War Letters, 1861–1865

New York Public Library
    John Bigelow Papers
    Charles P. Daly Papers
    Horace Greeley Papers
    Miscellaneous Personal Papers Collection
    Henry J. Raymond Papers
    John Francis Ruggles Papers
    Samuel J. Tilden Papers

Ohio Historical Society, Columbus
    Samuel Sullivan Cox Miscellaneous Correspondence

Pennsylvania State Archives, Harrisburg
    MG-6, Diaries and Journals Collection
    MG-7, Military Manuscripts Collection
    MG-8, Pennsylvania Collection (Miscellaneous)
    MG-15, Hiram C. Alleman Papers
    MG-22, William Bigler Collection
    MG-41, John A. J. Cresswell Collection
    MG-54, J. Alexander Fulton Papers
    MG-95, Daniel Musser Papers
    MG-188, Woods Family Collection
    MG-189, Kelly Family Collection
    MG-198, Stokes L. Roberts Papers
    MG-200, Poster Collection
    MG-221, Samuel P. Glass Collection
    MG-222, Jacob Sigmund Collection
    MG-223, Francis W. Reed Collection
    MG-224, John S. Garrett Collection
    MG-225, L. M. Anderson Collection

MG-226, Christian Geisel Collection
MG-227, Solomon Fox Collection
MG-228, William C. Armor Collection
MG-229, R. W. Penn Collection
MG-230, David W. Howard Collection
MG-231, Jacob R. Hill Collection
RG-7, Records of the General Assembly
RG-19, Records of the Department of Military and Veterans Affairs
RG-26, Records of the Department of State
RG-33, Records of the Supreme Court of Pennsylvania
RG-47, Records of the County Governments

Pennsylvania State University, Special Collections, Paterno Library, University Park
James A. Beaver Papers
Samuel Gramly Diaries
John S. Pulsifer, Union League of America Papers
Evan Williams Civil War Letters

Pennypacker Mills, Schwenksville, Pa.
Samuel W. Pennypacker Papers

Princeton University, Special Collections, Firestone Library, Princeton, N.J.
Civil War Letters of Adam Badeau
George B. Bacon Papers
Augustus W. Bradford Papers
Benjamin H. Brewster Papers
William L. Dayton Papers
Hubbell Family Papers
Civil War Papers of Symmes H. Stillwell

The Huntington, San Marino, Calif.
Henry Douglas Bacon Papers
Samuel L. M. Barlow Papers
Brophy-Beeson Papers
Colver Collection
Cave Johnson Couts Papers
Thomas Haines Dudley Papers
Eldridge Collection
Huntington Miscellaneous Collection
Ward H. Lamon Papers
Francis Lieber Papers
John Page Nichols Papers

U.S. Army Military History Institute, Carlisle, Pa.
 Arnold Family Papers
 Civil War Miscellaneous Collection
  John Quincy Adams Diary
  Oscar Adams Letter
  Anderson-Caperhart-McCowan Family Papers
  G. E. Andrews Letters
  Ashley Family Papers
  John W. Bates Diary
  John C. Baum Diary
  James Beard Letters
  Samuel H. Beddall Diary
  Nathaniel Belknap Papers
  Benton Family Papers
  Adam Jasper Best Letter
  Allan L. Bevan Letters
  George C. Booze
  Boucher Family Papers
  Thomas C. Bowman Letters
  John Brandon Collection
  John R. Bricker Collection
  Samuel Brooks Letters
  James Baldwin Burrows Letters
  John Preston Campbell Papers
  Malcolm Campbell Essays
  Thomas Campbell Diaries
  Morris W. Chalmers Letters
  Jasper B. Cheney Letters
  Nathaniel A. Conklin Letters
  Bayard Taylor Cooper Letters
  Lucius B. Corbin Letters
  Edward Cotter Letters
  Charles A. Coward Letters
  Jacob B. Dannaker Letters
  George Davis Letters
  James W. Davis Diary
  Leaner E. Davis Letters
  Hannah Eliza Delp Collection
  Frank Wilberforce Dickerson Letters
  Jonas Denton Elliott Letters
  Nancy Bowden Ellis Letters
  John D. Fish Letters

Oliver B. Fluke Letter
Brigham Foster Letters
Foster Family Papers
Joel F. Frederick Letters
Charles J. Fribley Diaries
D. M. Garland Letters
William B. Gates Letter
Ezra Getschell Letters
John Gourlie Letters
Graham Family Papers
Robert N. Greenfield Diaries
John Guest Correspondence
Charles W. Gurney Letters
William C. Hacket Letters
John Halloran Letters
Heald Family Papers
Paul Hersh Letters
Robert Hill Letters
Freland N. Holman Letters
Orrin D. Holmes Letters
Henry Hoyt Letters
Napoleon Bonaparte Hudson Letters
Henry S. Jay Papers
Frederic Henry Kellogg Letters
Andrew Knox Letters
George L. Lacey Letters
William H. Lambert Letters
Robert E. Lassman Letters
Reynolds Laughlin Papers
Jacob Mohler Leidigh Diaries
Fernando Coltrain Lewis Letters
Albert Liscom Papers
Andrew J. Lorish Letters
Paul Lounsbury Letters
Charles H. Lutz Letters
Lyman Family Papers
Samuel J. Marks Letters
Benjamin F. Marshall Letters
William M. Martindell Letters
Charles Maxim Letters
Samuel Z. Maxwell Letter
Cary E. McCann Letters

James McIlwain Letters
John S. McVey Letters
James E. Mitchell Letters
Harrison Montague Letters
George F. Morse Letters
Annesley N. Morton Letters
John Morton Letters
James H. Nugent Letters
Aaron Overstreet Letters
B. Theodore Parks Letters
Miles Peabody Letters
Letters, Articles and Reminiscences of the 149th Pennsylvania Vol. Infantry
Richard A. Plotts Collection
James B. Post Letters
Lorenzo N. Pratt Letters
James L. Rea Letters
Richards Family Papers
John H. Rippetoe Letters
Samuel H. Root Letters
James B. Rounsaville Letters
William Ryan Letters
Franz Schwenzer Papers
Sexton Family Papers
William T. Shimp Letters
George Shingle Letters
James Randolph Simpson and George Simpson Papers
George G. Sinclair Papers
Francis M. Skillin Letters
Charles H. Smith Letters
David Smith Letters
Harry F. Smith Letters
Hosea Smith Letters
Southard Family Papers
Spencer Family Papers
Benjamin F. Stalder Papers
Steffan Family Letters
Stern Family Papers
George Tate Letters
John Van Verhten Letters
John M. Waggoner Family Papers
William Henry Walling Letters
Richard H. Watson Letters

    Jacob Weiker Letter

    D. Cameron White Letters

    Richard Williams Letters

    George A. Wilson Letters

Civil War Times Illustrated Collection

    Nelson Chapin Correspondence

    E. B. Doane Correspondence

    Featherstone Collection

    Wilbur Fisk Letters

    John W. Ford Letters

    Marcus O. Ford Letters

    Liberty Foskett Letters

    Vernon F. Henderson Diary

    Henry Henney Diary and Letters

    William S. Keller Papers

    Jacob Reser Letters

    Norman D. Smith Correspondence

    Perry R. Smith Correspondence

    Daniel Sterling Correspondence

    James P. Stewart Correspondence

    Charles Marshall Stone Letter

    E. P. Sturges Correspondence

    Adolphus P. Wolf Letters

Civil War Times Illustrated Collection, 2nd series

    Newton Adams Letters

    Willie Rool Diary and Letters

James S. Davis Papers

Harrisburg Civil War Round Table Collection

    Benjamin F. Ashenfelter Letters

    John W. Bailey Diary

    Bernhard Family Papers

    Gregory A. Coco Collection

    Clement Hoffman Letters

Lowry Hinch Papers

George Miller Collection

Pennsylvania "Save the Flags" Collection

    Alexander W. Acheson Letters

    Gideon Mellin Letters

Smith-Kirby-Webster-Black-Danner Family Papers

Western Reserve Historical Society, Cleveland, Ohio

    Vallandigham-Laird Family Papers

Wisconsin Veterans Museum, Research Center, Madison
    Martin G. Ellison Papers
    James G. Knight Papers

Wistar Institute, University of Pennsylvania, Philadelphia
    Isaac J. Wistar Civil War Collection

Newspapers

Illinois
    Chicago Tribune (Proquest)

Massachusetts
    Pittsfield Sun (America's Historical Newspapers)

New York
    New York Daily Tribune
    New York Times (Proquest)
    New York World

Ohio
    Highland Weekly News

Pennsylvania
    Bellefonte Central Press (Penn State Digital Collections)
    Bellefonte Democratic Watchman (Penn State Digital Collections)
    Bucks County Intelligencer (Doylestown)
    Chambersburg Franklin Repository (Penn State Digital Collections)
    Doylestown Democrat
    Harrisburg Patriot and Union (Penn State Digital Collections)
    Lancaster Intelligencer (Penn State Digital Collections)
    Lebanon Advertiser (Penn State Digital Collections)
    Luzerne Legal Observer
    Mifflinburg Telegraph
    Pennsylvania Daily Telegraph (Harrisburg) (Penn State Digital Collections)
    Philadelphia Age
    Philadelphia Daily Evening Bulletin (Penn State Digital Collections)
    Philadelphia Inquirer
    Philadelphia North American and United States Gazette
    Philadelphia Press (Penn State Digital Collections)
    Pittsburgh Daily Commercial (Penn State Digital Collections)

Union County Star and Lewisburg Chronicle
Wellsboro Agitator (Penn State Digital Collections)
West Chester Village Record
Wilkes-Barre Luzerne Union

Modern Newspapers (accessed through ProQuest)
Atlanta Constitution
Austin American Statesman
Florida Times Union (Jacksonville)
Virginian-Pilot (Norfolk)
Wall Street Journal

Constitutional Documents

Ambler, Charles H., Frances Haney Atwood, and William B. Mathews, eds. *Debates and Proceedings of the First Constitutional Convention of West Virginia (1861–1863)*. 3 vols. Huntington, W.V.: Gentry, [1939–40].

Cary, George W., and James McClellan, eds. *The Federalist: The Gideon Edition*. Indianapolis: Liberty Fund, 2001.

Illinois. *Journal of the Constitutional Convention of the State of Illinois, Convened at Springfield, January 7, 1862*. Springfield: Charles H. Lanphier, 1862.

Kansas. *Constitutional Convention*. Topeka: Imri Zumwalt, 1920.

Lord, William Blair, and David Wolfe Brown, eds. *The Debates and Proceedings of the Constitutional Convention of the State of Michigan, Convened at the City of Lansing, Wednesday, May 15th, 1867*. 2 vols. Lansing: John A. Kerr & Co., 1867.

Lord, William Blair, and Henry M. Parkhurst, eds. *The Debates of the Constitutional Convention of the State of Maryland, Assembled at the City of Annapolis, Wednesday, April 27, 1864*. 3 vols. Annapolis: Richard P. Bayly, 1864.

Maryland Constitutional Convention Commission. *Constitutional Revision Study Documents*. Baltimore: King Brothers, 1968.

Ryan, Frank J. *Constitution of the State of Kansas and Amendments and Proposed Amendments Submitted*. Topeka: Ferd Voiland Jr., 1946.

Shanahan, Elwill M. *The Constitution of the State of Kansas with Amendments*. Topeka: Robert R. Sanders, 1973.

Steinglass, Steven H., and Gino J. Scarselli. *The Ohio Constitution: A Reference Guide*. Westport, Conn.: Greenwood, 2004.

Underhill, E. F., comp. *Report of the Proceedings and Debates of the Constitutional Convention for the Revision of the Constitution of the State of New York, 1867–'68*. 5 vols. Albany: Weed, Parsons & Co., 1868.

U.S. Constitution (1787).

Congressional Documents

Appendix to the Congressional Globe
Congressional Globe
Congressional Serial Set
Journal of the House of Representatives
House of Representatives Bills and Resolutions
Senate Bills and Resolutions
Senate Executive Journal
Senate Journal
U.S. Statutes at Large

State Legislative Documents

Bergner, George, ed. *The Legislative Record: Containing the Debates and Proceedings of the Pennsylvania Legislature for the Session of 1864.* Harrisburg: "Telegraph" Steam Book and Job Office, 1864.
———. *The Legislative Record: Containing the Debates and Proceedings of the Pennsylvania Legislature for the Session of 1866.* Harrisburg: "Telegraph" Steam Book and Job Office, 1866.
Kansas. *1974 Session Laws of Kansas.* Topeka: Robert R. Sanders, 1974.
Maine. *Maine Legislative Manual, 1865.* Augusta: Stevens and Sayward, 1865.
———. *Resolves of the State of Maine, from 1866 to 1868, Inclusive.* Augusta: Owen and Nash, 1868.
Maryland. *Documents of the General Assembly, 1864.* Annapolis: Richard P. Bayly, 1864.
———. *Journal of the Proceedings of the House of Delegates, 1864.* Annapolis: Bull and Tuttle, 1864.
———. *Journal of the Proceedings of the Senate, 1864.* Annapolis: Bull and Tuttle, 1864.
———. *Documents of the General Assembly, 1865.* Annapolis: Richard P. Bayly, 1865.
McElroy, W. H., and Alex. McBride. *Life Sketches of Government Officers and Members of the Legislature of the State of New York for 1875.* Albany: Weed, Parsons and Co., 1875.
Michigan. *Acts of the Legislature of the State of Michigan, Passed at the Regular Session of 1867.* 2 vols. Lansing: John A. Kerr, 1867.
New Hampshire. *Laws of the State of New-Hampshire, Passed June Session, 1866.* Concord: George E. Jenks, 1866.
New York. *Journal of the Senate of the State of New York at Their Eighty-Sixth Session.* Albany: Comstock & Cassidy, 1863.
———. *Laws of the State of New York, Passed at the Ninetieth Session of the Legislature, Begun January First, and Ended April Twentieth, 1867, in the City of Albany.* Albany: Weare C. Little, 1867.

———. *Documents of the Senate of the State of New York, Ninety-Eight Session—1875.* 6 vols. Albany: Weed, Parsons and Co., 1875.

———. *The Revised Statutes of the State of New York*, Vol. 1. Albany: Banks and Brothers, 1889.

Ohio. *General and Local Laws and Joint Resolutions Passed by the Fifty-Sixth General Assembly of the State of Ohio, at Its Second Session, Begun and Held in the City of Columbus, January 3, 1865, and in the Sixty-Third Year of Said State.* Columbus: Richard Nevins, 1865.

Oregon Revised Statutes (available at www.oregonlaws.org/).

Pennsylvania. *Acts of the General Assembly of the Commonwealth of Pennsylvania.* Philadelphia: John Bloren, 1813.

———. *Laws of the General Assembly of the Commonwealth of Pennsylvania.* Harrisburg: Packer, Barrett and Paree, 1839.

———. *Journal of the Senate of the Commonwealth of Pennsylvania, of the Session Begun at Harrisburg, on the First Day of January, A.D., 1861.* Harrisburg: A. Boyd Hamilton, 1861.

———. *Legislative Documents. Miscellaneous Documents Read in the Legislature of the Commonwealth of Pennsylvania.* Harrisburg: Boyd Hamilton, 1862.

———. *Journal of the Senate of the Commonwealth of Pennsylvania of the Session Begun at Harrisburg, on the Sixth Day of January, 1863.* Harrisburg: Singerly & Myers, 1863.

———. *Journal of the House of Representatives of the Commonwealth of Pennsylvania, of the Session Begun at Harrisburg, on the Fifth Day of January, 1864.* Harrisburg: Singerly and Myers, 1864.

———. *Journal of the Senate of the Commonwealth of Pennsylvania, of the Session Begun at Harrisburg, on the Fifth Day of January, 1864.* Harrisburg: Singerly & Myers, 1864.

———. *Miscellaneous Documents Read in the Legislature of the Commonwealth of Pennsylvania.* Harrisburg: Singerly and Myers, 1864.

———. *Laws of the General Assembly of the State of Pennsylvania, Passed at the Session of 1866, in the Nineteenth Year of Independence.* Harrisburg: Singerly and Myers, 1866.

Vermont. *Acts and Resolves Passed by the General Assembly of the State of Vermont, at the Annual Session, 1866.* Montpelier: Freeman Steam Printing Establishment, 1866.

Wisconsin. *General Laws Passed by the Legislature of Wisconsin, in the Year 1865, Together with Joint Resolutions and Memorials.* Madison: William J. Park, 1865.

———. *General Laws Passed by the Legislature of Wisconsin, in the Year 1866, Together with Joint Resolutions and Memorials.* Madison: William J. Park, 1866.

———. *General Laws Passed by the Legislature of Wisconsin, in the Year 1868, Together with Joint Resolutions and Memorials.* Madison: Atwood and Rublee, 1868.

———. *Journal of Proceedings of the Twentieth Annual Session of the Wisconsin Legislature, for the Year 1868.* Madison: Atwood and Rublee, 1868.

———. *General Laws Passed by the Legislature of Wisconsin, in the Year 1869, Together with Joint Resolutions and Memorials.* Madison: Atwood and Rublee, 1869.

Ziegler, Jacob. *A Manual for the Government of the Senate and House of Representatives of the Commonwealth of Pennsylvania.* Harrisburg: "Telegraph" Steam Print, 1864.

Official Documents and Statistical Sources

Bates, Samuel P. *History of Pennsylvania Volunteers, 1861–5*. 5 vols. Harrisburg: B. Singerly, 1869–71.

Dubin, Michael J. *United States Congressional Elections, 1788–1997: The Official Results of the Elections of the 1st through 105th Congresses*. Jefferson, N.C.: McFarland, 1998.

Gould, Benjamin A. *Investigations in the Military and Anthropological Statistics of American Soldiers*. New York: Hurd and Houghton, 1869.

Indiana. *Report of the Adjutant General of the State of Indiana*. 8 vols. Indianapolis: Alexander H. Conner, 1868–69.

Michigan. *Annual Report of the Adjutant General of the State of Michigan, for the Year 1864*. Lansing: John A. Kerr, 1865.

———. *Annual Report of the Attorney General of the State of Michigan for the Year 1866*. Lansing: John A. Kerr, 1866.

New York. *Annual Report of the Adjutant-General of the State of New York*. 43 vols. Albany: James B. Lyon, 1893–1905.

Ohio. *Annual Report of the Secretary of State to the Governor of the State of Ohio, for the Year 1864*. Columbus: Richard Nevins, 1865.

Pennsylvania. *Report of the Adjutant General of Pennsylvania Transmitted to the Governor in Pursuance of Law for the Year 1863*. Harrisburg: Singerly & Myers, 1864.

———. *Report of the Adjutant General of Pennsylvania Transmitted to the Governor in Pursuance of Law for the Year 1864*. Harrisburg: Singerly & Myers, 1865.

———. *Reports of the Heads of Departments, Transmitted to the Governor of Pennsylvania, in Pursuance of the Law, for the Financial Year Ending November 30, 1864*. Harrisburg: Singerly & Myers, 1865.

Stryker, William S. *Record of Officers and Men of New Jersey in the Civil War, 1861–1865*. 2 vols. Trenton: J. L. Murphy, 1876.

United States Bureau of the Census. *The Statistical History of the United States from Colonial Times to the Present*. New York: Basic, 1976.

War Department. *Revised Regulations for the Army of the United States, 1861*. Philadelphia: J. G. L. Brown, 1861.

War of the Rebellion: A Compilation of the Official Records of the Union and Confederate Armies. 128 vols. Washington, D.C.: Government Printing Office, 1880–1901.

Wisconsin. *Message of the Governor of Wisconsin, Together with the Annual Reports, of the Officers of the State, for the Year, A.D. 1865*. Madison: William J. Park, 1866.

Pamphlets

Bailey, Alexander H. *Allowing Soldiers to Vote. Mr. Bailey's Speech on the Bill to Extend the Elective Franchise to the Soldiers of this State in the Service of the United States. In Senate, April 1, 1863*. N.p., 1863.

Biblicus [pseudonym]. *The Bible View of Slavery Reconsidered: A Letter to the Right Rev. Bishop Hopkins.* 2nd ed. Philadelphia: Henry B. Ashmead, 1863.

Black, Chauncey F. *Speech of Chauncey F. Black, of York, To the Democracy Assembled at Hawley, Wayne County, Pa., Sept. 21, 1863.* N.p., [1863].

Black, Jeremiah S. *The Doctrines of the Democratic and Abolition Parties Contrasted: Negro Equality: The Conflict between "Higher Law" and the Law of the Land. Speech of Hon. Jeremiah S. Black, at the Hall of the Keystone Club, in Philadelphia, October 24, 1864.* Philadelphia: Age Office, 1864.

———. *Speech of Hon. Jeremiah S. Black, at the Democratic Mass Convention, in Lancaster City, September 17, 1863.* Harrisburg: Patriot and Union Steam Print, 1863.

A Black Record! Gov. Curtin's Portrait Drawn by a Black Republican Editor. Who Clothed Our Soldiers in Shoddy? Who Plundered Our Brave Volunteers? Voters Read! Philadelphia: Age Office, [1863].

Chandler, William E. *The Soldier's Right to Vote. Who Opposes It? Who Favors It? Or, The Record of the M'Clellan Copperheads Against Allowing the Soldier Who Fights, the Right to Vote While Fighting.* Washington, D.C.: Lemuel Towers, 1864.

Christianity versus Treason and Slavery. Religion Rebuking Sedition. Philadelphia: H. B. Ashmead, 1864.

Cook, William A. *Hon. Geo. W. Woodward and the Gubernatorial Contest in Pennsylvania. Review of his Speech in Independence Square, Philadelphia, December 13, 1860. A True Exposition of His Principles and Purposes.* [Washington, D.C.]: Chronicle Print, 1863.

Democratic Opinions on Slavery! 1776–1863. N.p., [1863].

Democratic Party (Pa.). State Central Committee. *Soldiers Read!! Citizens Read!!! Address of the Democratic State Central Committee. Letter of Major Geo. A. Woodward. Letter of Judge Woodward.* Philadelphia: Age Office, 1863.

Hopkins, John Henry. *Bible View of Slavery.* 1861. Reprint, New York: Society for the Diffusion of Political Knowledge, 1863.

Kemble, Fanny A. *The Views of Judge Woodward and Bishop Hopkins on Negro Slavery at the South: Illustrated from the Journal of a Residence on a Georgian Plantation.* [Philadelphia]: N.p., 1863.

Lundy, John Patterson. *Review of Bishop Hopkins' Bible View of Slavery, by a Presbyter of the Church in Philadelphia.* [Philadelphia]: N.p., 1863.

May, James. *Remarks on Bishop Hopkins' Letter on the Bible View of Slavery.* N.p., 1863.

Opinions of a Man Who Wishes to be Governor of Pennsylvania: Extracts from a Speech of Judge Woodward, delivered on Thursday, December 13, 1860, at Independence Square, Philadelphia. Philadelphia: C. Sherman Son & Co., 1863.

A Picture of Slavery, Drawn from the Decisions of Southern Courts. Philadelphia: Crissy & Markley, 1863.

Political Dialogues: Soldiers on Their Right to Vote, and the Men They Should Support. Washington, D.C.: Chronicle Print, [1864].

The Political Portrait of Andrew G. Curtin, By One of His Own Party. N.p., [1863].

Vail, Stephen M. *The Bible against Slavery, with Replies to the "Bible View of Slavery," by*

John H. Hopkins, D. D., Bishop of the Diocese of Vermont; and to "A Northern Presbyter's Second Letter to Ministers of the Gospel," by Nathan Lord, D. D., Late President of Dartmouth College; and to "X," of the New-Hampshire Patriot. Concord: Fogg, Hadley & Co., 1864.

Wallace, William A. *Reasons of Hon. Wm. A. Wallace, of Clearfield, For His Vote on Amendments to the Constitution.* N.p., 1864.

Whiting, William. *The War Powers of the President, and the Legislative Powers of Congress in Relation to Rebellion, Treason and Slavery.* Boston: John L. Shorey, 1862.

———. *War Powers under the Constitution of the United States,* 10th ed. Boston: Littleton, Brown & Co., 1864.

Woodward, George W. *Speech of Hon. George W. Woodward: Delivered at the Great Union Meeting in Independence Square, Philadelphia.* Philadelphia: Ringwalt & Brown, 1860.

———. *Speech of Hon. George W. Woodward, Delivered at the Great Union Meeting in Independence Square, Philadelphia, December 13th, 1860: The Democratic Platform, Adopted by the State Convention at Harrisburg, on the 17th June, 1863.* Philadelphia: Age Office, 1863.

Woodward in 1860 & 1863. Philadelphia: Crissy & Markley, 1863.

Woodward on Foreigners. Philadelphia: H. B. Ashmead, 1863.

Periodicals and Almanacs

American Law Register
American Periodicals Series (ProQuest)
Monthly Law Reporter
The Old Guard: A Monthly Journal, Devoted to the Principles of 1776 and 1787
Tribune Almanac and Political Register
United States Service Magazine

Court Reporters

Brewster's Reports (Pennsylvania state cases)
California Reports
Grant's Reports (Pennsylvania state cases)
Kansas Reports
Maine Reports
New Hampshire Reports
New York Reports
Ohio Reports
Pennsylvania Reports
Philadelphia Reports

U.S. Reports (U.S. Supreme Court cases)
Wisconsin Reports

Additional Published Primary Sources

Adams, Lois Bryan. *Letter from Washington, 1863–1865*. Edited by Evelyn Leasher. Detroit: Wayne State University Press, 1999.

Alderson, Kevin, and Patsy Alderson, eds. *Letters Home to Sarah: The Civil War Letters of Guy C. Taylor, 36th Wisconsin Volunteers*. Madison: University of Wisconsin Press, 2012.

Aldrich, C. Knight, ed. *Quest for a Star: The Civil War Letters and Diaries of Colonel Francis T. Sherman of the 88th Illinois*. Knoxville: University of Tennessee Press, 1999.

The American Annual Cyclopaedia and Register of Important Events. 14 vols. New York: D. Appleton, 1862–75.

Anderson, David L., ed. "The Letters of 'Wilhelm Yank': Letters from a German Soldier in the Civil War." *Michigan Historical Review* 16 (Spring 1990): 73–93.

Bailey, Judith A., and Robert I. Cottom, eds. *After Chancellorsville, Letters from the Heart: The Civil War Letters of Private Walter G. Dunn & Emma Randolph*. Baltimore: Maryland Historical Society, 1998.

Bartlett, William H., ed. *Aunt and the Soldier Boys*. Santa Cruz, Calif.: Privately printed, 1973.

Bates, Edward. *Diary of Edward Bates*. Edited by Howard K. Beale. Washington, D.C.: Government Printing Office, 1933.

Baumgartner, Richard A., ed. *The Bully Boys: In Camp and Combat with the 2nd Ohio Volunteer Infantry Regiment, 1861–1864*. Huntington, W.V.: Blue Acorn Press, 2011.

Beatty, John. *Memoirs of a Volunteer, 1861–1863*. 1879. Reprint, New York: W. W. Norton, 1946.

Bennett, Stewart, and Barbara Tillery, eds. *The Struggle for the Life of the Republic: A Civil War Narrative by Brevet Major Charles Dana Miller, 76th Ohio Volunteer Infantry*. Kent, Ohio: Kent State University Press, 2004.

Bigelow, John. *Retrospections of an Active Life*. 5 vols. New York: Baker and Taylor, 1909–13.

Bird, Margaret McKelvy, and Daniel W. Crofts, eds. "Soldier Voting in 1864: The David McKelvy Diary." *Pennsylvania Magazine of History and Biography* 115 (July 1991): 371–415.

Boag, Peter G., ed. "'Dear Friends': The Civil War Letters of Francis Marion Elliot, A Pennsylvania Country Boy." *Pittsburgh History* 72 (Holiday 1989): 193–98.

Bobrick, Benson. *Testament: A Soldier's Story of the Civil War*. New York: Simon and Schuster, 2003.

Bogue, Allan G., ed. "William Parker Cutler's Congressional Diary of 1862–63." *Civil War History* 33 (December 1987): 315–30.

Bonner, Robert E., ed. *The Soldier's Pen: Firsthand Impressions of the Civil War*. New York: Hill and Wang, 2006.

Bradley, Susan Hinckley, ed. *A Soldier-Boy's Letters, 1862–1865*. Boston: Privately printed, 1905.

Bridge, Carolyn S., and Marilyn Bridge Brown, eds. *Letters from Elmira's Trunk: An Indiana Family in the Civil War*. West Lafayette, Ind.: Twin, 2002.

Brown, Joseph E. *Message of His Excellency Joseph E. Brown, to the Extra Session of the Legislature, Convened March 10th, 1864*. Milledgeville: Boughton, Nisbet, Barnes and Moore, 1864.

Brun, Christian, ed. "A Palace Guard View of Lincoln: The Civil War Letters of John H. Fleming." *Soundings: Collections of the University [of California at Santa Barbara] Library* 3 (December 1971): 18–39.

Burlingame, Michael, ed. *Lincoln's Journalist: John Hay's Anonymous Writings for the Press, 1860–1864*. Carbondale: Southern Illinois University Press, 1998.

Burlingame, Michael, and John R. Turner Ettlinger, eds. *Inside Lincoln's White House: The Complete Civil War Diary of John Hay*. Carbondale: Southern Illinois University Press, 1997.

Butler, Benjamin F. *Butler's Book: Autobiography and Personal Reminiscences of Major-General Benjamin F. Butler*. Boston: A. M. Thayer, 1892.

Chase, Salmon P. *Sixth Report of Historical Manuscripts Commission: With Diary and Correspondence of Salmon P. Chase*. Washington, D.C.: Government Printing Office, 1902.

Clarke, Hermon. *Back Home in Oneida: Hermon Clarke and His Letters*. Edited by Harry F. Jackson and Thomas F. O'Donnell. Syracuse, N.Y.: Syracuse University Press, 1965.

Cole, Donald B., and John J. McDonough, eds. *Witness to the Young Republic: A Yankee's Journal, 1828–1870*. London: University Press of New England, 1989.

Collier, John S., and Bonnie B. Collier, eds. *Yours for the Union: The Civil War Letters of John W. Chase, First Massachusetts Light Artillery*. New York: Fordham University Press, 2004.

Colton, J. Ferrell, and Antoinette G. Smith, eds. *Column South: With the Fifteenth Pennsylvania Cavalry from Antietam to the Capture of Jefferson Davis*. Flagstaff: J. F. Colton, 1960.

Connolly, James A. *Three Years in the Army of the Cumberland: The Letters and Diary of Major James A. Connolly*. Edited by Paul M. Angle. Bloomington: Indiana University Press, 1959.

Cox, Samuel Sullivan. *Eight Years in Congress, from 1857 to 1865: Memoir and Speeches*. New York: D. Appleton, 1865.

Crist, Lynda Lasswell, et al., eds. *The Papers of Jefferson Davis*. 15 vols. projected. Baton Rouge: Louisiana State University Press, 1971–present.

Daly, Maria Lydig. *Diary of a Union Lady*. Edited by Harold Earl Hammond. New York: Funk and Wagnalls, 1962.

Dana, Charles A. *Recollections of the Civil War*. New York: Collier, 1963.

Davis, David Brion, and Steven Mintz, eds. *A Boisterous Sea of Liberty: A Documentary History of America from Discovery through the Civil War*. New York: Oxford University Press, 1998.

Dee, Christine, ed. *Ohio's War: The Civil War in Documents.* Athens: Ohio University Press, 2006.

Depew, Chauncey M. *My Memories of Eighty Years.* New York: Charles Scribner's Sons, 1924.

The Dismissal of Major Granville O. Haller of the Regular Army, of the United States by Order of the Secretary of War. Paterson, N.J.: Daily Guardian, 1863.

Dittenhoefer, Abram J. *How We Elected Lincoln: Personal Recollections.* 1916. Reprint, Philadelphia: University of Pennsylvania Press, 2005.

Drake, Julia A., ed. *The Mail Goes Through or Civil War Letters of George Drake.* San Angelo, Tex.: Anchor, 1964.

Driver, Robert A., and Gloria S. Driver, eds. *Letters Home: The Personal Side of the American Civil War.* Roseburg, Ore.: Privately printed, 1992.

Engs, Robert F., and Corey M. Brooks, eds. *Their Patriotic Duty: The Civil War Letters of the Evans Family of Brown County, Ohio.* New York: Fordham University Press, 2007.

Everstine, Barbara Schilling, ed. *My Three Years in the Volunteer Army of the United States of America, from August 12th, 1862, to June 10th, 1865: Edw. Schilling, Co. F, Fourth Md. Vol. Infty.* N.p., 1985.

Finsley, Charles E., ed. *Hannah's Letters: Civil War Letters of Isaac E. Blauvelt, Friends and Other Suitors.* Dallas, Tex.: Kings Creek Press, 1997.

Flower, Milton E., ed. *Dear Folks at Home: The Civil War Letters of Leo W. and John I. Faller with an Account of Andersonville.* Carlisle, Pa.: Cumberland County Historical Society and Hamilton Library Association, 1963.

Ford, Worthington Chauncey, ed. *A Cycle of Adams Letters, 1861–1865.* 2 vols. Boston: Houghton Mifflin, 1920.

———. *War Letters, 1862–1865, of John Chipman Gray and John Codman Ropes.* Boston: Houghton Mifflin, 1927.

Freidel, Frank, ed. *Union Pamphlets of the Civil War, 1861–1865.* 2 vols. Cambridge: Harvard University Press, 1967.

Gates, Betsey, ed. *The Colton Letters: Civil War Period, 1861–1865.* Scottsdale: McLane, 1993.

Geary, John White. *A Politician Goes to War: The Civil War Letters of John White Geary.* Edited by William A. Blair. University Park: Pennsylvania State University Press, 1995.

Gilmor, Harry. *Four Years in the Saddle.* New York: Harper and Brothers, 1866.

Gooding, James Henry. *On the Altar of Freedom: A Black Soldier's Civil War Letters from the Front.* Edited by Virginia M. Adams. Amherst: University of Massachusetts Press, 1991.

Goodsell, James H., ed. *Official Proceedings of the Democratic National Convention, Held in 1864 at Chicago.* Chicago: Times Steam Book and Job Printing House, 1864.

Gould, Joseph. *The Story of the Forty-Eighth [Pennsylvania Infantry].* Philadelphia: Alfred M. Slocum, 1908.

Graf, Leroy P., Patricia P. Clark, and Marion O. Smith, eds. *The Papers of Andrew Johnson.* Vol. 7, *1864–1865.* Knoxville: University of Tennessee Press, 1986.

Grimsley, Mark, and Todd D. Miller, eds. *The Union Must Stand: The Civil War Diary of John Quincy Adams Campbell, Fifth Iowa Volunteer Infantry.* Knoxville: University of Tennessee Press, 2000.

Guroski, Adam. *Diary.* 3 vols. 1862–66. Reprint, New York: Burt Franklin, 1968.

Ham, Gerald, ed. "The Mind of a Copperhead: Letters of John J. Davis on the Secession Crisis and Statehood Politics in Western Virginia, 1860–1862." *West Virginia History* 24 (January 1963): 173–200.

Hancock, Harold B., ed. "The Civil War Diaries of Anna M. Ferris." *Delaware History* 9 (April 1961): 220–64.

Harris, Robert F., and John Niflot, eds. *Dear Sister: The Civil War Letters of the Brothers Gould.* Westport, Conn.: Praeger, 1998.

Hartwell, John F. L. *To My Beloved Wife and Boy at Home: The Letters and Diaries of Orderly Sergeant John F. L. Hartwell.* Edited by Ann Hartwell Britton and Thomas J. Reed. Madison, Wisc.: Fairleigh Dickinson University Press, 1997.

Hastings, William H., ed. *Letters from a Sharpshooter: The Civil War Letters of Private William B. Greene, Co. G, 2nd United States Sharpshooters (Berdan's), Army of the Potomac, 1861–1865.* Belleville, Wisc.: Historic Publications, 1993.

Henry, Guy V. *Military Record of Civilian Appointments in the United States Army.* 2 vols. New York: Carleton, 1869–73.

Herdegen, Lance, and Sherry Murphy, eds. *Four Years with the Iron Brigade: The Civil War Journals of William R. Ray, Co. F., Seventh Wisconsin Infantry.* Cambridge, Mass.: Da Capo Press, 2002.

Hinsdale, Burke A., ed. *The Works of James Abram Garfield.* 2 vols. Boston: James R. Osgood, 1882.

Hoadley, J. C., ed. *Memorial of Henry Sanford Gansevoort.* Boston: Franklin Press, 1875.

Holmes, Oliver Wendell. *Touched with Fire: The Civil War Letters and Diary of Oliver Wendell Holmes, Jr., 1861–1864.* Edited by Mark DeWolfe Howe. 1947. Reprint, New York: Da Capo Press, 1969.

Hopkins, Vivian C., ed. "Soldier of the 92nd Illinois: Letters of William H. Brown and His Fiancée, Emma Jane Frazey." *Bulletin of the New York Public Library* 73 (February 1969): 114–36.

Hudder, Jean Anne W., ed. *Dear Wife: Captain Joseph Adams' Letters to His Wife, Eliza Ann, 1861–1864.* [s.l.]: J. A.W. Hudder, 1985.

Johnston, Gertrude K., ed. *Dear Pa—And So It Goes.* Harrisburg: Business Service, 1971.

Kamphoefner, Walter D., and Wolfgang Helbich, eds. *Germans in the Civil War: The Letters They Wrote Home.* Chapel Hill: University of North Carolina Press, 2006.

Kellogg, Mary E., ed. *Army Life of an Illinois Soldier: Including a Day-by-Day Record of Sherman's March to the Sea.* 1906. Reprint, Carbondale: Southern Illinois University Press, 1996.

Laas, Virginia J., ed. *Wartime Washington: The Civil War Letters of Elizabeth Blair Lee.* Urbana: University of Illinois Press, 1991.

Lambert, Lois J., ed. *Ninety-First Ohio Volunteer Infantry: With the Civil War Letters of Lieutenant Colonel Benjamin Franklin Coates and an Annotated Roster of the Men of Company C.* Milford, Ohio: Little Miami, 2005.

Larke, Julian K. *General Grant and His Campaigns.* New York: J. C. Derby and N. C. Miller, 1864.

Levstik, Frank, ed. "The Civil War Diary of Colonel Albert Rogall." *Polish American Studies* 27 (Spring/Autumn 1970): 33–79.

Lincoln, Abraham. *The Collected Works of Abraham Lincoln.* Edited by Roy P. Basler et al. 9 vols. New Brunswick, N.J.: Rutgers University Press, 1953–55.

Lincoln, Charles Z., ed. *State of New York: Messages from the Governors.* 9 vols. Albany: J. B. Lyon, 1909.

Longacre, Edward G., ed. "'Come Home Soon and Dont Delay': Letters from the Home Front, July, 1861." *Pennsylvania Magazine of History and Biography* 100 (July 1976): 395–406.

Lusk, William Chittenden, ed. *War Letters of William Thompson Lusk.* New York: Privately printed, 1911.

Lyman, Theodore. *Meade's Headquarters 1863–1865: Letters of Colonel Theodore Lyman from Wilderness to Appomattox.* Edited by George R. Agassiz. Boston: Atlantic Monthly Press, 1922.

Maness, Donald C., and H. Jason Combs, eds. *Do They Miss Me at Home? The Civil War Letters of William McKnight, Seventh Ohio Volunteer Cavalry.* Athens: Ohio University Press, 2010.

Marks, Bayly Ellen, and Mark Norton Schatz, eds. *Between North and South: A Maryland Journalist Views the Civil War.* Rutherford, N.J.: Fairleigh Dickinson University Press, 1976.

Marshall, Jeffrey D., ed. *A War of the People: Vermont Civil War Letters.* Hanover, N.H.: University Press of New England, 1999.

McCalmont, Alfred B. *Extracts from Letters Written by Alfred B. McCalmont.* [Franklin, Pa.]: Privately printed, 1908.

McClure, Alexander K. *Lincoln and Men of War Times.* 1892. Reprint, Philadelphia: Rolley and Reynolds, 1962.

———. *Old Time Notes of Pennsylvania.* 2 vols. Philadelphia: John C. Winston, 1905.

McKelvey, Blake, ed. *Rochester in the Civil War.* Rochester, N.Y.: Rochester Historical Society, 1944.

Meade, George Gordon. *The Life and Letters of George Gordon Meade, Major-General United States Army.* 2 vols. New York: Charles Scribner's Sons, 1913.

Meier, Louis A., ed. "The Diaries of Hiram Corson, M.D.: Civil War Years, 1862–1865." *Bulletin of the Historical Society of Montgomery County* 33 (Fall 2002): 192–290.

Molyneux, Joel. *Quill of the Wild Goose: The Civil War Letters and Diaries of Private Joel Molyneux, 141st P. V.* Edited by Kermit Molyneux Bird. Shippensburg, Pa.: Burd Street Press, 1996.

Moore, Frank, ed. *The Rebellion Record: A Diary of American Events.* 12 vols. New York: G. P. Putnam, 1861–68. Reprint, New York: Arno Press, 1977.

Moore, Hugh. "A Reminiscence of Confederate Prison Life." *Journal of the Illinois State Historical Society* 65 (Winter 1972): 451–61.

Nelson, James G. "'My Dear Son': Letters to a Civil War Soldier." *Filson Club History Quarterly* 56 (April 1982): 151–69.

Nevins, Allan, and Milton Halsey Thomas, eds. *The Diary of George Templeton Strong, 1835–1875.* 4 vols. New York: Macmillan, 1952.

Niven, John, et al., eds. *The Salmon P. Chase Papers.* 5 vols. Kent, Ohio: Kent State University Press, 1993–98.

Noe, Kenneth W., ed. *A Southern Boy in Blue: The Memoir of Marcus Woodcock, 9th Kentucky Infantry (U.S.A.).* Knoxville: University of Tennessee Press, 1996.

O'Brien, Thomas M., and Oliver Diefendorf. *General Orders of the War Department, Embracing the Years 1861, 1862, and 1863.* 2 vols. New York: Derby and Miller, 1864.

Orr, Timothy J., ed. *Last to Leave the Field: The Life and Letters of First Sergeant Ambrose Henry Hayward, 28th Pennsylvania Volunteers.* Knoxville: University of Tennessee Press, 2011.

Overfield, Joseph M., ed. *The Civil War Letters of Private George Parks, Co. C, 24th New York Cavalry Volunteers.* Buffalo: Gallagher Printing, 1992.

Osborn, Thomas Ward. *The Fiery Trial: A Union Officer's Account of Sherman's Last Campaigns.* Edited by Richard Harwell and Philip N. Racine. Knoxville: University of Tennessee Press, 1986.

Parker, Thomas H. *History of the 51st Regiment of P. V. and V. V.* Philadelphia: King & Baird, 1869.

Patrick, Marsena Rudolph. *Inside Lincoln's Army: The Diary of Marsena Rudolph Patrick, Provost Marshal General, Army of the Potomac.* Edited by David S. Sparks. New York: Thomas Yoseloff, 1964.

Pease, Theodore Calvin, and James G. Randall, eds. *The Diary of Orville Hickman Browning.* 2 vols. Springfield: Illinois State Historical Library, 1925.

Pelka, Fred, ed. *The Civil War Letters of Colonel Charles F. Johnson, Invalid Corps.* Boston: University of Massachusetts Press, 2004.

Pennsylvania State Agricultural Society. *First Annual Report of the Transactions of the Pennsylvania State Agricultural Society.* Harrisburg: A. Boyd Hamilton, 1854.

———. *Second Annual Report of the Transactions of the Pennsylvania State Agricultural Society.* Harrisburg: A. Boyd Hamilton, 1855.

Porter, Horace. *Campaigning with Grant.* New York: Century, 1897.

Proceedings of the Officers and Soldiers of the Indiana Regiments in the Army of the Cumberland, on the Memorial and Resolutions to the Indiana Legislature. Indianapolis: Joseph J. Bingham, 1863.

Puck, Susan T., ed. *Sacrifice at Vicksburg: Letters from the Front.* Shippensburg, Pa.: Burd Street Press, 1997.

Raus, Edmund, ed. "'Dear Brother Isaac . . .': Letters from George Edgcomb, 15th New York Engineers." *Military Images* 8 (May–June 1987): 14–15.

Raya, Michael David, ed. *Letters from the Front: Three Years in the Civil War.* N.p., 2001.

Redkey, Edwin S., ed. *A Grand Army of Black Men: Letters from African-American Soldiers in the Union Army, 1861–1865.* New York: Cambridge University Press, 1992.

Reed, George Edward, ed. *Pennsylvania Archives, Series 4, Vol. 8: Papers of the Governors, 1858–1871.* Harrisburg: William Stanley Ray, 1902.

Reid, Harvey. *Uncommon Soldiers: Harvey Reid and the 22nd Wisconsin March with Sherman.* Edited by Frank L. Byrne. Knoxville: University of Tennessee Press, 2001.

Rosenman, Samuel I., comp. *The Public Papers and Addresses of Franklin D. Roosevelt. 1944–45 vol.: Victory and the Threshold of Peace.* New York: Harper and Brothers, 1950.

Sauerburger, Dona Bayard, and Thomas Lucas Bayard, eds. *I Seat Myself to Write You a Few Lines: Civil War and Homestead Letters from Thomas Lucas and Family.* Bowie, Md.: Heritage, 2002.

Schurz, Carl. *Speeches, Correspondence and Political Papers of Carl Schurz.* 6 vols. Edited by Frederic Bancroft. New York: G. P. Putnam's Sons, 1913.

Scott, Robert Garth, ed. *Fallen Leaves: The Civil War Letters of Major Henry Livermore Abbott.* Kent, Ohio: Kent State University Press, 1991.

Sears, Stephen W., ed. *The Civil War Papers of George B. McClellan: Selected Correspondence, 1860–1865.* New York: Ticknor and Fields, 1989.

———. *On Campaign with the Army of the Potomac: The Civil War Journal of Theodore Ayrault Dodge.* New York: Cooper Square Press, 2001.

Seymour, Horatio. *Public Record of Horatio Seymour.* Edited by Thomas M. Cook and Thomas W. Knox. New York: I. W. England, 1868.

Shannon, Fred Albert, ed. *The Civil War Letters of Sergeant Onley Andrus.* Urbana: University of Illinois Press, 1947.

Silber, Nina, and Mary Beth Sievers, eds. *Yankee Correspondence: Civil War Letters between New England Soldiers and the Home Front.* Charlottesville: University Press of Virginia, 1996.

Simon, John Y., et al., eds. *The Papers of Ulysses S. Grant.* 31 vols. Carbondale: Southern Illinois University Press, 1967–2009.

Skipper, Marti, and Jane Taylor, eds. *A Handful of Providence: The Civil War Letters of Lt. Richard Goldwaite, New York Volunteers, and Ellen Goldwaite.* Jefferson, N.C.: McFarland, 2004.

Smith, John David, and William Cooper Jr., eds. *A Union Woman in Civil War Kentucky: The Diary of Frances Peter.* Lexington: University Press of Kentucky, 2000.

Soman, Jean Powers, and Frank L. Byrne, eds. *A Jewish Colonel in the Civil War: Marcus M. Spiegel of the Ohio Volunteers.* Kent, Ohio: Kent State University Press, 1985.

Stevens, Harriet, ed. *The Graybeards: The Letters of Major Lyman Allen, of the 37th Regiment Iowa Volunteer Infantry.* Iowa City: Camp Pope Bookshop, 1998.

Stevens, Thaddeus. *The Selected Papers of Thaddeus Stevens.* 2 vols. Edited by Beverly Wilson Palmer and Holly Byers Ochoa. Pittsburgh: University of Pittsburgh Press, 1997.

Styple, William B., ed. *Generals in Bronze: Interviewing the Commanders of the Civil War.* Kearny, N.J.: Belle Grove, 2005.

Sumner, Charles. *The Selected Letters of Charles Sumner.* 2 vols. Edited by Beverly Wilson Palmer. Boston: Northeastern University Press, 1990.

Sylvester, Lorna Lutes, ed. "The Civil War Letters of Charles Harding Cox." *Indiana Magazine of History* 68 (March 1972): 24–78.

Tappan, George H., ed. *The Civil War Journal of Lt. Russell M. Tuttle.* Jefferson, N.C.: McFarland, 2006.

Tatum, Margaret Black, ed. "'Please Send Stamps': The Civil War Letters of William Allen Clark, Part I." *Indiana Magazine of History* 91 (March 1995): 81–108.

———. "'Please Send Stamps': The Civil War Letters of William Allen Clark, Part II." *Indiana Magazine of History* 91 (June 1995): 197–225.

———. "'Please Send Stamps': The Civil War Letters of William Allen Clark, Part III." *Indiana Magazine of History* 91 (September 1995): 288–320.

———. "'Please Send Stamps': The Civil War Letters of William Allen Clark, Part IV." *Indiana Magazine of History* 91 (December 1995): 408–37.

Testimony Taken by the Joint Select Committee to Inquire into the Conditions of Affairs in the Late Insurrectionary States. 13 vols. Washington, D.C.: Government Printing Office, 1872.

Thornbrough, Gayle, and Paula Corpuz, eds. *The Diary of Calvin Fletcher.* 9 vols. Indianapolis: Indiana Historical Society, 1972–83.

Thorson, James A., ed. *Pontius Family Letters, 1861–1933.* Omaha, Neb.: Privately printed, 1999.

Throne, Mildred, ed. *The Civil War Diary of Cyrus F. Boyd, Fifteenth Iowa Infantry, 1861–1863.* Iowa City: State Historical Society of Iowa, 1953.

Tocqueville, Alexis de. *Democracy in America.* Translated by Gerald E. Bevan. New York: Penguin, 2003.

Tomlinson, Helyn W., ed. *"Dear Friends": The Civil War Letters and Diary of Charles Edwin Cort.* N.p., 1962.

The Trial of Hon. Clement L. Vallandigham, by a Military Commission: And the Proceedings under His Application for a Writ of Habeas Corpus in the Circuit Court of the United States for the Southern District of Ohio. Cincinnati: Rickey and Carroll, 1863.

Trimble, Richard M., ed. *Brothers 'Til Death: The Civil War Letters of William, Thomas, and Maggie Jones, 1861–1865.* Macon, Ga.: Mercer University Press, 2000.

Vallandigham, Clement L. *Speeches, Arguments, Addresses, and Letters of Clement L. Vallandigham.* New York: J. Walter, 1864.

Wainwright, Charles S. *A Diary of Battle: The Personal Journals of Colonel Charles S. Wainwright.* Edited by Allan Nevins. New York: Harcourt, Brace and World, 1962.

Walters, Sara Gould, ed. *Inscription at Gettysburg: In Memoriam to Captain David Acheson, Company C, 140th Pennsylvania Volunteers.* Gettysburg, Pa.: Thomas, 1991.

Weaver, Henry Clay. "Georgia through Kentucky Eyes: Letters Written on Sherman's March to Atlanta." Edited by James M. Merrill and James F. Marshall. *Filson Club History Quarterly* 30 (October 1956): 324–59.

Weller, Edwin. *A Civil War Courtship.* Edited by William Walton. New York: Doubleday, 1980.

Welles, Gideon. *Diary of Gideon Welles: Secretary of the Navy under Lincoln and Johnson.* Edited by Howard K. Beale. 3 vols. New York: Norton, 1960.

Westervelt, John H. *Diary of a Yankee Engineer: The Civil War Story of John H. Westervelt, Engineer, 1st New York Volunteer Engineer Corps.* Edited by Anita Palladino. New York: Fordham University Press, 1997.

White, Jonathan W. "The Civil War Disloyalty Trial of John O'Connell." *Ohio Valley History* 9 (Spring 2009): 2–20.

———, ed. "A Pennsylvania Judge Views the Rebellion: The Civil War Letters of George Washington Woodward." *Pennsylvania Magazine of History and Biography* 129 (April 2005): 290–316.

———. *A Philadelphia Perspective: The Civil War Diary of Sidney George Fisher.* New York: Fordham University Press, 2007.

Wightman, Edward King. *From Antietam to Fort Fisher: The Civil War Letters of Edward King Wightman, 1862–1865.* Edited by Edward C. Longacre. Madison, Wisc.: Teaneck, 1985.

Wistar, Isaac J. *Autobiography of Isaac Jones Wistar, 1827–1905: Half a Century in War and Peace.* 1914. Reprint, New York: Harper and Brothers, 1937.

Woodring, Jacqueline Weaver, ed. *The 1861–1864 Civil War Letters of General Erastus Barnard Tyler.* Ravenna, Ohio: Portage County Historical Society, 2009.

SECONDARY SOURCES

Books

Alotta, Robert I. *Civil War Justice: Union Army Executions under Lincoln.* Shippensburg, Pa.: White Mane, 1989.

Ayers, Edward L. *In the Presence of Mine Enemies: War in the Heart of America, 1859–1863.* New York: W. W. Norton, 2003.

Baker, Jean H. *Affairs of Party: The Political Culture of Northern Democrats in the Mid-Nineteenth Century.* Ithaca, N.Y.: Cornell University Press, 1983. Reprint, New York: Fordham University Press, 1998.

———. *The Politics of Continuity: Maryland Political Parties from 1858 to 1870.* Baltimore: Johns Hopkins University Press, 1973.

Barrett, John G. *The Civil War in North Carolina.* Chapel Hill: University of North Carolina Press, 1963.

Battle, J. H., ed. *History of Columbia and Montour Counties, Pennsylvania.* Chicago: A. Warner, 1887.

Belz, Herman. *Abraham Lincoln, Constitutionalism, and Equal Rights in the Civil War Era.* New York: Fordham University Press, 1998.

———. *Emancipation and Equal Rights: Politics and Constitutionalism in the Civil War Era.* New York: Norton, 1978.

——. *A New Birth of Freedom: The Republican Party and Freedmen's Rights, 1861–1866.* Westport, Conn.: Greenwood Press, 1976.

——. *Reconstructing the Union: Theory and Policy during the Civil War.* Ithaca, N.Y.: Cornell University Press, 1969.

Bennett, Brian A. *Sons of Old Monroe: A Regimental History of Patrick O'Rorke's 140th New York Volunteer Infantry.* Dayton, Ohio: Morningside House, 1992.

Bensel, Richard Franklin. *The American Ballot Box in the Mid-Nineteenth Century.* New York: Cambridge University Press, 2004.

Benton, Josiah H. *Voting in the Field: A Forgotten Chapter of the Civil War.* Boston: Plimpton Press, 1915.

Berlin, Ira, Joseph P. Reidy, and Leslie S. Rowland. *Freedom's Soldiers: The Black Military Experience in the Civil War.* New York: Cambridge University Press, 1998.

Bernstein, Iver. *The New York City Draft Riots: Their Significance for American Society and Politics in the Age of the Civil War.* New York: Oxford University Press, 1990.

Blackmar, Frank W. *Kansas: A Cyclopedia of State History, Embracing Events, Institutions, Industries, Counties, Cities, Towns, Prominent Persons, Etc.* 2 vols. Chicago: Standard, 1912.

Blair Harry C., and Rebecca Tarshis, *The Life of Colonel Edward D. Baker, Lincoln's Constant Ally.* Portland: Oregon Historical Society, 1960.

Blight, David W. *Race and Reunion: The Civil War in American Memory.* Cambridge: Harvard University Press, 2001.

Bradley, Erwin Stanley. *The Triumph of Militant Republicanism: A Study of Pennsylvania and Presidential Politics 1860–1872.* Philadelphia: University of Pennsylvania Press, 1964.

Brandt, Dennis W. *From Home Guards to Heroes: The 87th Pennsylvania and Its Civil War Community.* Columbia: University of Missouri Press, 2006.

Brasher, Glenn David. *The Peninsula Campaign and the Necessity of Emancipation: African Americans and the Fight for Freedom.* Chapel Hill: University of North Carolina Press, 2012.

Brummer, Sidney David. *Political History of New York State during the Period of the Civil War.* New York: Columbia University Press, 1911.

Campbell, Jacqueline Glass. *When Sherman Marched North from the Sea: Resistance on the Confederate Home Front.* Chapel Hill: University of North Carolina Press, 2003.

Castel, Albert, *Tom Taylor's Civil War.* Lawrence: University Press of Kansas, 2000.

Ceaser James W., and Andrew E. Busch, *The Perfect Tie: The True Story of the 2000 Presidential Election.* Lanham, Md.: Rowman and Littlefield, 2001.

Chaffin, Tom. *Pathfinder: John Charles Fremont and the Course of American Empire.* New York: Hill and Wang, 2002.

Collins, Lewis, and Richard H. Collins. *Collins' Historical Sketches of Kentucky: History of Kentucky.* Rev. ed. 2 vols. Covington: Collins, 1878.

Costa, Dora L., and Matthew E. Kahn. *Heroes and Cowards: The Social Face of War.* Princeton: Princeton University Press, 2008.

Coulter, E. Merton. *The Civil War and Readjustment in Kentucky.* Chapel Hill: University of North Carolina Press, 1926.

Curti, Merle. *The Roots of American Loyalty.* New York: Columbia University Press, 1946.

Davis, Stanton Ling. *Pennsylvania Politics, 1860–1863.* Cleveland, Ohio: Western Reserve University Bookstore, 1935.

Davis, William C. *Lincoln's Men: How President Lincoln Became Father to an Army and a Nation.* New York: Free Press, 1999.

Dearing, Mary R. *Veterans in Politics: The Story of the G.A.R.* Baton Rouge: Louisiana State University Press, 1959.

Dell, Christopher. *Lincoln and the War Democrats: The Grand Erosion of the Conservative Tradition.* Madison, N.J.: Fairleigh Dickinson University Press, 1975.

Dershowitz, Alan M. *Supreme Injustice: How the High Court Hijacked Election 2000.* New York: Oxford University Press, 2001.

Dobak, William A. *Freedom by the Sword: The U.S. Colored Troops, 1862–1867.* Washington, D.C.: Center of Military History, 2011.

Donald, David Herbert. *Lincoln.* New York: Simon and Schuster, 1995.

Eddy, T. M. *Patriotism of Illinois.* 2 vols. Chicago: Clarke and Co., 1866.

Fellman, Michael. *Inside War: The Guerrilla Conflict in Missouri during the American Civil War.* New York: Oxford University Press, 1989.

Fields, Barbara Jeanne. *Slavery and Freedom on the Middle Ground: Maryland during the Nineteenth Century.* New Haven: Yale University Press, 1985.

Foote, Lorien. *The Gentlemen and the Roughs: Violence, Honor, and Manhood in the Union Army.* New York: New York University Press, 2010.

Frank, Joseph Allen. *With Ballot and Bayonet: The Political Socialization of American Civil War Soldiers.* Athens: University of Georgia Press, 1998.

Franklin, John Merryman. *Recollections of My Life.* Baltimore: Reese Press, 1973.

Frederickson, George M. *The Inner Civil War: Northern Intellectuals and the Crisis of the Union.* New York: Harper, 1965.

Gallagher, Gary W. *The Union War.* Cambridge: Harvard University Press, 2011.

Gallman, J. Matthew. *Mastering Wartime: A Social History of Philadelphia during the Civil War.* New York: Cambridge University Press, 1990.

———. *The North Fights the Civil War: The Home Front.* Chicago: Ivan R. Dee, 1994.

Garraty, John A., and Mark C. Carnes, eds. *American National Biography.* 24 vols. New York: Oxford University Press, 1999.

Geary, James W. *We Need Men: The Union Draft and the Civil War.* Dekalb: Northern Illinois University Press, 1991.

Gibbs, Joseph. *Three Years in the Bloody Eleventh: The Campaigns of a Pennsylvania Reserves Regiment.* University Park: Pennsylvania State University Press, 2002.

Gillette, William. *Jersey Blue: Civil War Politics in New Jersey, 1854–1865.* New Brunswick, N.J.: Rutgers University Press, 1994.

Glatthaar, Joseph T. *Forged in Battle: The Civil War Alliance of Black Soldiers and White Officers.* New York: Free Press, 1990.

——. *The March to the Sea and Beyond: Sherman's Troops in the Savannah and Carolinas Campaigns.* New York: New York University Press, 1985.

——. *Soldiering in the Army of Northern Virginia: A Statistical Portrait of the Troops Who Served under Robert E. Lee.* Chapel Hill: University of North Carolina Press, 2011.

Gordon, Ann D. *The Trial of Susan B. Anthony.* Washington, D.C.: Federal Judicial Center, 2005.

Green, Michael S. *Freedom, Union, and Power: Lincoln and His Party in the Civil War.* New York: Fordham University Press, 2004.

Grimsley, Mark. *The Hard Hand of War: Union Military Policy toward Southern Civilians, 1861–1865.* New York: Cambridge University Press, 1995.

Grimsted, David. *American Mobbing, 1828–1861: Toward Civil War.* New York: Oxford University Press, 1998.

Guelzo, Allen C. *Lincoln's Emancipation Proclamation: The End of Slavery in America.* New York: Simon and Schuster, 2004.

Hancock, Harold Bell. *Delaware during the Civil War: A Political History.* Wilmington: Historical Society of Delaware, 1961.

Hess, Earl J. *Liberty, Virtue, and Progress: Northerners and Their War for the Union.* New York: New York University Press, 1988. Reprint, New York: Fordham University Press, 1997.

——. *The Union Soldier in Battle: Enduring the Ordeal of Combat.* Lawrence: University Press of Kansas, 1997.

Hicken, Victor. *Illinois in the Civil War.* 2nd ed. Urbana: University of Illinois Press, 1991.

History and Roster of Maryland Volunteers, War of 1861–5. 2 vols. Baltimore: Press of Guggenheimer, Weil, and Co., 1898–99.

Holt, Michael F. *Political Parties and American Political Development from the Age of Jackson to the Age of Lincoln.* Baton Rouge: Louisiana State University Press, 1992.

Holzer, Harold. *Emancipating Lincoln: The Proclamation in Text, Context, and Memory.* Cambridge: Harvard University Press, 2012.

Horrall, S. F. *History of the Forty-Second Indiana Volunteer Infantry.* Chicago: Privately printed, 1892.

Hunt, Roger D. *Colonels in Blue: Michigan, Ohio and West Virginia: A Civil War Biographical Dictionary.* Jefferson, N.C.: McFarland, 2011.

——. *Colonels in Blue: Union Army Colonels of the Civil War: New York.* Atglen, Pa.: Schiffer Military History, 2003.

——. *Colonels in Blue: Union Army Colonels of the Civil War: The Mid-Atlantic States: Pennsylvania, New Jersey, Maryland, Delaware, and the District of Columbia.* Mechanicsburg, Pa.: Stackpole, 2007.

——. *Colonels in Blue: Union Army Colonels of the Civil War: The New England States.* Atglen, Pa.: Schiffer Military History, 2001.

Hyman, Harold M. *A More Perfect Union: The Impact of the Civil War and Reconstruction on the Constitution.* New York: Knopf, 1973.

Keyssar, Alexander. *The Right to Vote: The Contested History of Democracy in the United States.* New York: Basic, 2000.

Kirkland, Edward Chase. *The Peacemakers of 1864.* New York: Macmillan, 1927.

Klement, Frank L. *The Copperheads in the Middle West.* Chicago: University of Chicago Press, 1960.

———. *Dark Lanterns: Secret Political Societies, Conspiracies, and Treason Trials in the Civil War.* Baton Rouge: Louisiana State University Press, 1984.

———. *The Limits of Dissent: Clement L. Vallandigham and the Civil War.* Lexington: University of Kentucky Press, 1970.

———. *Lincoln's Critics: The Copperheads of the North.* Shippensburg, Pa.: White Mane, 1999.

Lathrop, George Parsons. *History of the Union League of Philadelphia, from Its Origin and Foundation to the Year 1882.* Philadelphia: J. B. Lippincott, 1884.

Lawson, Melinda. *Patriot Fires: Forging a New American Nationalism in the Civil War North.* Lawrence: University Press of Kansas, 2002.

Leonard, Elizabeth D. *Lincoln's Forgotten Ally: Judge Advocate General Joseph Holt of Kentucky.* Chapel Hill: University of North Carolina Press, 2011.

Linderman, Gerald F. *Embattled Courage: The Experience of Combat in the American Civil War.* New York: Free Press, 1987.

Long, David E. *The Jewel of Liberty: Abraham Lincoln's Reelection and the End of Slavery.* Mechanicsburg, Pa.: Stackpole, 1994.

Long, E. B. *The Civil War Day by Day: An Almanac, 1861–1865.* Garden City, N.Y.: Doubleday, 1971.

Lonn, Ella. *Desertion during the Civil War.* Gloucester, Mass.: American Historical Association, 1928. Reprint, Lincoln: University of Nebraska Press, 1998.

Lowry, Thomas P. *Don't Shoot That Boy: Abraham Lincoln and Military Justice.* Mason City, Iowa: Savas, 1999.

———. *Tarnished Eagles: The Courts-Martial of Fifty Union Colonels and Lieutenant Colonels.* Mechanicsburg, Pa.: Stackpole, 1997.

———. *Utterly Worthless: One Thousand Delinquent Union Officers Unworthy of a Court-Martial.* Lexington, Ky.: N.p., 2010.

Mach, Thomas S. *"Gentleman George" Hunt Pendleton: Party Politics and Ideological Identity in Nineteenth-Century America.* Kent, Ohio: Kent State University Press, 2007.

Manning, Chandra. *What This Cruel War Was Over: Soldiers, Slavery, and the Civil War.* New York: Random House, 2007.

Matthews, Gary Robert. *Basil Wilson Duke, CSA: The Right Man in the Right Place.* Lexington: University Press of Kentucky, 2005.

Matthews, Richard E. *The 149th Pennsylvania Volunteer Infantry Unit in the Civil War.* Jefferson, N.C.: McFarland, 1994.

McPherson, James M. *Drawn with the Sword: Reflections on the American Civil War.* New York: Oxford University Press, 1996.

———. *For Cause and Comrades: Why Men Fought in the Civil War*. New York: Oxford University Press, 1997.

———. *Ordeal by Fire*. 3 vols. New York: McGraw-Hill, 1982.

———. *Tried by War: Abraham Lincoln as Commander in Chief*. New York: Penguin, 2009.

Mitchell, Reid. *Civil War Soldiers*. New York: Viking, 1988.

———. *The Vacant Chair: The Northern Soldier Leaves Home*. New York: Oxford University Press, 1993.

Neely, Mark E., Jr. *The Fate of Liberty: Abraham Lincoln and Civil Liberties*. New York: Oxford University Press, 1991.

———. *Lincoln and the Triumph of the Nation: Constitutional Conflict in the American Civil War*. Chapel Hill: University of North Carolina Press, 2011.

———. *The Union Divided: Party Conflict in the Civil War North*. Cambridge: Harvard University Press, 2002.

Nelson, Larry E. *Bullets, Ballots, and Rhetoric: Confederate Policy for the United States Presidential Contest of 1864*. Tuscaloosa: University of Alabama Press, 1980.

Nelson, William E. *The Fourteenth Amendment: From Political Principle to Judicial Doctrine*. Cambridge: Harvard University Press, 1988.

Newlin, William H. *A History of the Seventy-Third Regiment of Illinois Infantry Volunteers*. [Springfield, Ill.]: Published by the Authority of the Regimental Reunion Association of Survivors of the 73d Illinois Infantry Volunteers, 1890.

Niven, John. *Salmon P. Chase: A Biography*. New York: Oxford University Press, 1995.

Partridge, Charles A., ed. *History of the Ninety-Sixth Regiment Illinois Volunteer Infantry*. Chicago: Brown, Pettibone and Co., 1887.

Porter, George H. *Ohio Politics during the Civil War Period*. New York: Columbia University Press, 1911.

Prominent Democrats of Illinois. Chicago: Democrat Publishing Co., 1899.

Ramold, Steven J. *Across the Divide: Union Soldiers View the Northern Home Front*. New York: New York University Press, 2013.

———. *Baring the Iron Hand: Discipline in the Union Army*. DeKalb: Northern Illinois University Press, 2010.

Randall, James G. *Constitutional Problems under Lincoln*. Rev. ed. Urbana: University of Illinois Press, 1964.

Reid, Whitelaw. *Ohio in the War: Her Statesmen, and Generals, and Soldiers*. 2 vols. Columbus, Ohio: Eclectic Pub. Co., 1893.

Rowell, John W. *Yankee Cavalrymen: Through the Civil War with the Ninth Pennsylvania Cavalry*. Knoxville: University of Tennessee Press, 1971.

Samito, Christian G. *Becoming American under Fire: Irish Americans, African Americans, and the Politics of Citizenship during the Civil War Era*. Ithaca: Cornell University Press, 2009.

Sandow, Robert M. *Deserter Country: Civil War Opposition in the Pennsylvania Appalachians*. New York: Fordham University Press, 2009.

Sawrey, Robert D. *Dubious Victory: The Reconstruction Debate in Ohio*. Lexington: University Press of Kentucky, 1992.

Schmidt, Lewis G. *A Civil War History of the 147th Pennsylvania Regiment.* Allentown, Pa: Privately printed, 2000.

Scrugham, Mary. *The Peaceable Americans of 1860–1861: A Study in Public Opinion.* New York: Columbia University Press, 1921.

Sears, Stephen W. *Chancellorsville.* Boston: Houghton Mifflin, 1996.

———. *George B. McClellan: The Young Napoleon.* New York: Ticknor and Fields, 1988.

Sauers, Richard A., and Peter Tomasek. *The Fishing Creek Confederacy: A Story of Civil War Draft Resistance.* Columbia: University of Missouri Press, 2012.

Scott, Sean A. *A Visitation of God: Northern Civilians Interpret the Civil War.* New York: Oxford University Press, 2011.

Shankman, Arnold M. *The Pennsylvania Antiwar Movement, 1861–1865.* London: Associated University Presses, 1980.

Siegel, Alan A. *Beneath the Starry Flag: New Jersey's Civil War Experience.* New Brunswick, N.J.: Rutgers University Press, 2001.

Silbey, Joel H. *A Respectable Minority: The Democratic Party in the Civil War Era, 1860–1868.* New York: W. W. Norton, 1977.

Smith, Adam I. P. *No Party Now: Politics in the Civil War North.* New York: Oxford University Press, 2006.

Smith, John Day. *The History of the Nineteenth Regiment of Maine Volunteer Infantry, 1862–1865.* Minneapolis: Great Western Printing, 1909.

Smith, Rogers M. *Civic Ideals: Conflicting Visions of Citizenship in U.S. History.* New Haven: Yale University Press, 1997.

Speed, Thomas. *The Union Cause in Kentucky, 1860–1865.* New York: G. P. Putnam's Sons, 1907.

Speed, Thomas, R. M. Kelly, and Alfred Pirtle. *The Union Regiments of Kentucky.* Louisville: Courier-Journal Job Printing Co., 1897.

Stampp, Kenneth M. *Indiana Politics during the Civil War.* Bloomington: Indiana University Press, 1949.

Swan, James B. *Chicago's Irish Legion: The 90th Illinois Volunteers in the Civil War.* Carbondale: Southern Illinois University Press, 2009.

Swanson, James L. *Manhunt: The 12-Day Chase for Lincoln's Killer.* New York: William Morrow, 2006.

Tap, Bruce. *Over Lincoln's Shoulder: The Committee on the Conduct of the War.* Lawrence: University Press of Kansas, 1998.

Thomas, Benjamin P., and Harold Hyman. *Stanton: The Life and Times of Lincoln's Secretary of War.* New York: Alfred A. Knopf, 1962.

Tredway, G. R. *Democratic Opposition to the Lincoln Administration in Indiana.* Indianapolis: Indiana Historical Bureau, 1973.

von Spakovsky, Hans, and M. Eric Eversole. *America's Military Voters: Re-enfranchising the Disenfranchised, Legal Memorandum No. 45.* Washington, D.C.: Center for Legal and Judicial Studies, Heritage Foundation, 2010.

———. *A President's Opportunity: Making Military Voters a Priority, Legal Memorandum*

No. 71. Washington, D.C.: Center for Legal and Judicial Studies, Heritage Foundation, 2011.

Wagandt, Charles L. *The Mighty Revolution: Negro Emancipation in Maryland, 1862–1864*. Baltimore: Johns Hopkins University Press, 1964.

Wang, Xi. *The Trial of Democracy: Black Suffrage and Northern Republicans, 1860–1910*. Athens: University of Georgia Press, 1997.

Warner, Ezra J. *Generals in Blue: Lives of Union Commanders*. Baton Rouge: Louisiana State University Press, 1964.

Warshauer, Matthew. *Andrew Jackson and the Politics of Martial Law: Nationalism, Civil Liberties, and Partisanship*. Knoxville: University of Tennessee Press, 2006.

Waugh, John C. *Reelecting Lincoln: The Battle for the 1864 Presidency*. New York: Crown, 1997.

Weber, Jennifer L. *Copperheads: The Rise and Fall of Lincoln's Opponents in the North*. New York: Oxford University Press, 2006.

Wiley, Bell Irvin. *The Life of Billy Yank: The Common Soldier of the Civil War*. New York: Bobbs-Merrill, 1952.

Williams, Frank J. *Judging Lincoln*. Carbondale: Southern Illinois University Press, 2002.

Williams, T. Harry. *The Selected Essays of T. Harry Williams*. Baton Rouge: Louisiana State University Press, 1983.

Wittenberg, Eric J. *The Union Cavalry Comes of Age: Hartwood Church to Brandy Station, 1863*. Washington, D.C.: Brassey's, 2003.

Work, David. *Lincoln's Political Generals*. Champaign: University of Illinois Press, 2009.

Wubben, Hubert H. *Civil War Iowa and the Copperhead Movement*. Ames: Iowa State University Press, 1980.

Zornow, William Frank. *Lincoln and the Party Divided*. Norman: University of Oklahoma Press, 1954.

Edited Volumes

Cashin, Joan E., ed. *The War Was You and Me: Civilians in the American Civil War*. Princeton: Princeton University Press, 2002.

Cimbala, Paul A., and Randall M. Miller, eds. *An Uncommon Time: The Civil War and the Northern Home Front*. New York: Fordham University Press, 2002.

———, eds. *Union Soldiers and the Northern Home Front: Wartime Experiences, Postwar Adjustments*. New York: Fordham University Press, 2002.

Longacre, Edward G., and Theodore J. Zeman, eds. *Beyond Combat: Essays in Military History in Honor of Russell F. Weigley*. Philadelphia: American Philosophical Society, 2007.

McDonough, Daniel, and Kenneth W. Noe, eds. *Politics and Culture of the Civil War Era: Essays in Honor of Robert W. Johannsen*. Selinsgrove, Pa.: Susquehanna University Press, 2006.

McPherson, James M., and William J. Cooper Jr., eds. *Writing the Civil War: The Quest to Understand.* Columbia: University of South Carolina Press, 1998.

Moreno, Paul D., and Johnathan O'Neill, eds. *Constitutionalism in the Approach and Aftermath of the Civil War.* New York: Fordham University Press, 2013.

Sheehan-Dean, Aaron, ed. *The View from the Ground: Experiences of Civil War Soldiers.* Lexington: University of Kentucky Press, 2007.

Slap, Andrew L., and Michael Thomas Smith, eds. *This Distracted and Anarchical People: New Answers for Old Questions about the Civil War Era North.* New York: Fordham University Press, 2013.

Ural, Susannah J., ed. *Civil War Citizens: Race, Ethnicity, and Identity in America's Bloodiest Conflict.* New York: New York University Press, 2010.

Wilson, Joseph T. *The Black Phalanx: A History of the Negro Soldiers of the United States in the Wars of 1775–1812, 1861–'65.* Hartford: American Publishing Co., 1890.

Articles and Essays

Abzug, Robert H. "The Copperheads: Historical Approaches to Civil War Dissent in the Midwest." *Indiana Magazine of History* 66 (March 1970): 40–55.

Baker, Jean H. "A Loyal Opposition: Northern Democrats in the Thirty-Seventh Congress." *Civil War History* 25 (June 1979): 139–55.

Berlin, Ira. "Who Freed the Slaves? Emancipation and Its Meaning." In David W. Blight and Brooks D. Simpson, eds., *Union and Emancipation: Essays on Politics and Race in the Civil War Era,* 105–21. Kent, Ohio: Kent State University Press, 1997.

Bestor, Arthur. "The American Civil War as a Constitutional Crisis." *American Historical Review* 69 (January 1964): 327–52.

Blair, William. "A Record of Pennsylvania Deserters." *Pennsylvania Magazine of History and Biography* 135 (October 2011): 537–38.

Burcher, William M. "A History of Soldier Voting in the State of New York." *New York History* 25 (October 1944): 459–81.

Cardinal, Eric J. "Disloyalty or Dissent: The Case of the Copperheads." *Midwest Quarterly* 19 (October 1977): 24–35.

Carson, Jamie L., et al. "The Impact of National Tides and District-Level Effects on Electoral Outcomes: The U.S. Congressional Elections of 1862–63." *American Journal of Political Science* 45 (October 2001): 887–98.

Coleman, Charles H. "The Use of the Term 'Copperhead' during the Civil War." *Mississippi Valley Historical Review* 25 (September 1938): 263–64.

Cowden, Joanna D. "The Politics of Dissent: Civil War Democrats in Connecticut." *New England Quarterly* 56 (December 1983): 538–54.

Curran, Daniel J. "Polk, Politics, and Patronage: The Rejection of George W. Woodward's Nomination to the Supreme Court." *Pennsylvania Magazine of History and Biography* 121 (July 1997): 163–99.

Curry, Leonard P. "Congressional Democrats, 1861–1863." *Civil War History* 12 (September 1966): 213–29.

Downs, Lynwood G. "The Soldier Vote and Minnesota Politics, 1862–65." *Minnesota History* 26 (September 1945): 187–210.

Dunkelman, Mark H. "Through White Eyes: The 154th New York Volunteers and African-Americans in the Civil War." *Journal of Negro History* 85 (Summer 2000): 96–111.

Fehrenbacher, Don E. "The Making of a Myth: Lincoln and the Vice-Presidential Nomination in 1864." *Civil War History* 41 (December 1995): 273–90.

Fields, Barbara J. "Who Freed the Slaves?" In Geoffrey C. Ward et al., comps. *The Civil War*, 178–81. New York: Alfred A. Knopf, 1990.

Geary, James W. "Civil War Conscription in the North: A Historiographical Review." *Civil War History* 32 (September 1986): 208–28.

Graber, Mark A. "Voting Rights and Other 'Anomalies': Protecting and Expanding Civil Liberties in Wartime." In Thomas E. Baker and John F. Stack Jr., eds., *At War with Civil Rights and Civil Liberties*, 153–76. Lanham, Md.: Rowman and Littlefield, 2006.

Guelzo, Allen C. "Defending Emancipation: Abraham Lincoln and the Conkling Letter, 1863." *Civil War History* 48 (December 2002): 313–37.

Haller, Theodore N. "Life and Public Services of Colonel Granville O. Haller: Soldier, Citizen and Pioneer." *Washington Historian* 1 (April 1900): 102–9.

Hallock, Judith Lee. "The Role of the Community in Civil War Desertion." *Civil War History* 29 (June 1983): 123–34.

Harris, William C. "Conservative Unionists and the Presidential Election of 1864." *Civil War History* 38 (December 1992): 298–318.

Herrera, Ricardo A. "Self-Government and the American Citizen as Soldier, 1775–1861." *Journal of Military History* 65 (January 2001): 21–52.

Hutter, W. H., and Ray H. Abrams. "Copperhead Newspapers and the Negro." *Journal of Negro History* 20 (April 1935): 131–52.

Hyman, Harold M. "The Election of 1864." In Arthur Schlesinger, ed., *History of American Presidential Elections*, 2 vols., 2:1155–244. New York: Macmillan, 1971.

Klement, Frank L. "Civil War Politics, Nationalism, and Postwar Myths." *Historian* 38 (May 1976): 419–38.

———. "Middle Western Copperheadism and the Genesis of the Granger Movement." *Mississippi Valley Historical Review* 38 (March 1952): 679–94.

———. "Midwestern Opposition to Lincoln's Emancipation Policy." *Journal of Negro History* 49 (July 1964): 169–83.

———. "The Soldier Vote in Wisconsin during the Civil War." *Wisconsin Magazine of History* 28 (September 1944): 37–47.

Lerch, Kathryn W. "Prosecuting Citizens, Rebels & Spies: The 8th New York Heavy Artillery in Maryland, 1862–1864." *Maryland Historical Magazine* 94 (Summer 1999): 132–71.

Levine, Peter. "Draft Evasion in the North during the Civil War, 1863–1865." *Journal of American History* 67 (March 1981): 816–34.

Longacre, Edward G. "The Union Army Occupation of New York City, November 1864." *New York History* 65 (April 1984): 133–58.

Martin, Boyd A. "The Service Vote in the Elections of 1944." *American Political Science Review* 39 (August 1945): 720–32.

McKitrick, Eric L. "Party Politics and the Union and Confederate War Efforts." In William Nisbet Chambers and Walter Dean Burnham, eds., *The American Party Systems: Stages of Development*, 117–51. New York: Oxford University Press, 1967.

McPherson, James M. "War and Politics." In Geoffrey C. Ward et al., comps., *The Civil War*, 350–53. New York: Alfred A. Knopf, 1990.

McSeveney, Samuel T. "Re-electing Lincoln: The Union Party Campaign and the Military Vote in Connecticut." *Civil War History* 32 (June 1986): 139–58.

———. "Winning the Vote for the Connecticut Soldiers in the Field, 1862–1864: A Research Note and Historiographical Comment." *Connecticut History* 26 (November 1985): 115–25.

Milano, Anthony J. "The Copperhead Regiment: The 20th Massachusetts Infantry." *Civil War Regiments* 3 (1993): 31–63.

Morrison, Trevor W. "Constitutional Avoidance in the Executive Branch." *Columbia Law Review* 106 (October 2006): 1189–259.

Neely, Mark E., Jr. "The Civil War and the Two-Party System." In James M. McPherson, ed., *We Cannot Escape History: Lincoln and the Last Best Hope of Earth*, 86–104. Urbana: University of Illinois Press, 1995.

———. "The Constitution and Civil Liberties under Lincoln." In Eric Foner, ed., *Our Lincoln: New Perspectives on Lincoln and His World*, 37–61. New York: W. W. Norton, 2008.

———. "'Seeking a Cause of Difficulty with the Government': Reconsidering Freedom of Speech and Judicial Conflict under Lincoln." In Phillip Shaw Paludan, ed., *Lincoln's Legacy: Ethics and Politics*, 48–66. Urbana: University of Illinois Press, 2008.

Nelson, Larry E. "Black Leaders and the Presidential Election of 1864." *Journal of Negro History* 63 (January 1978): 42–58.

Parks, George E. "One Story of the 109th Illinois Volunteer Infantry Regiment." *Journal of the Illinois State Historical Society* 56 (Summer 1963): 282–97.

Ray, P. Orman. "Military Absent-Voting Laws." *American Political Science Review* 12 (August 1918): 461–69.

Robertson, John. "Re-Enlistment Patterns of Civil War Soldiers." *Journal of Interdisciplinary History* 32 (Summer 2001): 15–35.

Roche, John P. "The Loss of American Nationality—The Development of Statutory Expatriation." *University of Pennsylvania Law Review* 99 (October 1950): 25–71.

Rodgers, Thomas E. "Republicans and Drifters: Political Affiliation and Union Army Volunteers in West-Central Indiana." *Indiana Magazine of History* 92 (December 1996): 322–45.

Royster, Charles. "'The Nature of Treason': Revolutionary Virtue and American Reactions to Benedict Arnold." *William and Mary Quarterly* 36 (April 1979): 164–93.

Russ, William A., Jr. "The Struggle between President Lincoln and Congress over Disfranchisement of Rebels (Part 1)." *Susquehanna University Studies* 3 (March 1947): 177–205.

Sandow, Robert M. "The Limits of Northern Patriotism: Early Civil War Mobilization in Pennsylvania." *Pennsylvania History* 70 (Spring 2003): 175–203.

Sears, Stephen W. "McClellan and the Peace Plank of 1864: A Reappraisal." *Civil War History* 36 (March 1990): 57–64.

Shankman, Arnold M. "For the Union As It Was and the Constitution As It Is: A Copperhead Views the Civil War." In James I. Robertson Jr. and Richard M. McCurry, eds., *Rank and File: Civil War Essays in Honor of Bell Irvin Wiley*, 93–111. San Rafael, Calif.: Presidio Press, 1976.

———. "Soldier Votes and Clement L. Vallandigham in the 1863 Ohio Gubernatorial Election." *Ohio History* 82 (Winter/Spring 1973): 88–104.

Smith, Adam I. P., and Peter J. Parish. "A Contested Legacy: The Civil War and Party Politics in the North." In Susan-Mary Grant and Peter J. Parish, eds., *Legacy of Disunion: The Enduring Significance of the American Civil War*, 81–99. Baton Rouge: Louisiana State University Press, 2003.

Smith, Paul S. "First Use of the Term 'Copperhead.'" *American Historical Review* 32 (July 1927): 799–800.

Tapp, Hambleton. "Incidents in the Life of Frank Wolford, Colonel of the First Kentucky Union Cavalry." *Filson Club Historical Quarterly* 10 (April 1936): 82–99.

Towne, Stephen E. "Killing the Serpent Speedily: Governor Morton, General Hascall, and the Suppression of the Democratic Press in Indiana, 1863." *Civil War History* 52 (April 2006): 41–65.

Trennery, Walter N. "Votes for Minnesota's Civil War Soldiers." *Minnesota History* 36 (March 1959): 167–72.

Verter, Bradford. "Disconsolations of a Jersey Muskrat: The Civil War Letters of Symmes H. Stillwell." *Princeton University Library Chronicle* 58 (Winter 1997): 231–72.

Vorenberg, Michael. "'The Deformed Child': Slavery and the Election of 1864." *Civil War History* 47 (September 2001): 240–57.

Wagandt, Charles L. "Election by Sword and Ballot: The Emancipationist Victory of 1863." *Maryland Historical Magazine* 59 (June 1964): 143–64.

Weber, Jennifer L. "All the President's Men: The Politicization of Union Soldiers and How They Saved Abraham Lincoln." In Orville Vernon Burton, Jerald Podair, and Jennifer L. Weber, eds., *The Struggle for Equality: Essays on Sectional Conflict, the Civil War, and the Long Reconstruction*, 76–90. Charlottesville: University of Virginia Press, 2011.

Williams, T. Harry. "Voters in Blue: The Citizen Soldiers of the Civil War." *Mississippi Valley Historical Review* 31 (September 1944): 187–204.

Winther, Oscar O. "The Soldier Vote in the Election of 1864." *New York History* 25 (October 1944): 440–58.

White, Jonathan W. "Canvassing the Troops: The Federal Government and the Soldiers' Right to Vote." *Civil War History* 50 (September 2004): 290–316.

———. "Citizens and Soldiers: Party Competition and the Debate in Pennsylvania over Permitting Soldiers to Vote, 1861–64." *American Nineteenth Century History* 5 (Summer 2004): 47–70.

———. "An Unlikely Database: Using the Internet Creatively in Historical Research." *Perspectives on History: Newsmagazine of the American Historical Association* (March 2006): 52–53.

———. "'Words Become Things': Free Speech in Civil War Pennsylvania." *Pennsylvania Legacies* 8 (May 2008): 18–23.

Young, Ernest A. "Constitutional Avoidance, Resistance Norms, and the Preservation of Judicial Review." *Texas Law Review* 78 (1999–2000): 1549–614.

Zornow, William Frank. "Treason as a Campaign Issue in the Re-election of Lincoln." *Abraham Lincoln Quarterly* 5 (June 1949): 348–63.

———. "The Union Party Convention at Baltimore in 1864." *Maryland Historical Magazine* 45 (September 1950): 176–200.

Dissertations and Theses

Altavilla, Keith Fellows. "Can We Call It Anything but Treason?: Loyalty and Citizenship in Ohio Valley Soldiers." Ph.D. diss., Texas Christian University, 2013.

Horner, Jennifer Ruth. "Blood and Ballots: Military Voting and Political Communication in the Union Army during the United States Civil War, 1861–1865." Ph.D. diss., University of Pennsylvania, 2006.

Robertson, John Gordon. "Rich Man's War, Poor Man's Opportunity? Civil War Re-Enlistment and the Right to Rise." Ph.D. diss., Carnegie Mellon University, 2009.

White, Jonathan W. "With Ballot and Bullet: The Union Army and the Reelection of Abraham Lincoln." Master's thesis, University of Maryland, College Park, 2003.

———. "'To Aid Their Rebel Friends': Politics and Treason in the Civil War North." Ph.D. diss., University of Maryland, College Park, 2008.

Young, William Lewis. "Soldier Voting in Ohio during the Civil War." Master's thesis, Ohio State University, 1948.

INDEX

African Americans: enlistment of, 36, 39–40, 45–48, 55–57, 63–68, 71, 80, 89, 93, 191n34, 202n53; mistreatment of by white soldiers, 62–63, 195n96–98, 204n89; and self-emancipation thesis, 39–40; and suffrage, 8, 21, 98, 129–31, 139–40, 157–58, 220n10, 220n5, 222n28, 223n42; white Union soldiers' views of, 8–9, 39–40, 45–47, 49–57, 62–69, 71, 74–76, 80–90, 92–94, 97, 104, 107–8, 121, 129, 190n22, 194n81, 201n47, 202n53, 204n86, 204n89, 212n43, 217n104. *See also* Emancipation Proclamation; slavery

Agnew, Daniel, 146–47, 224n55, 225n66

Articles of War: described: 7, 10, 54, 82, 188n2, 195n97, 218n125; violated by soldiers, 38–39, 46, 50–51, 56, 72, 92, 121, 190n19

Atlanta, 5–6, 54, 99, 102–3, 106, 127–28, 153, 209n16, 210n27, 210n30, 215n89

Baker, Edward D., 38, 57

Baker, Jean H., 1, 212n53

Banks, Nathaniel P., 71

Barlow, Samuel L. M., 14, 98, 102

Belmont, August, 14, 100–102

Bennett, Thomas W., 44–45, 79, 179n12

Benton, Josiah H., 153, 155, 173, 213n53

Berlin, Ira, 39

Biddle, Charles J., 19, 29, 55

Blair, William A., 26, 145

Brough, John, 25–26, 35, 184n63

Browning, Orville H., 13

Buchanan, James, 101

Buckingham, William A., 24–25

Buell, Don Carlos, 44, 61

Burbridge, Stephen, 66

Burnside, Ambrose, 40–42, 86

Butler, Benjamin F., 49, 86, 129

Cameron, Simon, 27, 46

Chamberlain, Joshua Lawrence, 138

Chase, Salmon P., 44, 98, 130

Chase v. Miller, 16–17, 19, 31

Chicago Convention. *See* Democratic National Convention

citizenship, rights of, 65–66, 208n10, 220n11, 222n24; for African Americans, 8, 21, 98, 129–31, 139–40, 157–58, 220n10, 220n5, 222n28, 223n42; denied to soldiers, 1, 20–21, 54, 57–58; deserters deprived of, 8, 131–51, 221n12; deserved by soldiers, 4, 7–8, 21–24, 26, 33, 37, 73, 82, 155, 157–58, 164–65; of southerners, 29, 34, 124–25, 134, 221n12; for women, 129–30, 135, 140, 222n28, 223n42

civil liberties, 4–6, 18, 20, 25, 34, 36–37, 41, 100, 124, 143, 154–55, 220n2, 221n15. *See also* habeas corpus, suspension of the privilege of

Congress, 38, 65, 67, 90, 195n97, 221n21, 224n56; criticism of, 7, 10, 43, 49, 198n19; disfranchises deserters, 8, 131–38, 143–51, 221n23, 224n45; elections for, 5–6, 17, 115–17, 119–20, 127, 153–54; members of, 13, 19–20, 25, 31, 41, 46, 69, 76, 82, 100, 109; and promotion of officers, 57, 59, 211n42; and punishment of soldiers, 39, 42; and the right of soldiers to vote, 23–24, 110, 156–60, 162–63, 165, 183n54

conscription: in the courts, 225n66; opposed by Democrats and supported by Republicans, 5, 14, 32, 36–37, 78, 95, 178n8, 179n14; and the

271